CADETS, CANNONS and Legends

CADETS, CANNONS *and* Legends

THE FOOTBALL HISTORY OF
MORGAN PARK MILITARY ACADEMY

JOE ZIEMBA

gatekeeper press

Columbus, Ohio

Cadets, Cannons and Legends:
The Football History of Morgan Park Military Academy

Published by Gatekeeper Press
2167 Stringtown Rd, Suite 109
Columbus, OH 43123-2989
www.GatekeeperPress.com

ISBN: 9781642373417

Printed in the United States of America

To
Marcia Thomas and Sharon Eichinger
The Angels of the Archives

Margie Ann Schaaf
You Would Have Loved This Stuff

Carol
Always the Inspiration

TABLE OF CONTENTS

PREFACE

Leaves from the Tree of Loyalty

Back in 1926, acclaimed Broadway playwright and author C. Frederick "Fred" Herendeen fired off a letter to Colonel H. D. Abells, the Superintendent of Morgan Park Military Academy (MPMA) in Chicago.

Herendeen, a graduate of the Academy in 1912 and a devoted supporter of the school, was concerned that the Academy (then over 50 years old), did not possess a reliable history in printed form. Herendeen noted in his correspondence that there was "a lack of any real concrete traditions in connection with the old school. This is all the more striking to me in view of the fact that few schools have such a rich fund of school lore and traditions as Morgan Park has."

Apparently, this failure to properly document the history of his *alma mater* was becoming bothersome to Herendeen, and he was not bashful in proposing a viable solution: "I have been trying to figure out ways and means whereby the academy's glorious past might find expression in some permanent form...that such an end might be accomplished through the medium of a pamphlet or book wherein the doings of our past heroes might be set forth..."

Herendeen then offered to write the book (and publish it at his own expense) and even provided two brief sample chapters for Col. Abells to review—both focusing on football players Herendeen had played with on the football team at MPMA. "Not because they were outstanding heroes particularly," explained Herendeen, "but because they serve to illustrate... the finest attributes which Morgan Park brings out in cadets."

In his concluding paragraph in the missive to Col. Abells, Herendeen even suggested a title for the book: "If such a book were printed it might well be under the title of **Leaves from the Tree of Loyalty**."

If Herendeen had a soft spot in his heart for MPMA, perhaps he was even more sentimental about the Academy's solid football program, after starring for the team as an "All Western Academic" center in 1911 and then returning to coach the team for one season in 1914.

Herendeen never faltered in his support for the Academy throughout his bright literary career, even penning the school "fight" song called "MPMA Loyalty" in 1934 and sponsoring many campus events, including a track meet. Yet, his dream of prompting a written history of the school itself never materialized during his lifetime.

There were, of course, some internal efforts to document the school's revered history. For example, in 1935, the campus-based student newspaper called *The Academy News* began to uncover the history of the school. In the June 12, 1935 issue, the editors announced that "*The Academy News* wishes to present an accurate a history of the school as it can find. None was available as such. What was available was scattered, meager, and living solely in the minds of 'old timers' and yellowed relics of treasured newspapers of the day."

The Academy News still managed to compile an early, and invaluable, history of the school and we must acknowledge the authors of that project: Cadet Wilmer Esler (Class of 1936) and faculty member Captain Jean L. Taylor. Many other snippets of school history appeared over the years but all paled in comparison to the exhaustive and precise **Morgan Park Academy, A History (Volume I)** authored in 2007 by long-time faculty member and school archivist Barry Kritzberg. Kritzberg carefully reconstructed the history of the Academy from 1873-1907, while also personally assuming a leadership role in both the preservation of the Academy's historical documents and establishing a more formal archive for this critical collection. Kritzberg unleashed a flood of articles, recollections, and insight into the productive early years of the institution in "An attempt to recover the life of the place." He certainly succeeded in that objective...

As such, this book is not intended to delineate the entire history of the school, but will touch upon that history as the colorful escapades of its football program are discussed.

In the following pages, the author will share his interpretation of the rich football history of Morgan Park Academy, an astute institution that placed emphasis on a grand education and the moral high road including athletics--but the successful football team persistently elevated and supported the prestigious reputation of the Academy. Thanks to the visionary work of Academy employees and archivists (particularly in the past two decades), the important history of the school has been both "saved" and preserved. Often it is convenient to "toss" ancient pieces of paper or artifacts from bygone years, but the Academy has not only retained critical matter, it has embraced its history.

Still, the story of the football program required further study and examination. Very few school or academic athletic programs were as prosperous for such a lengthy period of time. Accomplishments have been uncovered and history refurbished to present a hopefully reliable documentation of the names, faces, and legends of the Morgan Park Military Academy football program.

While a complete published history of the legendary Academy as suggested by Fred Herendeen (from 1873 to today) remains as a possible exercise for future authors, the objective of this project has been to focus on the history of the football program at the Academy from 1893 to 1958. One may question why have the spirits of a forgotten athletic past been reconvened for this purpose? Or, is there any good reason why such time and effort have been invested in a football program that remains largely forgotten and quietly swept aside by the annals of time? Also, did not the school itself drop football in 1978?

Yet amid the rubble of discarded years and memories, a trend began to emerge. It was a trend that revealed much more than just the history of a football program at one tiny preparatory school on the south side of Chicago...

What emerged was a startling array of characters and teams that not only represented the Academy, but also influenced the national game of football itself in its formative years. As the decades flew by and the little school continued to dominate on the gridiron, it began accumulating an impressive roster of football "graduates" that eventually included (among others) four members of the College Football Hall of Fame, many collegiate players and coaches, professional athletes, prominent businessmen, an NFL official, an Olympian, and even a United States Senator!

Although it is acknowledged that the football program continued at the Academy until 1978 (and it was not always a military school in the early years), the focus of the project was narrowed to include all years encompassing the Morgan Park Military Academy name along with the football seasons prior to when the military school aspect was lastly instituted (1959). As such, we have attempted to accurately document the history of the football program from 1893 through the 1958 season, after which the Academy discontinued its military affiliation.

Football was so popular at Morgan Park Military Academy that most students were able to participate in the sport on a variety of levels. Over the years, the school has sponsored intramural, bantamweights, lightweight, and heavyweight teams, along with (later) the traditional freshman, sophomore, junior varsity, and varsity squads. As such, a priority needed to be established and this book will focus only on the heavyweight (or varsity) teams from 1893-1958.

Owing to the prominence and visibility of the Academy football program, we were able to identify the schedules, players, and games throughout the history of the program via newspapers, books, yearbooks, the Academy archives, and other extant materials. The results allowed us to recreate those forgotten early years and to establish a verified basis for the football tales that follow.

It should also be mentioned that the author spent his early years residing on the campus of Morgan Park Military Academy where his father was an instructor, football coach and athletic director. This publication is not intended to be an investigation of his father's time at the school, although his influence on the football program certainly could not be disregarded.

Hopefully, the following pages will help to partially fulfill the dreams of Fred Herendeen nearly a century after his insightful letter to Col. Abells. In that note, Herendeen suggested that a book about the Academy might provide inspiration in "some way that the incoming cadets might realize at once, the school spirit which has in the past meant so much to Morgan Park Academy." We also hope that this book will contribute some sense of pride to past, present, and future students of the Academy by sharing the monumental, and largely forgotten, incredible history of the school football program.

Perhaps Fred Herendeen stated it best at the conclusion of his plea for a documented school history: "Of course, this (book) may be all wrong but I truly feel that loyalty in the cadet core can best be served and promoted by a better knowledge of our school's splendid past."

What follows, then, is a trip through the storied history of the football program at Morgan Park Military Academy...a past that was interrupted by two World Wars, a national influenza outbreak, the Great Depression, and the Korean War. It was, as Mr. Herendeen so accurately stated so many years ago, a "splendid" past—and one that does indeed merit resurrecting.

ACKNOWLEDGEMENTS

With a project such as this, which spans over 125 years of history, we must gratefully thank the many individuals and organizations that have provided assistance.

Indeed, there would be no book about the football program at Morgan Park Military Academy without the guidance and insight of the individuals who oversee the exceptional Archives at the current Morgan Park Academy. For their wonderful cooperation and assistance, we thank Marcia Thomas and Sharon Eichinger, who on countless occasions, cheerfully scanned a needed photo or located a forgotten document. In addition to being skilled in the art of quilting, Marcia and Sharon are also expert researchers! There simply would not have been a book without the dedication of these two talented individuals. Others from the Academy who were very generous with their time and contributions were Katie Zimmerman, Vincent Hermosilla, Allie Bowles, Julie Cuadros, Linda Cuadros, and Head of School Mercedes Sheppard.

We are also grateful to Morgan Park Academy graduate David Honor for his contribution of the exceptional cover design for this book, as well as for his careful guidance in salvaging aging photographs that were both fragile and invaluable. In terms of pursuing the finished product, we thank "readers" Rosemary Otten, Mary Geismann, Michael Coffeen, Annie Choi, and Margaret Achenbach for their valuable insight and advice. Final editing was completed by attorney Steven Thomas whose keen suggestions ensured that each detail was relevant and accurate. Steve's vast interests in art and literature include numerous genres and cultures. We hope that his first foray into football will not be his last!

Many authors of related publications have shared their expertise and knowledge including: Robert Pruter (**The Rise of American High School Sports and the Search for Control: 1880-1930**); Lewis Bowling (**Wallace Wade: Championship Years at Alabama and Duke**); Frank Maggio (**Notre Dame and the Game That Changed Football: How Jesse Harper Made the Forward Pass a Weapon and Knute Rockne a Legend**); Robin Lester (**Stagg's University**); and Barry Kritzberg (**Morgan Park Academy, A History Volume One**). We thank them for both their insight and their excellent counsel.

Family members of individuals mentioned in the history of the Academy, along with other individual experts, have been most helpful including: Denise Hill, great-granddaughter of former Academy player and coach Jonathan Webb; Michelle Myers Berg, a local historian and professional tour guide in St. Paul, Minnesota; Dr. George E. Bryar, a physician with unique ties to both the Academy and Chicago history; Betty Reichel, daughter of Academy football player Bernard Kormann Reichel; and Chuck DiCola, the grandson of the founder of DiCola's Seafood, a respected business located near the Academy.

Research material was generated from the following locations: Chicago History Museum (Ellen Keith, Lesley Martin); Special Collections Research Center, The University of Chicago Library; The University of Illinois Archives (Linda Stahnke Stepp, Katherine Nichols); The University of Notre Dame Archives (Joe Smith); Bentley Historical Library, University of Michigan (Greg Kinney); The John A. Logan Museum, Murphysboro, Illinois (P. Michael Jones); the Chicago Heights (Illinois) Public Library; Governor's State (Illinois) University; Frankfort (Illinois) Public Library; Blue Island (Illinois) Public Library; the Abraham Lincoln Presidential Library, Springfield, Illinois (Debbie Ross); the Lemont (Illinois) Public Library (Paul Dobersztyn); North Olympic Library System, Port Angeles, Washington (Victoria Townsley); Ridge Historical Society, Chicago, Illinois (Edris Hoover, Jessica Gradolf, Dogmara Mosiniak); and of course, the Archives at Morgan Park Academy.

We also must include representatives from various academic organizations who were very generous with their time and resources: Joan Sweeney, Viatorian Community; Jeff Kenney, Culver Academies; Adam Maser, Hastings College; Sarah Fetters, Duke University; Andrew McDonnell, Wayland Academy; Gene Ambroson, Christie Vos, and Adam Fullerton, Morningside College; and Stew Salowitz, Illinois Wesleyan University. All were very helpful in tracking down information that was critical in the construction of this book.

Many, many graduates of Morgan Park Military Academy shared their memories of both the football program and the Academy itself. The list is lengthy, and all are mentioned in the following pages, but we do wish to specifically thank Pete Voss, Frank Fonsino, Ed Madsen, Mike McClure, Ambassador Al Hoffman, and Dr. Frank Burd for generously sharing an abundance of time to relate their experiences at the Academy. Their patience and commitment in the face of numerous inquiries was greatly appreciated. Mr. Fonsino went above and beyond by helping to locate numerous graduates and helping to organize the various interview sessions with former students and football players.

In addition, we acknowledge and thank our partners at Gatekeeper Press including Rob Price, Sarah Borich, and Tony Chellini for guiding this project to a successful conclusion. Their professionalism and expertise were certainly appreciated...

Finally, a special thanks to my family for their patience and assistance throughout this lengthy process. To my children, Joseph and Angela, your support and encouragement have been gratifying as well as comforting. And to my wife, Carol, once again your guidance and inspiration slows down the merry-go-round enough to bring sense and direction back into focus. Thank you is never enough...

—Joe Ziemba

"Morale — the will to win, the fighting heart — are the honored hallmarks of the football coach and player. Likewise, they are characteristic of the enterprising executive, the successful troop leader, the established artist and the dedicated teacher and scientist."

—President Dwight D. Eisenhower

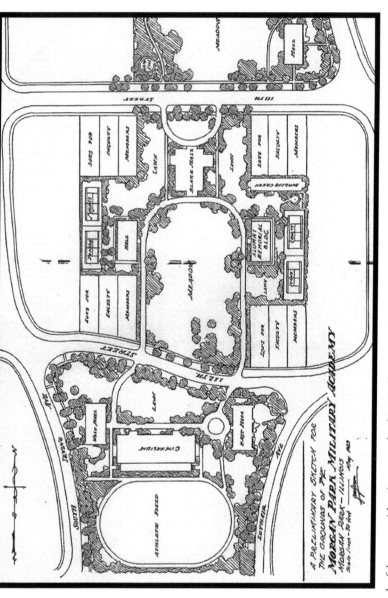

The preliminary sketch of the campus (above) was completed in 1923 by noted landscape architect Jens Jensen. It was intended to provide a futuristic view of where the proposed new buildings (Alumni Hall and Hansen Hall) would appear in 1928. On the right (north) side of the campus, 111th Street serves as a natural boundary. Abells Field would be built on the north side of 111th Street in 1934. To the left (south) end of the campus, the gymnasium and the athletic fields were separated from the main campus by 112th Street. Football games were played on this field until 1934. (All photos in book courtesy of Morgan Park Academy except where noted)

CHAPTER 1

More Brutal Than Prize Fighting

"No malaria, no boys of vicious habits, nor boys
expelled from other institutions received."
—Academy Catalog, 1881

NOVEMBER 20, 1894

After exiting the train at the Morgan Park station, the 14 members of the Englewood High School football party from Chicago gathered to review the final directions to their destination. There was some warmth provided by the large fireplace in the spacious, three-story building, which was just completed in 1891 by architect John T. Long.

It would be an easy walk of a block or so to the football field at Morgan Park Academy. The directions advised the group to head west down Morgan Avenue (now 111ᵗʰ Street) to the Academy grounds, and then stroll through the center of the Academy property to the temporary gymnasium directly ahead on Rinaldo Avenue (now 112th Street). The playing field would be found behind the gym building.

Easy enough, agreed the team members, until the march "down" Morgan Avenue proved to be both challenging and …intimidating! Looming ahead was a very steep hill, a hill that was nowhere to be found in the sparse directions provided to the team. The suburb of Morgan Park itself rested on one of the highest points in the Chicago area (a remnant of the last glacier period, about 12,000 years ago) and the journey up the hill

1

on Morgan Avenue was the only way to access the Academy campus from the train station.

So up they went, grumbling and shuffling, until they reached the summit. The cold November wind slammed into the party without mercy and the players' legs began to ache a bit under the strain of the sharp uphill climb. After all, climbing steep hills was not a common occurrence in the very flat precincts of Chicago! Yet the young football players moved forward, adorned in similar, but not identical uniforms. Within moments, the group reached the Academy property and soon found its way to the field itself.

Although high school football competition was still in its infancy in 1894, Englewood was considered one of the pioneers of the prep game in Chicago, beginning play in 1889 as a charter member of the Cook County League in Chicago. The game of football itself in 1894 bore little resemblance to the modern game of the 21st century. It was a brutal, controversial display that was more of a curiosity rather than the obsession it remains today on many levels.

PITCHING INDIVIDUALS HEADLONG TO EARTH

In his autobiography (**Touchdown**), legendary coach Amos Alonzo Stagg (1862-1965) of the University of Chicago included a quote (page 86) from an unnamed New York newspaper that seemed to accurately describe the early days of football. In this case, the reporter covered an encounter between Yale and Princeton in 1884:

> The spectators could see the elevens hurl themselves in kicking, writhing heaps. They had a general vision of threatening attitudes, fists shaken before noses, darting hither and thither, throttling, wrestling and the pitching of individuals headlong to earth; and all this was an exceedingly animated picture which drew from them volley after volley of applause.
>
> Those inside the lines, the judges, reporters, and so on, were nearer and saw something more. They saw real fighting, savage blows that drew blood, and falls that seemed as if they must crack all the bones and drive the life from those who sustained them.

Many newspapers found the sport of football to be classless and clueless, and certainly beneath the interest of the normal citizen.

In particular, the *Chicago Daily News* launched a withering campaign against the uncivilized nature of football on November 3, 1893, snagging at any ripe opportunity to besmirch the game:

> According to Macon McCormick the sporting writer, football is more brutal than prizefighting, and he wonders why the one is protected and the other condemned. The answer is very plain. Football is the product of colleges and is cultivated as a sport; prizefighting is a relic of barbarism and is fostered by gamblers and turf men. None familiar with sports doubts that football is more brutal than prize-fighting. It is not manly, and the camp follower of the game is the college tough.

The *Chicago Daily News* returned with still another indictment against the game on November 18 with the following broadside:

> The great claim in its favor that it was a game and the product of seats of learning. There is little in the game as now played to cause admiration. It is a free fight. Published reports of recent football performances point to a state of affairs discreditable to a high degree. It is plainly said that certain young men in different "teams" were many times over squarely struck in the face and elsewhere with clinched fists and came out of the game carrying the same marks they would have borne from a drunken street brawl.

In the 1890s, the players wore very little, if any, protective equipment (and no full-face protection), referees were often ill informed, and game scheduling was haphazard at best. The Englewood group traveling to Morgan Park consisted of just 14 players. Since those participating in the game played on both the offensive and defensive sides of the ball the need for substitutes (unless due to injury) was rare. Usually a team manager would accompany the team and would be available to play in an emergency.

Passing the ball was not yet recognized as a valuable offensive weapon (especially since the football itself was much more oval and bulky) and coaching was non-existent. Author and Chicago area high school football history expert Robert Pruter noted that "Englewood like most Chicago schools during this era relied either mainly on the team captain or an alumnus to coach its team each year. Such a situation left every season in an ad

3

hoc situation with regard to coaching, as high school elevens searched for recent grads in local colleges to direct the team for the season and often from game to game."

Englewood, from the south side of Chicago, captured the Cook County league title in 1891 and was so respected that the team was invited to play the University of Illinois in 1892 when the University of Wisconsin was unable to participate. Although Illinois defeated Englewood 38-0, the game was somewhat competitive and exemplified the capabilities of the Englewood club against a much tougher, and older, collegiate opponent.

LADIES ARE GALLANTLY ADMITTED FREE

Games between universities and high schools were not uncommon in the early days of competition. Englewood High School opened up its 1894 season with an exhibition loss to the powerful University of Chicago squad. Chicago's *Inter Ocean* newspaper (September 8, 1894) even managed to softly promote the contest by announcing that "An admission of 10 cents will be charged, but ladies are gallantly admitted free."

The 1894 football game between Morgan Park Academy and Englewood High School was a bit quizzical since it pitted a tough, experienced city opponent with a large enrollment (over 1,000 students) against a small "suburban" institution with a student body of just 108, with just 78 of those being male students. In addition, Morgan Park was rather new to the game of football and 1894 marked the first full season of competition for the team. It was clearly a step up in terms of competition for the Academy, a theme that would characterize the football program at Morgan Park Academy for years to come…

The scheduling of the game with Englewood High School was quite noteworthy for the Academy, according to author Robert Pruter:

> Football as a formally organized sport in the high schools was still young in 1894, when Morgan Park Academy organized its first team, so the school did not yet have any league affiliation and had to search for competition. The school found itself having to compete against the very best, notably Englewood High School, which won the Cook County championship that year, one of five league titles the state's top football power would win in the decade.

Whereas Englewood initiated its schedule against the University of Chicago, the Academy dropped a 12-4 decision in its opener to the Englewood YMCA. It should be noted that in 1894 a touchdown was worth just four points while a goal after a touchdown earned two points, as did a safety. Unlike today's game, teams usually played on a field without goal posts, so teams could add a pair of points, usually by running, for the "extra" score.

Prior to the Englewood contest that would conclude its initial season, the Academy compiled a respectable 3-3 mark, including knocking off the "second" team of Lake Forest University 12-6. A late season 8-6 defeat suffered at the hands of the University of Chicago second team indicated that the Academy gridders were developing into a respectable unit.

SCHOLASTIC PLAYERS QUARREL

Indeed, the Englewood game itself proved to be quite entertaining, albeit brief. Perhaps angered by the trudge up the hill, or even by the voracity of the Academy players, Englewood seemed to dip into its share of mayhem on the field as described by the *Chicago Tribune* (November 21, 1894) under the headline "Scholastic Players Quarrel:"

> Englewood High School and Morgan Park Academy played yesterday on the academy grounds at Morgan Park. After a series of end runs and bucking the line in the first half Dickey (Morgan Park) made a touchdown and Taylor kicked goal. Continued and persistent "slugging" of Englewood's left guard and right end marked the play.

As the game moved into the second half, tempers continued to flare, according to the *Chicago Tribune*: "In the second half Morgan Park carried the ball far into the opponents' field early, and after a strong 'buck' at the line the ball was called down. The Englewood men got it and ran down the field. After a sharp controversy over the play the captains called the game off, the score standing: Morgan Park 6, Englewood 0."

Fred Lowenthal was a member of that first team and later a controversial head coach of the football squad in 1902 at the Academy. However, by 1905 he was a columnist for the *Chicago Tribune* and used his position to recall that Englewood game under the headline "Story of a Former Morgan Park Captain." To its credit, Morgan Park Academy was both integrated and co-educational in 1894 and Lowenthal praised the abilities of his former teammate, George Bell, in the article. Bell was African-American and the Lowenthal article (although very politically incorrect today) is quoted here as it was written November 5, 1905:

> Bell was an embryonic theologian, and of course, very devout. This, though, did not prevent him from playing as rough a game as the rules allow. In a stiff contest with the team from Englewood High School, the colored lad was pitted against a player who at that time had some reputation as a weight tosser. For a while there was a terrific duel going on between the two, but finally Bell put his opponent hors de combat with a neck hold which was a cross between Evan Lewis' favorite and a straight choke.

> "O!-!-! My neck is broke," cried the opponent, writhing in pain. "The_____broke my neck." "Get up," said the dusky giant, without raising his voice, "get up; yo' neck ain't broke, o' you couldn't swear like that."

And so ended the first full season of football at the Academy. While the team managed an overall 4-3 mark with that final victory, the Englewood game began what would become a regular tradition at the Academy: success against larger schools, both in Chicago and in the Midwest. The performance of the football team was a source of internal pride for the Academy for several decades. As the teams continued to dominate over the years, the tremendous support for the players was unwavering, especially by the students and the entertaining Academy campus newspapers. *The Philolexian*, an Academy student publication (October 1895) quickly took up the call to stir up support for the football squad with the following editorial:

> It has been well said that the best way to advertise a school is to give it a successful football team. It might be as truthfully said that the best way to develop a good football team is for everyone to encourage it. We trust this interest on the part of the students in the game will continue, and now that the season has just begun, that every student will consider himself under obligation to aid and encourage our team. If they win laurels, let us be the first to bestow them. If they are unfortunate, let us not upbraid, but rather offer a sympathetic and cheerful encouragement.

NO MALARIA, NO BOYS
OF VICIOUS HABITS

It is unlikely that football, or any other game, was considered when the school was founded (as indicated by the Academy archives) in 1873 as the Mt. Vernon English, Classical, and Military Academy (see the complete listing of school names throughout the years at the end of this chapter). The land used to create the campus was previously owned by the Blue Island Land Company. As *The Academy News* noted in its school history article in 1935 [mentioned in the "Preface" to this book]: "The founder was Professor S.S. [Samuel Sheldon] Norton, who besides being the first headmaster, was the owner as well, for the obvious reason that he donated $16,000 of the necessary $30,000 that the building cost. The rest of the money was subscribed by property owners in the village of Morgan Park."

A school catalog published in 1874 by Mt. Vernon Military Academy still exists in the Academy archives and provides a glimpse into the early objectives of the administration:

> It is aimed to imbue them (the students) with high-minded, Christian and gentlemen-like sentiments, truthfulness, honor, candor, and doing right because it is right. By appealing to the moral sense, discipline is often a means of elevating the character, and a cheerful obedience to rules is secured.

Basic costs for boarding students would be $400 per year, but of course, that would include "Instruction in all branches taught in the English course, board, washing, mending under-clothing, lights, fuel, etc."

By 1877, the institution became independently known as Morgan Park Military Academy and remained that way until 1889 when it was renamed as the Illinois Military Academy.

Other early annual school catalogs share insight into the fledgling days of the institution. For example, in the catalog from 1881-82, the school sharply promoted the positive aspects of the campus, including "No malaria, no boys of vicious habits, nor boys expelled from other institutions received." The catalog further stated that "runaways are not wanted in our school, no guard is placed to stop the cadets from running away, and no time is wasted in looking after them if they do."

In addition, the catalog encouraged each of the students to bring "one Bible, one umbrella, two nightshirts, one knife, one plated fork, one tea-spoon, one napkin ring, one paper of needles, and one spool of strong, black thread." Meals were provided to the boarding students as part of the overall tuition package and students were required to wear uniforms.

Then, in 1892, after experiencing some financial difficulties, the school became part of the newly established University of Chicago and was renamed again as Morgan Park Academy of the University of Chicago. The military aspect of the school was dropped; the school was integrated, and women were now welcome to enroll. The *Chicago Tribune* described the grounds of the Academy as follows on October 2, 1892:

> The academy of the university is located at Morgan Park, and all preparatory work is done there. Five good size buildings are used, four of which are owned by the university. The building formerly owned by the Illinois Military Academy has been rented. The academic work was begun in August, and many students have been taking a summer course to prepare them for the university work.

The impetus behind this unique partnership was Dr. William Rainey Harper, President of the University of Chicago, who strongly pushed for a university prep school to be located in Morgan Park (then a suburb of Chicago).

With solid financial backing from the eminent John D. Rockefeller, both the University and the Academy flourished under the guidance of Harper. Students seeking a classical education at the Academy were also offered the opportunity to participate in sporting venues and other non-academic pursuits. On Sunday, March 19, 1893, *The Inter Ocean* reported that Morgan Park Academy and the University of Chicago participated in a basketball game: "This new game is becoming very popular with Western football teams, because it can be played indoors and lacks some of the rougher features of the rugby games." Nine players were on the court for each team and the University eventually prevailed by a score of 8-6. The **Encyclopedia of Chicago** designated this contest as the first game of basketball ever played by a high school team in the State of Illinois. In his landmark book **The Rise of American High School Sports and the Search for Control** (page 103), Robert Pruter contends that "The earliest schoolboy basketball in Illinois thus was played by Morgan Park Academy in 1893 and 1894…the school appears to have been the first secondary school in the country to have taken up the sport…" In reality, the first basketball game ever played by a high school team was mentioned by *The Inter Ocean* on February 18, 1893 when the newspaper reported on an upcoming basketball game scheduled for February 24, 1893 between the Academy and the West Side YMCA in Chicago.

On November 5, 1893, the *Chicago Tribune* stated that the "Morgan Park football team defeated the Lake Front Academy team by a score of 14-12 yesterday." No additional information was provided and since a school named Lake Front Academy was not in existence at the time, the opponent was probably Lake Forest Academy. This was likely the first football game played by the Academy since its partnership began with the University of Chicago. As noted previously, the school would begin its first full season in 1894.

In 1895, Morgan Park Academy "named" H.W. Dickinson its first football coach. Dickinson was likely a student since he was included (and named) ln an early photo of that 1895 Academy team. By now the Academy football team was also under the somewhat watchful eye of Coach Amos Alonzo Stagg of the University of Chicago.

Stagg, an All-American football player at Yale, arrived at the University of Chicago in 1892 after a stint as football coach at Springfield (Massachusetts) College. It was President William Rainey Harper himself who encouraged Stagg to join the faculty at the University of Chicago. Harper was a professor at Yale during Stagg's time at that institution and Harper hand-picked Stagg to both start the University of Chicago gridiron program in 1892, as well as to serve as Associate Professor and Director of the Department of Physical Culture and Athletics.

While Stagg was engaged to establish the football program at Chicago, he was also aware over the next few years of the gridiron possibilities at Morgan Park. In a sense, he was hoping that the Morgan Park team might serve as a type of "feeder" system for the University football program. Eventually, Stagg actively served as the coach of the Academy team, aggressively selected former players to coach at the Academy, and also arranged for the Academy teams to both scrimmage with the University of Chicago, as well as to play Chicago in regular season games. As the *Chicago Tribune* stated on September 19, 1895: "The (Morgan Park) team is being coached by H.W. Dickinson and after October 1 will play one or two practice games each week with Stagg's eleven at the university."

AND THEN THE FUN BEGAN

By the time the 1895 season rolled around, the Morgan Park Academy squad was a bit more experienced, and a great deal more organized than the previous year. Patching together a schedule that included a local athletic club, a YMCA, a university and an academy, the Morgan Park Academy team rolled to a successful 6-2 record. Although the club failed in a rematch with Englewood High School (dropping a 6-0 decision), victories over Northwestern Academy (58-0), Lake Forest Academy (6-0), and the Lake Forest University second team (34-0) were highlights of the season. In the Lake Forest Academy victory, the lone Morgan Park touchdown was tallied by Joseph Chalmers Ewing. Ewing would later play for the University of Chicago, but he is perhaps best known as being both the head football and baseball coach at Baylor University in Texas, part of a long line of Morgan Park Academy players who later coached at the collegiate level.

Aside from the blemish suffered in the Englewood game, the only other defeat suffered by the Academy in 1895 occurred in the wildly weird final game of the season at the Gibson City (IL) Athletic Club. The scheduling of this game remains a bit perplexing. In order to reach Gibson City, the Morgan Park players needed to embark on a long train ride downstate to Gibson City (in Ford County), and then grab the nearest taxi (which looked a lot like a horse and wagon) to find the football field.

The *Gibson City Courier* (November 22, 1895) kept the locals updated as the town prepared to welcome the visitors:

> The football game with Morgan Park, which has been arranged to take place here tomorrow, will be played at Pearces's race track east of town. Without doubt it will be the most interesting game of this fall as the Morgan Park team plays a smart scientific game.

It should be noted that by 1895, the Chicago newspapers were aware of the growing popularity of football and usually provided fairly extensive coverage of each high school game played in the area. Away games were included if the team from the Chicago area was able to contribute somewhat accurate information to the newspapers. In the case of the distant Gibson City contest, representatives from the Academy used the telegraph system to relay the lineups as well as the game results.

As such, *The Inter Ocean* dropped in a comprehensive game summary of the Gibson Athletic Club's 4-0 victory:

> Gibson, in the first half, made the first touchdown, but failed to kick goal and then the fun began. Morgan Park claimed a foul and threatened to leave the grounds, but after a great deal of wrangling the game was resumed...Dr.

Lovell was referee and proved unsatisfactory. It looked at times if he would be mobbed. The Morgan Park men left the grounds in anything but in the best of humor claiming that the game was stolen from them.

As expected during those early times, the capabilities of the referees were often minimal. The game was still fairly new, and the referees were generally supplied by the home team. So, it was not unusual if the referee might exhibit behavior on the field that might be considered partial to the host squad.

A friendlier viewpoint on the game later appeared in January of 1896 in *The Philolexian*, a campus publication published by the Philolexian Society at Morgan Park Academy. In its review of the football season, *The Philolexian* inserted some additional editorial insight into the result of the Gibson City game:

> The Gibson City game was characterized by knavery and trickery on the part of the opposing team, but in spite of off-side plays, unfair decisions and general slugging, our men managed to hold them to one touchdown, and the player who made this one touchdown afterwards acknowledged that he ran out of bounds to do it. The score, as one of our boys put it, was
>
> Morgan Park   0
> Gibson City   0
> Umpire   4

Despite the hard feeling about the loss to Gibson City, the proud *Philolexian* paused to shower the 1895 team with platitudes:

> The past autumn has been an important one in the history of our football team. The games played were not many, but the scores will go on record and serve as an inspiration to the boys next year. Taking it all in all, Capt. (George) Bell and his men are to be congratulated for the brilliant record they have made. But the one thing that brings special pride to every member of the Academy is their reputation for fairness and honesty.

As mentioned in Fred Lowenthal's 1905 article, George Bell was an exceptional student as well as a rugged figure on the gridiron. Academy records indicate that Bell (who entered the school in October of 1892 from Nashville, TN), easily took on a challenging academic schedule which included English, Latin, Greek, French, and German along with more traditional coursework. Following his graduation from the Academy in 1896, Bell entered the University of Chicago where he decided to drop football to focus on his academic pursuits. Unfortunately, Bell passed away in 1898, but he must be considered as one of the founders of the formidable football program that would prove to be a remarkable asset to Morgan Park Academy in the coming decades.

EXTRA POINT

School "spirit" and the favorable support of the football team quickly became prominent on the Morgan Park Academy campus early in the existence of the team. It was a movement that would continue through the existence of the Academy football program through the next several decades. As an early example, just after the start of the 1895 season, *The Philolexian* spoke boldly of the importance of having a successful football team at the Academy:

> It has been well said that the best way to advertise a school is to give it a successful football team. It might be as truthfully said that the best way to develop a good football team is for everyone to encourage it. The Academy has reason to be proud of the teams she has put forth in the past, notwithstanding the fact that we have never yet been given the advantage of a good regular coach . . . We trust this interest on the part of the students in the game will continue and now that the season has just begun, that every student will consider himself under obligation to aid and encourage our team. If they win laurels, let us be the first to bestow them. If they are unfortunate, let us not upbraid, but rather offer a sympathetic and cheerful encouragement. With such encouragement we will have a team who will do their utmost to give the Academy a high rank in the list of football teams this season.

FORMAL NAMES OF THE ACADEMY (1873-1959)

(Courtesy of Morgan Park Academy)

1873	Mount Vernon English, Classical and Military School
1874	Mount Vernon Military Academy
1877	Morgan Park Military Academy
1889	Illinois Military Academy
1892	The Morgan Park Academy of the University of Chicago
1898	The Academy of University of Chicago
1900	The Academy of the University of Chicago for Boys
1907	Morgan Park Academy on the Ridge
1909	Morgan Park Academy
1915	The Morgan Park Preparatory School
1918	Morgan Park Military Academy
1959	Morgan Park Academy

CHAPTER 2

Drawing Rooms and Locker Rooms

---

*"Football enthusiasm is plentiful about the school and in
many cases, is accompanied by considerable skill."*
—The Autocrat, Morgan Park Academy, 1896

In 1896, the lads of the Morgan Park Academy football squad were once again without a coach, but that minor distraction failed to hinder one of the finest seasons in the history of the school.

Ollie Mann was elected team captain, and the responsibilities for managing the team—as well as finalizing its schedule—were primarily thrust on his strong shoulders. The schedule included another "difficult" road game in the young program's tenure when a contest was scheduled at St. Charles High School, in St. Charles, IL on October 17. Captain Mann was required to help decipher an assortment of travel options, such as train schedules as well as horse and wagon transportation.

Players would be required to carry their own equipment for the long (nearly 60 mile) trip to what is now a far western suburb of Chicago. In addition, Mann would need to arrange meals and something resembling a locker room where the players could change into their uniforms.

A very welcome solution to the locker room dilemma was accepted when a private home in St. Charles was offered to the players according to *The Autocrat* (October 1896):

> At St. Charles, our eleven was given the freedom of the
> spacious Miller home, the parlors and drawing rooms of

which were turned into dressing rooms in short order. The
boys declare they were never in more pleasant quarters!

Despite the plush "locker room" accommodations, the undefeated
(3-0) Morgan Park team was faced with both a tough foe and an early
season snowfall as the contest began with St. Charles. Playing in a combination of snow and slush, the two teams battled back and forth in a rugged
affair that was typical of the time.

With no passing game in evidence, both clubs subscribed to the
"mass" style of play that stacked two lines of opposing players nose-to-
nose as each play began. The linemen would stand straight, and teammates
would be positioned very close together (often holding on to the person
next to them) and then surge forward in a group in an effort to pave the
way for the ball carrier to gobble up some very valuable yardage. While only
five yards were needed for a first down, just three downs were permitted
to achieve that objective—or the ball would simply be turned over to the
other team at the spot of the failed third down.

Needless to say, this type of cramped, physical play was very rough,
but the players seemed to prefer it that way, no matter what the conse-
quences. Although the pace—and speed—of the game was much slower,
injuries were still prevalent due to the rugged play, scarce rules, and the
lack of proper equipment. Pushing, shoving, and fighting were not only
common, but expected.

It was the responsibility of the officials to determine the placement
of the ball after each play, and to assist them, fields were generally marked
with horizontal lines every five yards. This prompted some observers to
note that the football field itself now resembled a cooking "gridiron," a
term which remains to this day to describe a football field, and to define
those who played the game as "gridders."

NO UNNECESSARY
WRANGLING OR SLUGGING

Surprisingly, the Academy game with St. Charles side-stepped the usual
physical shenanigans on the field as the *Autocrat* slyly reported: "There was
no unnecessary wrangling, and 'slugging,' as it is called, was not resorted to
by any player of either team."

One of the best offenses in 1896 was indeed the defense...This was
the result of another quirk of the times where the punt was often used in an

attempt to secure better field position. The punt could be launched by the offense at any time, whether it be first, second, or third down. If a team felt that it was too deep in its own territory to risk its offensive attack (and/or a fumble), it would simply punt the ball to the other team and hope that its defense could "hold" the other team's offense. Unfortunately, this often led to a dreadfully boring football game (especially in bad weather) where teams might receive a punt, only to immediately punt the ball back to the opposition.

Another odd strategy was the option for a team to kick the ball away (instead of receiving it) after its opponent scored. Again, the trend was to secure better field position rather than to initiate an offensive attack deep in its own territory. The scoring system was still undergoing experimentation with touchdowns worth four points and successful extra point attempts counting for two points.

THEY WENT IN TO DO OR DIE

All of these elements appeared in the precise reporting that appeared in the *Autocrat* following the St. Charles game:

> St. Charles, early in the first half, forced the ball to within three feet of the Morgan Park goal, but they then lost it on downs, after which a well-placed kick by Riley, which was fumbled by the other side and gathered in by Smith, so cheered our boys that they scored about five minutes later. The goal was missed and St. Charles kicked off. Morgan Park did not lose the ball until they had again scored and kicked goal.

The hosts jumped back in the game early in the second half to slice the lead to 10-6, before the *Autocrat* ascertained that "Prospects were not exceedingly bright just then for the Park boys but after readjusting their shin guards and nose masks they went in to do or die...and another figurative scalp adorns the belt of Captain Mann."

The final result of the game remained 10-6 in favor of Morgan Park to which the *Chicago Tribune* (October 18, 1896) attributed the victory to advantageous field position: "Riley's punting relieved several critical situations. The academy bucked hard but were loose on the defensive. The terrific rushing of Powers was the feature of his team's work."

A MORE EXALTED OPINION OF
PREPARATORY FOOTBALL TEAMS

With that key victory secured against St. Charles, the Academy rolled through its remaining six games undefeated, while allowing just six points during that span. Two weeks after the St. Charles game, Morgan Park knocked off the University of Chicago "second" team 12-0 in what might be described as a significant upset. The Academy *Autocrat* was even more elated than usual in its game summary (October 1896):

> The University Reserves, i.e. the scrubs, proved easy victims for our team on Wednesday, October 21ˢᵗ. The score was 12-0 in our favor and the sophs, and seniors, from the U. went home with a more exalted opinion of preparatory football teams.

The Academy was originally scheduled to play the Chicago varsity team as part of the university's unusual schedule that also included Iowa, Wisconsin, Northwestern, and Michigan. All those teams are powerhouses today, but in 1896, the Chicago students clamored for a tougher schedule that included stronger teams in the Midwest such as Minnesota and… DePauw University of Greencastle, Indiana!

Yet, the students were also irked by the fact that Stagg scheduled two other prep schools (English High and Armour Institute) in addition to the Academy. While Stagg promised to squeeze in a game with the University of Illinois, the fans were still not happy as *The Inter Ocean* reported on September 16, 1896:

> While the rooters, however, appreciate the fact, they are nevertheless inclined to think that Stagg might have secured much better teams than Armour Institute, English High School, and Morgan Park Academy. None of these teams are strong enough to compete with the varsity men, and hence the games threaten to be more or less one-sided affairs.

Stagg managed to quickly adjust the schedule according to the *Chicago Tribune* on October 20, 1896:

> Secret practice will be inaugurated by Coach Stagg in order to prepare his Maroons for the coming struggle with

Northwestern. This sort of practice will be kept up all week, with the exception of tomorrow, when a practice game will be played with Armour Institute. The date with Morgan Park Academy for this afternoon will be filled by the second eleven tomorrow at Morgan Park.

And just like that, Stagg helped ease some of the outward criticism of scheduling prep opponents, although high school teams like Englewood, Hyde Park, and others remained on the Maroons' schedule until 1905. In his autobiography (page 159), Stagg recalled the difficulty of finalizing both a competitive squad and schedule in the 1890s, owing largely to the lack of nearby competition. "The game was so new that it had not yet caught the public's interest, the gate receipts were trivial, and there were no prep schools and few high schools to feed the colleges with trained material."

STAGG COACHED FOOTBALL AT BOTH INSTITUTIONS

Oddly enough, Stagg was likely the impetus behind the formation of the very first football team at Morgan Park in 1894 and probably became a very active (albeit mostly uncredited) part of the Academy grid program. The current Academy web site acknowledges the unique partnership between the University of Chicago and the Academy back in the 1890s when the school was known as the "Morgan Park Academy of the University of Chicago…teachers at the Academy held university rank and one of them, Amos Alonzo Stagg, coached football for a time at both institutions."

While Stagg's autobiography fails to specifically mention the Academy, the Academy yearbook lists Stagg as the coach (or more likely the co-coach) in 1903, 1908, and 1909. In his physical absence, however, Stagg sent an endless stream of former players to coach the Academy football program for several years. This process would ensure that players at the Academy would be familiar with the University's football system should they decide to matriculate at that institution. In a sense, the Academy served as a football "farm" club for the powerful University program, at least until the careful partnership between the two academic entities dissolved in 1907. The fact that Stagg was mentioned as the Academy football coach in 1908 and 1909 indicates that the veteran coach was inclined to continue to cultivate the football arrangement with the Academy, even after the break-up between the two schools. Meanwhile, the roster of the University football squad was continually sprinkled with Academy graduates throughout this period.

But back to the 1896 season…

Additional incentive for the future was provided to the football team when representatives of the Academy expressed interest (in January of 1896) in participating in the establishment of a new athletic conference in that would include only private prep schools, similar to Morgan Park Academy. The other possible circuit candidates were Lake Forest Academy and Northwestern Academy. Although the "Academy Athletic Association" did not launch in time for the 1896 football season, it did set the groundwork for the initial season of something called the Inter Academic League in 1897. The creation of this conference would provide a more fixed schedule of adequate competition for the private prep schools who were still challenged to fill out their same dates from a wide assortment of opponents in 1896. For example, the Academy competed with such varied teams as the Auburn Athletic Club, the Chicago Theological Seminary, and the YMCA Training School. The steady presence of a formal league would certainly help stabilize the scheduling process each year. Ironically, the April 1896 issue of *The Autocrat*, published by Morgan Park Academy, identified Stagg as one of the driving forces behind the development of the new league, and that "Stagg…represented our Academy" at the initial meeting.

PLAYERS REFUSING TO GROVEL IN THE MUD

While league formation discussions were on the back burner in 1896, the Academy shuffled through the remainder of its ten-game schedule without a blemish. An anticipated tough contest against powerful Englewood High School resulted in an impressive Academy showing according to the *Chicago Tribune* on November 8, 1896:

> To the surprise of all except those who are acquainted with the spirit of win or die prevailed in the academy at Morgan Park. Englewood High School was not only defeated but outplayed at every point. For forty minutes, the men of the two teams took turns falling down in the mud and ice water, with the score 10-0 when time was finally called.

Weather was again a factor when the Academy traveled to Austin Village in Chicago a week later and grabbed a 16-6 victory. *The Inter Ocean* (November 15, 1896) described the messy terrain thusly:

The field was covered with mud and the play of both teams was exceptionally slow. The Austin team was handicapped by five substitutes, the regular players refusing to grovel in the mud for honors.

A final 22-0 win over Armour Institute on Saturday, November 21 capped the first perfect football season for Morgan Park Academy. The team finished with a 10-0 record and outscored its opponents 144-18. It was the first of twelve undefeated seasons for the Academy, the last occurring in 1975.

By 1897, the influx of Academy players to the University of Chicago became even more apparent as Coach Stagg began to more fully develop the athletic pipeline from Morgan Park Academy to the University of Chicago.

With lax rules regarding the age of players (both on the high school and collegiate levels), the age of individual members of the University of Chicago football team might be met with some surprise in the 21ˢᵗ century. *The Inter Ocean* unveiled its pre-season preview of the Chicago team on October 3, and singled out several key players who had graduated from the Academy:

> John Webb, who played left guard on the varsity last year, will probably be seen in his old position this fall. He weighs 173 pounds and is 27 years old. Webb played on the academy team at Morgan Park before he entered the university…Frank Clayton Cleveland comes from Morgan Park where he played on the academy team for three years. He is 24 years of age…Ray Johnson entered the varsity from Morgan Park this autumn. He is 20 years old and weighs 167 pounds…

Another potential varsity stalwart named in the article was Craig Bowdish, a 27-year-old alumnus of Yankton College in South Dakota. Indeed, it was not uncommon for players to enjoy a fulfilling varsity career at one college, and then simply enter another university and repeat the entire athletic process.

This challenging transfer concept was not restrained until 1922 when the National Collegiate Athletic Association (NCAA) adopted its "Ten Point Code" by which major issues such as transfers and freshman eligibility were addressed. For football players, this resulted in freshmen not being eligible to play on the varsity level, while varsity players were limited to three years of eligibility, and restrictions were established to impact players transferring easily from one school to another. Perhaps most importantly, athletes could only play for the school that they currently attended.

Since collegiate players were older at this time, it might be assumed that this would also be the case for high school athletes in the late 19th century. In an interview for this book, author and MPA historian Barry Kritzberg discussed the age issue in the early days of MPA football:

> This was probably fairly common, for there were no universally acknowledged restrictions about the ages or affiliation of the players. The ages do suggest, however, that a number of those players may not have had any connection with the university beyond the football field. Games may have been organized under the auspices of a university, but most were probably more like sandlot pickup games, where anyone who turned up might be allowed to play.

> High school football teams operated in much the same way. Many of the teams (particularly in the public schools) did not have coaches; it was the captain of the team who handled all the responsibilities of arranging for playing fields and finding suitable opponents. When there were "adult" coaches, they were more than likely volunteers, not salaried employees of the schools.

> The existence of ringers was obviously a problem for high school and college programs and it was not until state high school athletic associations began to form (1900 in Illinois) that problems such as this were discussed, if not immediately regulated. Much of it in those early days depended on the honor and integrity of the individual schools, for enforcement was not always practical or possible.

> Most independent schools had athletes who were typically older than some of their high school peers. A defense was made of this, however, that is plausible, but perhaps also an ingenious excuse: it was considered "normal" for boys who had attended public high schools to take an extra year or two of work at a preparatory school (like Morgan Park Academy) to prepare for the college entrance exams. But what coach would not have liked to pick up a "freshman" player with four years of experience under his belt?

With this consideration, it was likely not such a surprise when Stagg unveiled his 1897 football schedule that included Notre Dame, Michigan, Wisconsin, Illinois, and…Morgan Park Academy!

The game took place on Tuesday, October 19 on Marshall Field at the University of Chicago. The Academy entered the fracas with a 0-1 record following a season-opening 8-0 loss to the long-forgotten Eggleston Athletic Association, and the prep school boys proved to be no match for the varsity Maroons (4-0), who won easily 30-0. Morgan Park Academy put up a strong showing in the first half, trailing just 4-0 at the intermission, before the University club pulled away in the second half. Nonetheless, *The Inter Ocean* (October 20, 1897) praised the efforts of the losing team: "The Morgan Park eleven put up a good, fast game, and at times made surprising gains against their much heavier opponents." Following its mismatch with the Academy, Chicago then bounced Northwestern (21-6), Illinois (18-12) and Notre Dame (34-5) the next three weeks on the way to a final 8-1 record (although the Morgan Park game was not included in the official records of the university).

THIS GIVES MORGAN PARK THE CHAMPIONSHIP

But the real prize for the Academy during the 1897 season was the battle for the championship of the infant "Inter Academic League." With just three teams in the conference, the pennant race was over in a mere two weeks.

On October 30, Morgan Park routed Lake Forest Academy 28-0, and then followed that victory with a 17-0 decision over Northwestern Academy on November 6. "This gives Morgan Park the championship of the Inter-Academic League," proclaimed *The Inter Ocean* following the game, "having won from Lake Forest by a score of 28-0."

With shutout wins over the University of Chicago Scrubs (6-0) and Lewis Institute (21-0), Morgan Park finished the 1897 campaign with a respectable 4-2 record.

While the football team continued to position itself as one of the most respected prep clubs in the city, the year 1897 also marked some serious physical growth on the Morgan Park campus. Although overall registrations for the academic year dropped to 147 (100 boys and 47 girls) from 171 the previous year, the Academy dedicated some significant new property additions, including a dormitory. Also, the school purchased eight adjoining acres and developed this land into an enviable athletic field.

The new field was later described by the *University of Chicago Weekly* (September 8, 1898): "This field has been prepared by putting in a thorough system of drain-tile, grading to a perfect level, laying out around the edge of the oval and excellent bicycle and training track one-fifth of a mile in length, and offering the best of facilities for both football and baseball."

GIRLS RESCUE THEIR CHATTELS

With the new facilities in place for the 1898 school year, the Academy continued to promote its capabilities, especially for Chicago area students and their parents seeking an alternative to the increasingly crowded public schools in Chicago.

An advertisement for the Academy from 1897 found in the school archives promoted "A thorough preparatory school for both sexes. Eight buildings. New hall and athletic field. Accessible by two railroads and electric cars for day pupils on the south side. Boarders from Chicago may spend Saturday and Sunday at home."

Yet, with all of the optimism on the campus, there appeared to be some underlying dissension regarding the continuation of the co-ed educational opportunities on campus. On one hand, administrators noted, the female students helped pay the bills, while on the other, the girls occupied valuable dormitory space that might be used to attract more male boarders to the school.

The "space" issue had become even more critical after a frightening fire swept through the girls' dormitory (Park Hall) in December of 1895. While there was no loss of life or any reported injuries, the students and employees living and working in Park Hall lost many of their personal possessions. Due to the fire, the Academy scrambled to find housing for the ladies. The *Chicago Tribune* observed (December 16, 1895) under the sub-head "Girls Rescue Their Chattels" that the fire started on the third floor of the building while the students were enjoying dinner on the first floor. Apparently, one of the girls "lit her lamp before going downstairs, and sometime after, it exploded spreading its flames to the articles of furniture in the room and later bursting into a blaze of startling proportions."

As murmurs regarding the demise of the co-educational system at the Academy continued to surface over the next couple of years, the Academy Dean, Charles Thurber, was quoted in the *Chicago Tribune* (June 4, 1898) stating that "The girls are now, and forever, a part of our school." To justify that position, the Academy announced that the "Old Morgan Park Hall" would be updated and improved to serve as a girls' dormitory prior to the opening of the 1898-99 school year. For the moment, the controversy seemed to diminish…

EVANSTON MANAGER TOOK TEAM OFF FIELD

Back to football…

When the 1898 season began, the Morgan Park Academy football team welcomed its first "official" coach: Frederick R. (F.R.) Nichols. Nichols was a savvy halfback for Coach Stagg at the University of Chicago who graduated in 1897 and who would be the first of several former Chicago players who would take over the football helm at the Academy over the next few years. "Fred (Nichols) was one of the all-time 'greats' of the university baseball and football teams," praised then Morgan Park Academy Superintendent Harry D. Abells later in an undated document found in the Academy archives.

For Stagg, this would be a convenient opportunity to ensure that a loyal, watchful eye would be kept on the gridiron activities at the Academy. Nichols proved to be a natural educator both on and off the field as he led the Academy to a satisfying 4-1 record in his first campaign, including a quirky championship in the Inter Academic League. In 1898, the conference still consisted of just three teams: Northwestern Academy, Lake Forest Academy, and Morgan Park Academy. While the Academy easily handled Lake Forest 29-0 late in the season, the only other scheduled conference game (October 29) against Northwestern was never played!

When Northwestern arrived 30 minutes late from Evanston, Illinois for the start time at Morgan Park, the latter team apparently "refused to play only an exhibition game. The Evanston (Northwestern) manager took his team off the field," reported the *Chicago Times-Herald* (October 30, 1898).

Three weeks later, the aforementioned Lake Forest contest was staged at Lake Forest and the *Chicago Times-Herald* (November 20th) described the action as "one-sided" in the easy 29-0 romp. The victory left the Academy with a 4-1 record for the season, prompting the *Chicago Times-Herald* (November 22) to proclaim the Academy as having "One of the best football records among minor and secondary schools of the west."

In addition, the newspaper focused on one of Coach Nichols' biggest concerns entering the season: the lack of size on the team's roster: "The lightness of the team is worthy of notice in comparison with the large scores made by these academy 'feather weights' against heavy and fierce elevens."

Nichols returned to coach the Academy football team for his second, and final, season in 1899. As part of his new responsibilities as the school's athletic director, Nichols was instrumental in securing funds for the football squad. Early in the school year, Nichols addressed the student body to report on the overall athletic program at the institution, including fund raising. "A committee is at work raising funds," noted the *Chicago Times-Herald* (October 7), "and they have been very successful. The plan this year is to sell season tickets instead of asking for voluntary contributions." Nichols concluded his remarks by reminding the students to support the football team at its home opener against the South Side Academy later that day.

It turned out to be a wildly successful debut for the '99 squad as it steamrolled the South Side Academy club 50-0, pushing *The Academy News* coverage (October 10) to the point of giddiness:

> That our team would defeat their opponents was a foregone conclusion, but that they should so gloriously "put it all over them" exceeded even the highest expectations. The result was, indeed, very gratifying to the lovers of football at Morgan Park, and augers well for the games that are to come.

The Academy News was also quick to praise the role and influence of coach Nichols: "Mr. Nichols deserves great credit for putting the team in shape in so short a time." A final observation by *The Academy News* politely described an opponent's apparent foray into a bit of rough play late in the game: "One of their players unfortunately gave way to his 'scrappy' tendencies. It was very foolish of him and had he been more careful he would doubtless have been saved that severe headache. This was the exception, however, and the South Side players as a whole are clean and gentlemanly."

NO SECOND TEAM TO PRACTICE WITH

The same issue of *The Academy News* also published an insightful letter from Martin Schryver, captain of the football team. In his note, Captain Schryver identifies a distinctive trait of some of the early prep football teams—the lack of players, skilled or not. After all, the game was still very new and most, if not all, Academy players did not participate in any formal football program until arriving on campus. As such, Coach Nichols was not only outlining strategy and conditioning efforts, but also providing basic gridiron skills and techniques to his players.

While Schryver's letter expressed gratitude for the existence of the football program, it also sharply requested more students to actively participate in the sport:

> We have received elegant financial support and have no complaint to make on the rooting, but we must have a strong second team if we are to expect success…The outlook of this direction, I must confess, is rather gloomy. For the last two weeks, the 'regulars' have had no second team to practice with and even a Morgan Park team cannot win without practice. Mr. Nichols has shown a great interest in the team and has spent no little time teaching the fellows good football. Let the scrubs show their appreciation and turn out strong this week.

Although the club (with or without some new faces!) was stopped a week later by the University of Chicago Scrubs 5-0, the Academy then reeled off four straight wins to set up a season-ending final game with a new and very prominent opponent: Culver Military Academy of Culver, Indiana.

Still a well-regarded prep school to this day, Culver proved to be a challenging adversary throughout the history of the football program at Morgan Park (Military) Academy. While the opening contest in this long rivalry resulted in an 18-6 Culver victory in 1899, it tipped off an extraordinary and intense competition over the next 50 years between the two academies. The loss to Culver on November 18, 1899 capped off a 5-2 record in the final year of the Coach Nichols' era.

In the Culver defeat, the sole touchdown tallied by the Academy was the only score allowed by Culver during the season, according to *The Inter Ocean*:

> Morgan Park played a snappy, aggressive game, and scored a touchdown in the first half, the first scored against the cadet team this season. Morgan Park used the Chicago revolving mass on tackle and pushed the ball across the line before Culver succeeded in solving the play. Both teams played a good article of football.

Nichols concluded his brief coaching stint at the Academy with an overall record of 8-3, but more importantly pushed the school's football program to a level of competitive respect in both the Chicago area and the Midwest. He went on to establish himself as both an instructor and administrator in the Chicago Public School system for over 40 years, including serving as the principal at the Hendricks, Marsh, and Bright schools in Chicago. He passed away on December 7, 1950 at the age of 86.

EXTRA POINT

Over the years, numerous graduates of Morgan Park (Military) Academy have left an impact on the game of football at various locations. The first of these may have been Joseph Chalmers (J.C.) Ewing (1875-1965). A native of Gibson City, Illinois, Ewing graduated from Morgan Park Academy in 1898 and then played football and baseball for A.A. Stagg at the University of Chicago during the 1899-1900 school year.

His academic career took a bit of a detour when he was named as the head football coach at Colorado College (1900 and 1901 seasons) where he compiled an 11-3 record. Chalmers then moved on to become head coach for the football program at Baylor University in Texas in 1902. Earlier in 1902, Ewing also started the baseball program at Baylor.

He did return to the University of Chicago to complete his law degree in 1903 and then established a legal practice in Greeley, Colorado, where he became a successful business man. He served several years as the U.S. Collector of Customs for Colorado and Wyoming and operated several business interests in both Colorado and California. Ewing passed away in San Diego in 1965 at the age of 89.

The 1896 football team of the Morgan Park Academy of the University of Chicago finished with a spotless 10-0 record while playing high schools, colleges, and athletic clubs. Only three touchdowns were allowed by the club all season. The odd objects worn around several of the players' necks are actually nose guards in an era when very little body protection was utilized on the field.

Coach F.R. Nichols (second row with tie) led the 1899 squad to a 5-2 mark after captain Martin Schryver begged students to join the team. Front row (from left): Lodge, Brinton, and Pratt. Second row: Morgan, Ellsworth, Schryver, Coach Nichols, Schroeder, and Beckett. Third row: Freeman, Oberg, Dickson, Paddock, Reniff, Preston, and Schnur. In 1900, George Schnur scored six touchdowns and kicked seven extra points in one game!

CHAPTER 3

Too Hot to Handle

"Dean Wayland Chance turned the regular chapel time over to the athletic association, in an effort to raise money for the football team."
— Chicago Daily Journal, 1900

One of the hopefuls of the 1900 football team was a slight, inexperienced, but very determined halfback from Iowa who transferred to the Academy for his final two years of prep school. His appearance on the Morgan Park campus apparently was heavily influenced by the presence of inexpensive rail transportation from his home in Mason, Iowa to Chicago.

In later life, he recalled that the decision was quite simple: "We lived in Iowa and my father was in the cattle business. I could always get a free ride into Chicago on a cattle train. For that reason, I went to Morgan Park Academy," reported author Frank Maggio in his book **Notre Dame and the Game That Changed Football** (page 65).

Jesse Harper was a quiet kid who spent most of his initial days at the Academy patiently explaining that his first name was pronounced "Jess" and not "Jessie." His initial impact on the football team was minimal with limited playing time. In fact, his first appearance in an Academy uniform was with the "scrub" team as it was smoked 17-0 by the University School on October 3, 1900. Harper's brother Floyd (who graduated in 1899) had been a star receiver for the Academy, once grabbing a pair of touchdown catches against Lake Forest during the 1898 season. In time, Jesse Harper would become one of the most influential individuals in the history of football. Unfortunately, in 1900 it would take Jesse a bit longer to make his mark on the field under the watchful eye of new coach (and alumnus) Jonathan Webb...

Webb was an ebullient, thoughtful individual who graduated from Morgan Park Academy in 1896. While at the Academy, Webb undertook an ambitious classroom schedule, excelling in math, chemistry, and botany, while slipping a bit in Greek and Latin. He then played four years at tackle under Coach Stagg at the University of Chicago. The 1899 UC squad (16-0-2) was undefeated and captured its first Western Conference (now Big Ten) championship while Webb gained all-league honors for his performance on the field. It appears that Webb was a favorite of Stagg's as well, since the respected coach recalled Webb's toughness when he referred to the UC team of 1897 years later in his autobiography (**Touchdown**, page 206):

> The group of which I speak was the wildest crew I ever skippered. The animal spirits which later helped to bring home the championship [1899] bacon were devoted in quarters to a continuous rough housing that made life interesting for the other tenants.

> Jonathan Webb, solid, loyal, sober citizen and star tackle, being hit in the ear by a steaming hot potato, the most of which stuck there, refused to dig the potato out, although it was blistering that sensitive organ, as a lesson to his rowdy associates.

It was now becoming normal for Stagg to insert one of his former players into the football helm at the Academy and Webb was the logical choice when F.R. Nichols departed after the 1899 campaign. Webb likely jumped at the opportunity to coach at his alma mater, especially when offered a faculty position at the Academy as well.

Eager to begin his professional career, Webb first engineered a major change in his personal life by marrying Miss Eva Miriam Cleveland of nearby Mokena, IL (another graduate of Morgan Park Academy) on August 22, 1900. However, when the young couple returned to the Academy for the start of the 1900-1901 school year, there was one glaring difference in the campus from which they had both departed just a few years earlier.

THE PEOPLE OF MORGAN PARK ARE STIRRED UP

After years of rumors, discussion, and debates, the management of the University decided to no longer accept women as students at the Academy. This decision, which took effect on July 1, 1900 was met with sadness by the female students but there was no flexibility or recourse in the decision. According to Academy records, 49 females (out of 154 students) were enrolled for the 1899-1900 school year. The decision followed a legal review of the female exclusion possibility by members of the Board of Trustees of the University of Chicago under the auspices of the "Committee on Academy." In a letter (February 25, 1900) to Chicago president William R. Harper from T. W. Goodspeed, Secretary of the Board of Trustees, Goodspeed outlined the recommendation of the Committee:

> At a meeting of the Committee on Academy held February 23, a legal opinion was presented to the effect that there was no legal obstacle in the way of making the Morgan Park Academy an exclusively boys school. After a full discussion, it was voted that the committee report to the Board that it recommends the discontinuance of the co-educational feature at Morgan Park and the making of the Academy a boys school from and after July 1, 1900. (University of Chicago. Office of the President, Harper, Judson and Burton Administrations. Records (Box 3, Folder 11). Special Collections Research Center, University of Chicago Library.)

The Inter Ocean reported that "The people of Morgan Park are stirred up…over the announcement that the co-educational feature of Morgan Park Academy… is to be abandoned." Basically, there were few high school options for females in the area but a brief, albeit unsuccessful, appeal was launched to detour the decision. Overall attendance at the school slipped to 133 male students for 1900-1901, but by the 1902-1903 school year, 184 students were enrolled. The Academy would remain as an all-male student institution until 1959.

One of the challenges for both Coach Webb, and the Academy, was funding the growing—and very popular--football program. To this end, it was decided that a direct appeal be made to the students for a voluntary contribution that would be used to support the football team. Instead of the regular chapel service held on Wednesday, October 3, 1900, the session was altered to become a fund-raising effort for the squad. Wayland

Chase, the Dean of the Academy, offered the school athletic association the opportunity to seek direct support from the student body. Coach Webb was apparently persuasive in his comments, according to the *Chicago Daily Journal*: "One hundred and fifty dollars was asked, and inside of 15 minutes $270 was subscribed by the students and faculty."

Back on the football field, the Webb coaching regime tipped off with a rocky start, as the team stumbled out of the gate with an 0-2-1 mark. Part of this slow start may have been attributed to the absence of Captain Frank Schroeder, a tough tackle/fullback and graduate of Richmond High School in Illinois. Schroeder entered the Academy in the fall of 1899 and scored a pair of touchdowns in his very first game, a 50-0 win over the South Side Academy. He continued to dominate the action from both sides of the line during the season, including tallying four touchdowns in a 22-2 rout of Northwestern Academy, and his teammates honored Schroeder by selecting him as team captain for the 1900 campaign.

After spending the summer of 1900 back home, Schroeder returned to the Academy on September 18 to begin preparations for both the new school year and an ambitious football schedule. However, Schroeder was not in the lineup for the first game (a 0-0 tie on September 26 with the Morgan Park town team) and that absence was explained in the *Chicago Tribune* that same morning: "Captain Schroeder will not be back for a week or so owing to sickness, which is liable to keep him out of the game, the first of the season."

Sadly, on the same day (October 3) that the football team enjoyed its successful fund raiser, its captain, Frank Schroeder, passed away at home in Richmond, Illinois. The mysterious cause of death was not immediately noted until October 18, when the *Chicago Daily News* reported: "Frank Schroeder, who was playing at fullback, was taken sick with typhoid fever and died."

SCHNUR PLAYED THE STAR GAME

Perhaps distraught by the passing of Schroeder, MPA was winless in those first three encounters before engaging the YMCA Secretarial Institute on October 17. This game proved to be the stage that established the reputation of one of the school's first "superstar" players in halfback George Schnur. In the 57-0 romp over the YMCA squad, Schnur, a junior from Glencoe, Illinois, exploded for six touchdowns, and kicked seven extra points. With a touchdown worth just five points in 1900, Schnur still managed to personally score 37 points in the blasting of the YMCA. "Schnur played the star game," gushed the *Chicago Tribune*, "making six of the ten touchdowns and kicking seven goals. Schnur made a sensational touchdown after running the length of the field after he caught the ball on the kickoff."

Despite the brilliance of Schnur, Morgan Park followed the big win over the YMCA with a close loss (6-5) to the UC Scrubs and then a 5-5 tie with the Bennett Medical College which dropped the team's record to 1-3-2 midway through the season. It was during the Bennett contest on October 24 that Coach Webb initiated an unusual substitution noted by the *Chicago Tribune*: "Schnur played his usual good game but Coach Webb took him out in the second half to save him for Saturday's league game with the Armours." With Schnur idle on the sideline, Webb tossed unproven Jesse Harper into the Academy backfield, providing Harper with his first taste of varsity action for the season.

After a promising debut, Harper eventually claimed a permanent position in the starting rotation and helped the Academy conclude the season with a roar, grabbing victories in six of the remaining seven games to finish the season with a 7-4-2 mark despite the sluggish start. Two big wins over Northwestern Academy (24-0) and South Side Academy 17-12) brought the season to a successful conclusion, but not before some unusual circumstances involving the South Side contest.

Originally scheduled for November 17, the game with South Side spiraled into a comedy of errors when South Side initially requested a postponement due to its chosen field being unavailable.

The Academy insisted that the game be played when and where as scheduled and showed up at that location as planned. Since South Side could not secure the field as originally scheduled (and its team was not present at the appointed time after notifying Morgan Park), the Academy gleefully declared the game a forfeit and put another notch in its win column for the season. Meanwhile the South Side eleven was shocked that its offer to reschedule the game had been quickly rebuffed without any consideration of a new date or location.

The expected rebuttal protesting the result followed from South Side, but the two teams still could not reach a sensible solution regarding any alternative to the forfeit. This prompted a meeting of the Inter-Academic League Board of Control which solemnly directed that the game should be played (or re-played depending on your viewpoint) on December 8, so that a true champion of the conference could be determined. Naturally, there were some hard feelings on both sides regarding this decision. The *Chicago Tribune* reported on December 2 that "the dispute has aroused additional rivalry between the two academies and both have been working hard in preparation for the game. One of the odd features of the match is that both institutions are affiliated with the University of Chicago and have been trained in Chicago plays by former maroon players." In an effort to defuse any animosity on the playing field, it was agreed that University of Chicago Coach A.A. Stagg himself would be the referee for the game.

Prior to that big final game with rival South Side Academy, on December 2, the *Chicago Tribune* published a feature on the Morgan Park team, complete with photos of individual players, such as Schnur, quarterback Ralph Cobb, and team Captain Louis Paddock, a sturdy tackle. Readers also learned that right end Scott Mendenhall of the Academy had played the previous season at the University of Virginia. Regarding Harper, the newspaper stated: "Jesse Harper has shown himself to be a promising man in his playing at right half, but his slight weight has been a hindrance to his running this year." In another article, the paper described Harper as "nervy and fast."

After being thumped 50-0 by Morgan Park the year before, the South Side boys were itching for revenge. Various members of the University of Chicago varsity helped coach South Side the week before the game, including the talented All-American Clarence Herschberger, who also helped coach the undefeated 1899 University of Chicago team.

In a bitterly fought contest, Morgan Park prevailed 17-12 with the anticipated fisticuffs never emerging according to The Inter Ocean: "The playing consisted of masses on tackle and a lot of line bucking, while there was little kicking on account of the high wind. The game was clean throughout, and the decisions of the officials were never disputed, and the better team won." Schnur paced the victors with two touchdowns and a pair of extra points allowing the Academy to claim its fifth straight "Inter-Academic" title much to the elation of the student body.

But when the game ended, that's when the fun began!

BOYS SET FIRE JUST FOR FUN

Perhaps it was the thrill of victory, or avoiding the "agony" of defeat, but whatever "it" was prompted an unscripted celebration on the Academy campus that quickly escalated into a dangerous situation as the students joyfully celebrated the coveted championship victory over the South Side challengers. Although the Chicago papers were largely silent in reporting the incident, the raucous party evolved into a mini-riot causing considerable damage. The turning point arrived when the gleeful celebrants decided to torch an aging laundry building on campus. Actually, the far away *Rock Island Argus* provided the most intimate details of the ruckus that occurred following the South Side Academy game:

> Football yells, victorious players on the shoulders of their admirers, wild rushes between pupils and firemen and the whole scene lighted up by the shooting flames of the burning laundry building of Morgan Park Academy which the pupils had set on fire to celebrate their victory over the South Side Academy, marked the football demonstration at Morgan Park Saturday night. The mob finally drove away the firemen and dispersed to avoid a conflict with the police.

The laundry building was located at 11245 Crescent Avenue, just to the west of the gymnasium on the current campus. According to the *Argus*, the celebrating students might have used the football victory as a feeble excuse to address the unwanted presence of an ugly campus structure:

> The [laundry] building, a substantial two-story frame structure, was burned to the ground and the loss of $1,000 was not covered by insurance. This building, it is said, has long been an eye-sore to the pupils, who failed to see a desirable contrast between it and the six buildings on campus. The faculty is greatly incensed over the act of the pupils, and if the leaders can be discovered severe punishment will follow.

In addition to the loss of the building, the faculty could not have been pleased when word of the fiery destruction was picked up by media outlets around the country. The *Los Angeles Times* even turned the incident into an editorial, commenting that, "Students of the Morgan Park Academy burned one of the college buildings to celebrate a football victory. Well, this is better than murdering somebody, who knows but that this is the beginning of a blessed reform?"

The laundry building itself was never rebuilt…nor was it necessary to "rebuild" the football team as it prepared for the following season.

STAGG CALLS HIM THE STRONGEST PUNTER

With numerous key underclassmen returning from the 1900 team, including quarterback Cobb along with Harper and Schnur, there was a great deal of optimism heading into the 1901 season. Coach Webb returned to the University of Chicago after his single season at the helm to pursue a graduate degree as well as to help coach the football team under A.A. Stagg. For 1901, the coaching choice for the Academy was a bit unusual in that Reuben M. Strong was neither a graduate (nor a player) from the University of Chicago. Instead, Strong played for Oberlin College in Ohio where he distinguished himself as both an athlete and a scholar. During his collegiate career, Strong published an academic magazine called the "Journal of the Wilson Ornithological Chapter of the Agassis Association," that might have been a bit different from a normal football coach's expertise! He also earned a bit of notoriety on the gridiron when he broke both major bones in his right leg during a football game in 1895 and kept on playing! Following graduation from Oberlin, Strong was an instructor and football coach at Lake Forest Academy before he secured a PhD from Harvard in 1901. Returning to the Chicago area, Strong was hired by the Academy to teach physiology and botany, as well as coach both the football and track teams. As such, Strong was the only football coach in the deep history of the academy with a doctorate from Harvard University!

While becoming acquainted with his players, Strong helped prepare an ambitious schedule for the 1901 season that would include high schools, academies, colleges, associations and the first game ever to be played out of state by an Illinois prep school.

Excitement prevailed on the campus, and the potential of the football team was recognized by increased coverage in the Chicago newspapers. On September 19, the *Chicago Record-Herald* predicted that "The football prospects of the Morgan Park Academy are brighter this year than they have been for several seasons past." Meanwhile, the *Chicago Tribune* published a large photo of Captain George Schnur on that same day which included the caption stating that "He is considered the best halfback in the Academic League and Coach Stagg calls him the strongest punter among the preparatory school stars."

Even *The Academy News* chipped in with an optimistic flourish on September 25: "At this early date it would be foolish to predict too great things for the 1901 football team, but the prospects seem brighter this year than for several seasons past." Yet even as the ink was drying on this edition of *The Academy News*, the first dark cloud of the new semester drifted over the campus as youthful hijinks nearly turned into tragic circumstances.

THERE AIN'T ANY TWO OF YOU CAN HANDLE ME!

As part of the opening of the school year, it was traditional for the upper-classmen to "initiate" the resident members of the freshman class with a nocturnal application of hazing rituals, such as "hotfooting," which includes the battering of the soles of one's feet with a solid object (such as a wooden paddle) until the feet become "hot." In the wee hours of Tuesday, September 24, the annual rituals were largely completed and the faculty members overseeing the activity retired for the evening. It was then that one of the students in West Hall (now the tennis courts on the current campus) noticed that three boys from the town of Morgan Park were sitting on the second-floor fire escape and peering through the window of one of the dormitories. Upset with this unwanted intrusion, the Academy residents attempted to persuade the visitors from witnessing any more of the proceedings, and to leave their perch on the fire escape. If caught, it was possible that the visitors would also be subjected to the hazing ritual…

In order to facilitate the request to depart, one of the Academy students on the third floor unleashed a bucket of cold water onto the visitors, prompting two of them to surrender inside the second floor, while the third individual named James Etzler sprinted down the fire escape and defiantly challenged any takers to a fight by shouting, "There ain't any two of you can handle me!" Further insults were exchanged and to prevent Etzler from escaping, Albert "Ralph" Cobb, the quarterback on the football team, tackled Etzler and a fight ensued. "Etzler was severely beaten before he lost his temper," reported the *Chicago Tribune*, "Then, it is said, he cut his opponent in the back, tearing the sweater and running the blade in. Then he slashed Cobb's arm and hand. Weakened by the wounds, Cobb loosened his hold and Etzler rose to his feet." Dropping the knife, Etzler fled from the area and took a train to downtown Chicago. From there, he boarded a boat headed to Michigan in order to briefly ensure his escape from likely criminal charges.

Meanwhile, the injured Cobb was taken to the infirmary on campus for treatment of four stab wounds, two in the back, one in the arm, and one in the hand. Since Etzler was identified as the assailant (and fled the scene), a warrant was issued for his arrest should he be found. Fortunately, he did return to his nearby home later that week and was arrested but claimed that he acted only in self-defense. The *Academy News* was aghast at the circumstances and lamented the injustice done to Cobb:

> As to the dastardly crime everyone in school and in the village who knows the facts denounces it in the bitterest terms. A man must indeed be a villain of the blackest type who will unprovoked attack a student who is merely out for a frolic. To those who do not know Ralph Cobb we would say that he is the most popular fellow in school. He plays quarterback on the football team and is prominent in all athletics. He hasn't an enemy in the world and in short is a popular favorite and every student listens anxiously to every rumor that comes from his bedside.

While Cobb recovered, and missed the early part of the football season, Etzler was released on a lofty $500 bond following a preliminary hearing and the case was continued until October 5. An intense trial followed, with at least 11 witnesses testifying against Etzler. The defendant stood his ground by attempting to justify his self-defense claim and then launched counter charges against three Academy students, including Cobb. As the trial dragged into its third day, the defense attorney, perhaps seeking to salvage a lost cause, proposed a settlement to the prosecution. It was agreed that the charges against Etzler would be dropped. In return, Etzler would assume all court costs and drop his charges against the three Academy students. In *The Academy News*, Dean Wayland Chase explained that Etzler likely would have been subject to a conviction had the trial concluded as originally planned:

> Justice McKinnon, in declaring the case dismissed, pronounced it as his judgement that the evidence would have warranted his holding the defendant over to the grand jury as probably guilty of the serious charge against him. Yet, he said, that all things considered, he welcomed this way of ending the trial, believing that sufficient had been done to show the defendant the seriousness of his action.

With the agreement, both sides avoided additional legal fees and hopefully Etzler absorbed a key life-lesson. Cobb was doing well enough to testify in person at the trial, but still faced a lengthy recovery. Yet the real challenge now facing the Academy administration was a two-headed menace: negative national press as well as angry parents who didn't enjoy the traditional "hot footing" frenzy. With the laundry building fire of 1900 still fresh in the minds of many, the administration likely accepted the dismissal plea for Etzler in hopes that he, like the bigger story itself, would simply go away. Newspapers around the country picked up the regrettable incident, portraying the Academy as possibly an unsafe place to send one's child.

Then there was the issue of "hot footing" itself which basically prompted the stabbing incident. A year before the Cobb incident, several parents of freshmen students at the Academy visited the campus and "found their sons and heirs limping about as though suffering from gout, rheumatism, and soft corns. Inquiry revealed the fact that the freshmen were merely suffering from the 'hot foot.' The entire freshman class were on the casualty list, as it seems they made a concerted resistance to the upper classmen but were finally overpowered and subjected to the worst 'hot footing' ever visited by outraged upper classmen upon presumptuous freshman youth," reported the *Chicago Tribune*.

The faculty, at that time, announced that the "hot foot" custom would no longer be recognized on campus, yet it reared its ugly head again in 1901, quite possibly for the last time.

Meanwhile, the football season was about to begin on September 25, and Coach Strong scrambled to uncover a quarterback to replace the ailing Cobb. With the passing game largely non-existent at the time, the replacement for Cobb was not quite as difficult as it might be today when the quarterback oversees all aspects of the offense. However, there was also a limited roster and the myriad of running plays would need to be absorbed quickly by the new quarterback. After struggling through a listless 15-6 win over Lake View in the opener (Harper scored one of the touchdowns), Coach Strong settled on end Scott Mendenhall to assume the quarterbacking duties prior to the second contest with the Normal Park Athletic Association. Schnur scored twice in the 14-0 victory, including a 50-yard scoring romp over and through left tackle. Schnur was right back at it the following game, when the Academy rolled to a 65-5 decision over an outmanned Austin High School eleven. Schnur contributed five touchdowns and six extra points to personally account for 31 of this team's total of 65 which established a single game team scoring record for Morgan Park Academy.

In 1901, *The Academy News* was providing exceptional insight into the football team and its coverage of games was perceptive. The student newspaper eagerly accepted the dual role of both reporter and cheerleader for the team as it churned its way to one of the finest seasons in school history. Along the way, the *News* shared behind-the-scenes information that allows the current reader a generous peek into the management of a high school football team at the turn of the last century. For example, we learn that funding for the team did not come from the school itself, but rather from donations from the students and staff. In addition, players purchased their own uniforms and equipment, and likely chipped in for the transportation fees as well. *The Academy News* gratefully discussed the positive results of the annual fund raiser for the athletic department which occurred right after the convincing win over Austin:

> On last Thursday morning, the annual meeting of the students for the raising of money for the athletics was held after chapel. Many contributions were made which we know are at personal sacrifice, but this is the spirit that counts, and in it, perhaps, may be found the mighty something, known as the 'Morgan Park spirit.' The total amount secured was about $425.

Such funding helped facilitate the placement of new goal posts on the field in 1901, and the *News* hinted that the next big project would be the placement of "a wire fence around the entire gridiron. Such an improvement has long been needed and it will be appreciated by both players and spectators." The football team also welcomed an invaluable supporter in student team manager L. H. Fox, who helped arrange the schedule and also organized travel logistics. In an era when preliminary season schedules were sketchy and almost always changed on the run, Fox maintained the administrative stability needed to keep the talented team on track.

LOW ENOUGH TO CARRY A BIG GANG

As the football team continued to march through the season with an unblemished mark, Fox prepared for two significant road trips: one to Aurora, Illinois and the other to Cleveland, Ohio. Both would take considerable planning and organizational skills, as Fox would not only facilitate the football team's travel, but also offer the student body the opportunity to attend the "away" games. Just prior to the East Aurora High School contest, the Academy reeled off three straight shutouts, including a 28-0 pasting of St. Viateur's (aka St. Viator) College on October 9 where Harper tallied on a 70-yard scamper and Schnur accumulated 13 more points with a touchdown, three extra points, and a field goal (touchdowns and field goals/drop kicks each still counted for five points). However, Harper injured his left knee in this game and was expected to be lost for a portion of the remaining schedule.

Harper missed the next two wins over Chicago Eclectic College (29-0) and Armour Academy (39-0) as the team moved to 6-0 before the big game at Aurora on October 26. Although Harper was still out with the knee injury, *The Inter Ocean* reported on October 21 that Cobb would return to action after sufficiently recovering from the stab wounds suffered just prior to the opener: "The strength of the pennant winners of last year will be further increased by the return of Cobb, the star quarterback of last year's team."

Academy students were encouraged to attend the highly-anticipated battle in Aurora between the two undefeated teams. Manager Fox negotiated a special railroad fare price for attendees and *The Academy News* on October 23 expected its readers to show their support: "The fare ($1.50) to Aurora is low enough to carry a big gang…and all students who can afford the outing should take advantage of the opportunity. Aurora will be perhaps the hardest team we play this year and the eleven needs the rooters. Everybody turn out."

In an inside column, *The Academy News* offered some positive news regarding the injured players: "With Cobb in the game this week the team will be strengthened considerably and when Harper is back we will be 'It.'"

With a solid group of supporters in the stands, the Academy added East Aurora to its list of gridiron victims by tossing an 11-0 shutout described by the *Chicago Tribune* as "a desperately contested game…The score of 11-0 in favor of Morgan Park does not express the fierceness of the struggle." Three more victories followed in the next ten days to stretch the Academy record to 10-0. Harper returned to the lineup for the ninth game and scored three times in a 38-0 mauling of Lake Forest Academy. It was then that the Academy stepped away from the local competition for a week and ventured over to Cleveland, Ohio in a game that was historically significant for Illinois high schools according to author and historian Robert Pruter: *(A Century of Intersectional and Interstate Football Contests: https://www.ihsa)*

> In 1901, Morgan Park Academy actually inaugurated long-trip travel for Illinois schools, when it went to Cleveland to play the University School there for the private schools Midwestern championship. Neither team went home happy as the schools tied 0-0.

JOE ZIEMBA

GREATEST INTERSCHOLASTIC BATTLE EVER FOUGHT HERE

The *Chicago Tribune* covered the distant game and decided that it was "The greatest interscholastic battle ever fought here, and the result is important to Western secondary teams." Basically, the game indicated that the Academy club, as a representative of Midwest teams, proved that it could compete with more established programs from the eastern portion of the country. The *Chicago Tribune* added that "The field was slow and greatly retarded the fast plays which the Western boys hoped to win." In reality, the condition of the field might have been a huge factor in the outcome and perhaps an intentional home field "advantage." *The Inter Ocean* further reported that "The field at Cleveland was covered with loose sand, for which the local team had prepared by having cleats of extra length. Morgan Park was unable to use any of her end runs, on which she depends so much for gains." In other words, the hosts had utilized a unique way to slow down the quicker backs like Schnur, Harper, and Cobb of the Academy by simply "adjusting" the playing conditions.

Nevertheless, the Academy had one more piece of unfinished business as it closed out the season by hosting rival South Side Academy to conclude the 1901 schedule. Morgan Park prevailed 16-0 to complete a nifty 11-0-1 mark and claim still another Inter Academic championship. Even more impressively, the Academy outscored its opponents 300-16 to put an exclamation point on an outstanding year.

Unlike the previous season, when the final victory resulted in the torching of the laundry building, the student celebration after the South Side game was a bit more muted. There were speeches and fireworks, of course, with the evening capped off by just one lonely bonfire!

Schnur went on to star at the University of Chicago for Coach Stagg for two seasons, but then abruptly left school following his junior campaign to join his father's business enterprises. The other marquee name from the 1901 team was Jesse Harper, who also matriculated to the University of Chicago. Despite suffering from injuries and illness during his collegiate days, Harper did finally see action on both the football and baseball fields. But it was his career after graduation that pushed him into the national spotlight as he became the head football coach and athletic director at the University of Notre Dame. But more on that incredible story later…

Following the undefeated season, Coach Strong left the Academy for a teaching position at Haverford College (Pennsylvania), then began a ten-year stint in the Zoology Department at the University of Chicago. He

42

also served on the faculty at the University of Mississippi and at Vanderbilt University before securing a position as Chairman of the Department of Anatomy at the Loyola University School of Medicine (Illinois) in 1918. Dr. Strong remained in that role until his retirement in 1946. He passed away in 1964 at the age of 92 prompting William J. Beecher, Director of the Chicago Academy of Scientists, to write: "Dr. Reuben M. Strong was a bright and cheerful man with a sense of humor and kindly interest in younger scientists. What strikes one in retrospect is the large amount of work he accomplished by steady effort and the usefulness of his life. He started many things which will continue like the ripples going out on a quiet pond."

With that great, and only, season in 1901, Dr. Strong remains as an "undefeated" head coach as he takes his lofty place in the proud football history of Morgan Park Academy!

LOWENTHAL'S CRIME

Fred Lowenthal was a man of many talents. As noted previously, he was a graduate of Morgan Park Academy, a writer for the *Chicago Tribune*, a lawyer, union leader, theatrical representative, head coach of a fledgling professional football club, and briefly—the head coach of the Morgan Park Academy football team in 1902. Lowenthal, it seems, was the only Academy coach removed from his position in mid-season!

Yet it wasn't because of his skill, his knowledge, or his personality...

No, Lowenthal's "crime" was that he graduated from the wrong university. After becoming an All-American lineman at the University of Illinois in 1901, Lowenthal was expected to be named an assistant coach for that team following his graduation in 1902. However, when the Academy team returned to campus in September of 1902 without a coach, the school reached out to Lowenthal to fill the position. It seemed like a perfect match with an Academy graduate, who became an All-American, returning to his alma mater to coach. With Cobb back as captain and quarterback, Lowenthal jumped right in and led the team to quick victories over the Morgan Park Athletic Club and Chicago Manual High School. But it was the third game on October 11, against the University of Chicago Scrubs where the tenure of Coach Lowenthal crumbled. Facing a team that included Academy graduates (and brothers) Floyd (quarterback) and Jesse Harper (halfback), Lowenthal paced the sidelines as the Academy captured its third straight win with a tight 10-5 victory. Both Academy scores, including a 40-yard scamper, were made by William Newburn "the colored tackle of the Academy team," reported the *Chicago Tribune.*

The game was played at Marshall Field, home of the University of Chicago team, as a prelude to the Purdue-Chicago game later that same day. Homer J. Carr, a respected journalist and president of the influential Chicago Press Club, took the time to suggest a pragmatic marketing plan for the Academy and its formidable football team. Carr, an 1879 graduate of the "first" University of Chicago, fired off a note to University President William R. Harper on October 13 speculating that the visibility of the Academy playing at Marshall Field on a regular basis would be extremely beneficial: "In the way of advertising Morgan Park Academy…a vast amount of good can be obtained by having the academy team on Marshall Field as often as possible in the curtain raiser before the big games this fall. The advertising the Academy received last Saturday was worth hundreds of dollars no newspaper advertising could have called so forcibly to the minds of the spectators the existence of the academy as did the actual presence of its team." (Office of the President. Harper, Judson and Burton Administrations, Records [Box 3, Folder 12]) Carr's son, Frederick, was an Academy freshman at the time of this letter and eventually enjoyed an undefeated season on the academy tennis team.

However, Lowenthal's brief reign as coach of the team ended with a thud after the University of Chicago contest that had nothing to do with his team's fine performance on the field that day which had inspired Mr. Carr to forward his thoughts to President Harper. Apparently, Lowenthal's initial hiring was made by the Academy Athletic Association, and not by the administration of the University of Chicago, which still managed the Academy. As such, the University of Chicago administration (likely prompted by Coach Stagg) failed to "officially" approve the hiring of Lowenthal despite his gaudy resume. Instead, former Chicago quarterback August Holste (also an Academy grad) was brought in to head the football efforts for the remainder of the season.

There was some discussion that the Academy coach should be an individual "trained" by Stagg and thus familiar with the University of Chicago formations which would prepare any players hoping to play for Stagg in college. One might question why this unwritten rule did not apply in the hiring of Coach Strong, a graduate of Oberlin. The answer might lie in the fact that Lowenthal was a recent graduate of Illinois, a bitter rival of Chicago. There may have been a bit of paranoiac fear on Stagg's part that Lowenthal, once familiar with the University of Chicago football tendencies, might share that information with his former team—an adversary in the Western Conference. Despite the protests of his players and the Academy students, Lowenthal was replaced, but quickly found employment working with the Moline (Illinois) High School team.

Be that as it may, Holste, a 1902 graduate of the Northwestern University Law School, quickly grabbed control of the Academy club and stretched its unbeaten streak to 18 games (over three seasons) before Northwestern College defeated the Academy 11-0 on October 18. The team finished the 1902 season with a respectable 8-3 record, despite a slew of inexperienced players and an injury to Newburn that sidelined the star player for part of the season.

Following the successful 1902 season, both President William Rainey Harper and football coach Amos Alonzo Stagg of the University of Chicago were featured as speakers at the annual Academy football banquet. The *Chicago Tribune* covered this event and provided additional insight into the football relationship between the University of Chicago and Morgan Park Academy:

> Dr. Harper, in complimenting the team on its victories, endorsed football and athletics in preparatory schools as an aid to character building. He also said that a college was kept in the public eye by its teams and advertised by them. Coach Stagg said Morgan Park had the best academy team ever got together in Chicago. He thought the advance in high school and academy athletics had been wonderful of late, and that the Maroons [University of Chicago] look to the schools for material continually.

Coach Holste departed the Academy after just one season to become the coach of Rose Polytechnic (Indiana) in 1903, but soon became part of an emerging club of former Academy players and coaches who helped influence American football in the early part of the 20th century. Holste then moved on as the head football coach at Fairmount College (now Wichita State University) in 1904 and later coached at Hastings College in Nebraska from 1908-1912 and again from 1922-1925. "He coached our 1923 team to an undefeated 7-0 record," stated Adam Maser of Hastings College in an interview for this book. "This was the first Hastings College football team to be inducted into the Hastings College Athletic Hall of Fame." August Holste was individually inducted into the Hastings College Hall of Fame in 1991.

FOOTBALL IS A GOOD GAME

So, what about the dismissed Fred Lowenthal? Although he never publicly complained about the unusual circumstances of his departure, he quickly moved up the local football coaching ranks. He was named head coach at Englewood High School in Chicago in 1903 and by 1904 he was appointed co-head coach of the University of Illinois in the Western (now Big Ten) Conference. By 1905, Lowenthal was the sole head coach at Illinois and the team finished with a 5-4 record and 14-6-1 overall for his two-year stint.

But there was more to life that the energetic Lowenthal wanted to sample. While he kept his hand in football after leaving Illinois following the 1905 campaign, he also managed to taste a variety of other professional pursuits. Aside from his work as a writer for the *Chicago Tribune*, Lowenthal was also the "football expert" with the *Chicago American*. On the side, he completed law school, worked as a high school football referee and continued to assist with the coaching of the Illinois team as needed. In 1910, he was founder of the Theater Booking Corporation in Chicago which preceded his term as the Midwest legal representative of the Actors' Equity Association. In that role, Lowenthal pushed for the safety and protection of female actors, encouraged better sanitary conditions in dressing rooms, and supported separate dressing facilities for women.

In 1906, Lowenthal had the foresight to plant the seeds for a professional football league in Chicago. This was a vision well ahead of the status quo at the time, since professional football was not organized either regionally or nationally and, in most cases, was frowned upon. The initial version of the National Football League itself was not formed until 1920, so Lowenthal's effort in Chicago was both unique and far-sighted. Lowenthal explained his idea in an article in the *Minneapolis Journal* on September 21: "If football is a good game for colleges, it is a good game for others. If it is not a good game, it should not be played by colleges."

While the pro league failed to materialize immediately, Lowenthal was still a visible figure in the "prairie league" games played by organized local teams throughout the Chicago area. In particular, he was the long-time coach of the Thorn-Tornadoes from Chicago's south side, a club that in 1920, was said to have lost only three games since it was organized in 1908. The Thorns played most of the early NFL teams such as the Rock Island Independents and the Chicago Cardinals. Perhaps one of Lowenthal's more outstanding contributions to the game of football occurred in 1925 when he was an advisor to the legendary Red Grange of Illinois, who turned the football world upside down when he signed a contract to play pro football for the Chicago Bears immediately after his final collegiate game. The presence of Grange in the NFL, and two subsequent barnstorming tours in 1925 and 1926, pushed the sport of professional football to the front of the sports pages and marked the first time that huge crowds attended pro football games. After enjoying a full life with numerous accomplishments, Fred Lowenthal passed away from pneumonia on October 4, 1931 at the age of 52.

PUNCHING, GOUGING AND KICKING NOT UNCOMMON

After piling up 26 wins in the first three years of the new century, the Academy football team experienced something in 1903 that had not previously occurred in the brief history of the program: a losing season.

With Coach Holste gone after just a single campaign, the University of Chicago administration brought in another former Maroon player named John T. Lister to serve as the Academy football coach. Lister was captain of the football team and graduated from Butler College (now Butler University) in 1897. He then procured employment as a Professor of Modern Languages at Eureka (Illinois) College for two years before attending graduate school at the University of Chicago in 1899. Due to the accepted eligibility rules of the time, Lister was a reserve member of Stagg's championship team in 1899 as a grad student. While at Chicago, Lister was also a star on the track team, establishing the school record in the shot-put. From there, Lister spent three years as the football coach and athletic director at Colorado State Normal (now the University of Northern Colorado).

When the Academy football coaching position opened, Lister headed back to the Chicago area and assumed a faculty role at the Academy, teaching both French and German. Unlike others before him, Lister managed to stick around the football field for three seasons and worked tirelessly during the summers to complete his graduate degree at the University of Chicago. Ironically, the Academy annual catalog listed both Lister and A.A. Stagg as the coaches in 1903, although Stagg's contributions were likely minimal.

It should be noted that the interaction between coaches and players that are common in today's game was absent back in 1903. Coaches were prohibited from actively "coaching" during the games. Game officials could penalize a team for such infractions and even water boys were watched closely during time outs lest they bring in "helpful" instructions from the coach on the sidelines.

The game itself continued to be fairly brutal with punching, gouging, and kicking not uncommon. One of the favorite offensive formations was known as the "Wedge" where the offensive players (particularly on kickoff returns) would fix their fingers through the belt loops of the player next to them and march in unison downfield with their heads lowered and the ball carrier tucked in behind the human wall. Without helmets offering any type of protection, injuries were mounting and the public outcry against the brutality of football was rising.

THE REFEREE AND THE UMPIRE DISAGREED

Coach Lister hoped to instill his own strong work ethic into the Academy squad in 1903, which would be centered around sturdy William Newburn. While the team featured a staunch line, its offensive capabilities were in question for most of the season. After bouncing Harvey (now Thornton) High School 26-0 in the opener, the Academy could manage only two more touchdowns for the remainder of the season. The downward spiral on the offensive end left the squad with a final record of 2-3-3, but the season was not bereft of a few highlights (or lowlights) as follows:

- A game scheduled with the North Division High School on October 3 was cancelled when North Division refused to take the field without a player known only as Graham, its star lineman. Graham was attending his second high school during the 1903 season and the Board of Control for the public schools in Chicago suspended him, likely for using up his eligibility. On the other hand, if Graham somehow had regained his eligibility, the Academy would have refused to take the field against him!
- During a game on October 7 with Englewood High School, the competitors agreed to disagree and left the field of battle a bit early. With just about five minutes left in the second half of a scoreless tie, Englewood appeared to fumble near the Academy goal line. Here's what happened next, according to the Chicago Daily News: "The ball belonged to Englewood, but it was given to Morgan Park. The referee and umpire disagreed as well as the teams, as to who should have the ball and the outcome was that Englewood quit the game and came home."
- Sadly, a game with Culver Military Academy could not be arranged. The reason behind this, according to the *Chicago*

Tribune on November 2, 1903 was "because (William) Newburn, a colored boy, has been playing tackle for Morgan Park for two years and the (Culver) cadets drew the color line and refused to play against any team on which there was a colored player." Unfortunately, this policy was not limited to the Academy, nor the Academic League. A week later on November 12, The *Culver Citizen* remarked that "For the third time North Division has cancelled its date with Culver. Each time that a date was arranged, it was understood and agreed by North Division that their colored player should be left behind. In view of this clear understanding and definite agreement, Culver's objection to the colored player seems rather a flimsy excuse for North Division in cancelling their third date with Culver this season."

- As noted previously, Coach Stagg was listed in Academy publications as being one of the coaches of the football team in 1903. This was confirmed by an article appearing in the *Chicago Tribune* on November 3, which provided some insight into Stagg's management of both football teams: "Stagg left the [Chicago] second team entirely to assistant coaches Koehler and Harper, while he gave his attention to the Morgan Park Academy team, which the Chicago coach is preparing to meet Northwestern Academy next Saturday."
- The 1903 season concluded with a 16-0 loss to the University School of Cleveland, Ohio. In an odd year for offensive inefficiency, it was the fifth game in which Morgan Park was held scoreless—which matched the five shutouts of the defense! Overall, the Academy allowed just 48 points by its opponents over eight games but could manage only 38 tallies on offense for the year.

SERIOUS INFRACTION OF TRAINING RULES

With a woeful season plagued by injuries, controversy and blatant racism, the Morgan Park Academy squad looked hopefully to brighter results in the future. After all, things could have been worse…

And perhaps they were worse in Wisconsin, where the Racine College football team was disbanded after a serious breach of team rules.

Arrests?

Underage misbehavior?

Insubordination for signing autographs in the end zone?

No, the Racine team was ousted for a far more heinous reason than any of the above: the players were caught red-handed eating fudge! As we all know, this was a serious infraction of football training rules and the powers-to-be in Racine wasted little time in distributing swift punishment to the offending parties via invoking the "death penalty" for the football program!

EXTRA POINT

While Morgan Park Academy's Fred "Looie" Lowenthal was prominent in several fields, he initially became nationally known on the collegiate football field. An article in *The Tacoma* (Washington) *Times* (February 11, 1914) traced this awareness to an unnamed sports writer from Chicago, who himself was not too "aware" during one of Lowenthal's games at the University of Illinois:

> Lowenthal was one of the greatest guards the west ever produced, but he was with a weak team and no one would have known it but for the fact that a reporter from Chicago drank too much prior to a game at Urbana.
>
> The reporter had met several friends on the morning of the game and when he reached the reporters' coop he did not feel certain whether the players or the goal posts were running. Fortunately for him he drew a seat next to Mike Tobin, the inimitable critic and sage of the Illini.
>
> After each play the Chicago reporter would ask, "Who made that play?" "Lowenthal," Mike would respond, eager to boost his friend. "Who made the tackle?" "Lowenthal." "Who made the touchdown?" "Lowenthal." This continued through the entire game and the Chicago paper's report the next day read somewhat like this: "Lowenthal kicked off 50 yards to Lowenthal, who ran the ball back 25 yards before he was tackled by Lowenthal." From then on, Looie's fame was established!

The 1903 Academy team finished with a 2-3-3 slate under Coach John Lister (top row on left). Amos Alonzo Stagg was also listed as one of the coaches that season. This photo provides a glimpse at the flimsy padding worn by players at that time.

Jonathan Webb was a former all-conference tackle on the undefeated (16-0-2) 1899 University of Chicago squad. In 1900 (the year this photo was taken), he coached the Academy gridders to a 7-4-2 record. (Photo courtesy of Denise Hill)

Members of the undefeated 1899 University of Chicago football team gathered for a reunion in 1929. From left: Dr. Ralph Hamill, Chicago coach Amos Alonzo Stagg, Captain Walter Kennedy, and Jonathan Webb, Morgan Park Academy graduate and former Academy football coach. (Photo courtesy of Special Collections Research Center, University of Chicago Library)

CHAPTER 4

Flying Wedges, Orange Sox, and the Vice President

---

*"It is claimed that the Morgan Park boys are not in the
best of condition but that they think they will have a walk-
away when they line up against the fruit pickers."*
—The News Palladium (Benton Harbor, MI), 1905

Resting atop that vaunted hill on west 111th Street in Chicago, the Morgan Park Academy campus of today is not much different than it was over 100 years ago. Certainly, the buildings have changed, either through addition or destruction, but the center piece of the campus remains a lush, green open space that stretches cleanly from 111th Street to 112th Street.

Just to the south of 112th Street rests the venerable gymnasium/field-house, dedicated in 1901, but it no longer stands between the East and West Hall buildings—both of which have disappeared through the years. Behind the fieldhouse rests an expansive open field, now used primarily for baseball, softball and soccer, but it was once the home turf for the football team.

Two other main campus buildings, the Arts Center (built in 1968 on the site of Blake Hall) which faces 111th Street on the north end of the campus, and Hansen Hall (constructed in 1928) are "newer" edifices. Stately Alumni Hall still stands proudly on the east side of the campus, as it has since 1928.

In the fall of 1904, still another new head football coach with roots back to Coach Stagg and the University of Chicago, strolled through the open campus. However, Coach Floyd E. Harper was very familiar with the Academy, having graduated from there in 1899 after a stellar career on both the football and baseball fields. Harper, the elder brother of Jesse Harper, migrated to the University of Chicago following his graduation from the Academy and excelled on the baseball team (team captain for two years) and was a key substitute on the gridiron. Following graduation, Harper entered law school at the University of Chicago while also assisting with both the football and baseball teams under Stagg. When Stagg began to shed some of his responsibilities in the overall athletic department, Harper became the head baseball coach in the spring of 1905. One of his key players was second baseman Hugo Bezdek. Bezdek would later gain fame as a well-respected college and professional coach who remains as the only person in history who managed both a major league baseball team (Pittsburgh Pirates) and was the head coach of an NFL football team (Cleveland Rams) among his other accomplishments.

Meanwhile, during the 1904 football campaign, Harper assumed the dual role of assistant football coach at the University of Chicago while also serving as the head gridiron coach at the Academy.

Former football coach John T. Lister was still on the Academy faculty in 1904 and agreed to assist Harper with the team that season. Since Harper was listed more prominently in Academy documents regarding the football program, he was regarded as the head coach for that year with Lister as his able, and experienced, assistant.

A robust turnout of 25 players greeted Harper at the first day of practice on September 22, including a fullback from Milwaukee with an intriguing back story named Garry Williamson. Williamson originally headed south after high school to enroll at the University of Chicago and play football for Coach Stagg. However, after some difficulties verifying his eligibility, Williamson was sent over to the Academy for further academic seasoning. Once again, the strong bind between the Academy and the University football programs was exemplified by the shipping of Williamson to the Academy. During the academic year, Williamson took extra classes and attended summer school to ensure his collegiate eligibility while still maintaining his "freshman" athletic status for the 1905 football campaign at Chicago.

Having worked closely under Stagg, Harper was not opposed to innovative offensive sets, but also embraced the need for a stifling defense. Buoying the Academy defense was a large, but promising, junior named Albert Benbrook. A transfer from Armour Academy in Chicago, Benbrook was well over six feet and 200 lbs. even at this stage of his young career, when the towering guard solidified the line on both sides of the ball. Indeed, the 1904 Academy team stressed the defensive aspects by allowing just one touchdown (five points) for the entire season! Only a pair of ties with Englewood High School (5-5) and Northwestern College (0-0) stained an otherwise perfect year as the Academy rolled to a final 6-0-2 record. With the smothering defense in place, Harper's charges outscored their opponents 218-5 during this dominant season and grabbed the championship of the Western Athletic League. The team was so dominant that there were whispers and rumors as early as October that the Academy would insert itself into consideration for national recognition.

On October 30, just before Morgan Park vanquished its final four opponents by a combined 145-0 margin, the *Chicago Tribune* looked into its crystal ball:

> It is rumored that Morgan Park will meet Culver Institute November 19, in a game for the inter-academic championship of the west. The south side academy is scheduled for a game with the University High School of Cleveland and in the event of winning both games may arrange for a game with some "prep" team in the east to decide national supremacy.

NORTH DIVISION IGNORED HIS CHALLENGE

After blowing past the UC Freshmen 17-0 on October 29, Harper issued a challenge to the powerful North Division High School in Chicago for a game to decide the "Prep" championship of the west. North Division was already plotting a "championship" game with some unknown opponent on the east coast when Harper tossed some gas on the burgeoning competitive fire by telling *The Inter Ocean*:

> Before North Division goes east for a game, heralded as the prep champions of the west, they must prove their right to the title. At the present time, Morgan Park looks every bit as strong as North Division, and the local leadership should be settled before a game is scheduled with any Eastern team.

By November 5, the Academy improved to 4-0-2 when the squad traveled to Cleveland for a rematch with the undefeated University High

School. After floundering in a 16-0 defeat the previous year, the Academy erupted for a convincing 30-0 win that included a pair of touchdowns from fullback Williamson. Halfback Frank Garrett added two more scores, along with five extra points. Quarterback John Wrigley contributed the final touchdown.

After the Cleveland game, the *Chicago Tribune* provided an update on the MPA challenge to North Division High School:

> Morgan Park challenged the north siders earlier in the season, but a game could not be arranged. North Division has defeated most of the high schools of the city and will play Oak Park to decide the championship of the city high schools. Morgan Park plays University High School for the inter-academic honors, having defeated all other schools in the league. Morgan Park defeated Cleveland University school recently in Cleveland.

The *Chicago Tribune* hinted that the two powerful clubs could still meet later in the season, possibly at Marshall Field, home field of the University of Chicago. But first, the Academy needed to officially settle the Western Academic League title with University High School of Chicago on November 18. The pre-game hype proved groundless as the Academy white washed University High 57-0, behind four touchdowns from Wrigley and three from Williamson. In post-game comments the *Tribune* noted that, "Coach Harper and his Morgan Park protégés are now anxious to meet North Division, the team which claims to have won the high school championship. Harper said last night that North Division had ignored his challenge sent two weeks ago."

After a few more days of silence, *The Inter Ocean* (November 23) blasted the inactivity of North Division in an article that bordered on being a high school sports' editorial:

> North Division has been so busy looking about the country for some team to play for the championship of the nation they have overlooked a challenge from close home. Morgan Park Academy has a team this year that would call out the best the North Siders have. Why not have a post season game between these two elevens to decide the prep championship of the West? Morgan Park has won clear title in the academic league, and North Division in the

high school league. Morgan Park has challenged. Is North Division going to let the challenge go unnoticed?

HOODOO WAS COMPLETELY ROUTED

For whatever reason, North Division continued to ignore the local challenge and instead scheduled a game with Exeter Academy in Boston, Massachusetts on November 29. When this game did not occur, North Division played two more Illinois teams, winning against Rockford, but losing at Champaign. A response from North Division to the Academy challenge was never sent to Harper.

The undefeated Academy could thus claim its share of numerous mythical championships for 1904 but suffice it to say that the students were pleased just to capture the Academic League crown. In a post-season report, *The Academy News* happily honored the champions:

> For by its playing of clean victorious football the men who composed this team went through the season without losing a game, with only five points scored against them and scoring more points on their opponents than any other Morgan Park team ever managed to make in a season. In fact, the 'hoodoo' which for the past two years seemed to have such a full sway over our gridiron men was completely routed and some other more propitious element guided them to victory.

The 1904 season proved to be the final appearance on the Academy gridiron for Floyd Harper. After assisting Stagg once more in the fall of 1905, Floyd received his law degree from the University of Chicago in December of 1905. He headed west and opened a law office in Leavenworth, Kansas. In 1910, he was elected as Judge of the City Court and captured another election as County Attorney in 1914. Harper eventually moved to New York, and then to Chicago where he accepted a position in 1927 with the Midwest Utility Corporation. Finally, in 1932, Harper settled in Springfield, Illinois where he held various legal positions with the Central Illinois Public Service Company until his retirement in 1940. Harper found happiness in retirement as he operated a large farm of over 400 acres with his wife near Mechanicsburg, Illinois. Unfortunately, he passed away at the age of 62 from a heart attack on March 19, 1941.

THEY SERVE TOO MANY STEWS TO SUIT US!

When Charles Warren Fairbanks was sworn in as this country's 26th Vice President on March 4, 1905, his mind was focused on the business agenda established by President Theodore Roosevelt. Fairbanks realized that in his new position his privacy would be diminished, his name would be in the papers, and his family would always be expected to present themselves with dignity and decorum.

Someone forgot to tell his nephew, Loriston…

As the Morgan Park Academy student body sat down to lunch on Thursday, May 18, 1905 and the serving staff began distributing the luncheon selection, a slight murmur passed over the crowd, followed by an eerie silence.

It was almost as if one could hear a pin drop. Or a knife…

But a knife did drop, and almost as one, the entire group of students in attendance stood up and walked out the door.

It was the start of the great food strike of 1905 at Morgan Park Academy and young Loriston Fairbanks was one of the leaders of the campus revolt. He helped direct nearly 200 classmates in a "strike" called to protest the quality of the meals served to the students. "They buy the gravy by the barrel and serve too many stews to suit us," explained Fairbanks in an interview with *The Inter Ocean* on May 19. "We have too much roast beef also. Then the food is not clean. Frequently roaches and other bugs have been found in the food," he added.

Fairbanks claimed that the students had previously complained about these culinary delights to Academy Dean Wayland Chase, but Fairbanks and company did not experience any improvement in the fare. "We endured it as long as we could…there was no change, and so we decided that the next time anyone found cause for complaint, we would get up and go out. We agreed that a knife should be dropped on the floor as a signal. Today at noon we heard the knife drop and accordingly arose from our chairs and went out," concluded Fairbanks.

The strike lasted all of one day and the students returned for lunch on Friday, May 19 (after missing two meals) with the assurances of Dean Chase that improvements would be made. A student committee was established to monitor the situation and to address the following ominous, pre-strike concerns:

- Sour bread was served.
- Flies were sometimes found in the potatoes.

- Some of the food was too greasy.
- The table linen was not immaculate.

Of course, articles on the student strike itself—which was quite unusual for the time—appeared in numerous newspapers, and Vice President Fairbanks found himself squarely in the headlines such as in *The Inter Ocean* ("Led by Vice President Fairbanks' Nephew, Boys March From Morgan Park Academy") due to his ambitious relative, and the Academy student spokesman, Loriston Fairbanks!

PRICE INCLUDES OIL FOR LAMPS

As the administration dusted itself off from another negative student-inspired frolic in the media via the food strike, attention gradually returned to academics and the positive promotion of the school. Efforts were made, primarily through advertising and personal visits, to recruit students from outside the Chicago area. This endeavor was necessary since in the early part of the century, the Academy was bleeding money, showing deficits of $19,243 in 1903, $22,625 in 1904, and $16,940 in 1905. (University of Chicago. Office of the President. Harper, Judson and Burton Administrations. University of Chicago Library) At this time, the University of Chicago was already reviewing the numbers and considering viable alternative means for lifting the Academy out of its financial doldrums.

In 1905, the average cost for a student to attend the Academy was $371 for the 36-week school year. The 1905 *Morgan Park Academy Calendar* stated that accommodations were available in the Morgan, East, and West Halls (none of which exist today) and that "Students' rooms are lighted by lamps, as they furnish the best light for studying. Prices for rooms in all cases include heat, oil for lamps, care, and washing of towels and bed linen." All in all, the fees at the Academy were not cheap, but not uncommon in comparison with other private boarding schools. One positive source of pride--and recruitment--was the exemplary football team, which had bounced back from its first losing season in 1903 to achieve an undefeated season in 1904, with more bright prospects for 1905 and beyond.

The major Chicago newspapers continued to "cover" the Academy team in a time when major league baseball was king and professional football was basically non-existent. The University of Chicago football team was easily the most popular collegiate force in the area, and its affiliation with the Academy no doubt assisted in securing significant press coverage for the prep team.

With Floyd Harper now working solely with Stagg's team at the University in 1905, the Academy turned to Professor John Lister once again to head its football program. Flashy halfback Frank Garrett and intimidating lineman Albert Benbrook paced the team in its first outing, a 33-0 blanking of Lake View High School. It was the start of an unusual schedule patched together by Coach Lister in which the Academy would tangle with opponents from five different states: Illinois, Indiana, Wisconsin, Ohio, and Michigan. In fact, after the team rolled through its first four opponents (all via shutouts), the Academy ventured north to face Benton Harbor (Michigan) High School. According to the local newspapers, it was another inter-galactic match-up for the ages that would certainly settle any bragging rights for best team in the "middle west."

FAMOUS THROUGHOUT THE LAND

The pre-game hype from *The News-Palladium* in Benton Harbor was both confident and audacious: "If the Benton Harbor High School can defeat the Morgan Park Academy team (the champions of the Academic League) they will become famous throughout the land." The paper then eased into pure bliss by stating: "This no doubt will be the strongest team the boys will play this year and the game promises to be a spicy one. The capacity of the grandstand should be packed and there should be a thousand rooters on the sides of the field singing the old familiar tunes so cheerful to the heart of the moleskin stars."

From the Academy side, Lister realized that both teams were undefeated, and that Benton Harbor had not given up a single point to any opponent thus far in the 1905 season. It would be critical to unleash the talents of the swift Frank Garrett, who just two weeks previously had returned a 105-yard kickoff for a touchdown in a 53-0 win over Englewood High School.

Despite the poetic storm of words before the game, the contest itself was close, hard fought and riveting to the fans. It was also not without controversy...

The coach of the Benton Harbor High School team was one Clayton Tryon Teetzel, or, as he was known locally, Coach "Faster" Teetzel. Teetzel was a graduate of Englewood High School in Chicago who then played his collegiate football at the University of Michigan, receiving his law degree in

1900. Upon graduation, Teetzel decided to remain in the game by accepting the head coaching position at Michigan State Normal University (now Eastern Michigan). After serving three years at that gridiron outpost (finishing with a 6-14-1 record), coach Teetzel was convinced to take the reins of the prep football program at Benton Harbor in 1903.

His influence was immediate; the "Orange Sox," as the team was known, promptly captured the mythical 1903 state championship of Michigan. With a rabid fan base and overwhelming support from the town itself, Benton Harbor High School reached beyond the shores of the "Wolverine State" to solicit suitable gridiron competition. In particular, Benton Harbor focused on the Chicago metropolitan area in an effort to invite worthy opponents from both the high school and athletic club ranks to visit, such as Englewood High School and the Kershaw Athletic Club. By the time the Morgan Park Academy football team disembarked from its nearly 100-mile train trip to Benton Harbor on the morning of October 4, 1905, it was quite familiar with the powerful capabilities of the home team.

As the Academy players strolled through the streets before the game, they could not help but notice the abundant orange decorations in store windows, on street lights, and on landscaping that the townsfolk had carefully placed in honor of their local heroes. The school colors were proudly displayed throughout the downtown area, and the residents were abuzz with excitement for the upcoming match, probably fanned by the significant encouragement provided by the local press.

ROOTERS WERE WILD AND YELLED THEMSELVES HOARSE

Indeed, Benton Harbor had quickly become very, very good under the guidance of Coach Teetzel. So good—that other local high schools were beginning to walk away from scheduled games with Benton Harbor. In the week before the Academy game, *The News-Palladium* sadly reported that:

> The noted high school football team of Mt. Pleasant has received a severe attack of "cold feet" and will not play Benton Harbor. Our team was at one time laid up with the mumps, but they have never refused to play a game on account of sickness; certainly, not on account of "cold feet."

Later, the newspaper predicted that "if Morgan Park thinks they are going to find something easy to bet next Saturday, they will be very much surprised!" Speaking of "betting," that horrendous word that should never be offered in polite football society, *The News-Palladium* noted that "the sporting element is wagering that Benton Harbor will win by a good score and notices were posted this morning (day of game) offering $5 to $25 that Morgan Park would not score."

While *The News-Palladium* might be viewed cautiously for its insightful and partisan descriptions of the game itself, the reporting on the Morgan Park game was precise and literally a play-by-play account of the deliberations on the field. In addition, the article provided, albeit unknowingly, a solid glimpse into the strategies and techniques of the game of football in 1905. If we were to paraphrase the unique observational reporting of the game itself, it might be summarized as follows:

- On its second possession, Benton Harbor relied solely on short runs during a long drive to grab the first lead of the game 6-0 (five points for a touchdown and one for kicking the extra point). "The rooters were wild and yelled themselves hoarse," noted *The News-Palladium*.
- Morgan Park tied things up 6-6 in the second quarter with a rushing TD and the extra point, as the newspaper complained that the hosts "went to pieces."
- Although the Academy scored, it received the kick off from Benton Harbor, but promptly fumbled the ball allowing Benton Harbor to kick a field goal (four points) to secure a 10-6 lead at halftime.

From there, the ball game dissolved into an "exhibition of punting," where neither team could sustain any type of potential scoring drive. Each team decided to quickly punt the ball away on numerous occasions (no matter what the down) in an effort to secure better field position. In the end, there was no scoring in the second half, allowing Benton Harbor to claim the 10-6 victory as well as the title of champions of the "entire middle states." Coach Teetzel was rightfully ecstatic, and *The News-Palladium* joyfully captured the winning coach's exuberance near the end of the game: "The crowd in the grandstand was enthusiastic. Teetzel ran up and down the sidelines as happy as a little boy at the circus!"

But what about the pre-game hint about betting? After the contest, *The News-Palladium* gloated about the Academy's situation in light of losing its first game of the year: "All the more bitter was the taste of defeat because it not only cost them the title to the championship, but they were poorer in the pocket when the game was over than when it started."

However, in less than a month, the Benton Harbor hopes for a state championship were detoured when the Michigan state board bounced Benton Harbor from consideration for the top honors. Amid competitive charges of illegal players, illicit team management, and a professional coach (Teetzel), the decision was made despite a pragmatic defense presented by the Benton Harbor High School administration. According to the stunned *News-Palladium*, "Nothing can be done and Benton Harbor people will hold their sweet tempers knowing that they have a football team composed of strictly eligible members before which every other high school team in Michigan has taken to the woods."

Benton Harbor would finish the season with just one loss (38-0 to the University of Chicago freshman team), and then Coach Teetzel headed west to become the basketball coach and athletic director at Brigham Young University in Utah from 1905-1908. He later assumed the positions of football and track coach at Utah State Agricultural College (now Utah State) from 1908-1916. Teetzel eventually retired from coaching, returned to Chicago, and worked for the *Chicago Tribune*. He passed away on July 29, 1948 at the age of 71.

THE BOYS WORK AS DEMONS IN PRACTICE

As for the Academy, there was precious little time to rebound from the Benton Harbor disappointment. Morgan Park hit the rails once again the following week and renewed its rivalry with Culver Military Academy in Indiana on October 21, scorching Culver 51-5 as Garrett tallied four touchdowns. The *Morgan Park Post* stated that "This is the first time in five years that the Culver team has been beaten. The defeat at Benton Harbor made the boys work as demons at practice and judging from the score the same spirit must have been continued through Saturday's game [with Culver]."

A third straight week of travel to interact with an out-ot-state foe found the Academy team in Delafield, Wisconsin on October 28 to meet the Cadets of St. John's Military Academy. A challenging defensive struggle ended in a 0-0 stalemate that was quickly bemoaned by the supportive *Morgan Park Post*:

> The score, which with fair treatment should have been
> at the least calculation 24-0, in no way shows the relative
> merits of the teams, as the umpire, one of St. John's

faculty repeatedly penalized the Morgan Park team when within striking distance of the St. John's goal. Penalties, either deferred or inflicted, only at the particular moment when one's goal is in danger, not only show a lack of sportsmanship, but a rabid partiality, which is the greatest bane of a sport which may become, under such conditions, a curse not only to the player, but to the spectator as well. The simplest and best manner of preventing a repetition of this is to obtain officials who are not interested in either school.

This profound statement addressed the growing concern with the quality of officiating, where often the coach of the home team would absorb the officiating duties as well...or enlist the services of someone affiliated with the host team with at least a rudimentary understanding of the rules of the game. The officiating at this time likely was expected to favor the home team, although it was hoped that some thread of fairness would be evident as well.

Wins over Elgin Academy (45-0) and Northwestern Academy (18-6) followed, perhaps prompting the Academy to push itself back into consideration for the title of "Champions of the Midwest." In fact, during the week of November 6, the Academy challenged Benton Harbor High School to a rematch to be played on November 18 at the home field of the University of Chicago. While this game was never scheduled, a contest with the powerful University of Chicago freshmen was scheduled for November 11 as the opener prior to the Chicago-Purdue match that same day. Through a special arrangement with Coach Stagg of the University of Chicago, Academy students and friends received the special admission price of just $0.50 to witness both games. Although the Chicago freshmen had handed Benton Harbor its only defeat in a 38-0 pasting earlier in the season, the Academy threatened to pull off the upset before falling 6-4 to the University of Chicago. The only Academy score was from a 40-yard drop kick by Garrett.

The 1905 season concluded on November 25 as the Academy entertained the University School of Cleveland, the fifth state to be represented on the Morgan Park schedule. With the Benton Harbor loss in football limbo due to the penalties imposed on that school in Michigan, the Academy was once again poised to claim some type of championship honors. The *Chicago Tribune* decided that this game would be for the "championship of the western preparatory schools as the Cleveland school has met and defeated all the strong teams in Ohio and the Morgan Park team has undoubted claim to the championship in the vicinity of Chicago."

MICHIGAN AGENTS HAVE BEEN RUSHING HIM FOR EIGHT MONTHS

This one was over quickly, as Garrett and company blasted the visitors 27-0. Garrett scored on a 50-yard run, booted a 45-yard field goal, and added three extra points. For Garrett, it would be the last game of his brilliant career, and the *Chicago Tribune* speculated as to where the shifty halfback would land in college. In an early nod to football recruiting, the *Chicago Tribune* stated that "Next fall he will go to college, just where, he himself does not know. He leans toward Chicago, but Michigan agents have been 'rushing' him for eight months and a merry fight for the youthful prize is anticipated."

The team itself was feted by banquets and dances, and the players received sweaters with championship emblems for their efforts. The *Morgan Park Post* praised the results achieved by the coaching staff, noting that: "Coach Lister deserves great credit for the article of football which his protégés have been taught to play—an article which has once more brought the championship to Morgan Park." With established stars such as Garrett and Benbrook departing, the school would soon be seeking fresh players and a new head man for the football program as well…

With a 7-2-1 record for the season, Coach John Lister retired (again!) from his football coaching position, finishing with a 9-5-4 mark for his two seasons (1903 and 1905) as the head coach, while assisting Floyd Harper during the 6-0-2 campaign of 1904. A gifted linguist, Lister earned his doctorate while teaching and coaching at the Academy, and then embarked on an academic career at several colleges and universities before settling in as the Chairman of the Romance Languages at Wooster University in Ohio for over 20 years. He passed away in 1944 at the age of 72 without ever coaching another game of football.

Outside the gridiron, separate independent factions were moving in opposite directions that would certainly impact the Morgan Park Academy football team in 1906 and beyond. On a national level, the continuous slaughter of players on the football field was forcing many academic institutions to consider abolishing the sport altogether. On a more local level, but equally important, were the ramped-up discussions by the University of Chicago administrators who were fretting more than ever over the financial money pit that the Academy had become for the University. Could the Academy survive without the staunch support of the University? If so, would the game of football even be an option for future athletes at the Academy?

FOOTBALL IS A SAVAGE, BRUTAL, BLOODY FIGHT

The bloodshed and physical dismay endured by football players in the early days of the game was certainly not anything new. With little padding, archaic rules, and often ill-advised officials, the examples of horrific injuries and multiple deaths on the football field had become alarming. In 1904, there were approximately 21 fatalities on the field. By the conclusion of the 1905 season, that ghastly number was still significant, with 19 more players losing their lives. An article in the *New York Times* in 1905 decreed: "Football has degenerated into a savage, brutal, bloody fight between men…kick the ball or kick the head—it is all in the game." Many newspapers, particularly the *Chicago Tribune*, updated the disaster list on a regular basis helping to incite passionate discussions on both sides of the argument as to whether football should be abolished or not. Prominent universities such as Columbia, Duke, and Northwestern banned the sport and other institutions on different levels soon followed.

Still, more emphasis was being placed on changing the rules instead of abolishing the game itself. Feelings were so strong that the *Chicago Tribune* urged President Theodore Roosevelt to become involved in the overhaul of the rules and the game itself. A key target was the "mass" type of play where players would align themselves in a type of "wedge" by grabbing on to their teammates and moving forward as one "mass" with the ball carrier safely tucked back inside the wedge. Of course, helmet protection was minimal at best as the players surged downfield with their heads lowered like a ramming device as a chief component of the attack. Defensively, it was not uncommon for an entire team of defenders to pounce on the lone ball carrier, even if that person was already prone on the ground…since there were no rules against doing so. There was also concern over the lack of space created between the two opposing lines where the players would stand, and battle, toe-to-toe in an effort to claim or surrender real estate for their team. And, depending on the skill and insight of the officials, the game could also degenerate into the aforementioned display of punching, kicking, shoving, etc. that both intrigued, and appalled, the spectators.

With the clamor increasing to terminate the game due to the numerous deaths and serious injuries, the *Chicago Tribune* forwarded a very public telegram to President Roosevelt, appealing to his love of physical sport and support of athletic endeavors. The message was brief, but to the point:

> Hon. Theodore Roosevelt
>
> Washington, D.C., Nov. 25
>
> The 1905 football season practically closed today with two dead on the field of battle. Today's fatalities bring the total slain to nineteen, and the injured (record being made of accidents out of the ordinary) to 137. This year's record of deaths is more than double that of the yearly average for the last five years, the total for that period beingforty-five. A significant fact is that the teams playing an "open" game have escaped with less than their usual quota of accidents.

The *Chicago Tribune's* message practically begged the President to intervene on behalf of the game, and to push for significant changes in the rules. The *Chicago Tribune* took things a step further by contacting major colleges and universities in the country regarding the future of the sport. "Football as it is played must be immediately and radically reformed or abolished," was the message from the field reported by the newspaper on November 27. Actually, Roosevelt was keenly aware of the football safety issue and had already hosted a mini-summit at the White House in October of 1905 with coaches from three of the key football schools of Princeton, Harvard, and Yale. The President's message was clear and specific: clean up the game or risk the possibility of football being abolished in this country.

Eventually, Roosevelt helped prepare a football "reform" platform that proposed to define eligibility rules, reduce on-field brutality, and encourage administrative support of "clean" play. Then, in December, representatives (including Coach Stagg) of 62 collegiate institutions created a Rules Committee to evaluate and improve the current mandates of the sport. This committee evolved into the Intercollegiate Athletic Association of the United States (IAAUS), the forerunner to the National Collegiate Athletic Association (NCAA). As a result, several important rules changes were implemented for the 1906 season, including the following:

- The forward pass was legalized (although still with some restrictions, such as it must be thrown behind the line of scrimmage), opening up the field and creating the new "receiver" position.
- The so-called "mass" offensive formations, including the fearsome "wedge" were outlawed. Also, play was now stopped when the ball carrier was on the ground and anyone guilty of "slugging" could be immediately ejected.
- A neutral zone was established between the offensive and defensive lines and six individuals were required to play on each side of the line.
- The distance for a first down was extended from five yards to ten yards, although only three downs were still allowed to achieve the first down. This lessened the usage of the offensive line "plunge" which was designed to secure a yard or two as needed. Now, teams sought to force the play outside of the line of scrimmage in an attempt to secure more yardage per down.

These critical changes were designed to open up the field for play by reducing the mass collisions of bodies on the field. Deaths and injuries suffered on the football field were reduced sharply after the initiation of the new rules, although hardline, traditional followers of the game bemoaned the reduction of the close quarter skirmishes.

Ultimately, the game of football survived, improved and began to expand dramatically in the early years of the 20th century. The major rules changes drifted down to the high school level as well. The forward pass would still be viewed with some hesitancy until additional rules removed some of the restraints on that aspect of the game. However, in less than a decade, the innovative coaching techniques of a Morgan Park Academy graduate on the collegiate level would take advantage of the new passing rules and help propel the forward pass into a major offensive weapon for decades to come.

Meanwhile, Morgan Park Academy faced a future of uncertainty with rumors circulating that the partnership with the University of Chicago might soon be dissolved. Indeed, would there even be a Morgan Park Academy when the 1906 football season rolled around?

EXTRA POINT

The historic meeting between the Academy and Benton Harbor (Michigan) High School in 1905 was one of the most soundly covered football games in the history of the Morgan Park football program. Although most of the excitement was driven by the local Michigan newspapers, the publicity—in general—was positive for the emerging sport of high school football. The blanket of coverage continued well past the completion of the game as the town of Benton Harbor celebrated the biggest victory in its own football history. One unusual testament was a poem written about the game by someone named D.B. Edmunds and published in *The News-Palladium* in Benton Harbor on October 18, 1905. It is, perhaps, the only poem ever written about the Academy football team from the opposing teams' vantage point and one that again points to the apparent wagering done by the high school players:

Morgan Park and the Saturday Football Game
When Morgan Park came over
Our high school team to play
They thought they were in clover
And had a walk-away
They bet their money freely
Our high school would not score;
While they would roll up forty
At least, and maybe more.

But when the game was over
It was too late to kick;
The very thought of football
Made every player sick
That they were beaten fairly
Each player would admit
But dreaded, back at Morgan Park,
The roasting they would get.

I think the boys are wiser;
They should be, for they've seen
The way that "Faster" Teetzel
Can win with his "machine."
I heard one player saying,
"We could not win from them;
I'll wager twenty dollars
They could beat the U. of M. [Michigan]."

JOE ZIEMBA

Albert Benbrook (top row, fourth from right) was a towering presence on the
1905 Academy team (7-2-1) that claimed the title of "Academic Champions of
the Midwest." Benbrook was later a two-time All-American at the University of
Michigan.

CHAPTER 5

Coachless Wonders

"The Academy is experiencing great trouble in getting games this year, as every team wishes to meet an opponent which it is sure to defeat."
—Morgan Park Post, 1907

On the rather warm day of January 10, 1906, the staff and students of Morgan Park Academy learned of the passing of Dr. William Rainey Harper, the esteemed President of the University of Chicago. Many were surprised by this news, although Harper had privately shared the diagnosis of his cancer nearly a year earlier to close friends and family.

Determined to conquer the illness, Harper attempted to maintain the ambitious schedule for which he was known with extended hours, meetings, and travel that he deemed necessary to address the many needs of the growing University. Considered to be both brilliant and innovative, Harper had been hand-picked (at the age of 35) from his position at Yale by key university benefactor John D. Rockefeller to lead the institute when it was established in 1891. Harper worked to both organize and market the school, create a faculty, and develop a comprehensive curriculum.

Although an expert instructor in the Hebrew language, Harper exhibited a keen business sense as an administrator, carefully establishing correspondence courses to attract additional students, welcoming females to the university, recruiting international attendees, and establishing the respected University of Chicago Press. In the beginning, Harper intended to hire the very best faculty members available—and compensated them for their knowledge and skills. One of his first hires was All-American football player

Amos Alonzo Stagg from Yale, who was appointed to oversee the athletic and physical education programs at the University of Chicago.

Although Harper quietly battled yearly budget deficits at both the University (usually balanced by the generosity of Rockefeller) and the Academy, he proudly was part of an internal committee (including Rockefeller) that finally adopted a plan to balance the University budget in 1903. In his book **William Rainey Harper: First President of the University of Chicago**, author Thomas Wakefield Goodspeed shared the University's financial challenges from his position as the secretary of the Board of Trustees. In his book (page 193) Goodspeed stated that the committee released the following statement regarding the budget prospectus in December of 1903:

> If we shall demonstrate our ability to conduct the institution within its income and thus place it on an assured and permanent financial foundation we shall have placed the institution in a position to assure . . . not only the permancy of the institution, but that it can and will conduct its affairs without financial embarrassments and without financial crises...

Of course, part of the overall University budget difficulty was the continuing negative financial performance of Morgan Park Academy. While some corrective actions had been implemented in the past at the Academy, such as closing the doors to female students, Harper worked to keep those very same doors open for the current students, perhaps because he had a soft spot for the Academy. After all, Harper did maintain a home in the neighborhood and had spent several years as an instructor at the Baptist Union Theological Seminary (also known as the Morgan Park Seminary) prior to his stint at Yale University. In fact, Morgan Park Academy was now housed at the same location previously inhabited by the Seminary.

In retrospect, the experiences of Harper's stay in Morgan Park clearly influenced his future success as both an educator and visionary leader. Dr. G. W. Northrup, President of the University of Chicago Divinity School, indicated as much in his analysis of Harper in the Goodspeed book:

> The Morgan Park period, with its origination and experiment, is in a sense the key to Dr. Harper's later career. Those days of heroic struggle witnessed the uncertain beginning of educational ideas which afterward, proved and developed, became cornerstones of the university which he built.

CLASSED AS A STRANGER

So, with Harper's death in early 1906, along with the ongoing Academy financial crisis, there was considerable concern over the future support of the Academy by the University. University correspondence from April 9, 1906 predicted a deficit of $21,348 for the 1905-06 year at the prep school. Initially, no fiscal alterations at the Academy were evident under interim President Harry Pratt Judson (later named University President in 1907), although Judson was considered a very conservative financial manager. There was a slight decrease in some Academy faculty salaries, but no significant changes were revealed. (University of Chicago. Office of the President. Harper, Judson and Burton Administrations. Records, [Box 4, Folder 3], Special Collections Research Center, University of Chicago Library)

However, a surprising condition surfaced during the 1906 football season when the University refused to allow its freshmen to play Morgan Park Academy in their annual game. While the University of Chicago still supported the Academy, and Coach Stagg was certainly in favor of the game being played, the *Chicago Tribune* explained on October 23 that:

> When the case was put up to the faculty, the professors decided it would not be right to allow the contest. The "reform" rules forbid games between freshmen and "outside institutions," and Morgan Park, though a part of the university, was classed as a stranger.

From a football standpoint, the decision was mystifying to the Academy, which was in the midst of a very satisfying season. There was no shortage of competition for the team, which had entered the 1906 campaign with questions regarding its new head coach and the revised football rules in general, and then ended the season facing consternation over its roster and the abrupt ending to a traditional rivalry.

Stepping into the coaching vacancy was David S. Oberg. A 1903 graduate of the Academy, Oberg was a standout fullback and center for the 1902 team that finished 8-3. A native of Sweden, Oberg was a rugged individual who enjoyed the physicality in the trenches of football. So, it was no surprise that he was not supportive of the new rules which encouraged more creative rushing plays, passing the ball, and less violence at the line of scrimmage.

FORWARD PASS IS A DISAPPOINTMENT

In the aftermath of a 24-0 win over Chicago Heights High School in the second game of the season on September 26, the *Chicago Tribune* offered its interpretation of the revised on-field activity:

> The score was 24-0 in favor of the Morgan Park eleven and the new rules were given a trial... Forward passes were tried with more or less success...There was little resemblance of the old mass style of play and the plunging game which Morgan Park always has played was not a feature of its work yesterday.

Despite the win, Oberg was less than enthusiastic about the changes as noted in the same article. In fact, he was downright critical of the new rules, hinting that they would likely fail and perhaps yearning that some of the previous features of the game would be reinstituted:

> I was disappointed in the new rules according to the test we gave them this afternoon. I believed they (the rules changes) would simplify and make the game more open. Instead the game was no more than an exhibition of basketball. The forward pass is a disappointment. The game is too strenuous for an accurate pass forward of more than five yards...and I do not think it can be remedied in one season, if at all. There is no doubt in my mind that the new game will be rougher than the old...The old mass plays seldom hurt a man. The new tackling and standing so far apart will cause many more injuries, judging from what I have seen today.

If Oberg was not a fan of the changes, at least he was able to observe the battle from two different vantages, as both the coach of the Academy and as the referee of the same game! In future years, Oberg, as well as other fans of football, would come to welcome the forward pass. But in 1906 Oberg most definitely decided to pursue the ground game.

Part of that decision might be related to the presence of William Ames Robinson of Aurora, Illinois. Robinson spent just two years at the Academy but made more than a lasting impression on the football program during that brief stay. With Oberg concerned about the loss of the talented halfback Frank Garrett to graduation the previous year (and with only three experienced players returning), he was more than pleased to view the on-field gifts of the speedy Robinson. In the 24-0 game against Chicago Heights (now called Bloom High School), Robinson scored twice and added several long runs to quickly impress his new coach. During the season, the team also welcomed another talented ball carrier in James Albert Watts from Nashville, Illinois, another newcomer to the school. Both Watts and Robinson would anchor a mighty offensive unit for Oberg during the 1906 season.

As the 1906 campaign continued, and the altered style of play became more familiar, most reports found the game of football to be both safer, and more interesting. There were some unexpected challenges, such as when players sweeping around the ends were forced to avoid collisions with any spectators who had inched their way onto the field. (This was never a worry when the "mass" plays were predominant.) But on the whole, things seemed to settle down quickly as reported by the *Chicago Record-Herald* on October 1:

> Football, the 1906 brand, underwent a fairly severe test and as a result, the much-abused rule makers may look upon their work with some degree of satisfaction. Flaws were there, of course . . . but on the whole, the new rules worked well. Mass plays were eliminated, the games moved smoothly, the ball changing hands often, and the general effect in cases where the contesting teams took advantage of the new conditions was eminently pleasing to the spectators.

MORGAN PARK ACADEMY TO HOST NOTRE DAME

After defeating St. Ignatius College of Chicago 27-0 on October 18, the Academy moved to 4-0 without allowing a single point being scored against the defense. It was then announced that Morgan Park Academy would be hosting a game against a "new" opponent on October 24: the University of Notre Dame (second team).

For a variety of reasons, the game was never played, primarily because the Academy was scheduled to play at the University School in Cleveland, Ohio on October 27 in one of the big "rivalry" games of the time. Perhaps the Academy administration feared possible injuries in a game against Notre Dame that might influence the outcome of the important prep contest in Cleveland. Still, from a historical perspective, the scheduling of a football game between Morgan Park Academy and the University of Notre Dame remains a wonderful talking point, and certainly an unusual piece of gridiron trivia history!

Instead of hosting Notre Dame, the Academy squad headed east as planned to renew its rivalry with the University School of Cleveland on October 27. Despite slippery field conditions due to a 25-minute rain delay which hampered its exceptional offense, Morgan Park managed to upend the undefeated hosts 12-0. Unfortunately, this would prove to be the last game in the brief series between the two schools. During the off-season, a letter was received from the University School that effectively terminated the competition. The reasons, as shared during an Academy faculty meeting on February 1, 1907, mentioned that the Morgan Park Academy football team was "too old and mature in comparison with their own, for it to be desirable to continue the annual game held between the two schools."

ROBINSON'S WORK WAS SENSATIONAL

Upon its return from Cleveland, the Academy pummeled Wendell Phillips High School of Chicago 27-0 for its seventh straight shutout victory, despite missing several starters due to injuries. Robinson scored all five touchdowns for the Academy, earning the praise of the *Chicago Daily News*:

> Robinson, a Morgan Park halfback of varsity caliber, made every one of the five touchdowns for his team. Robinson's work was of a sensational order, the star dodging through the Wendell Phillips men on two occasions for almost half the length of the field, the result being touchdowns. His other scoring was done from lesser distances, but with equal brilliance.

As expected with an undefeated record this late in the season, the Academy began to formulate plans to capture the Illinois state title, keeping in mind that such an honor did not officially exist, nor were there any fixed post-season playoffs to help the best high school team secure that title. Instead, the rather flexible system of "challenging" another team to battle in a season-ending game for the right to claim the state title was acceptable. As in the past, the dreaded North Division High School (now Lincoln Park High School) in Chicago was identified as the other likely candidate to partner with in a "championship" game. The first salvo in this verbal process was fired by Captain John Wedow of the Academy in early November, who openly shared his intentions of scheduling a game on November 14 with North Division, the expected champion of Cook County. Apparently, North Division agreed to this contest, so it must have irked Wedow and his teammates when the *Daily News* reported on November 6, that North Division "will probably go east for a game with some eastern preparatory institution…and [the team is] making plans to cancel the game slated for November 14 with Morgan Park Academy."

This statement, then, appeared to open the proverbial can of worms, with Wedow igniting the fuse in the *Chicago Daily News* on November 7 by issuing "a formal challenge to North Division asking that the teams meet on Thanksgiving Day or the latter [North Division] forfeit its claim upon the Cook County championship." North Division countered by claiming that the Academy athletes were likely both ineligible and over-age, which prompted Wedow to respond by stating that the academic requirements were much more strenuous than the city high schools. But, it was to no avail, as North Division ultimately refused the challenge in the same *Chicago Daily News* article by stating: "Their eligibility rules are far different from ours and let it suffice to say that the matter must be dropped right here, for we (North Division) cannot accept a challenge from a school outside of our class."

After all the rhetoric off the field, the 1906 season meekly ended when the Academy bounced undefeated Culver Military Academy 18-6 and Lake Forest Academy 11-6, which were the only points scored against the Academy during its unscathed 9-0 season. The Culver game earned the Academy the fictitious western preparatory title, while the home game with Lake Forest decided the Inter Academic League Championship.

An interesting aspect of the Lake Forest game was the very welcome and positive support from the local newspaper, the *Morgan Park Post*, which shed its usual balanced reporting demeanor in order to urge local residents to attend the final contest:

> It is not often that the people of the village have an opportunity to witness such a game as this, and a large number ought to be present. Ladies can find comfortable seats on the balcony of the gymnasium. A fee of 25 cents will be charged spectators to help defray the expense of the game. The village ought to give strong support to the Academy team in this game.

After entering the season with little hope for success with only three players returning from the previous season, Coach Oberg (and assistant Tilden Stearns) guided the team to the fourth undefeated season in school history. After a one-year hiatus, Oberg returned to coach the team again in 1908. He remained in the Morgan Park area, serving as the Assistant Postmaster of Morgan Park from 1904-1909, and then moving to the position of Deputy Sheriff and Personal Bailiff for Judge Jesse A. Baldwin of the Circuit Court from 1909-1917. After graduating from the John Marshall Law School, Oberg was admitted to the Illinois bar in 1920 and eventually became a partner in the firm of Baldwin and Oberg in Chicago.

The football future looked very bright for Morgan Park Academy, but with the winds of change sweeping south from the University of Chicago campus, there was considerable doubt that there would even be a Morgan Park Academy when the 1907 school year rolled around. With the passing of Dr. William Rainey Harper, the Academy lost a valuable ally in the administrative towers of the University of Chicago. The parent institution continued to grapple with financial challenges, although the checkbook looked more promising due to significant changes initiated during Harper's final years as school president.

CHICAGO HAS DECIDED TO CLOSE THE ACADEMY AT MORGAN PARK

Yet no one could have been more surprised than the students of the Academy when the following statement was read at a school assembly on March 4, 1907 by Academy Principal Franklin Johnson:

> The Board of Trustees of the University of Chicago has decided to close the Academy at Morgan Park at the end of the school year in June next.

Of course, additional comments were made, but behind the scenes. University of Chicago President Harry Pratt Judson apparently provided no "warning" to Principal Johnson about this monumental decision but did forward a letter asking Johnson to "Please say to the faculty that their faithful and efficient work is appreciated fully, and that every endeavor will be used in their interest." However, nothing was suggested to placate the fears of the young students. (University of Chicago. Office of the President.

Harper, Judson and Burton Administrations. Records, [Box 4, Folder 3], Special Collections Research Center, University of Chicago Library, n.d.)

The plot to separate the Academy from the University had been discussed thoroughly during the University's Morgan Park Committee meeting on February 18, 1907. A letter on February 22 from attorney, and trustee, Jesse A. Baldwin to University of Chicago President Judson summarized the meeting's decision in one long, brutal sentence:

> At the meeting of the Morgan Park Committee, after a full discussion it was thought that to close the institution would be a great hardship, and one fraught with not only unpleasant, but harmful results, and, yet, Mr. Johnson stated that unless some arrangement could be made looking to a continuance of the life of the institution, for at least five years, during which all interested would unite in the endeavor to make the institution self-supporting, he should think it unwise to continue longer than this year. (University of Chicago. Office of the President, Harper, Judson and Burton Administrations. Records (Box 3, Folder 11). Special Collections Research Center, University of Chicago Library.)

Certainly, some last-ditch efforts were made to secure both funding (including a direct request to John D. Rockefeller) or a viable financial restructuring, but another meeting held on February 25 failed to consider any last-minute redemption for the Academy. And so, with no alternatives apparent to the Chicago Board of Trustees, the surprise announcement was prepared and shared with the Academy faculty and students on March 4.

As might be expected, the reaction to the closure decision was both swift and frightening. Students gathered that afternoon near West Hall (adjacent to the current gymnasium) where a crude likeness of University of Chicago President Judson was created. Then, according to *The Inter Ocean*, about 175 students escorted the pseudo President Judson into the village of Morgan Park:

> In front of the Rock Island train depot the procession stopped. A couple of the more athletic students climbed the telegraph pole and fastened the straw man to an arm of the pole. A match set the effigy on fire, and amid the hoots and jeers, and with the academy cheers as war-whoops, the students danced around the blazing effigy.

WE FEEL PRETTY BLUE ABOUT IT

Later, *The Inter Ocean* interviewed an unnamed student who explained the discontent of the student body:

> "We feel pretty blue about it," said one of the student leaders. "We are all loyal to Morgan Park, and we hate to see this order. We feel that Dr. Judson is more to blame than anyone else. And so, we expressed our disapproval in this manner."

On March 5, even *The New York Times* chipped in with a report on the closing, noting that Morgan Park Academy is "generally considered the best private college preparatory school west of Andover..." Overall the key reason for the closing was financial (although attendance at the Academy had been increasing). In addition, the Board of Trustees indicated that the need for a private school such as the Academy had been minimized by the advent of other strong, new public high schools in the Chicago area. Four days later, a group of Academy alumni met and pledged to raise $100,000-$400,000 in order to salvage the institution. Meanwhile, in April, a group of Morgan Park residents pursued the idea of transforming the Academy into a military school to simply be called Morgan Park Military Academy. This new version of the school would operate under the leadership of retired army officer Captain George Byrode.

When the Academy officially closed on June 1, it took only a few days for a new management plan to be put in place. After much discussion and fund-raising, the *Chicago Tribune* reported on June 5 that:

> Morgan Park Academy is not a thing of the past. Funeral obsequies and indignation meetings on the part of the students have all been in vain. It was announced yesterday that the institution will open again in the fall. It will continue to be known as Morgan Park Academy. Captain George L. Byrode and Professor Harry Delmont Abells have leased the buildings from the University of Chicago for a term of ten years.

And so, Morgan Park Academy survived, and continues to do so until this day. Buoyed by significant monetary contributions from the alumni and with a determination to establish its own independent academic credentials, the Academy was a place of furious activity during the summer of

1907. Recruiting advertisements were placed in various newspapers, and the creation of virtually an entirely new faculty was undertaken. As the school stumbled to the starting line to re-open as planned in September, only about 60 students were enrolled. But of that number, 14 hardy souls (according to a photo in the 1907-1908 **Morgan Park Academy Catalog**) elected to play football in 1907.

While lacking in both numbers and equipment, the players also soon discovered that no coach was available to help the team carry on its rich football tradition. Usually, Coach Stagg would remedy that issue, but with the separation of the schools, that solution no longer existed, at least temporarily. Following the perfect 9-0 season of 1906, the ragged bunch of athletes on the 1907 squad certainly faced an uphill battle in order to maintain the school's lofty gridiron reputation.

The key to the team's success quickly became apparent in the shape of the gifted William A. Robinson. Back for his senior year, Robinson assumed the roles of quarterback, captain, and coach in no particular order. Without an experienced adult on hand to direct, instruct, and train the players, Robinson absorbed those tasks, thus taking on a huge responsibility in addition to his on-field chores. Robinson received some logistical assistance from Rev. Robert J. G. McKnight, an instructor in modern languages at the Academy. Rev. McKnight was well-qualified in the academic arena after securing degrees from Geneva, Princeton, and the University of Chicago, including his Ph.D. from Chicago earlier in 1907. Rev. McKnight's presence was likely that of a chaperone, but his contributions and support were appreciated by both the team and the school administration.

With limited practice time and games scheduled on the run, the 1907 season was filled with new opponents and much uncertainty. Armed with just those 14 players, Robinson could do little to prepare the team for actual competition, such as holding live scrimmages. Although the first game on September 25 ended with a 24-0 win over neighboring Morgan Park High School, the overall lack of Academy players was not yet evident. Robinson started his season with two touchdowns in the victory.

HE GAVE THE FAT BOY PLENTY OF WORK

However, it was a scrimmage against the University of Chicago varsity on October 2 that pushed the Academy team into area football recognition. In a controlled scrimmage, the Academy defeated the Maroons 4-0, although the Academy offense was given advantageous field position on each drive to "test" Stagg's charges (Stagg also refused to allow his team to play offense). The *Chicago Tribune* observed that "the collegers were fooled time and again on the forward pass, which was worked admirably by the preps." Part of this success might have been attributed to the pass protection offered by towering (6'8", 225 lbs.) Academy guard George Harvey Gammon who worked opposite chunky lineman F. R. Handy of the Maroons. The *Chicago Daily News* stated that with Gammon "playing against Handy yesterday, he gave the fat boy plenty of work." Still, it was a surprising showing by the Academy against a team that would eventually capture the Western (now Big Ten) Conference championship that year. On another level, it appeared that Stagg was now allowed to work more closely with the Academy even if the two schools were no longer academic partners. Following the scrimmage, *The Inter Ocean* reported that "Stagg drilled the two squads on punting and drop kicking."

Returning to the prep level of competition, the Academy stormed past Chicago Heights (Bloom) 34-0, Englewood 67-4, and then embarrassed the U.S. Cavalry team out of Ft. Sheridan 92-0 in the highest offensive output in school history. As the *Morgan Park Post* reported: "The soldiers lack of practice as well as lack of spirit, being veritable toys in the hands of the local boys." In that game, the Robinson brothers combined to tally nine touchdowns with William garnering three and his sibling Arthur Robinson finishing with six scores, along with 11 extra points (41 points)!

Now 4-0, but still scrambling to fill out a full schedule, Captain Robinson managed to secure a home date with the Chicago Veterinary College. The game lasted a mere 25 minutes before it was mercifully concluded with the Academy far ahead 58-0. Once again, Arthur Robinson generated some excitement with three more touchdowns and eight extra points for 23 tallies. The *Chicago Tribune* drolly described the losers' situation: "The horse doctors presented a heavy team but were sadly lacking in team work. The Morgan Park lads ran rings around their heavy opponents and scored almost at will."

After a week off, the Academy eleven traveled to Culver Military Academy and escaped with a hard-fought 10-5 victory. Prior to the game, the *Post* hinted at an incentive for the team:

> The Academy plays Culver Military Academy at Culver, and will by defeating the soldier boys of Lake Maxinkuckee be able to lay undisputed claim to the academic championship of the west. Capt. Byroade (sic) and Principal Abells have promised the boys to go to Pittsburgh and play the All-Star

Academy and High School team just before Thanksgiving if they defeat every team they meet before that time.

And the Academy team did just that, blowing past St. John's Military Academy (24-6), Lake Forest Academy (58-4), and the Grand Prairie Seminary (12-0). After that final game, the *Chicago Tribune* stated that Morgan Park could now claim "the academic championship of the west." Arthur Robinson added two more touchdowns in that game, but it should be noted that halfback R.M. Allen had a game of historical proportions, succeeding on a drop kick field goal from 50 yards and "his punting averaged nearly 60 yards," according to the *Chicago Tribune*. Against Lake Forest, the Robinson brothers combined for a measly ten touchdowns, with the captain claiming six of those! However, Arthur Robinson added eight extra points to his four scores from the field (28 points).

THE TEAM HAS NO COACH

As usual, there was plenty of speculation regarding post-season games and honors. On November 14, the *Chicago Tribune* spoke of a climatic game with North High School of Minneapolis, Minnesota. This came a day after the *Chicago Daily News* finally "discovered" the exact lack of resources maintained on the football field by the Academy. In a front-page article, the *Chicago Daily News* marveled at the strength and size of the team despite its limited resources:

> Morgan Park, though one of the huskiest "prep" teams in the country, is also one of the most freakish. Its players range in weight from 126 lbs. to 226. B. Monroe, right end, is scarcely five feet tall and weighs only 126 pounds, while Gammon, right guard, is 6 feet 8 ½ inches in height and weighs 226 pounds. McKnight has only sixty students from which to select a team and much trouble was experienced in securing three substitutes. The team has no coach, Capt. Robinson, quarterback, mapping out the plays and drilling the men in their positions. The team never scrimmages except in games because of lack of scrubs and practices only once or twice each week.

Two large photos of the team (now showing 15 players) were included with the article which may have prompted readers to marvel at how much the team from the tiny school had accomplished with such limited resources and so few practices. On November 16, the *Morgan Park Post* hinted that the Academy was still in the hunt to play a team from Minnesota, but this time it would be the Central High School and that the *Chicago Tribune* "later wants them to go to Seattle to battle for the far western championship."

With a second straight unbeaten season, the Morgan Park Academy football team had now racked up 19 straight victories over three seasons, capped by the "imperfect" 1907 squad that defied all odds to fashion that perfect mark. This would be the last Academy team to conclude a season without a coach, but not the last football squad to finish its schedule unbeaten. With the school still struggling to achieve survival, optimism for the both the Academy—and the football team—continued to soar in 1908.

EXTRA POINT

With all the saber-rattling and conjecture surrounding possible post-season battles at the conclusion of the 1907 season, it was interesting to learn that the Academy team was definitely offered a "championship" game opportunity. *The Inter Ocean* revealed on November 20 that the North High School team of Minneapolis did attempt to arrange a meeting with the Academy: "The Minneapolis team was eager to meet the Morgan Park Academy eleven but was unable to reach an agreement with the academic champs on the question of a guarantee [i.e. cash]."

A few days later (on November 25), the *Morgan Park Post* provided information on another unsuccessful scheduling effort:

> The *Chicago Tribune* tried to arrange a game between the Academy and Central High School of Minneapolis for this Saturday, but as a game had already been scheduled (by the Academy) with Grand Prairie Seminary here, Manager McKnight did not wish to cancel the game at this late date. While the Academy team loses an opportunity of playing before four or five thousand people at Minneapolis, and thus advertise the school while enjoying a jaunt away from home, Mr. McKnight's point is undoubtedly well taken. Year after year such teams as Hyde Park High School and North Division High School, both of Chicago, have cancelled games with the Academy eleven just a few hours before the game, because they were reasonably certain of meeting defeat if they

played. Then they would make a great shout about going to Brooklyn or Seattle to play for the championship of the United States when as a matter of fact, they had not defeated their more formidable opponents at home.

And so, we will never know just how much of an impact the "coachless wonders" might have made on the national scene. Suffice it to say that the team with the sparse roster and no formal leader was extremely successful in its own local environment. It remains legendary among its counterparts in a school tradition where such labels are not easily attained.

The amazing 1907 "Coachless Wonders" finished undefeated (9-0) despite not having a coach! They outscored their opponents 379-19, including a 92-0 shutout of the U.S. Cavalry football team. The "Coachless Wonders" claimed the "Western Preparatory Championship."

This rare photo from 1907 shows the "Coachless Wonders" practicing on the Academy grounds. (Photo credit: SDN-006138, Chicago Daily News negatives collection, Chicago History Museum)

CHAPTER 6

A Stout, Spry Yankee Named John Kenfield

*"Morgan Park fought with a ripped and battered
lineup, but never did Culver have a chance."*
—The Academy News, 1910

Before he was profiled in *Life* magazine...

Before he (as rumored) named the Baby Ruth candy bar...

And well before a major sports facility was named after him...John
Kenfield was an inexperienced 17-year-old quarterback for Morgan Park
Academy in 1908.

Born in Louisville, Kentucky, Kenfield's family moved to the Morgan
Park area where John entered the Academy. Right after the first game of the
1908 season against the Morgan Park Village team, the local *Post* newspaper mentioned that residency:

> Great interest was manifested in the struggle because of
> the fact that there were four village boys in the Academy
> line-up: Roy Stephenson, Ellis Smith, John Kenfield
> and Lyle Startzman, whose playing, the town team were
> anxious to discount.

Kenfield wasted little time in positioning himself as a team leader,
as the swift quarterback scored early on a 40-yard run and the Academy
blasted its friendly neighbors by the score of 53-0. As the Academy struggled to continue to keep its doors open again in 1908, the football team

managed to schedule several "new" teams under the leadership of a quizzical coaching staff. Although the Academy 1908 catalog states that the coaches were none other than Amos Alonzo Stagg and former mentor David Oberg, there was no media mention of Stagg in connection with the Academy football squad throughout the season. Oberg, however, was lauded by *The Academy News* at the conclusion of the season when it noted that "David Oberg, an alumni football star, gave the team many pointers from which much of the team's success was derived."

In all likelihood, Oberg was the only coach that served the team that year, with Stagg probably overseeing the operation from a distance. It was odd that the Academy catalog mentioned Stagg as the coach, since there was no longer a formal partnership between the University of Chicago and Morgan Park Academy. Perhaps Stagg allowed the use of his name, and his limited presence, to help ensure that the highway for quality players would continue to stretch from Morgan Park to the University of Chicago campus.

Kenfield fit in nicely with returning halfback Arthur Robinson, who continued his torrid scoring pace in 1908. Robinson scored two touchdowns and Kenfield picked off a pass and returned it 80 yards in a 24-0 win over St. Ignatius College in the second game of the season. Three more easy victories left the Academy with a perfect 5-0 slate and 24 straight successes over parts of four seasons. However, during that stretch, five key players, including Robinson, were injured and ruled out of the next game against the always rugged Culver Military Academy. Still the Academy team was confident when it rolled into Culver, Indiana for the big matchup—only to absorb a shocking 39-10 loss to the Cadets. The 24-game winning streak was snapped, and Culver scored more points against the Academy in that game than any other opposing team in the school's history, surpassing the 30 points scored by the University of Chicago varsity in an 1897 game. Even more disturbing was the fact that Culver accumulated more points in one game than did the Academy's 24 previous opponents combined (37) during that long winning skein.

The schedule concluded with easy wins over Grand Prairie Seminary (16-0) and Evanston Academy (78-0) as the Academy finished with a very robust 7-1 mark. Kenfield scored four times against Evanston while Robinson ended his impressive career with a touchdown and an extra point. With Kenfield returning, *The Academy News*, in its post-season analysis, was anticipating an even better season in 1909: "Kenfield's drop kicking and ability in advancing the ball for touchdowns were superb. Kenfield has been elected captain for next season and it is hoped another championship team will be turned out."

VERY GOOD WORK WITH HIS TOE

With Kenfield back in command, the 1909 Academy team was superlative in scoring 346 points while allowing only eight. Yet, it was those precious eight points that cost the Academy another perfect season. Maneuvering behind the crafty Kenfield, Morgan Park powered past the Morgan Park Village team (45-0), Chicago Veterinary College (52-0) and Thornton High School of Harvey, Illinois (52-0) to open the season. Following the Veterinary College romp, *The Academy News* was effusive in its praise of Kenfield: "Captain Kenfield led his team on with great executive ability and he deserves a very great part of the credit for the victory, as he did very good work with his toe."

Yet it was in that fourth game of the season against always tough Culver Military Academy that Morgan Park stumbled for the only time that season. Outweighed by an average of 20 pounds per man, and playing in a driving rain storm, the Academy failed to muster any type of offense in a disappointing 8-2 loss at Culver. *The Academy News* (October 23, 1909), however, was generally supportive in its description of the pre-game atmosphere:

> Nearly all of the school went down to Culver with the team, and all were in the best of spirits, being positive of a victory although they knew that it would be a very hard-fought contest. When we landed at Hibbard [Indiana train station] some of the plebes [freshmen] were very much disappointed to find that the town was not quite as big as Chicago but that was nothing to their chagrin when they discovered the fact that there were only four conveyances [wagons], and that they would have to "hit the ties" for a few miles. However, that did not damper their ardor in the least and they made as much noise as any thunder storm.

Indeed, transportation was still a bit rugged in 1909 as the students (and team) would need to take the train on the old Nickel Plate Railroad to Hibbard, Indiana (a few miles northeast of Culver) and then obtain some type of transportation (or walk!) the rest of the way to Culver, usually by horse-drawn vehicles.

The Culver defeat was the only miscue in a 6-1 season for new Coach John Anderson, although the Academy catalog also listed A.A. Stagg as a coach. Once again, Stagg was never mentioned by local newspapers as having any type of affiliation with the Academy that year. The fact that Stagg did have a direct influence on the Academy football program throughout the years is undeniable; yet, it is mystifying as to what his specific role was with the institution. In an interview for this book, Mr. Robin Lester, author of **Stagg's University: The Rise, Decline, and Fall of Big-Time Football at Chicago**, provided his own insight into the Stagg-MPA relationship: "I do know that President [William] Harper valued the relationship to Morgan Park Academy and Stagg no doubt loved the idea that it would provide talented players for him."

So, even after both the death of President Harper, and the termination of the academic partnership between the University of Chicago and Morgan Park Academy, it certainly appears that Coach Stagg continued to be recognized as part of the Academy football program, albeit in a rather indefinable function. Stagg would be listed as an Academy football coach again in 1910 (along with Anderson), but that would be the final time that his name would be "officially" mentioned in an Academy publication.

However, a letter written by Academy grad James "Mark" Wade over 60 years after his playing days at Morgan Park ended seemed to clarify that Stagg was an active participant in the Academy football program. Wade, the older brother of legendary collegiate coach Wallace Wade, graduated from the Academy in 1912 after playing football from 1909-1911. The letter in question was written in 1975 to the Brown University Football Association where Mark Wade attended college following his graduation from Morgan Park. In the letter (published in the book **Wallace Wade**, page 24), Wade refers to his playing days at the Academy and specifically mentions the presence of A.A. Stagg:

> In 1912 I graduated from Morgan Park Military Academy in Chicago as president of the class and captain of the football team. During the three years I was at Morgan Park I was coached under the instruction of the famous coach, Alonzo Stagg…who, in my judgement, was the best coach in American history and a great builder of men.

Wade's letterclearly indicates that he, as a football player at Morgan Park Academy, was under the tutelage of Stagg. Although media reports from the time rarely indicated that Stagg was actively involved with the football program at the Academy, the listings in the school's catalogs referring to Stagg as a football coach can now be more comfortably relied upon as being accurate, thanks in part to the Wade letter. For the Wade correspondence, we can thank author Lewis Bowling, who included it in his definitive book **Wallace Wade**, which focused on Mark Wade's younger brother, Wallace. We will learn more about the superlative career of Wallace Wade in upcoming pages. Note that Mark Wade also referred to the school as Morgan Park Military Academy, although the institution did not assume that name until 1918. In 1912, the school was still called Morgan Park Academy, although the "military" connotation appeared several times in newspaper articles and the students were often referred to as "cadets."

Meanwhile, Anderson became the first "semi-permanent" Academy football coach in a career that extended through the 1913 season, although Anderson would return to coach again in 1919. He played three years for Coach Stagg at the University of Chicago (graduating in 1907), and then spent a season as an assistant coach for Knox College in Galesburg, Illinois before returning to the Chicago area as football coach at the Academy.

But in 1909, he found himself in charge of a spunky team that was a bit light on weight but generated a great deal of speed and efficiency on the field. Following the close loss to Culver, Anderson implemented some new offensive sets to unleash on St. Viateur's (later St. Viator) College. With Kenfield breaking free for a 90-yard score, the Academy burst out to a 27-0 halftime lead and cruised to an easy 54-0 victory. Kenfield and halfback Roy Stephenson each contributed three touchdowns in the romp. It seems that *The Academy News* (November 13, 1909) approved of the innovative plays from Coach Anderson as well: "A number of new plays were put in use to see if they were satisfactory; judging from the score at the end of the second half one would naturally think that they were."

The offensive fireworks continued through the final two games as the Academy blasted Evanston Academy 52-0 and then demolished Lake Forest Academy 90-0 in the second highest scoring game in school history. Stephenson scored two touchdowns and added seven extra points against Evanston, then added five touchdowns and a whopping ten extra points versus Lake Forest. With touchdowns worth five points in 1909, Stephenson totaled 52 points in those two last contests. Most importantly, with the victory over Lake Forest, Morgan Park Academy finished with a 6-1 record and grabbed the 1909 Inter Academic League championship, and "proved beyond dispute their right to the title of champions of Illinois," claimed *The Academy News.*

As part of the post-season coverage, *The Academy News* published an interesting article titled "Statistics On 1909 Team." Along with the roster itself, the newspaper included the height, weight, age, and the possible future college choices of each player. Captain Kenfield, still just a junior, was listed as 5'5" and 138 lbs., but already 18 years and seven months old. The eldest player was the aforementioned sophomore left guard Mark Wade at 21 years and seven months. Another new face on the team was soph center Fred Herendeen, the tallest player on the club at 6'1" and 178 lbs. The heaviest? Once again, Mark Wade was at the top in this category at 182 lbs. Overall, the players on the 1909 Morgan Park Academy squad averaged 159 lbs. each and ranged in age from 17-21 years old. This is quite the contrast to the modern high school player who would likely be in the 14-18 age group on a team that would probably average at least 50 lbs. more per man than in 1909. In terms of scoring statistics, Stephenson tallied 19 touchdowns and 38 extra points for a total of 133 points. Kenfield added 12 touchdowns, two field goals and four extra points.

TREATED TEAM AS IF THEY WERE HUMAN BEINGS

Three of the key players mentioned above (Kenfield, Herendeen, and Wade) eventually left lasting impressions on the Academy as proud graduates and with successful careers in their individual industries. Each would return for the 1910 season.

Coach Anderson would return as well, perhaps encouraged by a nicely veiled tribute from *The Academy News* (December 18, 1909):

> John E. Anderson is his name. The first week that he was here he looked us over in a quiet way and told us that we would have to get busy. With his help and advice, we did get busy enough to pull out a championship team. Anderson won his way into the hearts of all the fellows by the fairness and squareness of his methods. He really treated the fellows on the team as if they were human beings deserving of a certain amount of feeling. If we can have "Andy" next year, then nothing stands in our way for a championship team.

The diminutive Kenfield would once again anchor the squad at quarterback, although it is obvious that his eligibility somehow stretched into a fifth year in 1910. Kenfield was a superb football player, but also excelled in tennis, basketball, baseball, and track making him one of the most talented athletes in the history of the school. *The Academy News* provided more information about his talents, and his extended high school career, in its December 18, 1909 issue:

> John Kenfield, captain of the Academy championship football team of '09, is probably the most all-around athlete the school has at the present time. He started his work in the Academy four years ago. In his first year, he made a name for himself in tennis, where he won his first emblem [letter]. His second year was spent at Morgan Park High. While there Johnny was captain of the football and basketball teams. Last year, John returned to the Academy, becoming captain of tennis. During the year, he earned emblems in five different sports--football, basketball, baseball, tennis, and track. In his last year, he was captain of our football team and through his good generalship we were able to win the championship of Illinois.

Perhaps the year spent at Morgan Park High School was not included in his academic experience, for John Kenfield was back on the Academy football field to begin the 1910 campaign (his fifth year of high school). Kenfield was never a renowned scholar at the Academy, struggling with his classes in Latin, algebra, and history, according to his student records still maintained in the Academy archives. He did shine in courses related to the military, where he earned outstanding grades in his "Tactics" course which likely involved leadership skills. Still, most students probably assumed that Kenfield would graduate with the class of 1910. Even in the same issue of *The Academy News* noted above, the newspaper reported that M. H. Lockhart of Fulton, IL had been elected as the 1910 team captain "to fill the position left vacated by the graduation of Kenfield..."

Yet Kenfield was back in uniform in 1910 leading an impressive array of talent for Coach Anderson. Fred Herendeen returned at center, Mark Wade at guard, along with "the fastest squad of gridiron warriors the school ever has shown," according to the *Chicago Tribune*. One player that did not return for some reason was captain-elect M. H. Lockhart, and Herendeen was named to that important position. With such elated optimism, some may have been surprised that the Academy struggled to eclipse the Morgan Park Village team (5-0), St. Viator College (9-0), and Oak Park

High School (9-6) to open the season. However, the tight win over Oak Park would prove to be historically significant in the annals of Illinois high school football.

ZUPPKE WAS A NEAR-MARTINET

Oak Park High School had just hired a new football coach and history teacher from Muskegon, Michigan for the then astounding fee of $2,500.00 per year. His name was Robert Zuppke and his coaching reign (1910-1912) at Oak Park High School would result in unparalleled success. "The only game lost by Oak Park during the three years was the first game played during the first season that Zuppke had charge of coaching," stated author George Carr in *The Alumni Quarterly* (Volume 7, 1913) of the University of Illinois.

Indeed, that very first game was against Morgan Park Academy. While Zuppke was mustering his new troops, including right guard Bart Macomber, for its opening game, the veteran Academy team scored quickly in the first quarter on a 30-yard drop kick field goal by Kenfield. After Oak Park snatched a 6-3 advantage via a touchdown and then an extra point by Macomber, halfback J.W. Couchman crossed the goal line with only 46 seconds remaining to provide the Academy with a final 9-6 victory. Those would be the only points scored against Morgan Park that season. *The Academy News* was obviously happy with the hard-fought victory and heaped more praise upon Kenfield:

> By his rare selection of plays, by his kicking and handling of punts and by his individual playing during the game, Kenfield demonstrated that his reputation of being the best "prep" quarterback in the country was in no danger of slippage. It's there for good "Johnny," never fear. Suppose we all were as good as Kenfield?

Zuppke remained at Oak Park for just three seasons before embarking on a 28-year hall of fame career as the head football coach for the University of Illinois. At Illinois, Zuppke led the team to two national championships along with seven Big Ten titles. Among his legendary players were Harold "Red" Grange and George Halas, founder of both the Chicago Bears and the National Football League. Macomber followed Zuppke to Illinois in 1912 and became an All-American halfback/quarterback/kicker himself.

In an article written over 50 years later in *Sports Illustrated* (November 2, 1964), Macomber recalled the experience of playing for Zuppke:

> Zup was a near-martinet on the practice field," Bart Macomber recalls, "and wanted it strictly understood he was boss there at all times. He believed in thorough practice, monotonous drill, with perfection the goal. He was quick to criticize errors, but rarely given to praise. Off the field he was a mild, almost bland individual, about 5 feet 7, 165 pounds, light hair and complexion. Rather of the professor type, if you know what I mean.
>
> He earned a basketball letter at Wisconsin; football there amounted to four years of scrub. He taught history and coached football at Oak Park High, near Chicago. I believe he made about $2,500 at that job while I played for him there. We had three years undefeated, then he was offered the Illinois coaching post—at an increase in salary, of course. Our last year at Oak Park, the class of 1912, two on that team went on to All-America. They were Milton Ghee at Dartmouth and myself at Illinois. A third member of our team, Pete Russell, made All-Western at Chicago U.

While Macomber failed to mention that lone loss to the Academy in the article, he was accurate in his listing of his formidable teammates, all of whom were in the starting lineup against the Academy on October 22, 1910! Zuppke's charges finished the rest of the season undefeated and then claimed the state championship in both 1911 and 1912 as Oak Park failed to taste defeat in both of those campaigns.

Meanwhile, the Academy mauled the Chicago Veterinary College 47-0 in what might have been Kenfield's finest game. The tough quarterback scored four touchdowns, kicked a field goal, and added two extra points. The *Chicago Tribune* (November 6, 1910) covered the game and applauded Kenfield's work in the rout: "Much of the success of the victors was due to the generalship of Kenfield, who was able to pick plays that would gain against the heavy opponents."

The next big hurdle was a skirmish with Lake Forest Academy for a rare Monday game on November 14, 1910. Couchman was out of the lineup due to his mother's illness, but his teammates regrouped and spanked the hosts 25-0 to capture still another Inter Academic title. *The Academy News* added some more sparkle to the reputation of Kenfield when it stated:

"It might be said here that this little fellow played stellar ball throughout the contest and made the Lake Forest backfield smash records in their flights after his twisting punts." With little time to rest, the Academy traveled to Culver, Indiana five days later and returned with no decision in a 0-0 tie. The disappointing draw was likely due to the absence of both Kenfield and Couchman from the Morgan Park lineup, especially when Culver blocked a field goal that might have turned the tide for the Academy. Kenfield was normally accurate in those critical kicking situations.

THE SUB

Fifteen years after the Culver game, Fred Herendeen, by then a revered literary figure in the United States, wrote a touching remembrance of the scoreless contest. This mini memoir focused on the brave efforts of end Sam Beckwith who was injured that day and is printed here for perhaps the first time as it was written (no corrections were made to spelling or punctuation):

> Sam Beckwith was a substitute for three long weary years—
> He played the bench, but he could root with quite the
> loudest cheers—He never had a bit of luck for though he
> sure could play—The first-string ends both always stuck
> and finished every fray.

Now Sam you know was doggone good, he'd scrimmage with the best—He fought hard be it understood and passed in every test—He always was right on the spot to help in every way—But his it seems was just the lot to help but not to play.

Now Sam was always mad all through the Culver game—At other times a quiet lad, he never seemed the same—When one we started in to mix with the old C.M.A.—Sam never missed the smallest tricks he'd follow every play.

> *Sam fought for three long weary years to make that football*
> *team—But through he won a lot of cheers he never copped the*
> *cream—Till in his fourth and closing year he won his way to*
> *fame—He copped the job as star right end set for the Culver*
> *game.*

*He played just like a shooting star, all western end was he—
But then there came a blow to mark his well-earned victory—
Twas in the game with L.F. A. that we received the blow—For
though we won the game that day, they layed Sam Beckwith
low.*

*Our quarter back, our half back too, and Sam our star right
end—were all smashed up and we were blue, on that you may
depend—With Culver just one week away and raring for a
fight—Our skies were overcast and grey, and things looked
black as night.*

*Poor Sam was like a maniac, he'd bake his knee all day—
then hobble to the gym and back to cheer us in our play—He
took the sub right end each night and coached till taps had
blown—and then old Sam would douse the light, lie on his
bed and moan.*

*Well, Saturday came with a jump, we left for Culver's den—
And in each throat there was a lump for our three injured
men—For we knew what it meant to lose that chance that
meant so much, but Sam tried hard to chase our blues although
he wore a crutch.*

*That game I never shall forget, the fight of our careers—For
hard and fast each team was set, midst wave on wave of
cheers—But Culver had the strongest team, with fresh men
ever play—and we but fought to stem the stream and hold our
line that day.*

*Five minutes left, the score was tied, at naught to naught we
stood—Gosh how that Culver back field tried, and they were
more than good—And how our weary line stuck tight as shock
on shock they met—Twas Culver smash! M.P.A. fight! A very
even bet.*

*Three minutes left, our line swayed and staggered in their
tracks the game became one long parade of charging Culver
backs—Our forty yard—our thirty yard—our twenty yard—
and then—Another smashing, crashing, charge and we were
on our ten.*

One minute more our line was gone, all out upon their feet—For C.M.A. it meant a score, for M.P.A. defeat—When suddenly a whistle shrilled across the frosty air—The smashing play a moment stilled, we waited in despair.

Then out from where our subs had been (they now were in the game) there came a most unearthly din and then—Sam Beckwith came—he struggled like a fighting fool to shake the coach's touch—He kicked and fought just like a mule and even swung his crutch.

The tears were streaming down his face and as we looked again—We saw that he was making place for two more injured men—And how they fought to pass our coach and how they made their plea—they even faced a stern reproach of ump and referee.

Sam hobbled on his injured leg to prove he was all right—and both the others tried to beg they be allowed to fight—They wanted but to do their bit to help their team that day—Each man a sample of the grit we bred in M.P.A.

They got them off the field of play, though each was hopping wild—and as the ref passed where I lay I'll swear to you he smiled—The whistle blew the game again, four yards to go but say—We'd seen the fight of injured men, we held for them each play.

All this was fifteen years ago, but as I write I see—the face of Beckwith all a-glow as with a victory—They said it was our stonewall line that held for that surprise—But it was Beckwith—pal o' mine and two more injured guys.

STOUT, SPRY YANKEE NAMED JOHN KENFIELD

Two weeks later, the Academy capped its undefeated (6-0-1) schedule with a tight 6-0 win over another new opponent, Hinsdale High School. In an oddity for the time, the injured Kenfield was on the field…not as a player, but as the referee! Following the game, a string of dances and banquets celebrated the undefeated season and soon thereafter, Mark Wade was elected to serve as captain for the 1911 team as described by *The Academy News*:

Wade is a "southern gentleman," 22 years of age and tips the bar at 185 pounds. This is his second year at the Academy and he has the distinction of two years' service at left guard on two championship teams. This year he was considered one of the best guard men in the "prep business." In all of the title games this season he distinguished himself by his magnificent defensive playing. We all wish him all the luck in the world and we feel assured that under his able leadership Morgan Park Academy will continue her long list of title victories.

The 1910 season would mark the last appearance of John Kenfield in an Academy football uniform. Possibly the most talented athlete in the early history of the Academy, Kenfield excelled in several sports and also served as the school's basketball coach. Because of his participation on both the tennis and baseball teams in the spring, he usually chose baseball when there was a scheduling conflict. *The Academy News* (July 20, 1911) lamented the lost opportunities for the tennis squad: "Captain Kenfield would have helped along wonderfully in the team's play had he been able to compete in the various matches, but on account of his duties as captain of the baseball team, he was able to take part in a couple of contests only, and these he won for the team with ease."

So, what does an athletic superstar who stood only 5'5" do for an encore after his high school graduation? Perhaps as an acquiescence to his size, Kenfield drifted primarily towards tennis as his preferred sport and eventually became a national force in the National Clay Courts championships, reaching the final four on one occasion. Apparently, Kenfield never attended college full-time according to an article from *The Daily Tar Heel* in 1944:

> At 18, Mr. Kenfield went to work with the Andrew Jergens Co. as a salesman for toilet articles. Three years later he left Jergens to go into the piano business with the George P. Bent Co. in Chicago. He spent five years with this company and at one time was branch manager of the stores. During his leisure time, he continued with his tennis.
>
> Ambition pressed him forward and in 1914, he accepted a position with the Curtiss Candy Co., one of the largest companies of its kind in the world. Mr. Kenfield served as vice president during the eight years he was with the

company. It was in 1928, however, that Kenfield seriously went in for tennis as a life's vocation. He was appointed professional tennis instructor at the fashionable Lake Shore Country Club of Glencoe, Illinois.

Also, in 1928, Kenfield accepted the position as the head tennis coach at the University of North Carolina where he enjoyed an extraordinary career that stretched from 1928 to 1955. During that time, Kenfield's teams amassed 434 wins against only 30 losses. He captured 15 Southern Conference and two Atlantic Coast Conference championships. In 1948, his squad finished third in the country. His teams also established a then-record of 67 consecutive wins. As a result, Kenfield was named to the College Tennis Hall of Fame in 1986. However, an even bigger honor awaited in 1992 when the University of North Carolina named its new Cone-Kenfield Indoor Tennis Center after the Morgan Park Academy graduate (and also after a former North Carolina player named Caesar Cone II). Kenfield was profiled in *Life Magazine* (June 13, 1938) which described his impact on the North Carolina campus: "North Carolina, a proud southern institution, owes its tennis glory to the coaching of a stout, spry Yankee named John Kenfield. John Kenfield came to North Carolina in 1928. Promptly the university's teams began winning everything."

In a final tribute to the wonderful life of John Kenfield (1891-1958), the rumored story of his naming of the popular "Baby Ruth" candy bar was examined in the 2002 *University of North Carolina Men's Tennis* publication:

> Controversy about the origin of the [Baby Ruth] name continues to the present. A profile of John Kenfield, a vice president at Curtiss Candy in the early 1920s, reports that Kenfield claimed that he contacted Babe Ruth about licensing Ruth's name as a new moniker for the existing Curtiss' *Kandy Kake*. That product was being reformulated to become the five-cent bar that [Curtiss Candy] wanted to sell. Ruth demanded more money than Curtiss could pay at the time. Kenfield said that he then suggested the Baby Ruth name.

I CAME TO BUY 100 CARLOADS OF APPLES

With Kenfield finally graduating, the Academy football team looked for more success in 1911 under Coach Anderson but experienced an apparent tough blow when the talented Fred Herendeen suffered an appendicitis attack just prior to the season opening 18-6 win over Morgan Park High School. With medical treatments being a bit primitive compared to modern practices, Herendeen was thought lost for the season due to his balky appendix. However, Herendeen did return to the field briefly for the second game of the season, a surprising 15-0 defeat at the hands of the local Stingers Athletic Club, an independent football team. It was the first "home" loss for the Academy in five years, but a closer look at the Stingers' roster revealed familiar names such as Kenfield, Stephenson and other prominent graduates of the Academy football program. Instead of his normal center position, Herendeen operated out of the backfield as a fullback and proved to be a tough target for would be opposing tacklers with his 6'2", 191 lbs. frame.

Overall, a general lack of experience, along with some key injuries, crippled the Academy team in 1911 as the squad stumbled through its brief schedule with 3-3 record. The low point was a season finale shutout by Culver which resulted in a 32-0 stomping from the Indiana crew. "The local team outplayed the Morgan Park boys throughout the game and were in little danger at any time of being scored against," reported the *Culver Citizen*.

The Culver defeat marked the end of the Academy football playing careers for three-year starters Herendeen and Wade. Herendeen was introduced to readers in the Preface to this book as the distinguished Broadway playwright who, nearly 100 years ago, strongly urged Academy administrators to publish a history of the school. However, Herendeen would return to assist the football program following his graduation and we will learn more about this gifted supporter of the Academy shortly.

Mark Wade played briefly at Brown University in Providence, Rhode Island during the 1912 season, before leaving school to focus on his business career. He secured a spot at left tackle as a freshman and participated in several key contests for Brown, including a season-ending battle with the legendary Jim Thorpe and the Carlisle Indian School. But the lure of business began to pull Wade away from the football field, according to the same letter he penned in 1975 (from the book **Wallace Wade**, page 25):

> The only reason I didn't come back to Brown is that in 1913, I came to Wenatchee [Washington] to buy 100 carloads of apples. I expected to sell them and return to Brown. The only way to get 100 carloads was to buy direct

from the farmers and that required staying after the first of the term—too late for football.

Ultimately, Mark Wade devoted his career to the apple industry and eventually became the owner of one of the largest orchards in the country. Meanwhile, perhaps his greatest legacy to Morgan Park Academy was the fact that his younger brother, Wallace, followed him to Chicago in 1912. Born on June 15, 1892 in Trenton, Tennessee, William Wallace Wade attended both Peabody, and Fitzgerald and Clarke High Schools in Trenton, before heading north to finish his high school career. Author Lewis Bowling explained the reasons behind Wade's decision to attend the Academy:

> Even though Mark had graduated by the fall of 1912 when Wallace arrived, Wallace knew that this military boarding school was just what he wanted. Rigid discipline, high academic standards, and a love of sports were right in line with his interests.
>
> By the time Wade arrived, Coach Stagg had put John Anderson, one of his former Chicago players, in the position of head coach, but Stagg still attended practices occasionally. The knowledge that he would have an opportunity to be tutored by either Coach Stagg or his players, coupled with the fact that Mark had achieved such success there, played a significant role in Wallace's decision to go to Morgan Park.

Wallace, who had begun developing solid football skills during his previous high school stops, was one bright spot at left tackle for Coach Anderson during a tough 2-4 season in 1912. Included in those unsightly losses were a 33-0 shellacking by Rockford (Illinois) High School, and a 54-0 disaster against Culver, the worst defeat in Academy history at that time. While at the Academy, Wade also excelled in baseball and demonstrated that he was a solid student, achieving high grades in trigonometry, Greek, advanced algebra, and civics.

Wallace Wade graduated from Morgan Park Academy on June 12, 1913, and like his brother Mark, decided to enroll at Brown University. Before graduating from Brown in 1917, Wade (now a guard) helped his team to win 18 games against just seven losses and three ties. The team also participated in the second staging of the Rose Bowl in 1916, dropping a

14-0 decision to Washington State following an exhausting cross-country train trip. In an article in the *Chicago Evening Post* on December 24, 1930, Wade's contributions to Brown's success were still remembered:

> Wade was a player on the Brown group, the first Atlantic seaboard eleven that ever played a western team in the Rose Bowl contest. Brown was not undefeated in her own sector that year, but she had beaten Yale, Carlisle, and some others, and was regarded as a representative eastern team. And Wade was an important factor in whatever success Brown attained.

For Wade, his graduation from Brown was not the end of his football interests, but just the beginning, as he embarked on one of the most successful football coaching careers in the history of American collegiate football. Wade's football journey took him through both Alabama and Duke, where he won three national championships as the head coach at Alabama and he enjoyed further success at Duke, compiling a lifetime record (at both schools) of 171-49-10, good enough to earn Coach Wade a spot in the College Football Hall of Fame. In total, four members from the football program at Morgan Park Academy have been honored with inclusion into the College Hall of Fame, an exceptional number from such a small school. We shall examine the individual careers of these four gridiron legends more closely in the next chapter of this book.

MORGAN PARK GROUND ITS CLEATS INTO THORNTON

For the 1913 team, the last under Coach Anderson for a few years, it was either feast or famine on the offensive side of the ball. Although the final ledger of 3-2-1 returned the squad to a positive mark for the schedule, the team experienced a radical disparity on offense, being blanked twice while posting big numbers in the other four contests. John Kenfield returned to the bench in 1913, serving as Anderson's capable assistant coach, and helped the Academy finish with a flourish, routing Chicago Tech College 70-7 and Marshall High School of Chicago 67-0 in the final two games. Halfback Harold Fiske tallied five touchdowns in the Marshall game while quarterback Roy Ruehl added a pair of scores along with seven extra points.

By this time, interest among students in playing football at the Academy had increased significantly enough so that the school also fielded a "lightweight" team, usually composed of players under a certain weight threshold. Some schools also defined their fresh-soph or junior varsity teams as "lightweights." While this publication focuses only on the varsity or heavyweight aspects of the historical Morgan Park Academy football program, the lightweight squad of 1913 does rate a mention. The Academy lightweights roared through their schedule as champions of the Lightweight Suburban League and found themselves in the headlines after a wild 101-0 win over Thornton High School of Harvey, Illinois on November 15, 1913. It was the most points ever scored by a Morgan Park Academy team and enticed the *Chicago Tribune* to report that "Morgan Park Academy ground its cleats into Thornton High of Harvey 101-0, the largest score made this season. Morgan Park made fourteen touchdowns, followed by as many goals [extra points] by H. Monroe." With the modern football scoring system implemented in 1912, touchdowns were now worth six points, field goals earned three points, and extra points remained at one point each. A field goal earlier in the Thornton game completed the triple digit scoring.

Off the field, Morgan Park Academy helped form the Western Academic Athletic Association with seven other academies: Evanston, Culver, Lake Forest, St. John's, Northwestern, Elgin, and Wayland (Wisconsin). "This is this first time in the history of athletics that academies have been joined in one union," reported the *Chicago Tribune* on November 1, 1913:

> It was the culmination of preliminary plans suggested two years ago. One of the reasons for the formation of this league was to settle the different academic championships. Heretofore every school which had a claim took the title. According to the new rules, five football games must be played among teams of the league in order to get a standing.

Rules were also proposed that would require players to maintain academic requirements and to refrain from playing with a school other than the one that he might be attending. In the cloudy early days of prep high school football competition, these were sturdy ideals that would surely improve the image of the game as well as ensure that academic progression was an important partner in the academy football universe. Unfortunately, despite the wide-spread publicity surrounding the inception of the new league, it failed to emerge as expected.

MORGAN PARK ELIMINATES TANGO

Closer to home, the administration of the Academy hastily entered the area of social interaction for its students when it outlawed the "tango" dance. It remains unclear what prompted this decision, but the *Chicago Tribune* reported this mandate as a straight news story on November 14, 1913:

> The faculty of Morgan Park Academy has just voted to bar the tango and other new-fashioned dances from the parties at the school. Official word has gone out that the military two-step and waltz only will be danced at the academy parties. It is planned to instruct those of the student body who are interested in dancing in the old-fashioned steps.

Behind the scenes, the Academy itself was once again experiencing serious financial difficulties as 1913 stretched into 1914. In an effort to generate interest, the Academy initiated a substantial advertising campaign in newspapers across the country. A large ad in *The Pantagraph* In Bloomington, Illinois urged parents to "Train your boy as you plan your business...This famous boys' school ranks with the highest in the country in scholarship and athletics—its boys are acceptably prepared for any college, technical school, or for work."

In Iowa, and other areas, potential students were offered the opportunity to secure a scholarship to the Academy for the 1914-15 school year by selling subscriptions for newspapers—an unusual partnership between the school and assorted distant publications as promoted in *The Cedar Rapids Republican* on July 5, 1914:

> To some one boy there is a splendid reward awaiting for his summer's work—a $650 tuition scholarship to Morgan Park Academy of Morgan Park, Ill. This tuition-scholarship with take care of all the necessary expenses of the successful contestant for the school year of 1914-15, and it will go to the boy who does the most successful work during the months of June, July and August.

With enrollment resting at around 102 for the upcoming school year, the need for additional student tuition as a base fiscal resource was evident. Since the break with the University of Chicago, the Academy was largely the responsibility of Superintendent Clinton Everett Duncan who was visible in all decision-making at the Academy. One such decision likely involved the football coach, John Anderson. After graduating from the University of Chicago in 1907, Anderson received his law degree from there as well in 1912. The annual Morgan Park Academy catalog for the academic year of 1914-15 listed Anderson as the football coach once again. However, since the catalog was probably printed well in advance of the beginning of the school year it could be forgiven for including one small mistake: former player Fred Herendeen took over as the new gridiron mentor in 1914.

KEEP A STIFF UPPER LIP

The reason for this change remains unclear. In fact, Anderson's personal documents reviewed at the Chicago History Museum reveal that Anderson was bewildered by the surprise decision by Duncan. Anderson apparently wrote a letter in the late summer of 1914 to school principal Harry Abells seeking clarification on his football coaching position. Abells responded on August 1, 1914:

> I think nothing has been done as yet about the coaching for next year. As you know Mr. Duncan is in direct charge of the school. I left your letter with some other mail which came to me upon his desk. I think he must have seen it. Keep up a stiff upper lip. We all have to go through these strenuous times. In fact, I for one have never been out of them. But as I look back I can see that they have been fully as much a part of my education as my university training. Keep chuck full of courage, hope and fighting spirit and things are bound to come out all right.

It had been a busy year for Superintendent Duncan. Born in 1880 in West Virginia, he apparently attended Brown University for just one year, but was living in Chicago in 1900 and working as a servant and coachman, according to the U.S. Census. By 1910, he was employed as an instructor at Morgan Park Academy. On July 30, 1913, Duncan married wealthy Gertrude Wayte of Morgan Park (sister of former Academy football player Thomas Wayte) and their only child (John Everett Duncan) was born on June 2, 1914. However, on March 7, 1914, Duncan, along with John Elmer Berquist and James E. Dickinson, formed a new corporation called Morgan Park Academy. In reality, according to a document found in the Academy archives, the three partners did not enjoy equal ownership. Duncan owned 996 shares of the new corporation, while four others each owned one share.

While Duncan assumed the role of superintendent, Berquist became the Secretary and Dean of the organization—which was valued at $100,000.

ACTUAL CASH NEEDED RIGHT NOW

Unfortunately, the new corporation crumbled quickly and lost its lease on the Academy property (held by the University of Chicago) in November of 1914. With the real danger looming of the Academy permanently closing its doors, a hastily convened group of alumni and concerned friends met to discuss the future of Morgan Park Academy. Once again, a forgotten letter found in the John E. Anderson papers provided sorely needed insight into the situation as this small group of academic heroes (including former football coach David Oberg) reached out to the Academy community with an almost desperate "form" letter dated December 1, 1914:

> The privately owned and controlled school corporation headed by C. E. Duncan which has conducted M.P.A. the past few years was dispossessed of its lease to the school property November 20th, by the University of Chicago because of non-payment of rent. An emergency committee composed of quickly available alumni, village people, students' parents, and faculty members met. They decided unanimously that M.P.A. should not be allowed to pass out of existence in such a manner. The Academy has justified its existence in the past…

> The Emergency Committee decided upon a re-organization which gives the control of the school to a Board of Trustees, one-third of which are to be alumni. Mr. Abells is to be the Academic head . . . and the present faculty is to be retained.

> The Academy under sane business methods can be made to pay its way, but there are no funds present now to defray current expenses. The parents and village people are promising to help in a splendid manner. But actual cash is needed right now…Send what you can spare—many are giving ten dollars, several have promised a hundred.

Through the laudable efforts of the "Emergency Committee," the Academy once more prevailed over challenging financial difficulties and righted itself under the new management scheme. It was not an easy reversal as the school possessed only $1,840.76 in the bank in May of 1915, but several measures were implemented to balance the budget. One of the major contributors to the financial downfall of the Academy was the newspaper scholarship program (noted previously) initiated by Duncan. In exchange for "free" advertising, the Academy partnered with numerous newspapers in a circulation/scholarship scheme designed to attract new students from around the country. The prevailing thought, as expressed in a December 31, 1914 letter written by Duncan to his creditors, was that each scholarship winner would bring along one or more additional students who would pay full price for their tuition. Unfortunately, not one "paying" student was attracted to enroll at the academy, while 25 scholarships were awarded at $650 each. "Experts approved the plan, and it was reasonable to believe that each paper would draw at least one additional full paying boy," lamented Duncan in his missive. "It was reasonably and confidently expected that there would be at least $15,000 more in tuition this year, but not a single paying boy came through this extensive advertising campaign."

While enrollment was sorely needed, the new Board of Trustees and President Enoch J. Price (a local attorney and staunch supporter of the school) became personally involved in the careful financial reconstruction of Morgan Park Academy. In a letter written by Price on May 15, 1915 (found in the Academy archives), he summarized the first few months of the new regime:

> In general, we have exceeded our expectation in keeping the school together and in financing it from its own resources...changes were effected promptly in the management of the business affairs of the school resulting in considerable economies. It is and will be the policy of this Board to shape its budget to fit its revenue...

Much later, in July of 1944, with the school now quite successful as the Morgan Park Military Academy, Superintendent Harry Abells looked back at those difficult times in a report to the Board of Trustees:

> In 1914 our Board of Trustees was organized. The finances of the Academy were a minus quantity. Rigid economy, superior business management, and a remarkable growth in income through an increase in cadet [student] enrollment constituted the program...It was during these years that I came to know President E. J. Price as the Rock of Gibraltar

of Morgan Park Military Academy. He never wavered in our financial program. The school kept up its steady forward movement notwithstanding its temporary distress. Now we have another cycle of business prosperity.

Duncan eventually left the Chicago area in 1916 and settled in Weslaco, Texas where he worked as a farmer and real estate agent. He never returned to the educational field and passed away on October 31, 1953 at the age of 73.

EARLY SUCCESS SPOILED MY CAREER AS AN UNDERGRADUATE

Most likely, the absence of Coach Anderson from the football field in 1914 was the result of Duncan and his cohorts attempting to save money in view of the impending financial downfall. Away from the field, Anderson continued his legal practice and began to invest in real estate, both in Illinois and Florida. Always an innovator, Anderson also offered a "mail order" football coaching service which he began during his tenure at the Academy. In addition, he was the head football coach at Knox College in Galesburg, IL in 1917, compiling a 4-2-1 record for the season. He then returned to Knox as a line coach in 1921. Anderson passed away in Orinda, California in 1977 at the age of 94.

When the 1914 school year began, Herendeen (a 1912 Academy grad) was listed in the academic catalog as the Vice-President of the Alumni Association. At this time, Herendeen was already known for his creative skills, even though he was still a student at the University of Chicago in 1914. An article written in *The Brooklyn* (New York) *Daily Eagle* on February 25, 1934 recalled the auspicious start of Herendeen as a writer—and its effect on him:

> Mr. Herendeen is no novice on the stage. When he was a student at the University of Chicago, he had already become a successful dramatic writer. "Too early success spoiled my career as an undergraduate," mourned the writer. "I was 20 years old when my first play "The Spoilers" was produced. It ran eight months in Chicago, bringing in between $400 and $600 royalties every week. I had also written five vaudeville sketches, which

gave me additional royalties of between $75 and $150 a week." Naturally, when a 20-year-old boy receives such checks that run into four figures a week he begins to think that he knows more than the professors who are trying to teach him and whose salaries for a year are often not as much as he gets in two or three weeks.

With worker incomes in 1914 averaging about $25-$30 per week, the rookie football coach at the Academy was enjoying enormous earnings, while likely not receiving any compensation for his time with the football team! Working with his former teammate, Roy Stephenson, as an assistant coach, Herendeen and his crew were stunned 20-9 in the opener against Morgan Park High School. It marked the first time that the local high school had defeated the Academy in football competition. Herendeen's club rebounded behind the play of halfback Alfred Eissler to finish the season at 4-4, including a 59-0 bombardment of Deerfield High School and a 16-0 win over Loyola Academy. Hopes for a winning season were dashed in the finale, a 32-13 loss at Culver, which *The Culver Citizen* called "by far the most interesting for the spectators that has been played on the home grounds this year." The report also noted a familiar face assuming the role of referee: "The referee of the game was Kenfield, a famous quarterback of Morgan Park in the days when she used to come to Culver and win year after year." For now, the defeat marked the fifth straight winless (one tie) encounter with Culver in succession.

The 1914 season marked Herendeen's lone foray as a head coach in football. Instead, he began to focus solely on his blossoming composing career. He was particularly adept at creating school "fight" songs, authoring "Chicago's Honor" for the University of Chicago, and "MPMA Loyalty" for the Academy (in 1934). In addition, some of his popular plays for Broadway and elsewhere included "The Elopers," "Girl of Tomorrow," "The Web," "Orchids Preferred," and the film "All the King's Horses." Herendeen's literary output continued throughout his life and he regularly volunteered to assist the Academy with fund-raising, sporting events, and student stage projects. His rich and full life came to an end on June 4, 1962 at the age of 69.

EXTRA POINT

Finally, we share one more shining example of the writing talent of Fred Herendeen. In the following poetic verse, "Leaves from the Tree of

Loyalty," Herendeen likely recalls the 1911 football encounter with Culver, which resulted in a 32-0 Culver victory. In this verse, Herendeen spotlights the perseverance of one Samuel Cotrell, the smallish quarterback for the Academy team and one who personified the fighting spirit of Morgan Park Academy. There are just a couple of minor problems with the text: the actual score was not 36-0 as mentioned, and there was not a player named Sam Cotrell on the Academy football roster in 1911. However, the description of the size of the player, his position, and his talent lead us to believe that the author was actually talking about John Kenfield. Again, we have not changed any of the language in this beautiful tribute. It is printed as written by Fred Herendeen back in 1925.

LEAVES FROM THE TREE OF LOYALTY
By: F. Herendeen '12

Young Samuel Cotrell
This is not a song of winning
    That I'll sing to you tonight,
It is just a tale of grinning,
    Though you're beaten in the fight,
And it's such a tale of trying,
    That it gives me joy to tell,
Of that spirit never dying
    Of young Samuel Cotrell.

Now this Sam was just a shaver
    Weighed one twenty—soaking wet
But I'll say that ne're a braver
    Little rooster have I met
Through his grit and intuition
    He won everyone's esteem
And the quarter back position
    On our first string football team.

Well—that season we were winners
    Till we met the Culver test
We were keyed to fight like sinners
    For the banner of the west
It was by Lake Maxinkuckee
    That our championship hopes fell

But we smiled and cheered the plucky
        Little Samuel Cotrell.

That a game those fellows gave us
        All our rooters knew right then
There was nothing that could save us
        From those charging Culver men
Clean and hard those fellows pounded
        And though tooth and nail we fought
When the third quarter was rounded
        They led thirty-six to naught.

In the fourth our fellows held them
        Something made our line brace
But the signals as Sam yelled them
        Didn't get us any place
Then the Culver line started
        Kidding Sam cause he was small
Said that they were broken hearted
        Cause he didn't buck their wall.

Sam was crouching in position
        But he stood right up and glared
And he made a proposition
        Said, "Say, if you think we're scared
Pay attention to the next one
        Get this signal mark it well"
Then he yelled at the perplexed one
        "Line buck by Sam Cotrell."

Snap the ball came soaring to him
        Plunk! He hit that Culver line
Hit the guard—and went right through him
        Hit the quarter—spilled him fine
Dodged one Half, stiff-armed the other
        Crawled beneath a charging End
Riggled out of all that smother
        Carrying naught for foe or friend.

Down the field just like a rabbit
    With the Culver pack full chase
Sam fought on from force of habit
    Though he staggered in his pace
Just one man was left to stop him
    Twas the Culver safety Full
Though he came at Sam to drop him
    Sam just charged him like a bull.

Now that Full Back weighed two hundred
    Sam one twenty—soaking wet
And both rooting sections thundered
    As those charging players met
Neither dodged and neither faltered
    Came a crash—then came a cheer
For the outlook had been altered
    And young Sam Cotrell was clear.

Well that ends this little story
    There is nothing more to tell
Even Culver cheered the glory
    Of our Samuel Cotrell
Though the score was quite one-sided
    And though Culver won the fray
Everyone felt just as I did
    Victory for M.P.A.

So you see it's not the winning
    But the way you meet defeat
It's the way you keep on grinning
    As you cover your retreat
Scores themselves mean less than zero
    If you've fought your battle well
You'll be just a big a hero
    As young Samuel Cotrell.

In 1909, Coach John Anderson (upper left with "C" on jersey) and his club yielded only eight points while scoring 346 to snare another championship with a 6-1 mark. Some of the greatest names in the history of the Academy football program were affiliated with this team. Bottom row (from left): Radford, Stephenson, Kenfield (holding ball), Couchman, Reynolds. Second row: W. Marr, Lockhart, Hazlett. Third row: Beckwith (dark shirt), R. Marr, Herendeen, Mark Wade, Hubert. Top row: Coach Anderson, Young, Nichols.

Future College Football Hall of Famer Wallace Wade (bottom row, far right) was the starting left tackle for the 1912 Academy team.

CHAPTER 7

The Academy Immortals: Stagg, Harper, Wade, and Benbrook

"Winning isn't worthwhile unless one has something finer and nobler behind it. When I reach the soul of one of my boys with an idea, or ideal, or vision, then I have done my job as a coach."
—*Amos Alonzo Stagg*

How does one define a legend?

Every society deems to have its own "legends" who accomplished extraordinary feats in their lifetimes, or who became even more famous in death. The basis for depicting a legend appears to be those who seem larger than life because of their individual accomplishments in their specific field of endeavor.

For this book, we chose to designate the term "legend" for four individuals affiliated with Morgan Park Academy who are part of a very elite group: the College Football Hall of Fame. Much has been written about these Academy legends elsewhere during the past century or more, but we hope to adequately summarize their admirable careers, beginning with their experiences at the Academy.

The four legends we speak of include Amos Alonzo Stagg, Jesse Harper, Wallace Wade, and Albert Benbrook. Harper and Wade were inducted into the Hall of Fame based on their impressive coaching records on the collegiate level, while Benbrook was honored for his achievements as a player. Meanwhile, Stagg was a charter member of the Hall of Fame as both a player and as a coach. Long-time curator Kent Stephens of the

College Football Hall of Fame noted the impact of little Morgan Park Academy in comparison to other national high schools with representatives in the Hall of Fame:

> To have anyone from your high school in the College Football Hall of Fame is an honor. Morgan Park Academy is at the top of the list by having four people in the Hall of Fame. That is quite an accomplishment!

Stephens indicated that typically the Hall of Fame only tracks the high schools of "players" and two high schools in Ohio do have four players included in the College Football Hall of Fame, while the four Academy honorees include three coaches and a player. Still, the total of four representatives from Morgan Park Academy is certainly a remarkable achievement. The College Football Hall of Fame was founded in 1951 and according to its web site:

> Immortalizes the greatest of the amateur gridiron. 5.1 million people have coached or played the game and less than 1,300 are inductees in the Hall. This makes the College Football Hall of Fame an extremely selective group of individuals. Those (individuals)...have endured the blood, sweat and tears it takes to go from college greats to legendary sportsmen."

To include four members from one high school, such as Morgan Park Academy, is extremely rare and a further testament to the quality of individuals who participated in the Academy football program throughout the years. As such, we'll spotlight the successful football careers for each of these "legendary sportsmen."

ALL FOOTBALL COMES FROM STAGG

Amos Alonzo Stagg has been called many things during and after his lengthy coaching career, among them coach, innovator, mentor, grand old man, and curmudgeon. Born on August 16, 1862 in New Jersey, Stagg played football for five years at Yale University where his teams compiled a 53-2-1 record. Stagg was named to the very first All-American football team in 1889. After a couple of coaching stops at smaller schools, he was hired in 1892 by the fledgling University of Chicago as its Director of Physical

Culture and football coach. At the same time, he started the Chicago football team and even played on the team due to the loose participation rules at the time. Of course, Morgan Park Academy was an intricate part of the University of Chicago in the 1890s and when the football program was initiated at the Academy in 1893 and 1894, Stagg was a coaching presence for both teams. As previously noted, he was listed in the various Academy catalogs as the school's football coach for certain years (1903, 1908, 1909, and 1910) and some of his key players also referred to his physical presence with the Morgan Park team throughout the years.

At Chicago, Stagg was responsible for numerous football innovations, including the team huddle, the quick kick, the line shift, and the favorite for sandlot players of all ages—the Statue of Liberty. In this play the quarterback holds the ball as if about to throw the football, but instead, a teammate grabs the ball from behind and turns the fake pass into a running play. In 1895, he helped form what is now known as the Big Ten Conference. As a major national football power under Stagg, the University of Chicago captured national championships in 1905 and 1913, while also grabbing seven Big Ten titles during his tenure. His influence was so instrumental on a national level, that Notre Dame coach Knute Rockne once said: "All football comes from Stagg." Stagg loved coaching (he was also the school's baseball mentor for 19 seasons) and once told the United Press in 1932:

> Winning isn't worthwhile unless one has something nobler, and finer behind it. When I reach the soul of one of my boys with an idea, an ideal or a vision, then I think I have done my job as a coach.

Stagg's enormous tenure at Chicago lasted until he found himself battling both age and an indifferent administrator in University of Chicago President Robert Maynard Hutchins. In 1932, at the age of 70, Stagg was basically dismissed (effective June 30, 1933) in mid-season by new Athletic Director T. Nelson Metcalf with the support of President Hutchins. His age, not his ability, likely influenced the decision, according to the Associated Press on October 14, 1932:

> The reason given for Stagg's retirement, coming as a surprise to the intercollegiate athletic world and to Stagg himself, was that a rule was invoked which provides that no member of the faculty shall continue to hold a post after reaching the age of 70. Stagg became 70 years of age on August 16.

Behind the scenes, it was felt that Stagg, and football, had become too visible on the campus and both the coach and the team were compromising the intellectual reputation of the University. There was likely some grumbling from the alumni as well since Stagg's last three teams (1930-1932) finished with a combined 7-15-4 mark. Stagg approached this disappointing decision with grudging acceptance, but also refused the opportunity (prior to the dismissal) to accept a non-coaching administrative position with the school. His intention was clearly to coach again as he noted to the wire services:

> According to my present feelings, I expect to be good for 15 to 20 years more of active service. I feel too young and aggressive to step altogether out of my particular work, and, frankly, I am not content to do it. Whether I remain at Chicago or go elsewhere, I wish to be active in the field of coaching.

Determined to continue coaching after concluding his Chicago career with a remarkable 244-111-27 record at Chicago, he secured the head coaching job at the College of the Pacific in Stockton, California. In that position, Stagg added another 14 years to his thick coaching resume (1933-1946). Although his record (60-77-7) was not as lofty as it was in the early years at Chicago, Stagg was able to achieve even more coaching success according to author, and Stagg biographer, Robin Lester in his book **Stagg's University** (page 150):

> His subsequent coaching career at California's College of the Pacific promoted that small, unknown institution to undreamt athletic heights. Pacific adjusted quickly under Stagg to the realities of the competition for players. The local Pacific Alumni Club developed the Pacific Athletic Revolving Loan Fund, which was to "assist deserving athletes." Within six years, Stagg had lodged enough fine players at Pacific to schedule universities such as the University of Southern California and Notre Dame; within ten years, he was elected coach of the year when his team, now augmented by military trainees, became nationally ranked.

Stagg was ultimately forced out at Pacific in 1946 (despite being named national coach of the year in 1943), when Dean of Personnel James

H. Corson offered Stagg a retirement option: "We feel that it would possibly be better for him, the boys and the school if he let someone else take over the active coaching of the team, but that decision has to come from Mr. Stagg," reported *The Petaluma Argus*.

Stagg did acquiesce to the suggestion at Pacific, but then continued coaching in one form or another until 1958. He passed away on March 17, 1965 at the age of 102. Meanwhile, the football program at Chicago fell upon hard times after the demise of Stagg's coaching reign, never achieving a winning record in its final seven seasons following Stagg's departure. The school dropped football following the 1939 season. About the only bright spot from those final years was the selection of halfback Jay Berwanger as the winner of the very first Heisman Trophy (known then as the Downtown Athletic Club Trophy) in 1935. In 1936, Berwanger was the top choice in the very first draft of the National Football League, but he decided not to play pro football.

In death, Stagg continues to be remembered for his positive impact on the early days of collegiate football. Not only was he one of the foremost protectors of the game when President Roosevelt demanded changes in 1905, but he also will be recalled for his non-technical innovations such as the wearing of numbers on game jerseys and the offensive "huddle." Tributes were both heartfelt and numerous when he passed away, such as the one from former Northwestern Coach Lynn Waldorf who stated: "I don't know anyone who contributed more to football and I don't know anyone who enjoyed the absolute respect of his associates more than Mr. Stagg." Amos Alonzo Stagg was elected to the College Football Hall of Fame in 1951 as both a player and as a coach. For more on Stagg's prodigious career, we recommend Lester's comprehensive book **Stagg's University: The Rise, Decline, and Fall of Big-Time Football at Chicago**.

HARPER PLAYED THREE POSITIONS WITH EASE

Stagg coached numerous outstanding players at Chicago, including the legendary quarterback Walter Eckersall. With pro football not an option at the time, many of his players enjoyed successful coaching careers including Fritz Crisler (University of Michigan) and a skinny kid from Morgan Park Academy named Jesse Harper. Born on December 10, 1883, Harper graduated from the Academy in 1902 and followed his brother Floyd to the University of Chicago to play for Stagg. He spent two years at the Academy and was a solid performer on both the football and baseball fields. In the classroom, he struggled a bit, receiving average grades in classes such as German, Trigonometry, English, and Latin.

While Floyd Harper had sparkled on both the football and baseball fields for Coach Stagg, Jesse preferred the diamond, earning a starting spot his freshman year in the spring of 1903. Although he was the respected captain of the baseball team, Harper was on the slight side physically for football and avoided that sport until his senior year in 1905. He joined the team a bit late (on September 15th), but was in action immediately for the Maroons in the opening game against North Division High School the next day. According to the *Chicago Tribune*: "Jesse Harper, baseball captain last spring, joined the squad and will make a try for the backfield. He weighs 155 pounds and is fast." While not much was expected of Harper on the football squad, he saw action quickly, scoring a touchdown in a 15-0 win over Wabash College on September 30, 1905, then impressing everyone a week later in the 42-0 romp over Iowa as reported by *The Inter Ocean*:

> The feature of the game was the work of Jesse Harper, captain of the 1905 baseball team. Harper had never done much work at football until this year, but as soon as he donned a suit his work caught the eye of Coach Stagg, and the coach took special pains to teach the baseball man the rudiments of the Staggian system, with the result that yesterday Harper played three different positions with the ease and skill of a veteran. Harper started the game at left half, and from this position he gained consistently, making three touchdowns before he was shifted to end...

Harper also played some quarterback in that contest, spelling All-American Walter Eckersall late in the game. Although Harper was never considered a "star" on the football field, his leadership and determination were recognized by both Stagg and his teammates, who named Harper the captain of the "second eleven." In just a short period of time, the tenacious Harper had become an invaluable asset to the Chicago football team which finished the season with a lofty 11-0 mark. The Maroons outscored their opponents 271-5 and were recognized as the national champions.

DISPOSING OF 300 DOZEN HOT DOGS

Always resourceful, Harper apparently initiated a football-related business during the 1905 season while at the University of Chicago, as told by the *Chicago Tribune* in 1913:

> During his college course Harper took part in university and student activities, joined the Phi Delta Theta fraternity, and paid part of his expenses by his own efforts. One of his side lines was the refreshment privilege at the then Marshall Field. While Harper sat in gridiron togs on the side lines in the Michigan game of 1905, awaiting a possible call for emergency duty, his partner in the enterprise was disposing of 300 dozen, if you please "hot dog" sandwiches to appreciative customers at ten cents a throw or "two for a quarter," if they were in a hurry. As the cost of the sandwiches was one and one-fourth cents each, the profits [for Harper] can be estimated.

Following another stellar baseball campaign and graduation in 1906, Stagg helped Harper land the head football coaching position at Alma College in Alma, Michigan beginning in the fall of 1906. His responsibilities also included coaching the basketball, baseball, and track teams, as well as serving as athletic director. Yet, he maintained strong ties with Stagg, returning to Chicago to assist with pre-season training while still at Alma. In an interview for this book, Frank Maggio, author of **Notre Dame and the Game That Changed Football: How Jesse Harper Made the Forward Pass a Weapon and Knute Rockne a Legend**, commented on the influence of Stagg in the football universe of Harper:

> While at the University of Chicago, Jesse played for Amos Alonzo Stagg, one of the most important men in the early history of football. Stagg was not only an outstanding football coach but in Jesse's words was a "great character builder."

Harper remained at Alma for two years, compiling an 8-3-4 record on the football field and capturing the collegiate state title in baseball. His decision to continue at Alma in 1907 was greeted with great enthusiasm, both for his coaching success as well as for his insistence on molding his players into exceptional citizens, according to *The New North* newspaper

(June 27, 1907). "Harper is a believer in clean athletics. No unfair play has been allowed this year on any of the teams. A man must be a gentleman in athletic work, as well as in class work, he believes."

Following the conclusion of the 1907-08 school year, Harper returned home to assist his father with the family farming business in Iowa. During the 1908 season, Harper was out of coaching, but emerged as a highly touted referee of major college football games, serving as the field judge for the important Nebraska-Kansas game in late November. Harper, however, was anxious to return to the coaching fold and asked Stagg for his help in securing another position. Stagg agreed and wrote a favorable recommendation to the leadership at Wabash College in Indiana (from **Notre Dame and the Game That Changed Football**, page 74):

> Mr. Harper left his position at Alma in order to go into business with his father, but he writes me that he is planning to get back into coaching…He made a great success at Alma…He is a fine man personally clean and upright and will be thoroughly respected and liked wherever he goes…I consider that you will be fortunate if you secure him.

With the help of Stagg's letter, Harper was hired by Wabash in May of 1909 where he quickly encountered a much more difficult schedule than he had experienced at Alma. Harper finished 15-9-2 in four years at Wabash with opponents that included Purdue, St. Louis, Notre Dame, Butler, and Michigan Agricultural, now known as Michigan State.

NOTRE DAME WAS CONSIDERING TERMINATING ITS FOOTBALL PROGRAM

It was then (1912) that the University of Notre Dame became interested in Harper. Although he consented to conclude his Wabash coaching contract obligations for the spring of 1913, Harper agreed to terms with Notre Dame in December of 1912. His responsibilities would include becoming the school's first athletic director, as well as the head coach for football, basketball, track, and baseball. At that time, Notre Dame was certainly not considered a football powerhouse, and the University was even considering the possibility that football might be dropped, according to Maggio: "Before Jesse signed on at Notre Dame, the University was considering terminating its football program. They were losing money and they had difficulty finding opponents in their Midwest venue."

While still working at Wabash, Harper nonetheless began to immerse himself in the Notre Dame football culture and moved to upgrade the schedule as soon as possible. Overall, Harper looked to emphasize academic performance for his athletes, while developing a strong schedule with reputable schools that would generate interest in the football team while also providing much needed revenue via attendance. He initiated communications with several prominent schools in the hopes of attracting some of these prospective opponents to engage the small institution in South Bend, Indiana. Almost immediately, Harper landed a marquee name with the scheduling of the United States Military Academy (Army) at West Point, New York (including a substantial travel expense fee for Notre Dame) for November 1, 1913. Other recognizable schools were quickly added to the Notre Dame schedule according to Maggio:

> In his first year, Notre Dame traveled east to play Penn State and Army and into the southwest to play Texas. No college team had ever attempted such a travel schedule. Traveling the country became a hallmark of the Notre Dame program and Jesse was the originator.

The impact of Harper on the Notre Dame squad was dramatic. In that first season of 1913, Harper finished with a remarkable 7-0 mark, despite the rigorous railway travel schedule. Army fell 35-13, Penn State was defeated 14-7, and Texas was stunned 30-7. However, it was the Army game that elevated Harper's reputation and helped push Notre Dame to the upper fringes of collegiate gridiron recognition. Harper was grateful that Army would even schedule his club, being that Army was noted as a formidable football program on the national level, while Notre Dame was barely known outside of the Midwest. The loss to Notre Dame would be the only defeat in an 8-1 Army season.

While the scheduling of the Army game was a breakthrough for Notre Dame, it was what ensued on the field that day that remains historically significant. In the days when the forward pass was not considered a reliable weapon, Notre Dame quarterback Gus Dorais completed 13-17 tosses for an unheard of 243 yards during the rout of Army. His primary target was receiver Knute Rockne, who would soon pilot the Notre Dame program himself. Neither Maggio nor Notre Dame ever claimed that the team "invented" the forward pass or was even the first to successfully utilize the pass in collegiate competition. Yet one cannot deny that Harper was one of the first to use it as a positive alternative to the tried-and-true running game employed by just about every football team of the time in America.

HARPER FLASHED ACROSS THE ATHLETIC HORIZON

Harper eventually retired from Notre Dame after just five seasons, compiling a superlative 34-5-1 record. He opted to return to his first love of ranching and "Jesse left Notre Dame in 1918 to join his father-in-law in the cattle ranching business in southwestern Kansas," said Maggio. Harper was praised by the Notre Dame student newspaper (*The Notre Dame Scholastic*) on December 1, 1917 following the season when he finished 6-1-1 despite losing numerous players to the service:

> Harper has ever been progressive since coming to Notre Dame. He innovated the three-year eligibility rule, has advocated and co-operated with the faculty in obtaining high grade of scholarship, has shown himself relentless in enforcing all rules of amateurism. He has countenanced nothing but the highest grade of sportsmanship.

> Harper was a great man in 1913 when he flashed across the athletic horizon with an unbeatable team of veterans; he was a far greater man during 1917 when he molded a team from the greenest of material and battered his way through the heaviest schedule in the history of Notre Dame with just one defeat.

Upon Harper's recommendation, Notre Dame hired his key assistant, Knute Rockne, to continue the exemplary work established by Harper. Rockne and Notre Dame dominated college football during Rockne's tenure from 1918-1930. Prior to his untimely death in a plane crash on March 31, 1931 in Kansas, Rockne built a marvelous 105-12-5 record at Notre Dame. Following Rockne's passing, Harper returned to Notre Dame to serve as the Director of Athletics for two more years. After that brief stint, Harper returned to his 20,000-acre cattle ranch in the Cimarron River Valley in Kansas. Years later, he was asked by a reporter about ranch life and if there were any regrets from leaving football prominence at such a young age, to which Harper replied: "No, I've been happy. I've crossed Hereford cattle with oil wells, and you can't beat that!" Maggio, who worked closely with Harper's son James in the preparation of his book, stated that Harper's accomplishments were numerous:

> Jesse is the only coach in Notre Dame's history to have gone undefeated in his first season. He mentored Knute Rockne as a player and then hired Rockne as an assistant coach after Rockne's graduation. And, most importantly, Jesse lobbied Notre Dame and insisted that the university hire Rockne as his successor. Also, and very importantly, during his tenure at Notre Dame, Jesse emphasized academics and good character, traits Notre Dame has continued to emphasize to this day.

While Harper will be remembered for many positive accomplishments, Maggio pointed to the 1913 Army game that cemented Harper's recognition as a football legend:

> In the year 2000, ESPN compiled a series of lists of the best and the worst sporting events of the Twentieth Century. Jesse Harper's decision to pass against Army, resulting in Notre Dame's stunning defeat of Army in 1913, was ranked as the best coaching decision in football in the twentieth century, college or professional.

Maggio added one more remembrance of Harper from the 50th reunion celebration of Stagg's 1905 national champions from the University of Chicago. It was perhaps one of the final meetings between Stagg and Harper but demonstrated the continued influence of the old coach over his former (and aging) players:

> I cannot resist a story on "character" building. Stagg forbade his players to smoke, drink or use profanity. Can you imagine? Jesse carried that discipline on to Notre Dame. All lost long ago. But the point I want to get to is the story about Jesse's 50th reunion at the University of Chicago. Jesse, then in his seventies, was standing with his classmates having a drink . . . alcohol of course. Someone said here comes coach [Stagg] and they all immediately put down their drinks!

Harper passed away on July 31, 1961 at his ranch in Kansas at the age of 77. He was elected to the College Football Hall of Fame in 1971.

DON'T WANT ANYONE TO GET HOT AND SWEATY!

Like Jesse Harper, William "Wallace" Wade benefitted greatly from the coaching influence of Stagg. As noted in the previous chapter, Wade enjoyed a stellar playing career as a tackle at Morgan Park Academy and later as a guard at Brown University, including a trip to the Rose Bowl. Following graduation in 1917, Wade entered the military, serving from 1917-1919 in the army. His first coaching position followed when he was hired to lead the football team at Fitzgerald and Clarke High School in Tennessee. In his three seasons at Fitzgerald and Clarke, Wade lost just three games, and capped off his brief high school coaching career by capturing the Tennessee state championship in 1920. Leading up to that final game, Fitzgerald and Clarke knocked off Bryson College 21-13, with *The Tennessean* (November 21, 1920) lauding the leadership of Wade: "The strategy and skillful coaching of Coach Wade was a deciding factor, as was evident to all observers."

Based on this successful three-year stint on the high school level, Wade attracted the attention of head coach Dan McGugin at Vanderbilt University. In fact, McGugin was so anxious to add Wade to his staff that he offered to reduce his own salary. The athletic board at Vanderbilt politely refused the offer but added the popular Wade as the assistant football coach, as well as the head coach of both the basketball and baseball teams. It was hoped that Wade could help reverse the misery of a 4-3-1 grid campaign from 1920. Wade signed on before the 1921 season and in his two years with the Commodores, the team was undefeated with a 15-0-2 record. Wade quickly drew notice as a tough, relentless coach early in the 1921 Vanderbilt training camp as described in *The Tennessean* on September 16:

> Nothing is paramount to the feverish activity of the Commodores under the lash of the former Brown guard's scorching pace. Some of the more leisurely inclined Vandy candidates are still inclined to look askance at the steady application of whip and spur which Coach Wade insists be put into the work.
>
> The sarcasm of Wallace Wade is no soothing balm for folks who wear feelings on their coat sleeves. Yesterday a huge forward candidate was trailing the line at each charge by

about seven furlongs. He lacked the necessary enthusiasm. "Hey" yelled Wallace Wade. "What's the matter? Are you tired? If you are, go over and sit down. I don't want anybody to get hot and sweaty!"

Wade's success—and intensity—soon brought a head coaching offer from the University of Alabama in December of 1922. Wade agreed to a two-year pact with Alabama, starting at $6,000 per year, after also being pursued by Kentucky, Sewanee, and Texas. His meteoric coaching career was summarized by *The Tennessean* (December 17, 1922) when the somewhat clandestine signing was announced:

> In two years, Wallace has gone from a prep school tutor to the head of one of the largest institutions in Dixie, and at a salary which makes him one of the highest paid coaches in the south. Coach Wade expressed his sorrow at leaving Vanderbilt, where he has made a wide circle of friends… but felt that the opportunities offered at Alabama were too bright to be sacrificed. "At my age if a man ever expects to amount to anything as coach," stated Wade, "he must pull up and leave whenever such an opportunity presents itself. I hate to go. I have many friends at Vanderbilt and many in Nashville and I am very grateful to them for the encouragement they have given me."

Although Alabama had finished 6-3-1 in 1922 under coach Xen C. Scott, Wade was hired to coach the Crimson Tide when Scott's health deteriorated due to a cancer condition. In his first season (1923) Wade finished 7-2-1, and then improved to 8-1 in 1924 with a perfect 5-0 mark in the Southern Conference. This formidable start set the table for an undefeated 10-0 slate in 1925, including an impressive 20-19 win over Washington in the Rose Bowl. Alabama snared the national championship after being the first representative from the south to be invited to the Rose Bowl. With a rousing 25-3-1 record in the three seasons to inaugurate his career with the Crimson Tide, Wade was showered with accolades for his auspicious success. None other than the revered sports' scribe Grantland Rice acknowledged Wade in his national column on December 1, 1926 as Alabama prepared to grab its second straight national championship with a 9-0-1 record:

Wallace Wade, now coaching Alabama, was a guard at Brown nine or ten years ago. If anyone has a greater record for success in his eight or nine years the answer hasn't been printed yet. At Castle Heights [prep], Vanderbilt and Alabama, he has lost something like three out of seventy games and the list of defeats may be two in place of three… he has an average that will challenge even Knute Rockne's remarkable contribution to winning figures.

As Wade became more prominent as a collegiate football coach, his affiliation with Morgan Park Academy was often mentioned in articles such as the following excerpt from *The Monroe News-Star* on December 16, 1926:

Wallace Wade came from a football family. He attended Fitzgerald-Clarke prep in Tennessee and Morgan Park in Chicago. Then, following an older brother, he entered Brown University. Here he was an All-American tackle, playing three years on the team. "What the man says is alright with me," is the way members of Alabama's football team often speak of Coach Wallace Wade.

Overall, Wade led Alabama for eight seasons, compiling a 61-13-3 mark before resigning unexpectedly prior to the 1930 campaign. Wade agreed to coach the Crimson Tide for one more season but apparently was stung by local pundits who expected and demanded perfect records every season. Following a 6-3 record in 1929, Wade decided that the criticism was not worth the effort and that it was time to venture elsewhere. His decision to abandon Alabama for Duke University hit the newspapers on April 1, 1930 via the Associated Press:

Wallace Wade announced today he has resigned as head football coach at the University of Alabama and has signed a five-year contract with Duke University beginning in September 1931. Coach Wade gave no reason for leaving Alabama…Dr. George Denny, President of the university, commenting on the coach's resignation, said "Duke University is fortunate to obtain a coach of Wade's ability. It is with deep regret that I learn that Wade is going to leave us after 1930. He has made Alabama not only a great coach, but is a great leader of young men.

But first, the matter of the 1930 schedule needed to be addressed. As Wade fashioned perhaps his finest season (10-0 with a third national championship), more information regarding Wade's decision was flushed out by journalists, such as Ed Sullivan (the future television host) in the *Altoona Tribune* on December 8, 1930:

> Down in the Southland, an ironic situation exists at the University of Alabama, for the alumni of that school fell upon Head Coach Wallace Wade in a lean season, hounded him to the point where Wade signed a new contract with Duke University, and now the alumni are face to face with a pretty mess.
>
> Wade was hounded by the alumni on one occasion, this year turned out one of his greatest clubs, but like Humpty-Dumpty, the alumni find that no amount of cajoling or entreaty can put Wallace Wade together again. Wade, a silent fellow, uttered no pleas for mercy. Thoroughly burned up at the ingrates of Alabama, Wade announced that he would quit the school at the end of the 1930 season, when his contract expired. His last Alabama team is easily one of his best. Unbeaten in a hard-Southern schedule, it has been selected to face Washington State at Pasadena [Rose Bowl]. Alabama alumni are yelling for help. They are telling Wade now that they always believed in him to be a prince. The Brown University product has the last laugh, and I trust that Wade is indulging in the luxury of a snicker.

WADE ELEVATED DUKE FROM OBSCURITY TO NATIONAL PRESTIGE

The season-ending trouncing (24-0) of undefeated Washington State in the Rose Bowl finalized Wade's career at Alabama with that third national title. While the decision to take over the coaching reins at Duke might have been questionable from afar, Wade was an independent thinker and embraced a challenge. Certainly Duke (at the time) was not considered a national powerhouse like Alabama, but Wallace was ready to push his new team into the collegiate football limelight. He was also rewarded with a handsome salary (reportedly around $12,000 annually plus a share of the gate receipts at Duke home games). While Wallace was aware of the importance of a strong, winning football team at a major university, he also downplayed that perception in one of his early appearances on behalf of Duke. In a speech before the American College Publicity Association in April of 1931, Wade said: "It seems to me that the experience of institutions all over the country shows the way to increase student enrollment and endowment is to raise academic standards, improve equipment and secure better teachers." He added that football "should be emphasized only for the development and training it gives young men."

Wade immediately instituted his system at Duke and from 1931 through the 1941 season, built an 85-19-1 record before the interruption of World War II. Wade's squads appeared in two more Rose Bowl games and finished as high as #2 in the national rankings after a 9-1 mark in the 1941 season. In an interview for this book, Sarah Fetters, Associate Sports Information Director for Duke Athletics noted: "Wade elevated the Duke football program from obscurity to national prestige. Wade's 1938 Blue Devil team went undefeated, untied and unscored upon during the regular season before dropping a last second loss to Southern Cal in the Rose Bowl, 7-3."

Ms. Fetters added that "Current [Duke] head football coach David Cutliffe said this to *AL.com* in 2010 about Wallace Wade: 'He was the reason Duke developed into a national power. There was no accident that it coincided with him coming to Duke. The pursuit of excellence is kind of what I call it. You sense it in all the people I talk to about Wallace Wade.'" Wade's reputation was so strong that he was featured on the cover of *Time Magazine* on October 25, 1937 as *Time* reported on the emergence of football in the south under the title of "Southward the Course of Football Takes Its Way." In the coverage of the improving southern collegiate football landscape, *Time* provided an insightful look at Wade's coaching techniques:

> Drilling his men in every play down to the slightest movement of hand or foot, using a metronome to insure proper timing, sometimes rehearsing a play for two months before using it, crouching on the ground with any player to demonstrate exactly what he wants, Coach Wade is today esteemed by his colleagues as one of the most patient of football teachers. Above all things teacher Wade values economy of motion: "The best player is the one who does just what is necessary."

Duke's second trip to the Rose Bowl following the 1941 season was an unusual one. Due to the very recent outbreak of hostilities in WWII and fears of enemy attacks on California, the Rose Bowl game between Duke and Oregon State was moved to Durham, North Carolina. Duke was upset 20-16 in Wade's last game as a Duke coach until after the war concluded. Despite being nearly 50 years of age, Wade was commissioned as a major in March of 1942 and served as a field artillery officer during the war. Initially, he was assigned to coach a group of Army All-Stars in a five game exhibition series against various NFL teams. Wade was disappointed in this assignment since he preferred to do his part on actual battlefields. Later in the war, he received that opportunity and his contribution to the war effort was exceptional as noted in the book **Fields of Battle** (page 238):

> Wallace Wade Sr., at the age of fifty-two, fought in the European campaign without a day's leave, in constant range of enemy fire for nine months. He fought in the Battles of Normandy and on the Siegfried Line, in the Battle of the Bulge and the crossing of the Rhine. For his actions, Wade was awarded a Bronze Star and a *Croix de Guerre* with Palm from France.

Returning to Duke after the war, Wade elected not to coach in 1945, but was back on the sidelines a year later. He remained as coach of the Blue Devils through the 1950 season, finishing his two coaching tours at Duke with a combined 110-36-7 record. Overall, at both Alabama and Duke, Wade secured a sparkling mark of 171 wins against just 49 losses and ten ties. In retirement, Wade took on the role of commissioner for the Southern Conference from 1951-1960. However, his biggest honor followed in 1967 when the Duke football facility was renamed as the Wallace Wade Stadium.

Looking back on Coach Wade's long and successful career, author Lewis Bowling reflected on the early football influences on Wade. As with Jesse Harper, Amos Alonzo Stagg was a significant part of that early impression on Wade when he was a student at Morgan Park Academy:

> I think Wallace Wade benefitted from Coach Stagg by absorbing some of the knowledge Coach Stagg had, saw how he related to players and saw the presence of the man. I believe Morgan Park was coached by a former player of Stagg's, John Anderson, when Coach Wade arrived [in 1912]. Wade was following his brother, Mark, who had played at Morgan Park when Stagg was head coach at the University of Chicago and Morgan Park. But, of course, Coach Stagg was present around the Morgan Park team

quite a lot, as I understand it, and Coach Wade would have probably felt like Stagg was his head coach. I think Coach Wade's coaching mentors were W.A. Bridges when he played at Fitzgerald and Clarke in Tennessee, Coach Stagg, Edward Robinson at Brown, and Dan McGugin at Vanderbilt.

Overall, Bowling considers Coach Wade as one of the greatest collegiate football coaches of all-time. Indeed, his 171 victories still place him among the historical leaders, despite a career that ended almost 70 years ago and with fewer games played each season than under modern coaches. Bowling stated:

> I include Coach Wade among the very best college football coaches ever. He was a defensive genius, often employing an innovative 6-2-2-1 alignment, and the amount of shutouts his teams accumulated at Alabama and Duke testify to his defensive genius. Simply stated, he put Alabama football on the national map, he set the table for the great tradition that is Alabama football. He built Duke into a national powerhouse in football, taking them to two Rose Bowls. He was an innovator in football shoes, had one of the first coaches radio shows. His motivational skills were immense, as his players would literally "run through a brick wall" for him.

Wallace Wade passed away on October 7, 1986 at the age of 94. He was named to the College Football Hall of Fame in 1955.

FIRST WESTERN LINEMAN TO BECOME A TWO-TIME ALL-AMERICAN

If one looks hard enough for a really unique set of playing cards, you might discover the "Hero Decks" of the University of Michigan Wolverines. There are many names familiar to football fans in the package, including Tom Brady, Tom Harmon, and Jim Harbaugh. But one of the individuals included in this deck of "heroes" is from Morgan Park Academy. His name is Albert "Benny" Benbrook and he was the fourth representative from the Academy to be inducted into the College Football Hall of Fame.

Benbrook was a fearsome player and with just his sheer size at the time (240 lbs.), he was intimidating to opposing collegiate linemen. Add to that some elusive speed and lateral quickness and you have the makings of an All-American—which Benbrook became at the University of Michigan. Twice!

Prior to receiving national recognition at Michigan, Benbrook was an immediate sensation on the gridiron at Morgan Park Academy. Born on August 24, 1887, Benbrook transferred to the Academy on September 20, 1904 as a junior from Armour Academy in Chicago. He excelled as a student, particularly in classes such as algebra, mechanical drawing, and physics. All of this coursework no doubt prepared him for his engineering studies at the University of Michigan. During his two years at the Academy, the football team enjoyed fabulous seasons, finishing 6-0-2 (1904) and 7-2-1 (1905). Benbrook was also a standout on both the basketball and track teams, where he was superb on the latter squad with his performance with the weights.

For some reason, Benbrook delayed his entrance at the University of Michigan until September of 1907. Meanwhile, he apparently worked for a year and found an athletic home with the First Regiment Athletic Association on the south side of Chicago. During an indoor track meet on February 1, 1907 against the Evanston (Illinois) YMCA, Benbrook shattered the gym record in the shot put as reported by the *Chicago Tribune*:

> Benbrook raised the gymnasium record for the twelve-pound heave from 41 feet six inches to 48 feet seven inches. On the best of his three regular trials the big man dropped the leaden weight 46 feet six inches away from the circle and in an additional try granted for an attack on this new record, he succeeded in adding two feet and the odd inch to his newfound score.

In September of 1907, Benbrook finally arrived in Ann Arbor, Michigan for his freshman year which was noted by *The Inter Ocean*: "Benbrook, a big freshman from Chicago, has entered the university. Weighs 215 pounds and is said to be a star guard." Benbrook was a mainstay on the varsity line at Michigan by his sophomore season in 1908. He started the first three games of the season at right tackle, but after a 12-6 win over Notre Dame, he moved permanently to left guard on a club that finished 5-2-1. The Wolverines improved to 6-1 in 1909 as Benbrook was selected to football expert Walter Camp's annual All-American first team. It was an unusual honor for a team from the "west" since most All-American teams were stacked with representatives of the eastern powers such as Harvard, Princeton, and Yale. In fact, his biography at the College Football Hall of Fame notes: "A testament to the ability of Albert Benbrook was that he was the first western lineman to become a two-time All-American. Weighing over 200 pounds, he was considered huge for his time. What made Benbrook such a dominating force was his exceptional quickness."

Benbrook apparently developed a bit of an edge while dominating opposing linemen for the Wolverines and decided to channel his aggressive nature to another athletic outlet. In February of 1910 (after Benbrook's All-American junior year), he declared that he would become a professional heavyweight boxer. At the time, the intimidating Jack Johnson was in the midst of a seven-year run as heavyweight champion of the world. In what was termed the "fight of the century," undefeated former champion James Jeffries agreed to emerge from retirement to challenge Johnson. The fight was scheduled for July 4, 1910, but in February, Benbrook (although a totally inexperienced contender) announced that he would soon enter the sweet science of boxing and his intentions garnered national attention such as in the *Morning Register* in Eugene, Oregon:

> A new champion in the embryo state is scanning the pugilistic horizon. He is Albert Benbrook, captain of the University of Michigan football team this year. Al is a powerful chap and aspires to become heavyweight champion of the world. He declares that he will witness the Jeffries-Johnson fight from the ringside. "And if Johnson wins," says he, "I shall go into training at once and challenge him next winter." Benbrook has been examined by Floyd Fitzsimmons, the Benton harbor boxing promoter, who declares him all to the good. A newcomer, no matter how fast and strong, will have mighty hard picking landing a challenge. The old ring admonition is always forthcoming: "Aw, go get a reputation."

DIDN'T I TELL YOU TO GRAB BENBROOK'S LEGS?

Although Johnson successfully defended his title against Jeffries, the challenge from Benbrook was never forthcoming. Instead, he prepared himself for his final year at Michigan and once again proved to be an intricate part of the Wolverine football machine. The 1910 team was undefeated, but that mark was tarnished by three ties, leaving Michigan with a 3-0-3 record for the season. Benbrook went both ways and anchored a fabulous defense that allowed a mere nine points all season (and not a single touchdown). However, the Michigan offense could muster only 29 points itself. Still, it was enough for the Wolverines to be declared the "Western Champions" and Benbrook was named to several All-American teams for the second straight year. Walter Camp noted: "Benbrook is a born player. Last year he showed great strength and dash, and an ability to follow the ball; this year he has improved in every line and there is no match for him on the gridiron."

A few years later (on March 17, 1918), in his column in the *Chicago Tribune*, the respected sportswriter Walter Eckersall reminisced about the impact that Benbrook displayed during his career:

> During 1909, I [Eckersall] was elected to officiate in the Pennsylvania-Michigan game at Philadelphia. The first half was evenly fought with little to choose between the teams. The [Penn] players could not understand why ground could not be made through the Michigan line. I went to the Penn quarters to call the team out for the second half in time to hear [trainer] Mike Murphy say: "Didn't I tell you linemen to grab Benbrook's legs and hold them? He is playing the Michigan line alone." I returned on the train with the Michigan team and naturally the game was played over many times before Ann Arbor was reached. During the journey, I sat down beside Benbrook and asked:
>
> "How many times did they grab your legs when they had the ball?"
>
> "Every time," was his reply.
>
> "How did you shake them off?" I asked.
>
> "I simply used the knee of my free leg on their faces and went about my business." Benny answered: "And on one occasion I stepped on their hands before they got a chance to hang on."

Eckersall also marveled at Benbrook's ability to not only hold off the defense on running plays, but that he was quick enough to blast his opponent off his feet and then lead the runner downfield while picking off members of the defensive secondary. "Benbrook [is] the best guard in history," concluded Eckersall. Following the conclusion of his playing time at Michigan (pro football was not a viable option at the time), Benbrook made the transition to become a football referee, both on the high school and collegiate level, including as an official in what is now known as the Big Ten conference. During the day, he worked in sales for the family business--Monroe, Benbrook & Company in Chicago, an office furniture supplier.

BROKE A MAN IN TWO PARTS WHEN HE HIT HIM

Benbrook surfaced again in 1918 when he enlisted during World War I. He was joined by several other former All-American players who were inducted during a ceremony in Chicago. National newspapers picked up this unusual wire service story and focused on Benbrook:

> Al Benbrook, the old Michigan football star and regarded by many as the greatest guard ever developed in America, is soon to buck the Hun's [Germany] line in the greatest game of all. Benbrook in his prime was certainly the greatest guard Michigan ever developed and has been mentioned by many football experts as a linesman whose superior the game has never seen. The same spirit and strength that made him a world-beater in football will make him a hero in bucking the line of the enemy over there.

Benbrook survived the war and returned to the family business, eventually taking over the reins as president. In 1921, the *Chicago Tribune* profiled Benbrook in his post-playing days:

> Catching Albert Benbrook when there is not a smile on his face is quite a feat of photography. This giant athlete, who was one of the greatest football players ever developed in the west, is almost never without his smile, and is geniality personified. But in his collegiate days he was not noted for affability. Benbrook captained the University of Michigan team in 1910 and was the sort of a tackler who broke a man in two parts when he hit him.

In 1969, the Football Writers Association celebrated the first 100 years of football by naming Benbrook to the first team of the all-time greatest collegiate football honor squad for 1869-1918. Unfortunately, Benbrook was unable to experience that wonderful honor having passed away from a heart attack on August 15, 1943. At the time, he was a sales representative for the American Seating Company. Benbrook was just 55 at the time of his death.

Albert Benbrook was elected to the College Football Hall of Fame in 1971.

EXTRA POINT

In a final tribute to the College Hall of Famers from Morgan Park Academy, the following is a brief summary of each of their accomplishments as well as a final quote either from or about each of the Academy legends:

Amos Alonzo Stagg (1862-1965)

Listed as football coach at the Academy for four years while also guiding the University of Chicago for forty years and capturing two national championships, Stagg continued coaching into his 90s and finished with a 314-199-35 record.

"I once asked Knute Rockne where he got his football and the then almost magic Notre Dame system. 'I got it from Jesse Harper,' replied the immortal Rock. 'Harper got it from Stagg.'" –Harry Grayson, Newspaper Enterprise Association (NEA) Sports Editor

Jesse Harper (1883-1961)

A 1902 graduate of the Academy, Harper was an elusive halfback and solid baseball player during his time at Morgan Park. He is best known for his 34-5-1 record as head football coach at Notre Dame, where he fully promoted the use of the forward pass and pushed Notre Dame into national prominence.

"Football is to build men and to build good sportsmanship. You do not have any easy games. Every team that plays you is up. Every team that beats Notre Dame has a successful season."—Jesse Harper

Wallace Wade (1892-1986)

Wallace graduated from the Academy in 1913 after playing football and baseball during his senior season. He entered the coaching ranks and grabbed three national championships at Alabama and enjoyed additional success at Duke where the football stadium is named after him. Wade concluded his coaching career with an overall record of 171-49-10.

"Sure, academics eliminate some players, but football requires character and background. A chap with good grades has better potential to be a football player, as he has proven he is willing to work." –Wallace Wade

Albert Benbrook (1887-1943)

Benbrook was an all-around athlete at the Academy, starting in football, basketball, and track; became two-time All-American guard at the University of Michigan. Considered the best at the guard position of all time.

"I have seen nearly every guard of note play, but I never have seen the equal of Benbrook, every angle of play considered. Plays were sent anywhere at the line except toward Benbrook's position." –Walter Eckersall

Wallace Wade won three national championships as the head coach at Alabama, and then led Duke University to national prominence as well. He was a 1913 graduate of Morgan Park Academy and elected to the College Football Hall of Fame in 1955. (Photo courtesy of Duke University)

Albert Benbrook graduated from Morgan Park Academy in 1906 and later became a two-time All-American lineman for the University of Michigan. He was elected to the College Football Hall of Fame in 1971. (Photo courtesy of Bentley Historical Library, University of Michigan)

Jesse Harper (shown in 1931) graduated from Morgan Park Academy in 1902 and eventually became the head football coach at the University of Notre Dame. He compiled a 34-5-1 record at Notre Dame before turning over the reins to his assistant, Knute Rockne. He was voted into the College Football Hall of Fame in 1971. (Photo from the collection of the author)

Amos Alonzo Stagg was instrumental in starting the football program at Morgan Park Academy when the school was part of the University of Chicago. As the football coach at Chicago from 1892-1932, Stagg grabbed two national championships and compiled a sparkling 244-111-27 record. He was a member of the very first class of the College Football Hall of Fame in 1951, both as a player and as a coach. (Photo from the collection of the author)

CHAPTER 8

The Senator, the Flu, and the War

"Morgan Park has a well-known reputation as a first-class team and those who fail to see this game will miss an exciting time."
—The LaGrange (IL) Citizen, 1915

Dave Stewart was at a loss for words.

Almost…

"As yet, I really have not had time to realize that it is true," said Mr. Stewart. "Next to the surprise of the whole matter, the most pleasing thing about it is that the nomination came to me without any promise or trade and with no obligations except my duty to the citizens of Iowa and the nation." (Iowa City Press-Citizen, August 7, 1926)

Less than a decade removed from his position as head football coach at Morgan Park Academy, Stewart found himself at the pinnacle of political success on August 7, 1926 when he was appointed to fill the unexpired term of United States Senator Albert Cummins of Iowa, who had passed away suddenly on July 30, 1926.

So how did Senator Stewart move from celebrating a 1916 football victory over Lane Tech High School in Chicago to becoming part of probably the most exclusive club in America in just ten years? "I have always worked hard for what I got. This [the Senate appointment] was the easiest thing that was ever handed to me. I cannot say how much I appreciate the honor," Stewart told the *Greene* (Iowa) *Recorder* on August 11, 1926 following his selection.

Stewart was an energetic, ambitious individual who utilized his insight and intelligence to move ahead in all aspects of his life no matter what the circumstances. Stewart was born in New Concord, Ohio on January 2, 1887 and graduated from Geneva College (Beaver Falls, Pennsylvania) in 1911. He was a fullback on the 1910 Geneva football team that finished 2-5-2. After graduation, he taught and coached at high schools in Cherokee and Sioux City, Iowa (where he mentored a championship football team) until moving to Chicago in 1915 to pursue his law degree at the University of Chicago. In the fall of 1915, he joined the Academy staff with the simple title of "Athletic Coach." It was likely a part-time position for Stewart while he continued his law studies at Chicago. During the early years of his educational and employment activities, Stewart typically worked outside (or second) jobs to help defray his expenses, so his adding the coaching responsibilities while attending school full-time was not a surprise to those who knew Stewart.

GOOD SINGING IS ALWAYS PROVIDED

In 1915 Stewart may have noticed that the Academy was still struggling following its administrative reorganization of the previous year. Although not literally called a military school, the newly re-named Morgan Park Preparatory School did embrace that environment and its annual catalog promoted the strong suggestion that religion should be a major part of each student's experience:

> On every other Sunday, the Academy holds its own church service in the chapel. Leading ministers of Chicago, from all denominations, and laymen, who are interested in boys, address the school upon subjects of vital interest and importance. Good singing is always provided.

> On the Sundays when the Academy does not have its own church service, the battalion is divided into groups, each boy attending the church of his parents' choice. A boy may arrange to attend his own church in the village each Sunday. Each boy should bring a bible.

The military aspect of the campus was overseen by Lt. Col. Thomas Winfield Winston, an 1890 graduate of the U.S. Military Academy. An advertisement in 1915 promoted the school and promised "old fashioned scholastic standards" and "discipline." And what parent could ignore this statement? "True American citizenship requires this balanced training—you owe it to your boy."

As for his first football team, Stewart welcomed just 13 players and managed to schedule only five games during the 1915 season. The squad showed some promise with an opening 18-3 win over Parker High School of Chicago. This set up an early season showdown with distant LaGrange (Illinois) High School in what is now the western suburbs of Chicago. The *LaGrange Citizen* was lavish in its praise of the invading Morgan Park eleven:

> The big fighting team from the Morgan Park Academy will play LaGrange Saturday, October 9 on Emerald Field. The LaGrange boys will be pushed to the limit and have to fight like tigers. Morgan Park has a well-known reputation as a first-class team and those who fail to see this game will miss an exciting time. LaGrange will not only need the support of her student body in order to win, but that of the town's people as well.

Unfortunately, the pre-game hype vanished quickly as LaGrange inflicted a shocking 57-0 defeat on the Academy. More woe followed for Coach Stewart two weeks later when Evanston Academy blasted Morgan Park 67-9. With the victory, Evanston scored an astounding 280 points in its first three games, a surprising total that might have been attained by stretching the rules a bit as the *Chicago Evening Post* explained on October 30:

> In the Academy-Evanston game it was only a question of how large the score would be from the moment the Evanston team stepped on the field. The Morgan Park team was outweighed 40 pounds to the man, the Evanston line averaging 185 pounds. There is in all probability not a team around Chicago that could defeat Evanston. The team is heavier than any high school team and the players are much older. However, if Evanston conformed to the state high school rule that no one over 21 years of age could play, the team would not amount to much. The average age

of the players, according to one of the Evanston students, is 22 years. The team is not only heavy but fast, and the players are all experienced.

Contests against Lane Tech and Chicago Latin were cancelled during the two weeks following the Evanston debacle, leaving Stewart with just two "away" games in Wisconsin to conclude his first season. With wins over Northwestern Military Academy (31-7) and Racine College (7-0), Stewart managed to pull out a 3-2 record despite his abbreviated schedule. Along the way, one Academy team absorbed a horrific loss when the Lightweight squad (players under 150 pounds) was run over by the St. Viator College Lightweight squad 182-0, easily the ugliest loss in school history!

Stewart returned to coach again in 1916. With a mere 14 players on the roster, he still managed to return the football program to prominence with a successful 6-2 season. The Academy knocked off the Alumni 38-6, Hyde Park High School 12-7, and Lane Tech 9-0 to open the campaign with a spotless 3-0 mark. The fourth game was scheduled against a new opponent: Keewatin Academy of Waukesha, Wisconsin. Although Keewatin prevailed 12-0 despite the efforts of Captain Arthur Tetzlaff and tackle Lyall Beedy of Morgan Park, Keewatin found itself in the national news a few days later when a personal disagreement erupted into a fist fight between a teacher and an administrator. Apparently, instructor E. J. Lefebvre objected to the mandates established by recently hired business manager James Buchanan. The two squared off and Lefebvre was promptly arrested (and fired) after the battle and local deputies were called in to preserve order at the school when students joined in the fun. In court, more information was added to the story shared by the *Pittsburgh Post-Gazette*: "Lefebvre is in jail charged with assaulting Buchanan. Lefebvre accuses Buchanan of dishonesty. He says that students attacked Buchanan and turned a fire extinguisher on him. According to Lefebvre all the students are in revolt and ready to go home as soon as money arrives." Buchanan later resigned, and the crisis ended quietly.

Morgan Park bounced back to defeat University High School 31-7 as Tetzlaff tallied a touchdown and an extra point. Following a 32-0 shutout loss at Culver, Stewart's charges breezed past Morgan Park High School (40-6) and Northwestern Military Academy (21-0) to wrap up the season. Ultimately, Stewart graduated from the University of Chicago Law School in 1917 and decided to leave the Academy and become a partner in the law firm of Kindig, McGill, Stewart and Hatfield in Sioux City, Iowa. Stewart then served in the Marine Corps during World War I and returned to his law practice following the armistice.

As his career blossomed, Stewart became a very visible participant in local clubs and organizations, including serving as president of the Sioux City Chamber of Commerce beginning in 1925. Politically, Stewart became aligned in 1922 with the Woodbury County Republican Central Committee where he juggled allegiances within the party during a turbulent time in Iowa politics. As such, he was viewed as an ideal "compromise" candidate when there was a need to fill the unexpired term (until March 3, 1927) of the late Senator Albert Cummins. Stewart was appointed to the Senate seat on August 6, 1926 by Governor John Hammill as reported by the local *Greene Recorder*:

> Without anticipating political favors, a young attorney from Sioux City came to the state Republican Convention and emerged from it the party's nominee for the United States Senate to fill the unexpired term of the late Senator Albert Cummins.

Stewart was only 39 years old at the time of his appointment, but represented his state well during his minimal service in office as **The Biographical Dictionary of Iowa** noted:

> During his brief time in the Senate, Stewart became a strong supporter of the McNary-Haugen farm bill, which was passed during the following lame duck session but vetoed by [President Calvin] Coolidge. He also helped guide a bill to authorize continued navigational improvement on the Missouri River.

When his term was completed, Stewart did not seek another nomination, left politics and never looked back. He maintained his legal practice and was a steadfast contributor to local civic projects. During a time of significant growth for Morningside College in Sioux City, Iowa, Stewart served as chairman of the Board of Directors from 1938-1962. Stewart passed away on February 19, 1974 at the age of 87. In an interview for this book, Gene Ambroson, Director of Alumni Relations for Morningside College, reflected on the life, and impact, of Senator Stewart:

> David W. Stewart is considered to be one of the greatest movers and shakers of the northwest Iowa community of

Sioux City. Following his two-year stint as football coach at Morgan Park Academy while attending law school at the University of Chicago, Stewart re-settled in Sioux City, Iowa and became one of this state's and community's greatest leaders. His record of community and public service stands to this day as a shining example of what it means to give back in a very meaningful and productive way to the place where one lives and works. Though he left us a number of years ago, the Sioux City community shall never forget the tremendous contributions to excellence--particularly in education--that Stewart made here. That commitment was honed in places like Morgan Park Academy and Morningside College where he served on the board of directors for twenty-four years.

Teacher, soldier, lawyer, senator, and football coach...the legacy of David Stewart continues for this man of many talents, whose own magical journey through life touched many thousands more...

HIGH SCHOOL LADS ASCRIBED THEIR DEFEAT TO DARKNESS

Meanwhile, the start of the 1917 football season was initiated under the cloud of the United States' participation in World War I. Being a military school (except in name) the Academy would eventually make a significant contribution to the war effort in terms of graduates serving in the armed forces. The United States had maintained a position of neutrality since the outbreak of hostilities in 1914, but a prolonged series of malicious attacks by Germany on neutral (and U.S.) naval interests forced President Woodrow Wilson to seek a declaration of war. By April 6, 1917 both the United States Senate and the House of Representatives had voted to declare war on Germany and the war effort was underway.

With Coach Stewart moving back to Iowa (and eventual service in WW I), the Academy turned to Harry Schulte to handle the 1917 football program. On September 25, the *Chicago Tribune* suggested that the team was headed for a successful season:

With six of last season's players back for the 1917 football team at Morgan Park, and six of the lightweight regulars of a year ago heavy enough for play with the majors, the battle for berths of the Cadets' first eleven assures a highly successful gridiron campaign. The new students of good football caliber, also out for places, are helping Coach H. Schulte of Iowa University's 1910 varsity team weld a powerful eleven.

Ironically, the best player on the 1917 team was quarterback Paul Gates of Sioux City, Iowa, the exact location where former Coach Stewart now resided. Gates paced the club with three touchdowns in the opening 41-0 win over Austin High School of Chicago. But the early momentum for the team was stalled momentarily when a game scheduled with Loyola Academy on October 13 was cancelled by Morgan Park on October 12 due to a government inspection of the Academy's military programs also planned for October 13. In a sense, the war effort had hit home, but the team shrugged off this minor delay and grabbed three more quick victories over perennial power Englewood High School (33-0), St. Rita College (33-7), and St. Ignatius (13-0).

While still predominantly relying on a rushing offense, Coach Schulte toyed with the passing game behind the talented Gates. It was still difficult to pass the football accurately in 1917 with the ball itself much larger than it is today. Unless one was gifted with very large hands, it was indeed a challenge to throw a football accurately. An article appeared in the *Chicago Evening Post* that discussed the two most popular methods of tossing a football. Again, the football was much "wider" at this time:

> Forward passing is becoming more and more important as the game progresses. Each year finds teams more proficient with the use of the forward pass, largely because passers are becoming very skillful in throwing the ball. There are several ways of passing—one where the ball is laid on the hand with the palm upward, and a long, flat swing of the arm is pushing the ball forward. This form, I think, is not so safe and necessitates the starting of the ball on its flight too low down; in fact, so low down that it often is intercepted by the linemen and by the backs playing directly back of the line.

The most practical way seems to be to hold the ball in the hand, in the crotch made by the thumb and fingers, with the arm well above the head. When the ball is shot forward it starts from a higher elevation and has more accuracy and precision. As the arm is shot forward the hands should be allowed to turn inward, permitting the ball to slip off the end of the fingers, giving it a spin, which develops the spiral.

On November 3, the sporadic passing of Gates helped the Academy to garner its fifth straight win with a 19-7 waltz over local rival Morgan Park High School. "The game started late and dragged until darkness, to which the high school lads ascribed their defeat," reported the *Chicago Tribune*. The following week, Gates tallied all four touchdowns to lead the Academy over Northwestern Military Academy 24-13. However, the dreams for another undefeated season for the Academy were vanquished in the finale when old nemesis Culver steamrolled its way to an easy 47-14 victory. In Coach Schulte's only season with the Academy, he finished with a superlative 6-1 mark.

Already hobbled by the War, the United States faced another dangerous foe in 1918, and one that would not only cripple the football season, but nearly cripple the entire nation.

IT'S THE GRANDDADDY OF THEM ALL

Coaching the football team at the newly renamed Morgan Park Military Academy (MPMA) in 1918 was the last thing that Otho W. Ling wanted to do. A gifted musician, Ling was pleased to serve as the headmaster of the MPMA Lower (grade) School and also as the Band Director for the Academy. But football coach?

Yet strange times usually require sacrifices, and Otho Ling agreed to help his school wherever and whenever help was needed. In 1918, there was a huge void on the football field with no coach either ready, or available, to replace Coach Schulte. Band director Otho Ling slid somewhat uncomfortably into that position.

With the Academy now fully operational as a military school, the academic year opened in September with the real hope that the hostilities of World War I would soon be over. The Academy contributed deeply to the war (see "Extra Point" following this chapter) with 243 graduates of the Academy serving in the conflict, according to school archives. Of that significant number, seven former students made the ultimate sacrifice in defense of their country.

As the 1918 school year began, the U.S. Army was fully involved in the war in Europe and participating in the deadly Meuse-Argonne offensive in France. This six-week battle would prove to be the final, decisive offensive maneuver by the U.S. and its allies. By the time the football season opened on October 5, 1918, the Allies were overrunning the last German resistance at the infamous Hindenburg Line on the Western Front. Unbeknownst to those on the front lines, peace talks had quietly been initiated the day before. By the time the Armistice was declared on November 11, 1918, the shortest—and least productive—season in the history of the Academy football program had been completed.

The brief demise into an unsuccessful football campaign was certainly not the fault of Coach Ling. His efforts needed to be applauded, rather than criticized...and they were following the season. While Ling was faced with immersing himself into an entirely new culture (football vs. music), he was also staring at a vicious enemy that threatened every citizen of the world during that time: the deadly influenza epidemic of 1918.

Because of its severity and the threat of contagious exposure, large gatherings of individuals where discouraged, and in some cases, prohibited. The flu spread unceremoniously throughout the nation and since it seemed to affect younger people more adversely, events where large crowds of youths gathered (such as football games) were closely monitored or closed. Today, the sheer number of people affected by this illness seems almost unbelievable: 500 million taken ill globally, with 20-50 million deaths credited to the outbreak. But at the time, there were no antibiotics or vaccines available to fight this deadly disease, resulting in the rapid escalation of infected cases and deaths. "If you're in the business of infectious disease epidemics, you can't ignore the 1918 flu—it's the granddaddy of them all," noted Donald Burke, Professor of International Health at the Bloomberg School in the Fall, 2004 issue of the *John Hopkins Public Health* magazine.

The direct impact of the flu on the Academy's football program was the inability to construct a full schedule due to mandates imposed by civic and military administrators. With the flu reaching its most dangerous levels in the fall of 1918, most football games were simply cancelled rather than expose individuals to the flu from an innocent handshake or sneeze at an athletic event. In the Chicago area, St. Ignatius dropped its football program for the year, while Culver Military Academy created a ten-day ban on gatherings and "visiting," including football games.

The MPMA season did not push off until October 5, when the Cadets engaged in a scoreless tie at nearby Morgan Park High School. Then, on October 13, the *Chicago Tribune* reported on a cancelled game involving the Academy: "The epidemic caused the cancelling of another important game, Morgan Park Academy notifying Hyde Park High that it could not meet the local high school champs at Morgan Park."

Of course, colleges and universities were also affected by the flu and its accompanying restrictions. In early October, a wire report distributed across the country outlined new rules announced by Col. R. I. Rees, Chairman of the Committee on Education and Special Training for the Department of War:

> The war department took action today that will wipe out previously arranged college football schedules, but will enable the schools large and small, to have four games in November, two at home and two abroad. Practice is limited to one and one-half fours daily, including time spent for dressing and shower baths.

The Academy was unable to schedule another game in October as concerns regarding the influenza outbreak increased locally in the Morgan Park community according to the *Morgan Park Post*:

> Preventive measures undertaken by the Chicago health department and by individuals have had little effect in checking the spread of the Spanish influenza epidemic in the district this week. The list of local deaths is larger this week than any that had been recorded in a number of years. Every effort is being made to stop the spread of the disease. Most lodge meetings have been suspended by summary orders of the health department.

This was followed by a stern decision on October 22 from Chicago Health Commissioner Dr. Heath Robertson and Assistant Superintendent of Schools Edward Cole as reported in the *Chicago Tribune*: "All athletic activities must be discontinued until further notice," was the way the official edict read. According to Mr. Cole, Dr. Robertson stated that many of the influenza and pneumonia fatalities at Great Lakes Naval Training station (in nearby Glencoe, Illinois) were due to over exercising. "We feared the results of overheating in the various sports making students more prone to take cold," he said.

As the season stumbled to a close, even before it really got started, MPMA was drubbed by Lake Forest Academy 41-0 on November 2, and then fell to Northwestern Military Academy 6-0 in the final game on November 16. Historically, the 0-2-1 record will reflect the only time that an Academy team finished with a winless season, as well as the only instance where the team failed to score over an entire, albeit abbreviated, schedule. But there was no dishonor in that, nor was there any second-guessing. Instead, Ling was congratulated for his efforts for chaperoning a team that remained competitive despite being beset by injuries, illness, and an unpredictable schedule. In the 1919 Academy **Catalog**, an ample supply of recognition was served to the 1918 gridders:

> The football team of 1918 made a good record in spite of numerous injuries and the disorganization due to the prevalent influenza. At no time has the leadership of the coach and the strong MPMA spirit been more clearly shown. The Academy played throughout the season with increasing success.

Eventually, the flu epidemic disappeared, the soldiers returned home, and Otho Ling returned to his roots as the leader of the band. Ling spent several years at the Academy before finishing his academic career with a 32-year stint as an instructor and band director at Howe Military Academy in Howe, Indiana. He passed away at the age of 76 on June 14, 1964 in Naples, New York.

TAKE THE STREET CAR FOR MORGAN PARK NEXT SATURDAY

As the country returned to normal, so did Morgan Park Military Academy. The school turned to a familiar face when attorney John Anderson was tabbed to coach the football team in 1919. Anderson, who coached the team from 1909-1913 with an overall 20-10-2 record, was called upon to rebuild the football program which had been nearly lost to the influenza outbreak the year before. With a successful legal career, as well as a growing stable of local real estate acquisitions, Anderson provided the right blend of knowledge, experience, and familiarity with the program to resurrect the Academy's football fortunes.

Anderson scheduled an ambitious 11 game slate, added some tough new opponents, and set about adjusting the Academy's football fortunes. The coach was especially persistent on the defensive side of the ball and managed six shutouts during the season, reminding old-timers of his 1909 and 1910 squads which allowed a mere 14 points in 14 games over those two seasons. Unfortunately, the defense was a bit leaky in some of the other contests indicating that if the Academy failed to secure a whitewash on defense, the team might not prevail.

Following a humiliating 57-0 loss to Lake Forest Academy, the team's record rested at 3-3 with a tough home game looming with St. Charles (Illinois) High School on October 25. Despite the ugly loss the previous week, the *St. Charles Chronicle* (October 23) approached the game with Morgan Park with great anguish:

> The team (St. Charles) was idle last Saturday in order to give the men a much-needed rest and to get the cripples in shape for the Morgan Park game. The Cadets are reported to have a fast team this year and it will take all the football that the local boys have to put over a defeat.

Apparently, the scribes in St. Charles were onto something as Morgan Park bounced back from its 57-0 defeat against Lake Forest to trample St. Charles 57-7, the highest number of points for the Academy in a game in five years. Next up was a renewal of a rivalry with Bloom High School of Chicago Heights, Illinois that had been dormant since 1907. Bloom received exceptional local media coverage from the *Chicago Heights Star* newspaper which urged its readers to join the team on its venture a few miles north to Morgan Park:

> Next Saturday the boys play Morgan Park Academy. A much stronger resistance is expected at the coming game than has been met with by the home team this season. Last Saturday a good crowd witnessed the game and if anybody is wishing to see a real football game just take your auto or the street car for Morgan Park next Saturday.

The result of the Bloom outing was another surprising reversal for the Academy as Bloom captured an easy 32-0 decision. The *Star* was one of the first local newspapers to provide extensive coverage of local high school football games with pre- and post-game insight, including a near play-by-play account of the specific game. For example, the following is the *Star's* coverage of the second quarter of the Academy game:

> Second quarter—On the opening play, Kotal went 60 yards through tackle to a touchdown. On the point after, Schmeckpepper fumbled. Weiler kicked off. Bloom forced Morgan Park to punt and then carried the ball to the Academy's 20-yard line. Here Weiler was called back for a pass. Earl Davis got it and fell over the line. Brooks kicked goal. The quarter ended without further scoring. Score end of first half: Bloom 20. Morgan Park 0.

After two defensive bashings in three games, the Academy finished the season with three straight shutouts over Northwestern Military Academy (12-0), St. Alban's (7-0), and Morgan Park High School (13-0) to wrap up the campaign with a 7-4 mark. It would prove to be the final year of coaching at MPMA for Anderson, who concluded his staggered coaching career with a 27-14-2 record for his six seasons of work.

Anderson left the Academy with the most coaching wins (27) in school history, but his successor would not only better that achievement, but also initiate a new tradition for athletics at Morgan Park: a rather permanent football coach!

EXTRA POINT

Earlier in this chapter, the extreme sacrifices of Academy graduates during World War I were noted. In an effort to never forget these heroic individuals, the Academy created two memorials to honor the contributions of the former students. On November 15, 1921, a memorial service was held on campus to remember these soldiers by planting trees in their names. In addition, plaques were prepared to share the important stories of each of the graduates. While the passage of time often clouds our memories, respectful historians such as Barry Kritzberg battle to preserve them. In a moving article in the November 2002 issue of *The Academy News*, Kritzberg (then a senior member of the Academy faculty and the school's archivist) shared the very real interpretation of the seven Academy graduates who lost their lives in connection with World War I. Portions of his article are as follows:

***

They came late to the fray "over there" –to Fismes, to Argonne, to Verdun, to St. Etienne, to Aisne-Marne, names familiar to military historians as part of that final push toward Armistice—but some of them did not come back.

Five of the Morgan Park Military Academy cadets who enlisted in that "war to end all wars" were killed in action in an eight-week period in 1918. A sixth MPMA cadet was killed in a training accident in Texas earlier that year. A seventh cadet was killed in 1920, while with the army of occupation in Germany.

By December 1921 plans were underway to honor the seven slain in the Great War with plaques and memorial trees prominently displayed on the MPMA campus. The plaques were carefully worded and told the story of each cadet with simple eloquence:

> **Clarence Julius Bremer (Class of 1911)** enlisted in the aeroplane bombing service in December 1917. He trained initially at the University of Illinois and later at Ellington Field (Houston, Texas), where he was killed in an accident on March 2, 1918.

> **Charles Val Hoffman (Class of 1913)** entered aviation service in October 1917, but later transferred to a machine gun battalion. His company was sent to Europe in April 1918 and he was killed in action at Fismes, France, September 10, 1918.

> **John Rolfe Hubbard (Class of 1911)** enlisted in 1917 and became sergeant-major of an infantry battalion. He was killed in action September 26, 1918 in the first Argonne drive. (A copy of a letter in the World War I memorial file gives a slightly more detailed account of his death. Lieutenant Falls, his commanding officer wrote: "We regret that we cannot give you a story in greater detail of the circumstances surrounding Sgt. Major Hubbard's death, due to the fact that the group of which he was one is now either wounded or dead. On September 26, 1918, our regiment went over the top as a part of the American forces participating in what is now known as the Verdun drive. Our objective was the village of Cierges which we captured and held after a four days' flight, being relieved on the night of September 30 by the 32nd Division. Sgt. Major Hubbard was killed...by what we believed to have

been shell fire of an Austrian 88 field piece. He was buried within a few yards of where he fell…")

Lester William Allen (Class of 1917) joined the marine corps in January 1918. He was sent to France in May of that year and fought at Chateau-Thierry, Belleau Woods, St. Mihiel, Argonne, and the Champagne sector. He was killed in action near St. Etienne, October 3, 1918.

Walter Bogle Birkland (Class of 1914) enlisted in July 1917. His artillery company was sent to France in October 1917. He was killed in action at the Verdun front, October 11, 1918. He was buried in the American cemetery at Argonne. (A letter to his parents, from Lucien F. Boyles of his battalion, had this to say about Walter: "…the entire battalion has heard of the game, smiling way he died. I wish it could be repeated to the world as an example of how one American boy met his death…he said to the men who were bearing him to the dressing station, 'never mind me, fellows. You are going to too much trouble. Leave me here on the field. It will be all over in a minute.'…From the time he was hit…he refused to betray his suffering by a word or groan…only once did he seem to regret the wound that was costing him his life. And then he merely said: 'It's a little tough to get it, when it seems so nearly over.'")

Lloyd C. Bute (Class of 1914) entered military service in September 1917 and was in France by July 1918. He fought in the battle of Chateau-Thierry and was wounded on August 4, 1918 in the Aisne-Marne offensive. He died of complications from his wounds on November 3, 1918. (A printed account perhaps based on a letter from his parents, adds: "He got wounded with a piece of shrapnel on the left hip, from a trench mortar. He called to his sergeant who was a good friend of his, who gave him first aid and carried him over a mile to a first aid station. From there he was sent to a hospital where he wrote home that he was only slightly wounded, writing a very cheerful letter telling us not to worry that the wound would be healed in a couple of weeks; that he would not have told us at all only he knew we would see it in the paper. September 29, he wrote that it was all healed, and that was the last he ever wrote...")

Lothar R. Long (Class of 1910) was killed during the army of occupation, Coblentz, Germany, 1920.

***

It should be noted that Lester Allen, the youngest of the group mentioned above, was a member of the Academy football team for two years. Allen scored two touchdowns from his halfback position to pace the team to a 31-7 win over University High School in 1916.

David Stewart, the Morgan Park Academy football coach from 1915-1916, became a United States Senator from Iowa in 1926.

Football coach David Stewart (in tie) led the Academy to a 9-4 overall record in 1915 and 1916. He also served as the track coach at the school.

In 1918, the nation-wide flu epidemic limited Coach Otho Ling (standing right, in hat) to just three games in a shortened (0-2-1) season. It was the only winless campaign in the long history of the Morgan Park Military Academy football program. Ling, the school's Band Director, volunteered to coach the football team in its time of need.

CHAPTER 9

Tubby, Droegs, and Fielding Yost

"Our wet, muddy, happy boys nailed up forty points for MPMA."
—Maroon and White Yearbook, 1921

Since its inception in 1894, the Morgan Park Academy football program had relied heavily on short-term football coaches, usually ones with some connection to the University of Chicago. The coaches generally served for a couple of years and then departed to pursue other career opportunities or to complete graduate school studies.

In 1920, with the Academy fully independent of the University of Chicago as it raced into the "Roaring Twenties," the institution reached out to the Kentucky Military Institute to sign its next football coach: Floyd Fleming. Born on March 3, 1891, Fleming was a 1914 graduate of Indiana University, where he achieved a rare honor during his collegiate career by serving as the captain of both the football and baseball teams. Fleming, a stout, stern specimen, was a true loyalist to Indiana. In fact, in the team photos taken of the 1920 Academy football team, Fleming proudly poses in his Indiana letterman's sweater.

Fleming found himself in the national news in October 1913 when it was discovered that this multi-sport athlete was about to accomplish something totally bold and unusual on the collegiate football field. The *Indianapolis News* shared the following:

> When Indiana University meets the University of Illinois,
> it is believed Floyd Fleming, captain of the Crimson
> eleven last year, will establish the unique record of having

played in every position on the team in conference play. Fleming will start the Illinois game at center. He has played guard, tackle, and on both sides of the line, quarterback, both halves, and fullback. Besides his versatility on the gridiron, Fleming has played all the positions on the varsity basketball quintet, and has filled all the places on the baseball team, with the exception of pitcher and catcher. Athletic followers here say Fleming's record has never been equaled in the Western [Big Ten] Conference.

Fleming did bring a positive football mentality to Morgan Park and promptly found a way to both build his own future, as well as reverse the fortunes of the gridiron squad. During his early tenure at the Academy, Fleming witnessed a steady increase in enrollment, a broader "buy-in" by the alumni, and an almost uncommonly loyal fan base at the school itself. By 1920, the Academy had aligned itself with rules established for high school competition, including age requirements. As more and more high schools launched football programs, the newspaper coverage of the Academy's athletic ventures was not as extensive in the Chicago dailies. Instead of large game reports, smaller "summaries" were more common, but this coverage was identical for all area schools except for irregular longer features on a particular team. However, the student newspaper and yearbook at the Academy furnished its readers with in-depth coverage of both individual games and complete seasons, leaving a generous resource when and where those publications have been preserved.

HIS TASK LOOKED NEARLY HOPELESS

Things were not easy from the outset for Coach Fleming in 1920 as he greeted his initial squad that was small both in numbers and physical size. The Academy **Maroon and White** yearbook would later state: "At first his task looked nearly hopeless, but every night he was on the field working his very hardest that this school might succeed and those little fellows, for they were little comparatively, might learn enough football to outplay all larger opponents."

Leading the way would be a scrawny halfback named Walker "Tubby" Gorham who weighed a mere 135 pounds. But Tubby had plenty of company in the shallow weight area since the entire team averaged only 139 pounds, with quarterback Henry Sopkin checking in at just 115 pounds. Several other team members had never played the game before, so the challenge facing Coach Fleming was quite intimidating. Eventually 22 players participated on the team, and Fleming proved to be both an able "teacher" of the game, as well as a trusted mentor for his players. "His method of coaching is absolutely the most efficient to use for secondary schools," raved the school yearbook. "In football, our coach can run rings around any man on the team and show up the weaknesses of the team by exhibiting just where the deficiency may be found." Basically, Fleming evaluated the size of his squad (or lack thereof) and focused on conditioning and speed, pushing for any advantage that he might be able to create. But would speed and persistence successfully combine to overcome size and experience?

The opening contest against nearby Blue Island High School proved to be quite a pleasant surprise as the Academy waltzed over its opponent for an easy 79-0 win. It was likely a surprise for Coach Fleming as well since his emphasis on speed and deception could not be adequately graded during team practice segments. With an opposing team on the field, and one without previous knowledge of Fleming's tricky formations, the final score of the Blue Island game proved to be the ultimate gauge of success. Four more opponents fell in succession, including new adversaries such as Pullman Tech High School of Chicago, and De LaSalle, an original member of the Chicago Catholic League. Pullman was vanquished 14-0, while De LaSalle was toppled 45-0. In all. Fleming's charges had outscored those first five opponents by a 164-6 count, leaving a final contest at undefeated, and unscored upon, Northwestern Military and Naval Academy in Lake Geneva, Wisconsin. Although outweighed by an estimated 30 pounds per man, the plucky Academy team managed a 7-6 halftime lead when Tubby Gorham ripped off a 35-yard scoring dash. However, Gorham, now the starting quarterback, was injured in the second period and was unable to return until the final moments. By then, the hosts had scrambled back into the lead and held on to a 19-14 victory—spoiling the Academy's effort to complete an undefeated season.

The Academy News applauded the effort of the team (which finished 5-1 in Fleming's first campaign), but also praised the genial Northwestern hosts:

> The spirit shown by Northwestern was excellent. Our men were escorted to the school from Fontana [train station] by automobiles. At the school, guides were furnished to show the strangers about the campus, pointing out all buildings and points of special interest. During the game, Northwestern frequently cheered for our injured players and applauded our good plays. This courtesy and

sportsmanship was returned by our rooters, to as great an extent as possible. We appreciate what Northwestern did for us, the excellent sportsmanship and good fellowship which we received, but we plan an early revenge for the defeat administered to us.

HOLES BIG ENOUGH FOR AN ICE WAGON TO PASS THROUGH

As with most high schools, the end of the academic year coincides with the time-honored tradition of the distribution of the annual school yearbook. The 1921 version of the **Maroon and White** yearbook honored the football season with a tidy review of the results, along with full-length photos of each of the starters, with a brief biography of each of those players. This insight from nearly 100 years ago remains charming today, with the descriptive depictions of the players from a classmate's viewpoint, while the writer also strives to maintain journalistic decorum. Here are just a few biographic samples from the 1921 **Maroon and White**:

> **Vernon Horn** (Center): Playing every minute of our football schedule was "Bugle." We all rejoiced in a hearty voice to see him get there. Yes, it was Vernon breaking through center, and opening up holes big enough for an ice wagon to pass through.

> **Lawrence Amsler** (Tackle): Our opponents who attempted to gain on off tackle plays received the jolt of their young lives, for they would run into a fighting red-headed fellow. "Red" played a strong, fast tackle, playing in all but two quarters. The red-head was invincible. What more could we ask?

> **Walker Gorham** (Halfback): During this football season, Tubby was the individual star of the team. Playing right halfback, he scored 53 points out of a total of 178 points made all season. Besides his wonderful offensive ability, he was a defensive player of the highest order. He was the center of the scrap and fight all of the time, and it was his pep, enthusiasm, and spirit that was largely responsible for the fighting spirit of the team. Although he weighed only

135 pounds, Tub has played against men ranging anywhere up to 200 and beaten them at their own game.

YOU HAVE SENT US SOME VERY FINE FELLOWS

As Morgan Park Military Academy continued to grow in 1921, the school welcomed students from 27 states and three foreign countries, while Coach Fleming opened his training camp with 18 players on his football team. It wasn't "cheap" to attend the Academy, but intelligent and determined students dominated the enrollees, hoping to essentially prepare themselves for a challenging collegiate experience. Coach Fleming also had some "hope," in that some of those brilliant students might have some athletic ability as well.

To increase its visibility, the Academy began soliciting letters of recommendation for publication in the annual school catalog in 1921, which also served as a key promotional vehicle. For example, a representative from Brown University in Providence, Rhode Island, shared the following:

> You have sent us some very fine fellows during the last few years—the type we are glad to claim—men who become a big credit to Brown as they are to Morgan Park. You have perhaps already heard, but if not, will be glad to know, that the men you sent to us this year completed successfully their first semester's work, and we have not the slightest doubt that they will continue to do creditable work.

Academy students (and more importantly, their parents) could expect to remit $850 in 1921 for "the General Charge including tuition, board, room with necessary furniture, heat, light, laundry, infirmary, and use of arms and equipment," according to the 1921 catalog. Payments of $450 and $400 were due on September 14, 1921 and January 4, 1922 respectively.

There were still some challenges regarding the game of football itself, and the Chicago Public Schools struggled to balance the playing field in terms of competition and participation. Perhaps we could call this an early form of league "parity." An article in the *Chicago Daily News* reported on the league's activities, but also noted that there was an expectation for better officiating on the prep level:

> High schools situated in various districts of the city receive material for their teams which varies largely with

the character of the population in the district. In order to compensate for those regional diversities, height and weight restrictions have been placed in force, particularly in football, socker [sic] and basketball. What is called the "twenty year" rule provides that no student who has reached the age of 20 shall compete in any sport for his school.

Selection of competent football officials, which has been more or less a difficult matter, is to be made similar since the formation of an association of football officials. The association...gives applicants for membership a test on their ability before a committee. On a large chart of a football field various situations are diagrammed and the applying official is required to show a real knowledge of the game before he is admitted.

WHAT COULD BE SWEETER THAN TRIMMING OUR OLD RIVAL?

There were still a myriad of other challenges facing the game of football in 1921 and the Chicago area was ripe with wacky situations at individual schools and communities:

- In Zion, Illinois, 12 youths were arrested for playing football in a public park, thanks to a judge's ruling that asserted that playing football was prohibited in those locations. "The police force of the city has been enforcing the ordinance that makes football playing not only a crime, but one of the ten cardinal sins," reported the amused *Chicago Evening Post* on October 7.
- At Senn High School on Chicago's north side, the football roster was reduced from over 70 to 25 due to some questionable eligibility rules that some thought might have been initiated by the faculty simply to impede the popularity of the football program. A group of ineligible students called themselves "The Flunkers" and worked out with the team to allow scrimmaging, but the "Flunkers" were not eligible to participate in any games.
- Over in Oak Park, Illinois ten players were suspended for breaking training rules. Although the broken rules were not imme-

diately revealed, it was surprising that most of the players voluntarily "asked" to be suspended because of their indiscretions. Later, the coach of the Oak Park team did report that those suspended had been guilty of the dire crimes of smoking and staying out too late at night!

While Morgan Park Military Academy survived the 1921 season without any personnel or academic issues, the second edition of Coach Fleming's program struggled to stay afloat with a 2-2-1 record. With one game against Loyola Academy cancelled due to rain, the team made do with the abbreviated five game schedule. The highlight of the year was certainly the final game on the schedule, when the Academy scuttled the Northwestern Military and Naval Academy 40-0 to avenge the lone loss from the previous season. Team captain and quarterback Ted Arnold scored two touchdowns to pace the victors which made Arnold the "happiest man on earth," according to the school yearbook. The **Maroon and White** also added a joyous description of that final game:

> Then we hit Northwestern who bowed to us, and oh how low they bowed! Our wet muddy, happy boys nailed up forty points for MPMA and held Northwestern scoreless. What could be sweeter than trimming our old rival and doing it before the proud alumni who came back to honor the old school once more on homecoming day? The field was snowy and wet and by the best combination of backfield and line play ever seen, we sat upon Northwestern, who played a good clean brand of football but could not class with our boys.

Despite the average season, the love affair between the school and Coach/Captain Fleming (Captain being the coach's military title at the school) continued as stated in the 1922 version of the **Maroon and White**:

> Captain Floyd F. Fleming has completed his second year of coaching the football, basketball, and baseball teams of Morgan Park. His teams have been successful not only in winning a majority of their games but also in developing the individual in the essentials of team play and personal skill. With the kind of spirit that our coach instills in his men our athletes will carry on forever.

JOE ZIEMBA

MEN ARE IN THE MAKING AT MORGAN PARK MILITARY ACADEMY

As the 1922-23 school year began, an astounding statistic regarding the Academy appeared in the *Chicago Tribune* on September 29. While covering the prospects for the 1922 football season, the newspaper added some insightful information about the co-existence of the academic and athletic programs:

> Men are in the making out at Morgan Park Military Academy, whether it be for athletics or the more serious business of life. Just now, they're greatly concerned with whipping together a football eleven. There are about 200 students, 107 in the upper [high] school. Of the latter number, eighty-seven are engaged in football, a sufficient number for three teams, heavyweight, lightweight, and bantam. They have to be physically and mentally fit to enter Morgan Park, and even sounder both ways to play football.

The enthusiasm for football was evident at the Academy with the notation in the above article that over 80% of the high school students were actively engaged on one of the football teams. For several years, the school had offered "smaller" students the opportunity to participate on a lightweight or bantamweight squad. The players could learn the system and then perhaps literally grow into consideration for a heavyweight/varsity position by the time they became upperclassmen. In addition, those few students not actually playing football were encouraged to participate in other ways by *The Academy News*:

> Hitch your wagon to a star, is a fine motto, but the motto alone is not going to bring the results. The men who cannot go out for football should not remain idle. There are many small jobs that have to be done, and those jobs have to be done. The men on the side lines are the men to do them. The manager of football can use several men to help him. The trainer can use a good many men to rub the players and help him in general. The need of water boys was brought before our eyes very vividly...Only a few of the jobs to be done have been mentioned. The men who

166

do their job with cheerfulness are the men who are going to help make this season the best MPMA has ever had.

Once again, in 1922, the Fleming trademarks of speed and passion were observed by the *Chicago Tribune*: "The team isn't as heavy as most prep elevens. The line will average about 160 pounds and the backfield about 145 pounds. But there's speed and, judging from practice, plenty of aggressiveness and drive." Quarterback Ted Arnold and Captain Charles Terman (fullback) were expected to lead the Academy offense.

With the early schedule top-heavy with tough games against Catholic school opponents (De LaSalle, St. Rita, Loyola), the team wobbled out of the gate with a 0-2-2 mark. To add further distress, both Terman and Arnold were injured and unable to play as the team reached mid-season. Yet Coach Fleming managed to alter the fortunes of his team by grabbing three straight wins over St. Alban's (25-7), Pullman Tech (37-0) and Elgin Academy (7-0) before concluding the schedule with a 0-0 tie with fierce rival Northwestern Military and Naval Academy. The final 3-2-3 mark was likely disappointing for Coach Fleming, but the wait for another outstanding season was brief, as he positioned a stingy defense, along with a pair of incredibly talented athletes, to turn the tables in 1923.

A NORMAL LIFE IS A BUSY LIFE

Football continued its run of extreme popularity in 1923 as the Academy fielded teams in the heavyweight, lightweight, and bantam divisions, while also offering students the opportunity to participate in "Inter Company" (intramural) football games. The heavyweight/varsity squad was, of course, the brightest jewel in the Morgan Park football treasure chest, and the 1923 edition under Coach Fleming included 29 players on its roster. Games were still played behind the present gymnasium, where lucky fans could perhaps grab a seat on one of the two small balconies overlooking the field or stand anywhere around the gridiron to secure the best vantage point for a game. Many others elected to sit on the ground while the players could enjoy a single plank bench when not in the game.

When students were not involved in athletic endeavors, little time was left for anything except schoolwork. The 1923 Academy catalog provided some insight into the daily schedule of a cadet at a military school:

A normal life is a busy life. Indolence has no place in it. Reveille call sounds at 6:15 a.m. and from that moment until Tattoo, which is sounded at 9:15 p.m., the day is pregnant with wholesome activities. Fifteen minutes of brisk exercise is a fitting start for a strenuous day. Following reveille, quarters are policed and inspected. At 6:50 a.m. there is another formation for Mess One. The battalion is marched to the Mess Hall. On entrance, the whole battalion stands at attention while grace is said and until the command "Seats" is given. Each cadet sits erect in his chair with arms folded and remains in that position until the command "Rest" is given. A period from forty to fifty minutes is allowed for the meal. Police inspection follows at 7:40 a.m. and at 7:55 a.m. school call is blown. Recitation and study periods are continuous from 8:00 a.m. to 12:25 p.m., and from 1:20 p.m. to 2:55 p.m. At 3:05 p.m. the afternoon drill for one-hour duration begins. The sounding of recall is the signal for the recreation period continuing for those having good record until 6:00 p.m. Following the Mess Three, the rooms are put in order for a rigid inspection by the Commandant, and then the evening study hours begin. These continue from 7:15 p.m. until 9:15 p.m. Taps sound at 9:30 p.m. brings to a close a busy day.

MCAFEE QUELLED RALLY

William" Bill" Droegemueller was a lean, lanky (5'10") receiver who cemented his starting position as the left end on the 1923 Academy football team with good speed, intelligence, and soft hands. On the opposite side of the line, Bill McAfee lined up at right end and cast a large shadow over opponents determined to slip around his 6'2" frame. For that period of time, this was a pair of tall ends for a talented team that captured wins in its last four games to complete a satisfying 4-1-1 campaign. With Droegemueller and McAfee closing down the outside of the field, the Academy allowed just 16 points defensively in those six contests, while pitching four shut outs. One of those defensive gems occurred against emerging rival St. Alban's on November 3. Although team captain Frederick "Tanglefoot" Schmitz paced the offense with three touchdowns, Droegemueller was omni-present on the field, making tackles, returning punts, and downing a punt at the St. Alban's' own three-yard line. From there, the stingy Academy defense forced St. Alban's to attempt a punt from its own end zone as reported by *The Academy News* on November 16: "They made an attempt to kick from behind their goal line, but the kicker fumbled, and McAfee fell on the ball for the Academy's second touchdown." The win over St. Alban's was the second of four straight wins for the Academy and the Droegemueller/ McAfee combination helped the team snare two more victories over Elgin Junior College (14-7) and Northwestern Military and Naval Academy (19-0) to conclude the season. In the Elgin contest, McAfee grabbed a 30-yard touchdown reception for the winning score.

Although Droegemueller concluded his football days with that 1923 team, his athletic career was far from over—except that he, like McAfee, was superlative in another sport. For McAfee, his final years at the Academy were spent on the baseball field where his pitching prowess (only one loss in two seasons) paved the way for him to pitch at the University of Michigan. During the 1928 season at Michigan, McAfee finished with a sparkling 10-1 record, which, at the time, was the sixth highest single-season win total among Michigan pitchers in history. In addition, in 1956, his coach Ray Fisher looked back at his own 35 years of coaching at Michigan and named McAfee to his all-time Michigan team. McAfee was exceptional at the plate as well, hitting a robust .451 for the Wolverines in 1928.

All of this talent led McAfee to sign a major league contract with the Chicago Cubs, with whom he made his pitching debut on May 12, 1930. Although his time with the Cubs was brief, McAfee managed to stick around the major leagues for a few years, primarily as a relief pitcher with Washington (Senators), Boston (Braves), and St. Louis (Browns). His finest season was in 1932 when he finished the campaign with the Senators with a 6-1 mark and a solid 3.92 earned run average. If "saves" had been part of baseball's scoring criteria at the time, McAfee's contributions might have been more prestigious since he appeared to contribute strongly to many of the victories in which he participated. A prime example might have been his appearance against the Chicago White Sox on Saturday, June 24, 1933 when he effectively dominated the White Sox in the ninth inning of a Washington 7-5 win reported by the Associated Press:

> Relief pitcher Bill McAfee quickly quelled a ninth inning rally Saturday with the tying runs on base to give the American League-leading Washington Senators a 7-5 victory over the Chicago White Sox, their fourth straight in the series.

On February 13, 1935, McAfee announced his retirement from baseball in order to pursue a business opportunity with his father. Overall, McAfee concluded his five-year career with a 10-4 mark in 83 appearances. He enjoyed a successful career in business and eventually became mayor of Albany, Georgia. Unfortunately, McAfee was killed in a plane crash in July of 1958. Ironically, the private plane carrying the former big-league pitcher was heading north to watch the major league All-Star game in Baltimore. As such, Bill McAfee is likely the first Academy football player to make the successful journey to the world of major league baseball.

BEGAN POLE VAULTING WITH BAMBOO POLES

Bill "Droegs" Droegemueller was an exceptional student at the Academy and was awarded numerous honors, including the highest scholarship rank for the school year, and the Alumni Prize for "the most representative student during his junior and senior years." He enrolled at Northwestern University in Evanston, Illinois after his graduation in 1924. Aside from his football experience at Morgan Park, Droegemueller proved to be one of the state's top pole vaulters as well, despite rather rudimentary equipment. "I began pole vaulting as a kid, using my mother's old wooden curtain rods, or the bamboo poles out of rugs" recalled Droegemueller in an interview with the *Greeley Daily Tribune* in 1972. He vaulted "a little over 11 feet" at the Academy, and then joined the world's top vaulters while at Northwestern.

During his career at Northwestern, he captured a pair of Big Ten Conference pole vault titles and the NCAA national championship. Droegemueller also established new records for both the Big Ten as well as the United States. All of this success led to Droegemueller being named to the 1928 U.S. Olympic team which would be competing in Amsterdam. During the Olympic pole vaulting competition, Droegemueller and fellow American Sabin Carr were locked into an exciting duel for the gold medal after both athletes shattered the existing Olympic record of 13 feet, five inches set in 1920 by American F. K. Foss.

Droegemueller and Carr both cleared the bar at 13 feet, 5 7/16 inches, before Droegemueller blasted that mark away with a leap of 13 feet, 9 1/16 inches. In his next jump, Carr did even better, eclipsing the old record with a mark of 13 feet, 9 6/16 inches. Initially, it was announced that Droegemueller equaled Carr's performance, but later Olympic officials admitted their mistake and Droegemueller was credited with a final top vault of 13 feet, 5 7/16 inches. Though disheartened, Droegemueller received the silver medal for his second-place finish at the 1928 Olympic Games.

Following the conclusion of his athletic career, Droegemueller completed his medical studies at Northwestern in 1932 and eventually established an ophthalmology practice in Greeley, Colorado. He passed away in 1987, leaving behind his legacy as the only U.S. Olympic medalist from Morgan Park Military Academy!

THE ROAD TO SUCCESS IS STRAIGHT AHEAD

Late in the 1923-1924 school year, the students at the Academy were entertained by a surprise guest, the famous Fielding Yost, head football coach at the University of Michigan. Perhaps it was no coincidence that Yost was also the collegiate coach of Academy football legend Albert Benbrook, the College Football Hall of Famer who was a two-time All-American under Yost for the Wolverines. During his long coaching career, Yost compiled an outstanding 198-35-12 record with a sparkling 55-1-1 mark from 1901-1905 at Michigan. But the appearance of Yost on March 17 on the Morgan Park Military Academy campus was intended to inspire the Cadets, rather than to talk football. Through the next three decades, celebrity speakers (such as Knute Rockne and Lowell Thomas) would visit the campus on a regular basis, sharing their thoughts, influences, and often their adventures with the students. Perhaps Yost would prove to be inspirational for the 1924 Academy football team as he shared such sage advice (courtesy of *The Academy News*) as:

- We cannot be any better than we make ourselves.
- Everything is a day-by-day process.
- Serve yourself.
- Our bodies are our homes.
- Loyalty to friends, teachers, to country.
- The surest road to victory is straight ahead.

SUFFERING FROM STAGE FRIGHT

Coach Floyd Fleming, by now familiar with the year-round rigors of coaching the Academy football, basketball, and baseball teams, ramped up his 1924 schedule by adding a pair of powerful football foes on the road:

Michigan City (Indiana) and Danville (Illinois) High Schools. After an opening 6-6 tie with Michigan City, the Academy brought a 1-1-1 record into the fourth game at Danville and encountered something rather unexpected--a huge crowd. According to the *Southtown Economist* on October 29, more than 6,000 fans crammed into the Danville stadium to witness the event, with the hosts taking advantage of a sluggish Academy start to snare a 20-6 win:

> Apparently suffering from stage fright when playing in front before 6,000 spectators at Danville, Illinois, cadets from the Morgan Park Military Academy let the downstaters trim them 20-6. All of the victors' points were scored in the first half for in the third and fourth periods the cadets never allowed Danville to make a first down.

Just a week later, the Academy bounced back with a tough 14-6 victory over visiting St. Alban's Academy. The tightness of the contest impressed the local media (*Daily Chronicle*) covering the losing side from Sycamore, Illinois:

> The boys from the town showed a good fighting spirit and a good plan of attack. Morgan Park has a reputation of putting fighting aggregations on the gridiron and the fact that the game did not end with a victory for Sycamore does not mean that the St. Alban's team was an aggregation that is not a real crew of football players.

GIRLS TAGGED AT THE AUTOMOBILE ENTRANCE

Now 2-2-1, the Academy lurched into the final portion of the schedule in a most unusual setting--a forest preserve! Bloom High School of Chicago Heights, Illinois was the opponent, but one which (apparently) did not possess a suitable football field. Instead, the game was scheduled in a clearing of one of the local forest preserves. It was a festive event in the wilderness as the *Chicago Heights Star* newspaper (November 13) estimated that 1,300 attendees wrapped themselves around the temporary field of play. The host school even manufactured a method to secure some income in a situation where admission fees were not allowed:

More than 1,300 saw the game, according to the sale or disposal of tickets. As the forest preserve laws prohibit charges, girls of the school tagged [for donations] at the automobile entrance and throughout the crowd. Fans were tagged and given the opportunity to contribute what they wished, and by this source returns totaled over $200.

On the field, Bloom took advantage of a superior kicking game (along with two Academy fumbles on punts) to secure a hard-fought 16-6 victory. It is interesting to note the shift in suburban media coverage of high school football in the mid-1920s. When the Academy football program was initiated in 1894, the Chicago metropolitan newspapers usually "covered" every game, probably due to the fact that there were not many schools fielding teams for this still rather new sport. As more and more high schools opened in the city and suburbs, scores were still reported in the Chicago publications but the more "in-depth" reporting was done by the local newspapers such as the *Chicago Heights Star* which devoted nearly a full page to the Morgan Park Military Academy game and also published two other sidebars about the Bloom team in the same issue. It was coverage appropriate for a professional team in Chicago.

Following the Bloom loss, Fleming's charges were upended by Elgin Junior College 25-7, but then wrapped up the season finale with a resounding 23-0 advantage over Northwestern Military Academy. That final win brought the team's record to 3-4-1 for the 1924 season, but also paved the way for a quick return to glory amidst the finest two seasons in Coach Fleming's lengthy MPMA career.

EXTRA POINT

As the curtains closed on the 1924 football season, the final victory against Northwestern brought great joy to the MPMA students, most of whom accompanied the team to the game. *The Academy News* provided a comprehensive report on the game, but also shared some details on the trip itself, allowing the reader some insight into the adventures of high school football travel in 1924. The following is cited from *The Academy News* on December 5, 1924:

> The football team accompanied by the student body journeyed to Lake Geneva [Wisconsin] for the annual football game with Northwestern Military and Naval

Academy. For several weeks in advance they had been preparing themselves for this game and were in a state of high nervous tension as they realized that this would be a hard-fought game and success depended on their efforts. To show the depth of their loyalty the whole school agreed to go into strict training with the team. This agreement being closely adhered to by the great majority of the cadets. The cadets left campus at 7 o'clock on the day of the game, traveling to LaSalle Street Station [Chicago] in three special coaches over the Rock Island. At the station, they boarded five cars reserved on the Chicago, North Shore and Milwaukee Line to Kenosha, Wisconsin. The corps of cadets were met by a large part of the Kenosha police force and escorted to the Nash Motor Works, where Horace J. Mellum, an alumnus of the Academy, showed the corps through the plant. After the tour through the plant they had luncheon in the Nash Cafeteria. Besides the excellent food, Mr. Mellum also furnished a very good orchestra, which played intermittently throughout the meal.

When finished with their meal, the boys formed up outside the factory and had their picture taken in company formation. Later, the corps took ten buses belonging to the North Shore Line to the Northwestern campus. The only mishap encountered along the way was when one of the trucks developed carburetor trouble and was forced to put its passengers in another coach. The game started at 2:30. There was much rivalry all through the game as to cheering. The Academy displayed rooting of a superior order, due to the fact that this was the last game of the season and greater than all, must beat Northwestern.

There was much cheering at the end of the game, and it was some time before the cadets ceased to shout and boarded the buses for the return trip to Kenosha. The cadets were overjoyed at the final score and during the bus ride home sang songs and in every way conceivable showed the heights of their spirits over the victory. At the electric station, everyone joyously broke training. The corps arrived at LaSalle Street Station at 9:30 and home about 11:00.

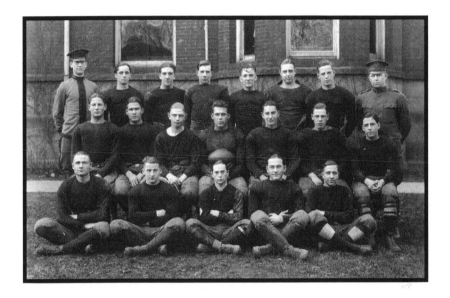

Coach Floyd Fleming (top row, far right) was a superb athlete at the University of Indiana who coached the football squad at Morgan Park Military Academy for 13 seasons and completed his career with a 49-33-12 record. Fleming's 1921 team (above) finished 2-2-1.

CHAPTER 10

Nothing Small About Shorty

"Why he weighs 260 now and made some so called
All-Americans look like stiffs!"
—Carl Brumbaugh Chicago Bears Quarterback, 1932

There was nothing small about Lloyd "Shorty" Burdick.

Not his size, his appetite, his personality, nor his gifted athletic ability.

Burdick, born August 8, 1908, entered Morgan Park Military Academy as a senior transfer student on September 16, 1925 just in time for the Academy's first football practice. Coach Floyd Fleming opened camp at 3:00 p.m. on the 16th and was a bit concerned over his prospects for the season since the Academy returned just three regulars from the previous year: Captain Harold Ollier, halfback Bill Kelly, and former center, but now a halfback, Dick Cass. Kelly was expected to be the squad's chief weapon, and on September 25 the *Southtown Economist* applauded his off-season work regimen in preparation for his senior campaign:

> Kelly is a south side boy. He proved to be a clever ground
> gainer in 1924. To get in shape for this fall he spent six
> weeks at Camp Custer following that up with some hard
> manual labor. He will be physically fit for the initial contest.

With little time to acclimate himself to his new team and teammates, Burdick easily captured a starting tackle position and promptly began forging his personal reputation in the first game against Michigan City (Indiana) High School on September 26. Although operating as a lineman, the sturdy Burdick morphed into a receiver and snared a 12-yard scoring pass for the only touchdown of the game in the Academy's 7-0 victory. His sturdy frame, estimated to be 6'5" and 230 pounds even in high school, had already landed Burdick the affectionate nickname of "Shorty." His heroic play in the Michigan City game was just the first stop in a boisterous athletic career that would take Shorty to acclaim on the gridiron at the University of Illinois and later as a member of the National Football League (NFL) champion Chicago Bears. But there's more...Burdick was also a boxer, a pro wrestler, a musician, a track star, an actor, and a real-life hero who once saved two children from near death.

There was never a dull moment around Shorty Burdick and there is much to share about his fascinating life. However, his rise to the top of the sporting world began when he transferred to the Academy from Stonington Community High School in central Illinois. He was at the Academy for just one year where he excelled in football, basketball, and track, but not in geometry!

It was a good time to be a student at the Academy. In 1925, an all-time high (to that date) of over 235 students were enrolled and the Academy administration (in the form of Superintendent/Colonel Harry Abells) established a "waiting" list for prospective attendees. In addition, the school purchased five acres of land for building expansion. The intent, according to Colonel Abells in the *Southtown Economist*, was to construct buildings (due to rapid growth) that would:

> Separate the upper and lower [grade] schools. This is to be made possible by the purchase of the five-acre plant...
> The construction of a large building which will completely house the younger boys is likely to be the next addition to the Academy.

As Burdick settled in to his dormitory room in the Academy barracks, it soon became apparent that he was receptive to trying all aspects of campus life. He eagerly posed for photos with his smaller classmates and even enjoyed a stint with the school band. Much of this activity was preserved due to the "Lloyd S. Burdick Papers" collection at the University of Illinois Archives in Champaign, Illinois. Burdick retained a scrapbook as well as numerous personal photos, some of which are shared in this book. It appears that he enjoyed each chapter of his career and never took himself too seriously, despite the fame that accompanied him throughout his life.

MORGAN PARK BATTERING RAM WAS INVINCIBLE

But back to football in 1925…

Next up for the Academy gridders was Pullman Tech High School from the far south side of Chicago. In a sloppily played game contested on a soccer field, the Academy prevailed 13-0 as Max Wortham scored twice on short rushes behind the over powering blocking of right tackle Burdick. Another shutout followed as the Academy trounced host Elmhurst Academy 34-0 on October 24. "The Morgan Park battering ram was invincible although the muddy field slowed up the action. More than once wide end runs ended disastrously when the ball carrier skidded in the mud. Nevertheless, Elmhurst was unable to stop the line drives," reported the *Southtown Economist* after the game.

In the first three victories, the Academy failed to allow a point scored by the opposition and manufactured a running game behind the staunch blocking of Burdick that appeared impossible to stop. Yet Coach Fleming had consistently demonstrated the ability to avoid predictable formations during his tenure, and the "trick" he unloaded against Chicago Latin School on October 31 must have seemed like a cruel Halloween treat to the Latin club. The game was scheduled to kick off at 11:00 a.m. at Cubs Park (renamed as Wrigley Field in 1927), home of the Chicago Cubs and the Chicago Bears. It was a thrill for both teams to take the field that morning, just a day before the Bears would entertain the Rock Island Independents in National Football League action.

What Coach Fleming plotted for Burdick and the Academy eleven that day was unusual, and a similar strategy might not receive such acclaim until Coach Mike Ditka of the Bears unleashed the huge lineman William "The Refrigerator" Perry from the Bears' backfield 60 years later during the team's Super Bowl XX championship season of 1985. Like Perry, Burdick was a large man, but also one with dexterity and quickness. During the first half, Morgan Park eased ahead 20-0, before the surprise weapon was unwrapped. Moved from his regular tackle position to the backfield, it was thought that Burdick would be used as an intimidating blocking back. Again, the sheer size of Burdick (6'5", 230) was impressive for a typical high school lineman in 1925. To place this type of athlete in the backfield where he could run or block with a full head of steam was frightening.

However, instead of playing the role of lead blocker for the offense to start the second half, Burdick happily accepted the handoff from quarterback John Arnold from his own 30-yard line and blasted through the Latin defense for a 70-yard score. "Burdick started on a rampage as soon as the second half was underway by running through the entire Latin team for a touchdown," reported the *Southtown Economist*. But Burdick was not finished: "Burdick, with one run of seventy yards and another of forty-five added twelve points to the score. Then Coach Fleming sent his second squad in to finish the game."

Burdick's "rampage" in the third quarter alone resulted in 175 yards gained on just three carries. An unidentified newspaper article found in Burdick's personal scrapbook in the University of Illinois Archives added: "The Latin School's attempts to stop the whirlwind lad had proved futile," while the *Southtown Economist* noted: "Shorty Burdick was the outstanding player of the Maroon outfit when he ran across the line for three touchdowns." For good measure, Burdick handled kick-offs and added an extra point in his abbreviated work day that resulted in a 48-0 win for the Academy.

Now 4-0 for the season, the Academy next entertained unbeaten St. Alban's on November 7. With Burdick bothered by injuries suffered in the Latin game and limited to playing only in the second quarter, the Academy relied on the running of Maxwell Wortham, who scored once and had three runs of over 50 yards each. Cass did tally three touchdowns as Morgan Park prevailed 30-0. The following week's game against Campion High School of Prairie du Chien, Wisconsin was cancelled due to rain, leaving the squad with one final game against Northwestern with the hope of completing an undefeated season. The last Academy team to accomplish this feat was the 6-0-1 club of 1910 under coaches John Anderson and A.A. Stagg.

By now the season-ending showdown with Northwestern was becoming a tradition, and the Academy viewed Northwestern as its chief rival. The date (November 21) would also be homecoming at the Academy with several pleasant activities planned to surround the football game for the "old boys." The *Southtown Economist* previewed the game, which promised to be a tight battle between two powerful prep squads:

As the two schools are old foes, the game will be the outstanding contest of this grid season. Northwestern has a record of only one defeat this season, while the Morgan Park boys have a string of victories and have not had their goal crossed.

It would be the last game for seniors such as Cass, Wortham, Ollier, Kelly, and Burdick and a victory in the finale would certainly add luster to the exceptional season that the team had compiled.

As he had been all season, Burdick was in the center of the action. Starting at right end against Northwestern, he moved over to the backfield in the first quarter and nearly scored after a 20-yard run. Burdick's big gainer set up the first tally of the day by Cass. The visitors knotted things up late in the half at 7-7, making these the first points allowed by the Academy all season. However, rushing touchdowns by Kelly and Wortham capped the scoring with the Academy finishing on top 21-7 at the end of the game. The win left the Academy with a perfect 6-0 record for the 1925 season. Even more impressive was the dominant nature of the team's wins, outscoring their opponents by a 153-7 margin in those six contests.

The 1925 campaign would prove to be the most successful of Coach Fleming's long tenure (1920-1932) as head football coach at Morgan Park Military Academy. It was also the school's first unbeaten and untied season since the "Coachless Wonders" of 1907 and would prove to be long remembered. In 1990, the *Academy Magazine* tracked down halfback Maxwell Wortham from the 1925 team. When asked about his favorite memories of his high school days, Wortham (82 at the time of the publication) quickly responded that his favorite recollection was "MPMA's 1925 Heavyweight football team which went undefeated, with only one touchdown scored by an opponent all year!"

Meanwhile Burdick, despite being at the school for just one year, managed to cram in a very busy schedule as he played football and basketball, participated in track (breaking the shot-put record), and also was part of the band. "Shorty is the big fellow who is responsible for all the oh's and ah's from the sidelines," praised the 1926 **Maroon and White** yearbook. "Although he had only one year at MPMA, he leaves a place hard to fill and we're sure that Illinois will welcome him as we did." Following his graduation from the Academy in 1926, Burdick did indeed head south to the University of Illinois to join the football team under coach Robert Zuppke. The legendary All-American Red Grange had finished his eligibility for the Illini in 1925 but Zuppke had already developed a powerful program that looked to continue the success that the team had achieved with Grange. Burdick quickly became a special part of the Champaign/Urbana campus, not only for his presence on the football field but also for other aspects of college life.

BURDICK IS BIG ENOUGH TO LICK THREE ARMY MEN

As a freshman in 1926 Burdick was not eligible to play varsity football, although he established a new freshman discus record for the track team in the spring of 1927. Despite several injuries, Burdick was a dependable varsity tackle for Coach Zuppke, including the 1927 season when the Illini finished 7-0-1 and were declared national champions. In 1928, Illinois once again captured the Big Ten championship and finished with a 7-1 mark. By Burdick's senior year, he was becoming as widely known as a wrestler as he was a football player. Shorty concluded his football career at Illinois with a 6-1-1 mark in 1929, leaving Burdick's teams with an impressive three-year record of 20-2-2. As in high school, Burdick was respected as both a determined competitor and a winner.

During his senior year of football, Burdick was injured in a game against Michigan prompting *The News-Herald* (Franklin, Pennsylvania) to report that "so valuable was his [Burdick's] ability that Coach Zuppke has been working two or three men in his position in an effort to learn just who can fill his shoes." Before the Army game in 1929 (a 17-7 Illinois victory), Zuppke praised the strength and ability of Burdick: "Burdick, our big tackle, is big enough to lick three Army men." His reputation on the wrestling mat was solidified in his senior year when Burdick finished in second place in the National Collegiate Association wrestling tournament at Penn State. That bout for the national championship was the only blemish on Burdick's senior season as he won 15 of 16 matches on his way to becoming the Big Ten heavyweight champion.

Shortly after the national tournament, Burdick decided to go pro— in wrestling! The *Chicago Evening Post* (August 20, 1930) reported on Burdick's initial foray into the world of professional wrestling:

> Lloyd Burdick, who starred on the mat and on the gridiron
> the last three years, has entered the professional wrestling
> ranks. Off to a good start, Burdick defeated Paul Harper in
> his first bout recently. It took him just nine minutes to win
> from the Houston, Texas wrestler.

At the time, Burdick was still completing his studies at Illinois with the intent of graduating with a degree in agriculture in February of 1931. He had also taken up another rugged sport in the form of boxing. In an unidentified source found in Burdick's scrapbook, he explained why he left the sport of boxing:

> I just got tired of having a headache every time an opponent
> tapped me on the jaw and decided it was made of glass. As
> I desired to engage in some combative sport, I turned to
> wrestling. I'm not sorry, either.

He wasn't a bad boxer, either, as Burdick knocked out 18 straight opponents and fought to one draw in his brief pugilistic career. As for his wrestling ambitions, Burdick participated in a "barnstorming" circuit during the winter of 1930 and 1931 and won all 14 of his matches.

But his promising football career was not over yet...

In 1931, Burdick signed with the Chicago Bears of the National Football League and soon earned a starting tackle spot. Once again, Burdick was positioned to be an integral part of a special team. As with the undefeated Morgan Park Military Academy team in his senior year, and the undefeated (and national champion) Illinois squad while in college, Burdick found himself with an enviable opportunity in the professional ranks. Owner George Halas had built a solid team on the north side of Chicago, and Burdick's teammates included future pro football Hall-of-Famers Red Grange, George Trafton, Link Lyman and Bronko Nagurski. Although the team struggled to an 8-5 record in Burdick's rookie season (1931), an unusual string of events left the Bears playing for the NFL championship in 1932—indoors! In order for this to happen, the Green Bay Packers failed to hold a commanding lead in the standings by dropping their final two games to finish with a 10-3 record. Meanwhile the Bears concluded their schedule with a wacky 6-1-6 mark while the Portsmouth Spartans ended up with a 6-1-4 finish. Since tie games did not count in the standings at the time, both Portsmouth and Chicago could claim 6-1 records (.857 winning percentage) which would place them both ahead of Green Bay 10-3, .769). Initially, the league looked at head-to-head competition between the Bears and the Spartans to identify the champion, but since both of those clashes ended in ties, it was decided to stage a playoff game in Chicago on December 18, 1932 to determine the league champion. Previously, the team with the best winning percentage was declared the champion each year, so this was the first time that the NFL conceived of a "playoff" for league honors since two clubs ended in a virtual deadlock.

QUITE LIKELY TO DEVELOP INTO A SCORING ORGY

Then, due to harsh weather and snow storms, the game was moved from Wrigley Field to Chicago Stadium, an indoor venue. A couple of years earlier, the Bears and the Chicago Cardinals played an exhibition game in this same location, so it seemed a logical solution to the weather problem. There were, however, some logistics that needed to be addressed prior to the game itself. Most importantly, the floor of the cavernous stadium would need to be adequately covered with a suitable playing surface. This was accomplished by dumping a six-inch layer of dirt and mulch over the floor "which insures good footing for the players and a cushion that will make hard tackling practical," wrote the *Chicago Herald and Examiner* the day before the game.

Next, rules to accommodate the smaller indoor field would need to be implemented. The two teams agreed that an 80-yard field would be acceptable along with normal playing rules. On the day of the game there was considerable excitement about the prospects of viewing pro football from an indoor vantage point, according to the *Chicago Herald and Examiner* (December 18, 1932):

> The Chicago Bears and Portsmouth Spartans will collide tonight in a post-season indoor professional football game at the Chicago Stadium, which appears to have stirred up the imagination of the natives considerably. There are several reasons for this state of affairs. In the first place, the game will determine the championship of the National League, 1932 variety. The prospect of viewing a steam-heated football game, particularly while sub-zero blasts are in evidence hereabouts also presents a novel appeal. The shortage of the field should be an aid to scoring and the game is quite likely to develop into a scoring orgy.

Burdick was a two-year starter at right tackle for the Bears and was once again in the lineup for the championship encounter. Burdick's blocking on offense, and his tenacious and overpowering defense, helped push the Bears to the 1932 NFL title with a 9-0 victory over the Spartans. It was Chicago's first championship since 1921, and the second of nine total team titles to date. An interesting sidebar to the game was the fact that the starting quarterback for Portsmouth, Dutch Clark, did not play in the game when he was unable to secure a leave from his regular job as basketball coach at Colorado College. Such were the challenges of the National Football League in 1932! Clark's absence certainly hurt the Spartans, since he was also the league's leading scorer during the regular season with 55 points. The championship "playoff" game in 1932 also led to a very important decision by the NFL. In 1933, the league decided to split its teams into two divisions, with the division leaders facing off in the post-season for championship honors. The Bears would return to the post-season in 1933 and defeat the New York Giants 23-21 in the first "official" league championship game—the granddaddy of today's alluring Super Bowl.

During the 1932 season, Burdick would receive high praise from his teammate, and football deity, Red Grange. In an article in the November 5 edition of the *Saturday Evening Post*, Grange showed his respect for Burdick by marveling: "Picture a fast, trimly built athlete . . . then imagine Jack Dempsey (heavyweight boxing champion) two or three inches taller and fifty pounds heavier, and you have Lloyd Burdick."

Another unidentified article in the Burdick scrapbook (most likely from 1932) includes a quote from Bears' quarterback Carl Brumbaugh regarding Burdick:

> Brumbaugh had many words of praise for Lloyd Burdick, who he says will be the greatest tackle in football next fall. "Why he weighs 260 now and what a game he played this past year. He made some so-called All-Americans look like stiffs. Dutch Clark of Portsmouth and Burdick were rated as the best prospects of the past year in pro football."

For some reason, despite the numerous accolades, a year later Burdick found himself as a member of the Cincinnati Reds of the NFL, which was actually a new franchise in 1933. The team lasted a mere two seasons in the league after finishing 3-6-1 in 1933 and 0-8 in 1934 before being barred from the NFL late in the 1934 season for non-payment of league fees. However, Burdick played only the 1933 schedule for the Reds where he quickly claimed the starting right tackle spot. The team, unfortunately, was awful, scoring just 38 points in those ten games. On December 27, 1933, Cincinnati announced (through the United Press) a blockbuster trade involving Burdick with the Portsmouth Spartans:

> The Cincinnati Reds of the National Football League completed a trade which sends lineman Lloyd Burdick to the Portsmouth Spartans for four players. Burdick, a former University of Illinois player who was with the Chicago Bears before coming to the Reds, weighs 257 pounds and is six feet, five inches tall.

Oddly enough, Burdick must have made up his mind about his football future as soon as he was informed of the big trade. A hand-written note (presumably Burdick's) in his personal scrapbook is dated December 27, 1933 and simply states: "This clipping writes *finis* to an active football career and concludes this book." There would be no more full-time football played by Lloyd "Shorty" Burdick…

PLAYING FOOTBALL WAS HARD, COACHING IS WORSE!

Instead, Burdick decided to try coaching, securing the position of head football coach at Knox College in Galesburg, Illinois prior to the 1934 season. At the time, Knox was wallowing in the depths of a 19-game losing streak. Burdick was an ideal candidate for the job and his former Illinois coach, Robert Zuppke submitted a strong recommendation (from the Burdick scrapbook) to the school's administration:

> You get a good idea of a man when he plays for your team three years as Burdick did. He is one of the finest boys I ever coached. He will be a good man for you off the field as well as on. The more you and your players see of him, the more you will like him. Coaching is not beating the tom-tom but is teaching. Burdick knows the technique and will be able to teach it.

Despite the glowing compliments and his own significant football playing success, Burdick was unable to stop the lengthy Knox losing streak as his club dropped all eight of its games to extend the negative streak to 27 straight losses. Even worse, the team failed to score a single point all season. It was the first football failure for Burdick, who decided to resign his coaching position on December 5, 1934 as reported by the *Chicago Tribune*. "I thought playing football was hard, but coaching is a lot worse," said Burdick. "I am pleased that it is going to be possible for me to go back to playing, and doubly so because I will be able to continue my law studies at the same time."

Burdick's intent was to sign with the Detroit Lions (previously known as the Portsmouth Spartans) and to attend a law school in the Detroit area. That part of the plan failed when Burdick, after a year off from playing, did not make the Lions' roster for the 1935 season. However, he was listed as a member of the team when the Lions played in an exhibition tilt after the season in Ogden, Utah in January of 1936. About that time, Burdick found permanent employment with the renowned Caterpillar Tractor Company of East Peoria, Illinois, eventually becoming the state manager for the organization. In his position, Burdick traveled widely and represented Caterpillar in such locales as Russia and Alaska. On August 9, 1945, while returning from a business trip to his home in Great Falls, Montana, Burdick was a passenger in a westbound train of the Great Northern Railroad's Empire Builder when the train was slammed from the rear by another westbound train near Michigan, North Dakota. The locomotive from the second train telescoped through the rear (sleeper) car of the first train causing horrific damage and losses. In all, 34 individuals lost their lives in the crash, including Lloyd Burdick. He was just 37 years old.

Maybe the only thing "short" about Lloyd "Shorty" Burdick was the amount of time he spent on this earth. From his undefeated high school football team at Morgan Park Military Academy, to his national championship at the University of Illinois, to his NFL title with the Chicago Bears, Burdick personified the definition of a winner. His enjoyment of life, and his inquisitive nature, enabled Burdick to continually address new challenges whether they were in the boxing or wrestling ring, or as the head coach of a college football team. He was even selected to play the role of "Pilate" in a Passion Play that was produced in Chicago for the 1933 World's Fair with a cast of 300. Ultimately, Burdick will be remembered for his big accomplishments, his large stature, and his huge personality…and, of course, as the only football player for Morgan Park Military Academy to enjoy an extended career in the National Football League!

EXTRA POINT

On February 20, 1940, Lloyd "Shorty" Burdick was seated in the lobby of a hotel in Marshalltown, Minnesota, finishing his breakfast and catching up with the news from the local paper. As he picked up his cup for a sip of coffee, Burdick noticed a ruckus out on the street, with excited citizens waving and pointing as a rusty old truck rumbled down the main street of the town. Whatever the people were agitated about, the truck driver paid no heed, and began to accelerate as the truck passed through a stop sign.

It was then that Burdick watched in horror as the truck chugged past the hotel front window. Dropping his cup of coffee, and tossing aside his newspaper, Burdick rushed out in the street and joined the others in shouting at the driver. When there was still no response, Burdick, clad in a business suit and dress shoes, began chasing the truck. Hoping against hope that he could reach the truck in time, Burdick made a wild dash to overtake the vehicle and jumped in front of it at a stop light, finally forcing the driver to stop. The angry driver jumped from his truck only to face the towering Burdick who then dropped to his knees and gently removed two young children huddled on the oversized front bumper of the truck. There, hanging on tightly to the giant, but gentle man, were the three-year-old twins of the driver who had crawled onto the truck before their father left for work. Not knowing the kids were there or in imminent danger, the driver had begun his day unaware of the frightful possibilities that could have resulted. The children were later described in national wire service articles as "crying and shaking with fright, but otherwise unhurt."

To which we may add one more attribute to the legend of Shorty Burdick—hero...

During his time at the Academy, future Chicago Bear Shorty Burdick (with tuba) was also a member of the school's band. (Courtesy of the University of Illinois Archives, Lloyd S. Burdick Papers, RS 26/20/27)

Lloyd "Shorty" Burdick was a rugged football player, but also a respected friend. Here Burdick (right) is shown with classmate Cadet Murphy Cohen in 1924. (Courtesy of the University of Illinois Archives, Lloyd S. Burdick Papers, RS 26/20/27)

At the University of Illinois, Lloyd Burdick was a nationally ranked collegiate wrestler, who also gave professional wrestling a try. As a football player, Burdick was a member of an undefeated high school team at Morgan Park Military Academy, a national collegiate champion at Illinois, and an NFL title winner with the Chicago Bears!

Football participation was offered to Morgan Park Military Academy students on a variety of levels: Heavyweight, Lightweight, and Bantamweight, as well as intramurals. Shown above is the 1925 Bantamweight team which likely required a weight limit of 125 lbs., while the limit for Lightweights was usually 150 lbs. In 1922, 83 of the 107 students in the high school grades played on one of the Academy football teams.

CHAPTER 11

The Magic Bus

"A rejuvenated aggregation swept an invading Indiana team off the field..."
—Maroon and White Yearbook, 1926

Coach Floyd Fleming was happy...or perhaps somewhat happy... when the 1926 football season began. The 1925-26 school year had been successful for Fleming, the coach of the football, basketball, and baseball teams for Morgan Park Military Academy. The football team finished undefeated with a 6-0 mark, with the basketball squad snatching second place honors in the National Academy Tournament in Madison, Wisconsin (14-4 record) and the baseball club (10-2) also enjoying satisfying results.

Now Fleming was facing a new challenge as he welcomed 50 candidates for the 1926 football team: only two starters returned from his powerful juggernaut of the year before. Looking at a bevy of new faces, Fleming would be forced to lean on those two veterans: quarterback/captain John Arnold and lineman John Sinclair.

But a new wrinkle was added to the Academy's arsenal in the summer of 1926 when the school purchased a summer camp near Traverse City, Michigan. Fleming, who also served as the school's Director of Athletics, helped promote student attendance at the camp by "encouraging" football players to participate in the camp's numerous activities. As such, Fleming could essentially operate a pre-season training camp for his club, allowing precious additional practice time during the summer months. Now, instead of a brief training session of a week or so when the players arrived on campus in the fall, Fleming could work with his players at a leisurely pace through part of the summer. The time would be used for conditioning, individual skills, and team bonding, all in a private, relaxed environment.

Also fresh in 1926 was a new athletic nickname for the school: the Warriors. Previously, the use of a nickname had been largely ignored. At times, Morgan Park Military Academy had been known as the Cadets (owing to the military presence), or as the Maroons (a nod to the University of Chicago).

By the end of the summer camp, Fleming had identified several viable and talented players to hopefully carry the Warriors through a rugged schedule in 1926. The fear of being non-competitive due to a lack of experience had swiftly disappeared during the heat of the rural Michigan workouts. *The Academy News* reported on October 6 that the team had endured a tough, no-nonsense practice schedule thus far in preparation for the season:

> With the greatest number of men out for positions on the team that ever aspired to carry the colors of M.P.M.A. on the gridiron, Coach Fleming is putting his army of fifty gridders through intensive training for the initial game of the coming season. Each day from the end of drill to Mess III [dinner] the heavyweight warriors are out on the field, rain or shine, getting in shape for the future tussles.

> The first week and a half was spent in getting in condition. Passing, tackling, and learning the fundamentals of the game took up the time during this period. On some days, weather not permitting outside drills, Coach Fleming went over the rules of the game for the coming season and explained them to the players.

GALAXY OF PIGSKIN CARRIERS

Fleming added another wrinkle to the demanding pre-season when he scheduled a scrimmage with tough Lindbloom High School of Chicago, in which no score was kept but the Warriors presented themselves well. The 1926 season started a bit late with the opener against Pullman Tech not scheduled until October 9. In a preview of the game, the *Southtown Economist* predicted big things for Coach Fleming's squad in 1926:

> Fifty Cadets went through a stiff scrimmage Saturday in lieu of a practice game to prepare them for their opening tilt this week with the Pullman Tech eleven. Coach Floyd Fleming is putting the finishing touches to what promises to be one of the strongest teams turned out at the military school in recent years. If the Cadets play true to form they should have little difficulty in rolling up a formidable count against the Techs.

The Academy club lived up to that hype by cruising past Pullman Tech 20-6 in the opener, with Arnold tossing two TD passes and rushing for the third score. Next up for the Warriors was a new opponent to the schedule, Onarga Military Academy (previously Grand Prairie Seminary) in Onarga, Illinois, about 30 miles southwest of Kankakee, Illinois. It would be Morgan Park's first long road trip of the season, but the school's emerging football team was already becoming noticed by the *Chicago Daily News*:

> Proficiency in military manners is not all that the boys at Morgan Park Military Academy acquire through their daily routines. Not a few of the future army dignitaries become so well acquainted with the dashing activities of the gridiron that they are constantly feared by rival elevens hereabouts. Much has been made of Knute Rockne's galaxy of pigskin carriers at Notre Dame, and here are fifty youths more than two-thirds of whom are football persons of no small talent. If there is strength in numbers, then Morgan Park has a football team that may need watching. Coach Floyd Fleming prides himself in the possession of no less than fourteen equally capable backfield men.

Ultimately, the Academy easily secured a 28-0 victory, which the *Southtown Economist* described as "(Red) Grange-like romps through enemy territory, and a fast-moving attack that proved too varied for the Onarga Military Academy defense, brought Floyd Fleming's Morgan Park Cadets to a 28-0 win in their first clash with the rival warriors."

However, the historical importance of the contest emerged the following Friday (October 20) when the student-managed *The Academy News* published a play-by-play account of the Onarga game. This was highly unusual. In fact, it was rare to discover a college or professional game with such astute coverage as provided by *The Academy News*. More importantly, it provided uncanny insight into the game itself, from its strategies to its statistics. *The Academy News* account of the game revealed an overwhelming rushing game by the Warriors, the more than casual use of the punt on early downs, and the unleashing of that barn-full of ball carriers by Fleming.

By charting the position of each play described by *The Academy News*, we can now (over 90 years later) visualize the on-field activity of a typical high school football game in 1926. With respect to the great writers who followed the Academy team in 1926, the following is a more modern take (followed by full game statistics) on the Onarga game, produced after creating a statistical chart based on game information published in *The Academy News*:

ACADEMY GROUND GAME OVERWHELMS ONARGA 28-0

Behind a stable of powerful running backs, Morgan Park Military Academy gave no quarter in its 28-0 romp over Onarga Military Academy yesterday in Onarga, Illinois. The bruising Warrior line pushed the Onarga defense to its limit, gobbling up 415 yards on the ground, including a 174-yard rushing effort by quarterback John Arnold. Arnold was just one of nine backs who gained positive yardage during the game, while his defensive counterparts held Onarga to a stingy total of just two yards.

Morgan Park elected to receive the opening kickoff and Glenn Kiskaddon made the return to his own 32. From there, an 11 play Academy drive stalled at the Onarga 25-yard line. Onarga decided to vacate its poor field position by punting on first down, but senior Jim Russell's punt traveled a mere 17 yards. However, the punt was fumbled by Morgan Park and recovered by Onarga on its own 42-yard marker. After a pair of rushing plays failed to gain even a single yard, Russell kicked it away again on third down, this time succeeding with a boot that was brought back to the Academy 36. After consistent rushing gains by Albert "Stewie" Stuart, Jim Hapeman, Glenn Kiskaddon, and Ed Lutomski, the ball rested on Onarga's 48. From there, Arnold bounced outside behind some fierce blocking and pranced all the way to the five-yard line, a 43-yard pickup. Three plays later, Arnold plunged in from the one, followed by a successful Kiskaddon kick, and the Academy grabbed its first lead of the day at 7-0.

On the ensuing kickoff, Onarga halfback Bob Hainline provided the home crowd with its biggest thrill of the day when he raced 45 yards with the return to midfield. But a five-yard penalty, followed by a five-yard loss, forced Russell to punt again on third down. His booming kick was good for a mighty

55 yards and left the Academy's offense in a deep hole at its own five-yard line. During the ensuing drive, the first quarter ended with Onarga trailing 7-0. Morgan Park piled up 155 yards on the ground (on just 17 carries) during the first stanza while Onarga managed to run only six official plays for minus five yards. Three of those plays were punts as Russell attempted to obtain better field position for his club.

Due to Onarga's unwillingness to send out its offense against the overpowering Academy defense, the hosts were once again limited in the second quarter with just eight plays (-16 yards), with four of those snaps being punts. Twice Russell punted on first down, but the Onarga strategy seemed to be working; its defense stiffened and held the visitors scoreless in the second period with the score remaining 7-0 at the break.

Early in the second half, Arnold lost a fumble on his own 45, enabling Onarga to mount its most successful drive of the contest. Assisted by a penalty and a ten-yard jaunt by Homer Crowden, Onarga pushed down to the Academy 30-yard line where a Russell toss on fourth down fell incomplete, turning the ball over to the Warriors.

After an 11-play Morgan Park drive into Onarga territory, Arnold overthrew his intended receiver resulting in an interception. Onarga attempted just one play from its own 37 (a two-yard loss) before Mr. Russell shanked a ten-yard punt on second down, leaving Arnold and company in excellent field position from the Onarga 45. From there, it took Arnold just one play to befuddle the defense as he swept off right tackle and raced in for the score, establishing a 13-0 lead for the Academy midway through the period. The extra point attempt failed.

The Academy scored quickly after Onarga decided to punt on first down following receipt of the kickoff. The Warriors set up shop on the Onarga 40-yard line. Two plays later, Karl "Boiler" Brusa exploded off tackle for a 37-yard score, but once again, the extra point was not good, leaving Morgan Park with a 19-0 advantage late in the third quarter. Lutomski's long kickoff was downed by Onarga on its own ten, before the hosts gave it right back via a Russell punt. With the ball on Onarga's 40, the Warriors marched downfield until Onarga intercepted a wayward pass by Stuart on its own five-yard line. As had been the habit all day, Onarga neglected its offense and sent Russell back to punt from his own end zone. An errant snap from center flew over Russell's head for a safety and the Academy margin grew to 21-0. The scoring concluded for the day on the ensuing free kick by Onarga when Hapeman gathered in the ball on his own 45, faked left, then moved back to the right side and rambled untouched for 55 yards and a touchdown. Evans was brought in to drop kick the extra point and was successful, building the final margin to 28-0 at the conclusion of the third quarter.

In a questionable coaching decision following the Hapeman score, Onarga kicked the ball off to Morgan Park instead of receiving the kick, thus negating any opportunity to cut into the large deficit. The Warriors ran off 19 plays to just one for Onarga in the fourth stanza with the ball ending up on the Onarga one-yard line as the final gun sounded the end of the game. The fourth quarter, although scoreless, was dominated by the Academy rushing game in an effort to gobble up time off the clock and preserve the lead. Overall, nine players carried the ball for the winners during the afternoon for a whopping 415 yards in total. Aside from Arnold's 174 yards, Brusa chipped in with 81 yards on eight carries, and Kiskaddon rushed for 45 yards in 14 attempts. Arnold, Stuart, and Lutomski combined to complete just one pass in eight attempts, with three interceptions. Those three interceptions, combined with one lost fumble, gave Onarga four turnovers which the losers were unable to capitalize upon. For Onarga, Russell's punting effort (11 for 313 yards/31.3 average) was about the only positive result for the contest. Overall, Onarga rushed 15 times for two yards, and failed in its only pass attempt. In contrast, Morgan Park rolled off 86 plays enroute to its dominant victory, moving the club to 2-0 on the season.

From the unwillingness of Onarga to test the Academy defense, to the over powering rushing attack of the Warriors, the in-depth reporting of *The Academy News* revealed an unusual peek at high school football strategy in the 1920s. One may attempt to grasp the thinking of Onarga's coaching staff, since it appeared to abandon any offensive efforts after just one series of downs. It must have been frustrating for the home fans to witness the excruciatingly long marches of the Academy offense, and then when the opportunity to respond presented itself to Onarga, the ball was usually punted right back to the Academy thus draining any hope for victory from the aspirations of the Onarga loyalists.

Would the rout have been any worse had Onarga chosen to initiate any type of offense? Or, was the hope of Onarga merely to keep the game close against an over-matched foe? Either way, we can only speculate regarding the intent of Onarga, but at the same time, appreciate the efforts of the editors of *The Academy News* for preserving this very unique piece of football history!

Onarga Academy Game Statistics
October 16, 1926
(Compiled from The Academy News Game Report)

Rushing Morgan Park Military Academy	Att.	Yds.	TD		Rushing Onarga Military Academy	Att.	Yds.	TD	
Arnold	22	174	2		Crowden	6	25	0	
Brusa	8	81	1		Songer	5	-6	0	
Hapeman	10	22	1		Hainline	3	-12	0	
Kiskaddon	14	45	0		Russell	1	-5	0	
Stuart	8	38	0		Total	15	2	0	
Lutomski	1	3	0						
Barber	7	25	0						
Carlson	7	24	0						
Korten	1	3	0						
Total	78	415	4						

Passing Morgan Park Military Academy	Comp.	Att.	Yds.	Int.	Passing Onarga Military Academy	Comp.	Att.	Yds.	Int.
Arnold	0	4	0	1	Russell	0	1	0	0
Stuart	0	1	0	1	Total	0	1	0	0
Lutomski	1	3	9	1					
Total	1	8	9	3					

Receiving Morgan Park Military Academy	No.	Yds.	TD		Receiving Onarga Military Academy	No.	Yds.	TD	
Drake	1	9	0		None				
Total	1	9	0						

Total Yards Morgan Park Military Academy					Total Yards Onarga Military Academy				
Rushing	415				Rushing	2			
Passing	9				Passing	0			
Total	424				Total	2			

Punting Morgan Park Military Academy	No.	Yds.	Avr.		Punting Onarga Military Academy	No.	Yds.	Avr.	
Lutomski	4	138	34.5		Russell	10	313	31.3	
					Bolt	1	28	28.0	

THE MERCIFUL WHISTLE SPARED A MORE TERRIFIC DRUBBING

If there was any doubt about the Academy offense in 1926, that inclination vanished the following week (October 23) when the Warriors blasted Elmhurst High School 63-0. Addison Barber, who was limited to seven carries for 25 yards against Onarga, exploded for four touchdowns, while another back, William Olsen, who failed to earn a carry the week before, added two more scores. The Elmhurst contest was one-sided from the start in the post-game coverage provided by the *Southtown Economist*:

> Using a battering line attack mingled with a fine open field running game and some clever passing, the Cadets swept down the field again and again. When the merciful whistle spared the Elmhurst eleven from a more terrific drubbing, the Warriors had crossed their opponents' goal line for ten touchdowns. From the opening kick-off until the close of the game the Cadets might have been in drill formation on their own campus instead of on a football field, so easily and without effort did they move up and down the gridiron for their scores.

In the excitement of the strong start to the season, a determined group from Wayland Academy (Beaver Dam, Wisconsin) strolled in to Morgan Park on October 30 and stung the hosts with an unexpected 7-0 defeat. The visitors arrived in a brightly painted school bus that could easily be identified on the Academy campus. Perhaps the bus was magical in nature, since neither the Academy, nor Wayland Academy anticipated such a result. Prior to the game, the Wayland administration sent out a missive to friends and alumni in the Chicago area seeking their support for the Wayland club. The tone of the letter was gloomy, in contrast to the exquisite colors of the bus. With injuries and lack of depth, the Wayland note moaned, there would be little chance for victory against powerful Morgan Park Military Academy, especially without the in-person support of the Wayland alumni in the Chicago region. The Wayland petition initiated a strong response, with over 100 supporters making the journey out to Morgan Park for the game. The *Wayland Greetings*, an alumni publication (November 1926), posted an update following the contest, including the sharing of a letter received from a prominent Wayland Academy parent commenting on the importance of the victory over the Academy (and his sheer happiness!) which follows:

> From several sources, including the Chicago press, I learned that the Morgan Park Academy has a football team which had not been defeated for two years. Your postal requesting the friends of Wayland to attend the game last Saturday told of your crippled team and confirmed the general opinion that Wayland was facing sure defeat. Wayland's bright colored bus which occupied a conspicuous place on the athletic field at Morgan Park was a joy to behold and was an important factor in dispelling the gloom of Wayland's rooters of whom there were a goodly number. I congratulate the artist. If the bus had been black instead of white and red, I would have bought some crepe before the game.
>
> When Wayland's fighting team went into action we realized that the Morgan Park team was to receive the surprise of its life, but the most optimistic of us could hardly hope for a victory. We were, however, treated to an exhibition of football which would have done credit to a major college team. On the whole, it was a fast, errorless and clean game, and was won by the best team. I have only one regret—no admission was charged for the best football game I ever saw. No friend of Wayland would dare say, publicly at least, that the game was not worth more than the Army-Navy game which will be played at the stadium in Chicago in a few weeks. It is morally, if not legally, wrong to get something for nothing and to ease my conscience I am enclosing a check for $50.00 for your athletic fund.

That $50.00 check mentioned above would be worth nearly $700 in today's dollars, but it also demonstrated the passion and support that the fan base possessed for the competing schools in 1926. For the Academy, the loss to stubborn Wayland Academy was a bit of a surprise, but the team redeemed itself the following week against another new opponent, Howe Military Academy from Howe, Indiana. After a scoreless first half, the Warriors bounced back to rout the visitors 35-0 behind a pair of touchdowns by Stuart. "By coming back in the second half, a rejuvenated aggregation," gushed the **Maroon and White** yearbook, "the heavies swept an invading Indiana team off the field."

The 1926 campaign concluded with a 0-0 tie with St. Alban's on November 13, and then a season-ending 20-0 shutout of rival Northwestern on November 20. "After the game was over everybody felt happy and the Cadets were driven to town where they had a cafeteria supper. The second largest score by which the Warriors have ever defeated the Lake Geneva cadets on Wisconsin soil was chalked up that day," remembered the **Maroon and White** in a fitting tribute to another crowning Academy football accomplishment.

With the season wrapping up with a 5-1-1 record, Fleming's gridders compiled a nifty 11-1-1 mark over the past two seasons (1925-26). More importantly, the Academy allowed only three touchdowns (20 points) over those 13 games while cranking out 319 points on offense. As such, Morgan Park Military Academy had reclaimed its status as one of the toughest high school football programs in the Midwest. But would Coach Fleming be able to continue his extraordinary winning touch in the future?

EXTRA POINT

In the fall of 1927, Morgan Park Military Academy published its annual school catalog, which provided prospective students, and their families, with everything they might need to know about the Academy, its campus, its expectations, and its opportunities. For the first time, the 1927 catalog seemed to utilize the renewed success of the football team as a recruiting tool, touting both the victories—and the spirit—of the gridiron program. The following is reprinted from that catalog and reflects nicely upon the reality and enthusiasm from the very noteworthy 1925 and 1926 seasons:

FOOTBALL SEASON

That first football practice is a stirring affair. Lads of all sizes gather on the athletic field to be culled over by the various coaches and sorted out so that they may practice with cadets of their own size. This preliminary sizing up is not final, for a person's capacity often is an outstanding factor in his being shifted to another team where his ability or lack of ability makes him better suited.

During the past two years it has been not at all an uncommon thing to find five or six inter-school football games being played on the various athletic fields during a single day. Thus, it can be seen that with all this competition with outside schools, every boy at Morgan Park has an opportunity to at least try for one of the squads. The team managers also are a necessity, and some boys who are compelled to give up active participation in the sport find their service to the school in this.

Naturally the first team games are the ones that draw the most interest, and on the day of the "big" game with a rival military school there is a real tension felt on the campus, as the zero hour approaches. With the cadet corps seated in the bleachers and a crowd of several thousand crowding around the sideline, the kickoff comes and the fight is on. Victories are all right, but the big thing is the fighting spirit, and it is no idle boast that every loyal cadet makes, when he says, "Every Morgan Park team fights!"

Coached by a man [Floyd Fleming] who has had years of experience with growing boys, the grid teams do not become a menace to health in any way. They are a remarkable developer for muscle and brawn, not to mention for nerves, and mental quickness.

CHAPTER 12

Wrigley Field, Camp Traverse and the Slippery Pigskin

"Several sideline attractions will be put on, featuring an Indian war dance by a group of Osage Indians, who will accompany the squad..."
—Southtown Economist, 1928

HERE WE ARE!

With that sound declaration, *The Academy News* proudly pushed out an unusual Saturday edition on October 8, 1927. Although the Academy football team had opened its season with a 7-7 draw with Onarga Military Academy just a few hours earlier, readers were delighted to see complete coverage of that game by six o'clock that same evening. It was a fantastic accomplishment for the student newspaper, especially considering that even the major metropolitan newspapers usually required at least an overnight stay to prepare for morning editions.

But here it was—on a cool autumn afternoon—and the students were able to gobble up all of the information on that day's game...and *The Academy News* was not shy about its major accomplishment:

> With Lindbergh and Chamberlin crossing the Atlantic and Goebel and Maitland winging their way to Hawaii in record time it was up to *The News* to try its wings in an effort to set a new speed record. Here we are! Thru the

cooperation of Mr. J. H. Volp and his loyal workers of the
Blue Island Publishing Corporation, *The News* believes it
has set a record for speed for high school publications. By
using modern speed machinery this paper is in your hands
even before the Chicago dailies have the dope! We are off
for a big year. Give us your backing.

In comparing its accomplishment to recent aeronautical feats by
Charles Lindbergh and Clarence Chamberlin in their rivalry to be the
first to fly across the Atlantic, as well as similar early Pacific flights from
the United States to Hawaii by Art Goebel, jr. and Lester Maitland, *The
Academy News* did break new ground in high school newspaper publishing.
Lindbergh won the race to be the first pilot to fly solo across the Atlantic
when he landed near Paris on May 20, 1927 and became an instant world-
wide celebrity. Chamberlin was the first to transverse the Atlantic with
a passenger when he set his plane down in Germany on June 4, 1927.
Military pilot Maitland, along with Albert Hegenberger, was the first pair
to cross the Pacific (from California) when they landed in Hawaii on June
29, 1927. Finally, civilian Arthur Goebel, Jr. (with navigator Bill Davis)
captured the Dole Air Race from California to Hawaii on August 17, 1927
to complete an exciting summer of aeronautical achievements in 1927.

SWIFT PLAY OF LUCK LET SLIPPERY PIGSKIN BOUNCE INTO HIS HANDS

Although publishing a student newspaper in an accelerated fashion certainly did not compare with non-stop flights across dangerous oceans at the
time, it was a singular distinction that *The Academy News* was able to effectively compete with the metropolitan daily newspapers in terms of local
sports coverage. The primary reason for the rapid publishing process was to
celebrate the opening of the 1927 Academy football season and to provide
same-day coverage of the opening game. Even the local area weekly, the
Southtown Economist was impressed by this accomplishment: "The editors
of the 'Academy News' accomplished a journalistic feat when they appeared
'on the street' with complete details of the game in their publication before
six o'clock." And, although rushed, the writing in that issue was not bad
either as the "lead" to the game account demonstrated:

It looked like a bad day for Morgan Park when Captain Hays of Onarga, with a light heart, turned his boys around on the gridiron for the start of the last quarter. But the downstate team hadn't counted on Robert Wallace's fleet heels or the swift play of luck which let a slippery pigskin bounce into his hands. Then too, the great interference he got as he galloped 75 yards thru the whole Onarga team wasn't in the plans that Onarga had made for the ending of this opening game of the newly formed Mid-West prep school conference.

But there was more progressive news included in this express issue regarding the school and the football program in the fall of 1927. For the first time in years, Morgan Park Academy agreed to participate in a new circuit, called the Mid-West Prep Conference, composed entirely of "academy" high schools. Joining Morgan Park in this effort were Onarga, St. Alban's, Elgin, Wayland, and Milwaukee Country Day School as indicated by the *True Republican* newspaper (April 30) in Sycamore, Illinois:

All these schools are private institutions and they are not eligible to join their state high school associations, but they may compete with high schools in every way except in tournaments and track meets. According to the bylaws of the Mid-West Conference members must play at least four of the schools in football to lay claim to the championship.

On campus, construction began on two major projects: Alumni Memorial Hall and Hansen Hall. A huge fund-raising campaign bolstered in part by high-profile alumni football players such as John Kenfield and Albert Benbrook, set its sights on the lofty goal of securing $50,000 to support the project. Alumni Hall was designed to accommodate 500 people in its dining facility and also featured a memorial staircase, both of which are in existence today. As the Academy planned for its future with the ambitious building projects, student enrollment (both Lower and Upper schools) jumped to 310 to start the school year, the largest number in history. And, just as Alumni Hall opened in late 1927, the Academy announced the imminent construction of still another building, this one to be called North Hall. Designated primarily as the barracks (or sleeping quarters) for about 150 boarding students, construction would begin in January of 1928 after initial design work by Ralph Oliver. The new building would be fire proof and would cost the princely sum of about $150,000.

With all of the construction activity around the campus, some students may have failed to notice that the football team struggled through a 2-3-1 season in 1927, with a concluding 20-6 win over St. Alban's being the highlight of a tough season. The talent of junior quarterback Robert Wallace helped the Warriors remain competitive, although depth and overall talent doomed the club to just a third-place finish in the inaugural season of the Mid-West Conference. The school yearbook, now called **The Skirmisher** summarized the season thusly:

> There being only two lettermen back from last year (1926), the coaches had an inexperienced team to start the season with. In mid-season, a good many of the players were visited by illness which reduced the spirit of the game... When the Cadets entered the field they found themselves considerably outweighed but they decided to fight all the way.

As the 1927 season wound down with few victories, the students were kept appraised of some recent graduates of the Academy who were making an impact on the collegiate football level that season. Among these players were Shorty Burdick at Illinois, Dick Cass at Navy, Max Wortham at Rice, and David Priess at Chicago. Perhaps the revered Coach Fleming hoped that the success of these members of the alumni would inspire his returning players as he plotted the means to reverse the team's gridiron fortunes in 1928.

HUSKY YOUTHS CARRIED SUITCASES
WITH LARGE LEATHER HELMETS

For Fleming, the easiest, and most visible, change was to formalize the pre-season training session at Camp Traverse in Michigan (approximately 300 miles from Morgan Park). In 1928, Fleming likely persuaded the administration to allow his "voluntary" football camp to become mandatory. The response was enthusiastic, as 22 players willingly registered for the program, according to **The Skirmisher**:

> There were a number of lettermen who returned and in order to get a good start and do away with the time

ordinarily spent in conditioning, a football camp was organized. The camp was held in the last two weeks of August at Camp Traverse. There were twenty-two aspirants to places on the team who attended, and they enjoyed the camp so much that it will be continued in future years.

The Academy News (September 12, 1928) provided an "inside" perspective of the camp schedule and activities:

> The old lodge at Camp Traverse probably breathed a sigh of relief on August 22, when the regular camp closed. But nobody thinks of a building and on Saturday morning, August 25, the entire camp was shocked out of its false security by the descent of a score or so husky youths who carried suitcases with large leather helmets strapped onto them. Football camp had started!

The first few days of camp were marked initially by arrival bed assignments, then by conditioning and long hikes, probably part of Coach Fleming's efforts to quickly round the players into football shape, according to *The Academy News*:

> Then one bright day (the field having been fixed the day before) football practice started in earnest. Up and down the field, time after time, charging and duck walking is hard work and none know it better than those who did it at camp. After everybody had begun to get in fairly good shape, Captain Fleming started to teach them how to tackle and block. "Hit him with your shoulder"— "Not that way—that's an arm tackle"— "Low, low, don't neck him"— "Hold him!! Why you had him and let him go;" these and other exclamations were heard all over the field. The squad soon began to look like something.

Fleming, along with assistant coach George Mahon, instituted a strict schedule for the campers, which included double practices balanced by leisurely swimming time and plenty of food:

6:30   First call

6:35   Reveille and dip

7:00   Mess I

8:45   First practice

11:00 Recall

11:05 Swim

12:30 Mess II

1:45   Second practice

4:00   Recall

4:15   Swim

6:00   Mess III

8:30   Taps

When the football camp finally concluded, *The Academy News* reported that the experience itself was certainly appreciated by the players:

> Every fellow felt glad that he had come. Both for the knowledge of football gained and for the feeling of being in good condition and good company. All in all, everyone feels that the camp was a great success and should be a great help in putting Morgan Park at the head of the conference.

As the school year began, there was speculation that the Academy would generate another very strong football team in 1928. The October 4 issue of the *Chicago Daily Journal* was particularly fond of the Warriors and the team's capable quarterback, Bob Wallace:

> Led by "Old Reliable" himself, Capt. Wallace, the Morgan Park Military Academy football team promises to leave ruin in its wake in prep circles this season. Playing his third season on the team, Wallace, who is by instinct a footballer, is expected to make an enviable rep. However, as far as that goes, he already has made a rep as a great ball carrier, quick thinker, and clever general. A natural born leader, Wallace will go down in academy gridiron history in the middle west. He is calling signals from the quarterback position on

one of the strongest, if not the most formidable, teams that ever represented the institution.

Despite the optimism heading into the season, Coach Fleming still needed to prepare his charges for what might have been the toughest schedule ever assembled for a Morgan Park Academy football team. Aside from the usual tough foes such as Wayland Academy and Northwestern Military Academy, Fleming also added three new challenging opponents: defending Chicago Catholic League (and city) champion Mount Carmel High School, St. Aquinas (Wisconsin), and powerful Missouri Military Academy from Mexico, Missouri. The last of those three new foes would be entertained at Wrigley Field, home of the Chicago Cubs. The game with Missouri Military Academy had been widely anticipated since the news of the looming clash was announced the previous March. Both Wrigley Field and Soldier Field were considered for the inter-sectional match-up before the schools agreed upon Wrigley Field and settled on the date of November 10 for the outing.

DOUBLE THICKNESS OF GLASS BETWEEN THE AUDIENCE AND THE STUDIO

The month of October would prove to be a busy one for the students of Morgan Park Military Academy. On October 3, the Warriors struggled through a 0-0 draw in the opening game with St. Aquinas as veteran quarterback Wallace was unable to unlock the stingy St. Aquinas defense. But the very next day, Coach Fleming enjoyed a brief brush with fame as he was invited to appear on mega radio station WLS in Chicago to discuss both football and sportsmanship. *The Academy News* (September 26, 1928) previewed the appearance with a tongue-in-cheek show of loyalty for the Academy coach on his eagerly awaited jump into the media spotlight: "The cadets will be on hand [at WLS] for the benefit of Captain Fleming. We are told there is a double thickness of glass between the audience room and the studio."

Freed from his media obligations following his appearance on WLS, Fleming re-focused on the second game of the young campaign against Catholic League power Mount Carmel. The "Carmelites" were was fresh off an undefeated (9-0-1) season in 1927 under Coach Tom Reardon and was well-prepared in a 13-6 decision over the Academy on October 6. But

Wallace and company reversed course a week later with a convincing 14-0 victory over stubborn Wayland Academy.

The following week marked the long-awaited dedication (on October 21) of the two newest buildings on campus: Alumni Memorial Hall and Hansen Hall. The completion of these two massive structures was a huge accomplishment for the growing academy, since the school was now adequately prepared for the future to offer more lodging space as well as sufficient classroom facilities. In addition, the largest existing building on campus, Blake Hall, was completely remodeled and ready for expanded usage. A gala celebration was planned to celebrate the dual dedications on October 21 as documented by the *Southtown Economist*:

> Gathering at the gymnasium, those participating in the exercises will parade to the Alumni building. Led by the school band and cadet corps, the alumni will head the procession followed by the faculty, trustees, and those guests invited to sit on the platform. Following the program, an inspection of the school, particularly of the new buildings and of Blake Hall, which is newly remodeled, will follow. A dress parade of the cadets will bring the day's program to a close. Alumni Memorial Hall houses the kitchen and dining room for the cadets, lounge, alumni club room, mothers' room, trophy room, library and occasional rooms for use of the alumni. Hansen Hall is the new barracks for upper school cadets. For the present, the two upper floors are used as barracks and the first floor for classrooms.

In 2017, Morgan Park Academy completed a special renovation of the forgotten top (fourth) floor of Hansen Hall. This spacious area had been unused for decades and served primarily as an "attic" for long-discarded fixtures and equipment such as old dormitory beds, furniture and even an aged automobile engine block! Although the fourth floor was always locked, over the years a few enterprising students managed to gain access to the attic and used this opportunity to scrawl their names or initials on the walls as proof of their presence. The remodeling of the area revealed huge one square foot support beams along with wonderful woodwork in certain locations. In a nod to its past, the Academy preserved the beams and enclosed two of the "autograph" areas in plastic so that future generations might remember the past history of the room, which is now a comfortable student lounge and study area.

208

OSAGE INDIANS WILL ACCOMPANY THE SQUAD

For the football team in 1928, two wins in the next three outings left the club with a 3-2-1 record leading up to the highly anticipated game at Wrigley Field on November 10 with Missouri Military Academy. Enthusiasm for the contest was rampant on the Academy grounds and all of the major Chicago metropolitan newspapers were avidly reporting on the game as well since it featured two schools with powerful football reputations, including one from a distant location outside the Chicago area. A special train was scheduled to leave the day before the game with the Missouri contingent, while the Academy arranged 20 buses to transport its students and followers to the north side of Chicago for the encounter. Instructions were posted around the Morgan Park campus indicating that the buses would depart at 12:30 p.m. for the game which was billed as the "Missouri-Illinois Military Academy Championship Game." Missouri Military entered the contest with a perfect 4-0 record without having allowed a single point scored against the team in those first four encounters. The *Southtown Economist* reported (November 6) that:

> Both squads stand high in their respective prep leagues and a fast game is in prospect. The entire student body of the Missouri school will be in the stands, while hundreds of Morgan Park alumni are expected to swell the crowd.

The *Chicago Daily Journal* was even more exuberant in its preview:

> The south side suburbanites (Morgan Park) are showing much class this season, in fact the eleven is the most formidable that has been developed at the school in several seasons, and, with reports to the effect that the "Show Me" outfit also is well organized, the battle promises to be a hummer. Several sideline attractions will be put on, featuring an Indian war dance by a group of Osage Indians, who will accompany the squad, which, by the way, will make the trip here by special train. The Missouri lads will not want for encouragement for the stage, either, as a good portion of the town of Mexico is planning to tail along.

Colorful marching displays by both sets of student corps added to the jovial atmosphere as nearly 5,000 attendees flocked to Cub's Park for the 3:00 kick-off. The game itself proved to be quite competitive as the visitors edged ahead 7-0 at the half. Both teams elected to punt early and often on their possessions. Entering the final period, Missouri still maintained a tight 13-7 lead, before an Academy fumble deep in its own territory enabled Missouri Military to score once more for the final 19-7 count. After the game, students and players from both schools enjoyed a banquet and dance at the Hotel Sherman in downtown Chicago where *The Academy News* (November 13) observed that:

> Although their goal-line had been crossed for the first time in two years, the spirits of the out-of-town cadets were at an exceedingly high level. After the food had been served, during which everybody sang songs, there were speeches by representatives from the two schools.

A dance followed dinner with the evening's festivities concluding at 11:00 p.m. according to *The Academy News*:

> Taps for Missouri was one half hour later. Those from M.P. came home on the eleven forty-five train. It might be said that the bugler was not loved the next morning when he blew reveille!

UNDOUBTEDLY THE WORK OF GANGSTERS

Unfortunately, the end of the evening's party became the beginning of a nightmare for a couple of brothers from the Missouri Military Academy group due to an accelerated case of what we might now call "road rage." Chester Acher, a 16-year old student at the Missouri school was in town for the Academy game and was pleased to have the opportunity to meet with his older brother John, a 21-year old fullback on the Northwestern University football team in nearby Evanston, Illinois. After the Missouri Military Academy prevailed in its joust with the Warriors, Chester arranged to meet John at the big dinner/dance at the Hotel Sherman. Meanwhile, John had played a key role in Northwestern's 7-6 win over Purdue University the same day.

When the evening's events concluded at the Sherman, the two brothers decided to borrow a car and sample some of downtown Chicago's night life. While driving down Michigan Avenue on the east side of Chicago's famed "Loop" area, the car driven by John Acher accidentally scraped the front fender of a passing vehicle, according to *The Sedalia* (Missouri) *Democrat* on November 12:

> A moment later the larger car overtook them. One of its occupants, waving a revolver, stood on the running board and ordered Acher to leave his car. Mr. Acher slumped to the ground as two bullets struck him. The sedan sped away through the loop and eluded police who gave chase. Commissioner of Police (John) Stege said the shooting was "undoubtedly the work of gangsters. The car they used, the fact that they carried guns, and their general behavior all point to that," he said.

Other early journalistic accounts indicated that Acher was either slain or paralyzed in the incident. However, he underwent immediate surgery but never recovered and passed away from his injuries at his home in Ft. Dodge, Iowa in May of 1929. Earlier in the evening at the banquet, the sponsor of the event, Mr. Jonas Mayer expressed his hope that the game between the two schools would become an annual event. Perhaps due to the attack on the Acher brothers in Chicago, the two schools never met again on the football field.

THE MUSIC WAS UNUSUALLY GOOD

With just two games remaining on the 1928 schedule, Wallace scored twice to pace the Warriors to a 24-0 win over visiting Howe Military Academy on November 17. The topsy-turvy season ended with a somewhat surprising 25-19 loss to St. Alban's of Sycamore, Illinois. The victory allowed St. Alban's to claim the conference championship as the Academy finished with that 4-4-1 record. About the only highlight of the week for the Academy was the inquisitive nature of the local citizens in DeKalb, Illinois who needed some explanation from the evening edition (November 24) of the *Daily Chronicle* newspaper:

> Many young men were noted on the street today, who were in uniform. It was a contingent from Morgan Park Military Academy of Morgan Park, Illinois. They came to witness

ANSWER :

a team for their own school.

And what better way for the Academy to celebrate a somewhat successful season in 1928? As usual, the last big event prior to the Christmas
break was the annual football dance, held in the school gymnasium on
112th Street (which still stands today). *The Academy News* (December 19)
captured the excitement of the festivities and aptly described the cheerful
decorations:

> Without a doubt, this affair takes its place as the best
> social event of the fall or early winter season. The music
> was unusually good and everybody had a good time.
> The usually bleak looking gymnasium was given color
> and school spirit in honor of the occasion. Over the two
> backboards were the scores of the Northwestern game.
> Maroon and white streamers hung from the ceiling to the
> floor and on these were placards bearing the names of all
> the prominent players. The dance floor was laid out in the
> form of a gridiron.

Among the 16 "emblem" winners from the 1928 football team was
a 147-pound two-year starter at guard by the name of William Cabrera.
As part of the expanded Academy recruiting process, Cabrera, a native of
Mexico, enrolled in the Academy Lower (grade) School in October of 1920
at the age of nine and graduated from Morgan Park Military Academy on
June 12, 1929. Cabrera was welcomed by both his fellow students and
teammates, who probably had no idea that his father, Luis (1876-1954),
a prominent lawyer and politician, was also the recent Secretary of the
Treasury under Mexican President Venustiano Carranza. Later in life, the
elder Cabrera twice turned down requests to run for President of Mexico.
William (born Guillermo) was a tough, albeit undersized lineman for the
Academy football squad, who earned high grades on the field and in the
classroom, excelling in American history and algebra. His presence at the
Academy was the positive result of aggressive marketing by the school since
the dire days of late 1914 when the Academy nearly closed its doors for
good. Its efforts to attract bright, determined students was evident since
the school first opened its doors in 1873 as the Mount Vernon English,
Classical and Military School. By 1928, the school was able to balance its

ANSWER

efforts to recruit students from prominent (i.e. wealthy) families as well as to meet the needs of educating less affluent local residents.

MORGAN PARK HAS A GREAT TEAM THIS YEAR

Once again in 1929, Coach Floyd Fleming chose to utilize the welcoming, but isolated, environs of Camp Traverse to prepare for the football season. This voluntary boarding session was open to all students who wished to secure a position on the upcoming football roster. Fleming anticipated that 30-40 athletes would register for the camp at the generous fee of $40 per person. As usual, *The Academy News* (August 13) provided all of the needed information for prospective campers:

> Camp will open Saturday, August 24th and will close Friday, September 6th. Boys will leave Chicago on Pere Marquette Railway from the Grand Central Station, corner Wells and Harrison Streets, August 23rd at 8:45 p.m. Daylight Saving Time. The railroad fare is $19 for the round trip, upper berth, $3 and lower berth, $3.75. The fee for the football camp is $40. A letter from Captain Fleming states that the camp is primarily a conditioning camp although fundamentals of play, instructions on the game and rules, take about half of the time.

Upon completion of the Camp Traverse practices, Fleming returned to campus to begin season drills in earnest, welcoming 125 candidates to the Heavyweight and Lightweight (generally under 150 lbs.) varsity teams. Assisting Fleming once again would be George Mahon, who would later become the head coach for what might be the school's greatest season ever in 1939. Fleming had hoped to avoid the slow start of the past two seasons but watched as his team faltered against Loyola Academy (13-6) and Calumet High School of Chicago (8-7) to open the season. Halfback Elliott Thrasher scored on an impressive 70-yard run but was later caught in his own end zone for a safety, allowing Calumet those two important additional points for the victory.

The first win was over a new opponent, Milwaukee (Wisconsin) University High School by a score of 13-7, before the Warriors settled for a scoreless tie with Onarga Military Academy in a game that was covered by the *Onarga Leader and Citizen*:

Onarga Military School's first football game away from home did not result in a way that was pleasing to all Onarga followers, yet it could be called a great success, considering their opposition. For Morgan Park has a great team this year. They are large and they know their football. A team that can match them has to be mighty good. Of the Morgan Park team, the play of Thrasher, their big fullback, was outstanding.

A week later (October 26), the Academy blanked the Harvard School of Chicago 20-0 to even its 1929 record at 2-2-1 at the half way point of the season.

And then the world changed…

On October 29, 1929, the stock market crashed—the first giant step towards pushing the United States into the Great Depression of the 1930s. Stock prices continued to slide and by 1933, about half of existing banks in the country had closed and unemployment was out of control. Ultimately, about 30% of the U.S. work force was out of work by 1933. Times were extraordinarily tough during this period and it took the vast military manufacturing initiative associated with World War II to finally pull the country out of this devastating economic downward spiral. While the Academy was not immediately affected by the crash of 1929, reduced enrollment in ensuing years along with the lack of significant contributions would force the Academy administration to face some harsh decisions in the early 1930s.

ELUSIVE AS A WET BAR OF SOAP!

In the first game after the crash, the Academy rolled over Wayland Academy 10-0 on November 2 in Beaverdale, Wisconsin to set-up the Homecoming match against arch rival Northwestern Military and Naval Academy from Linn, Wisconsin. Despite Northwestern's 0-3-1 record, the Academy team was wary of the visitors, especially in terms of the emotion that the rivalry typically inspired on the field. However, behind three touchdowns from halfback Guy Sinclair (including scoring jaunts of 30 and 50 yards), the Academy breezed past Northwestern by a 34-0 count. Now 4-2-1, the Warriors were beginning to generate some excitement, especially with hopes of snaring that elusive Mid-West Conference title. *The Academy News* started the parade of praise in its November 13 issue by complimenting the team on its solid performance following those two defeats to open the season:

> If ever an athletic record carried a moral to it, the record of our team does. At the start of the season things frankly looked bad. A defeat by a light but nevertheless fast team from Loyola could be passed off as a bit of hard luck at the first of a long schedule; but when the Warriors fell to an inferior team in the city league an air of gloom hung over the cadets. The corps was discouraged, but not so the team. These Warriors knew they were better than their record showed and they were out to prove it. The sting of the two earlier defeats was still there and with Northwestern in view a grim determination stood in their minds to prove once and for all the true caliber of their playing. They did so in a way that cannot be doubted. Northwestern is not a weak team. They are noted for trickiness and speed. They were in their element on a dry fast field. But our team fought and while they fought they found themselves amassing thirty-four points.
>
> A moral in this history is a fighting team. An epic of determination and the will to win. An epic of the underdog coming out from under. A team beaten, but not licked, down but not out, they came back. In a short month they have come up from a pre-season doping of an inferior team to a position which makes them the logical contender for the conference championship.

But the bright flowers of this football passion wilted quickly the following Saturday when the Academy traveled to Howe Military Academy in Howe, Indiana and dropped a 18-0 decision to the feisty Howe squad. It was the first time that Howe had defeated a Morgan Park team. *The Academy News*, which had been so full of admiration and praise for the Academy team just a few days before, unleashed a caustic attack on the club in its post-game coverage on November 29:

> They (Howe) had a little fellow by the name of Alter who was the smallest man on the field. He was as elusive as a wet bar of soap and covered considerable ground for Howe. In a game as devoid of thrills as a twelve-year-old

race horse and almost devoid of good football, the Morgan Park Warriors were trampled under the Howe Military Academy maroon and white by the score of 18-0…The Warriors had the game won two days before the battle. The time came and we know the result. Perhaps this trouncing was what the team needed. Perhaps it has served to show the players just how good they can rate themselves. We have a good team. We all know it. It's too bad that they thought so themselves.

The editorial freedom enjoyed by *The Academy News* served two opposite purposes: to lavishly praise the team in good times or to belittle it in bad. The stinging retort employed after the Howe fiasco may have served to inspire the gridders in the next contest against tough St. Alban's, with the Academy prevailing 26-13. Despite the frustration of an inconsistent season, the team prepared for its final game against Elgin Academy needing only a tie to capture the conference crown. Elgin entered the contest with a 2-1 conference mark, just behind the Academy's 2-0-1 slate.

Playing under dark skies and intermittent snow showers, the teams battled to a scoreless first half before Elgin pushed over a third quarter score to grab a 6-0 victory and secured the Mid-West Conference title. Certainly, the final 5-4-1 record was a disappointment to the Academy and its football team after entering the season with such high hopes. Unlike its sister publication, the Academy **Skirmisher** yearbook was unwavering in its support of the squad, focusing on the positives of the 1929 season: "Coming closer to winning the Mid-West Conference football title than any Morgan Park team has ever done, was the achievement of this year's heavyweight football team. This was due, in a large measure, to the efforts of Coaches Fleming and Mahon."

As the decade closed, difficult challenges would abound for both the Academy and Coach Fleming in the next three years—challenges that unfortunately would threaten the futures of both.

EXTRA POINT

One of the intriguing aspects of the Academy's athletic program was the number of opportunities for students to play organized football. This book focuses solely on the Heavyweight (Varsity) team as the main thread throughout the school's early history. However, the school also offered

Lightweight and Bantamweight squads which were limited by the physical weight of an athlete. While those weight restraints fluctuated through the years, the Lightweight teams of the 1920s and 1930s were likely placed at the weight of 150 pounds for the heaviest participant. Talented players could still be placed on the Heavyweight team as we have seen with the likes of 147-pound guard William Cabrera of the 1927 and 1928 Heavyweights. For the Lightweights, games were often scheduled as part of a double-header with the Lightweights playing immediately prior to the Heavyweight game, much like the sophomore/junior varsity would line-up just before the Varsity squad in today's high school competition. At other times, the Lightweights would be sent in a completely opposite direction to take on the best available competition.

While the Lightweight team often labored in obscurity at Morgan Park Military Academy, some of these teams were just too talented to stay out of the limelight. Such was the case with the 1929 Academy Lightweight club, which rolled through an undefeated season, without being scored upon! This was a rare accomplishment indeed for any level of football. The only blemish on an 8-0-1 season was a scoreless tie (naturally!) with Harrison High School of Chicago. Coached by Edward Bouma, the 1929 Academy Lightweights rolled over teams such as Thornton (18-0), Morton (22-0), Bloom (6-0), and Gary (Indiana) Froebel 18-0. Halfback Al Mancine was the captain and a terror in the backfield. In the opening win over Thornton, Mancine tallied three touchdowns. In the win over Kankakee (48-0), Mancine added four more touchdowns. And—it should be noted that the 1929 Lightweights were tough on the field as well. In a game against the Heavyweight Varsity "second" team of Pullman Tech, the **Skirmisher** stated that a total of seven Pullman players were "knocked out and had to be removed from the game."

The 1929 Lightweight team of Morgan Park Military Academy should be considered one of the greatest squads in the history of the school, especially with its undefeated record and by outscoring its opponents 192-0!

In 1928, the Academy coaches were (from left): George Mahon, Captain Hewitt, Floyd Fleming, and Edward Bouma. This photo was taken for use in the game program when Morgan Park Military Academy met Missouri Military Academy in 1928 at Wrigley Field in Chicago.

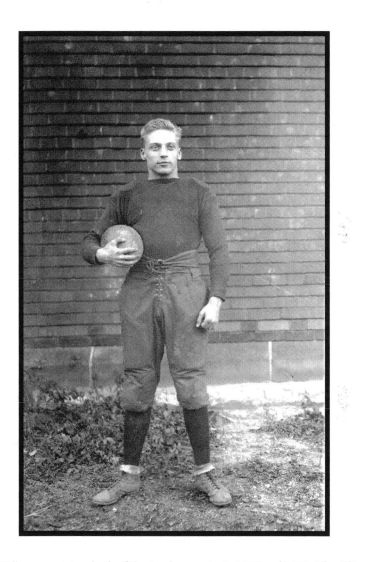

Bob Wallace was quarterback of the Academy team in 1927 and 1928. The *Chicago Daily Journal* described Wallace as a "great ball carrier, quick thinker, and clever general…who will go down in academy gridiron history in the middle west."

CHAPTER 13

Cheers, Fears, and Ransom Notes

"They were the kind of leaders that we all like to follow, full of pep and enthusiasm."
— The Skirmisher, 1929

Jerome "Benny" Factor loved to make people laugh…but all he really wanted to do was play football at Morgan Park Military Academy.

Ever since he entered the Academy's Lower School on February 3, 1925 as a seventh grader from Eugene Field Grammar School in Chicago, Benny was anxious to sample as many activities as possible that the school offered. During his time at the Academy, Factor enjoyed participating on the debate team, in the band, the annual minstrel show, and Bantamweight basketball. But at 5-4 and about 110 lbs., Jerome's future was likely not on the football field.

Yet, with the Academy's emphasis on physical participation and numerous football opportunities, Factor also played three years on the Bantamweight football team in high school and was captain of that team his junior year. **The Skirmisher** in 1929 described the basics of the Bantamweight program:

> This year's Bantamweight team led by Captain "Benny" Factor and coached by Captain De Grandpre was not as successful as might have hoped, however, considering the size of their opponents it was no disgrace to lose three of the five games scheduled. The Bantamweight team is composed of the smallest cadets in the Upper (high)

School who, when they go out for the team expect no more than to learn the rudiments of the game and to play an occasional contest. Because of their size it is usually hard to find other high school teams small enough to compete with. In most of this year's (1928) games the "Midgets" were greatly outweighed and we were just as proud of them as if they had won them all.

Ever the entertainer, Factor switched to the sidelines for his senior year as one of two cheerleaders for the Heavyweight football team, a prestigious position among students at the time as noted in the 1930 **Skirmisher**:

One of the reasons for the excellent cheering this season was the way in which the cheers were led. Marshall Levy and "Benny" Factor did the leading, and were very successful at it. They were the kind of leaders that we all like to follow, full of pep and enthusiasm. They were very successful in keeping up the same pep all the time, whether the team was winning or losing. This is a very hard task and much credit must be given to them for the way in which they did it.

HE HAS A GREAT NOSE FOR EVERYTHING

Over the years, the Academy has welcomed students from all walks of life. In an interview for this book, graduate Jerry Bowden (class of 1957) recalled that "students seemed to come from three types of families: those whose parents wanted them to receive a good education, those who came from broken homes, and those who might be described as kids who were in trouble." Pete Voss (class of 1955) added that "a lot of kids who were boarding students were from families that owned taverns or similar businesses. Their parents wanted to disconnect the kid from their business." In other words, students from wealthy families who could afford the advantages of a private school were always welcome and there is no evidence that the business background of any particular family was questioned. "A lot of families were 'connected,'" stated James Bowden (Class of 1956), "and it was great to go out with certain students. We received a different perspective from the different kids at the school."

Jerome Factor, the smallish, bespectacled kid with the rather large nose was one of those who entered the Academy by a parent who wished to secure the very best education for his son, but also desired to separate

Benny from the family interests. "Benny has a great nose for business. True, he has a great nose for everything—especially a dab of red grease paint," noted the 1928 **Skirmisher**. Because of his father's "business" Benny would soon become the central figure in one of the biggest Chicago underworld stories of the 20th century, and one that would stretch out for over twenty-five years, eventually presenting more questions than answers.

In early 1925 when Benny entered the Academy, his father John, known as Jake "The Barber" Factor was already a well-known con man with previous indictments for both stock and land fraud. Later he was responsible for gold mine scams in both Rhodesia and Canada, exemplifying his talents in various aspects of criminal deception. Factor was originally trained as a barber on the west side of Chicago, but through key contacts and an ability to soak up financial information, soon discovered that making money through questionable means could be personally gratifying. Meanwhile, his half-brother, Max Factor, had ventured west to Hollywood and created a massive cosmetics empire by working closely with the movie industry and then branching out to provide beauty products and services to consumers. It should be noted that the brothers did not work together, and that Jake Factor was not a part of the Max Factor cosmetic empire.

CHAUFFEURED AROUND CHICAGO IN A SILVER AND GOLD DUESENBERG

However, Jake Factor (who despised "The Barber" connotation) was never convicted for his early criminal adventures and in 1926, he partnered with the infamous underworld kingpin Arnold Rothstein in New York (and possibly Al Capone in Chicago) to plot an extraordinary stock scam in England (now known as a Ponzi scheme) that would eventually net Factor the incredible sum of about $8,000,000 before he fled back to Chicago to escape prosecution. But the fraud he inflicted upon thousands of trusting investors (rumored to include members of the royal family) would not be forgiven or forgotten. The long arm of the English law stretched over the ocean and demanded that Factor be returned for trial. In fact, with the delay in capturing and returning Factor to England, he was ultimately tried in absentia, found guilty, and sentenced to eight years of hard labor. Seeking to avoid extradition, Factor's army of highly paid lawyers sought to keep their client in the United States, but his case seemed hopeless and Factor appeared to be facing deportation in April of 1933.

Of course, Jake was certainly intent on maintaining both his freedom and his extravagant way of living as noted in John Tuohy's book (**When Capone's Mob Murdered Roger Touhy**, page 138) that detailed Factor's lavish lifestyle:

> He lived the good life with his stolen loot. He and his wife were seen in the smartest restaurants, chauffeured around Chicago in a silver and gold Duesenberg that cost more than most Chicagoans would earn in a lifetime. He lived in a roof-top bungalow at the Morrison Hotel where he also rented several suites as well as six additional rooms that he used as offices at $1,000 a week. He did all of this when the national income was $6,500 a year and one out of every three Americans was unemployed. The newspaper reported that…Jake the Barber had a net worth of at least $20,000,000…

Jake certainly enjoyed his ill-gotten riches but was in danger of losing it all unless he and his legal team could successfully argue his petition to avoid extradition before the United States Supreme Court. As Factor's representatives feverishly worked to prepare their case for the upcoming Supreme Court hearing on April 18, 1933, Factor privately contemplated his immediate future and any possible alternatives should his appeal fail. It appeared that there was little hope that Factor could bypass deportation. But just a few days before that hearing, his son (and Academy graduate) Jerome Factor was kidnapped on April 12 outside of his mother's apartment at 1215 Lunt Avenue on the north side of Chicago. The exact details were initially muddied by confusion and lack of accurate reporting, especially the reason why someone would seize the 19-year-old Northwestern University student. As more information became available, such as the fact that Jerome was already a millionaire due to a generous trust fund established by his father, there still was no indication that Jerome's captivity had anything to do with his father's legal struggles. It took until April 15 for the police to learn that Jerome Factor was missing and that the unknown kidnappers were demanding a $50,000 ransom. In a note received by the Factor family, the captors threatened harm to Jerome if their demands were not met:

> If you want your son Jerome home you will do as you are told. Get $50,000 in old money, small denominations, and have it ready on short notice. Do not notify the police

or we will send him home in parts. Be ready to follow instructions on a minute's notice. It's up to you. Do you want your son or your money?

On April 16, the *Chicago Tribune* published Jake's insistence that he was unable to pay the ransom:

> "The reports about my wealth have been greatly exaggerated," said Factor. "I would gladly give $50,000 for the boy's return if I had it, but I couldn't raise that much in six months. Two or three years ago it would have been easy, but now it's out of the question."

Instead, Jake the Barber decided to take matters into his own hands. As the days slipped by, a worried Factor ventured into his underworld realm of questionable friendships and solicited the services of members of the Capone gang, headed by Murray "The Camel" Humphreys, to help locate and "free" Jerome. This poorly kept secret irritated the Chicago Police Department as the prospect loomed that both law enforcement and gangland elements would be launching their own investigations into the kidnapping. In fact, the police were clearly befuddled by the lack of cooperation from Jake Factor in the investigation. On April 17 (according to the *Chicago Tribune*), acting on an anonymous tip, the police surprised a group of local gangsters who were apparently planning to quickly solve the disappearance of Jerome Factor:

> A police squad last evening raided a "hoodlum detective agency" in a suite of the Congress Hotel, arrested six men and uncovered evidence indicating that gangsters have been working to help John (Jake the Barber) Factor obtain the release of his 19-year-old son, Jerome, from the hands of kidnappers. The youth, a Northwestern University student, was kidnapped last Wednesday and is being held for ransom of $50,000. Sam Hunt, a leader of the remnants of the Capone gang, was one of those seized by the police. The others are Tony Accardo, Michael Spranza, Louis Cramer, Edward Guida, and Louis Romano, all of whom have been identified with Capone affairs in the past.

With Jerome still missing on April 18, Jake Factor was forced to miss his hearing before the Supreme Court, and who could blame him? The man was intent on finding his son quickly, and to do so he willingly passed on his own hearing that was to determine if he would indeed be returned to the United Kingdom to face an already determined prison term. Nonetheless, the Supreme Court agreed to reschedule Factor's hearing until May 29, 1933. Whispers among reporters and those close to the case indicated that Jake was close to a nervous breakdown, especially when the kidnappers raised their demands to $100,000. In an Associated Press article, the police quoted Factor as asking "Why did they grab the boy? Two years ago, they wanted me—why not now? Why the boy, I can't understand it."

Meanwhile, the arrested "members of the hoodlum investigation agency" were released on April 18 while Jake Factor continued to be evasive in terms of cooperating with the police. Certainly, he was relying more on the underworld parties for assistance in locating and freeing Jerome as explained in the *Chicago Tribune*:

> Murray Humphreys, Sam Hunt, and Tony Accardo are the leaders of this underworld investigation. All are holdovers from the old Capone gang regime and have the facilities to take care of any trouble that might arise in an encounter with the captors. Factor is said to be convinced that the gangsters have come much closer to a solution of the kidnapping mystery than have the police. It is understood that 125 known hoodlums, scattered over the state, are aiding Factor and doing so at their own expense. One of them explained their attitude is one of self-defense—that kidnappings create too much "police heat" and tend to interfere with their more orthodox rackets. In recruiting the 125 hoodlums a process of elimination has been worked out in which suspicion is directed against a minor kidnap gang whose members naturally refused to join the Humphreys-Hunt-Accardo searching corps.

CAPONE ORDERED THEM TO LAY OFF FACTOR

Although Al Capone had been convicted of tax-related offenses and imprisoned in late 1931, his "gang" continued to thrive in Chicago, except under a less "visible" business model. It seemed to make sense that the Humphreys investigative group would be receptive to helping Factor, thus discouraging any possible future kidnappings that cast a more negative public perception of the crime lords who were attempting to present themselves as legitimate business entrepreneurs after the demise of the more flamboyant Capone. Factor had already referred to an attempted plot to kidnap himself back in 1931. At that time, according to the Associated Press, "the extortionists… were expected to ask at least $500,000 ransom for [Jake] Factor and when intimations of the plan came to him, he went directly to Al Capone. The gang leader…summoned the plotters to his headquarters and ordered them to 'lay off Jake Factor—or else.'"

As the search for Jerome continued, the story was literally the main headline in most of the major Chicago newspapers, with the *Chicago Tribune* even including a photo of Jerome in his Morgan Park Military Academy football "cheer" outfit. Jake the Barber remained distraught: "Return my boy and I will gladly give up everything I have," he told reporters.

Then suddenly, Jerome Factor was released from captivity in the early hours of April 21. He told police that he had been seized the week before outside of his mother's apartment, forced onto the floor of a car with a coat over his head, and taken to an undisclosed destination according to the International News Service:

> It was there that I spent the last eight days," recalled Jerome Factor. "Each day one of the kidnappers would ask what sort of meal I wanted and bring magazines or papers which I was permitted to read. I never got a glimpse of the men holding me. They would just thrust food into the room… Then they took me in an automobile to another house and I spent a day there under close guard. Last night they put me in a car again and one of the men remarked, 'Buddy, we're going to release you now. And we didn't get any money for all this trouble. He seemed mad."

Denying that he was aware Jerome had been released, Jake the Barber didn't show up immediately after Jerome had been freed, but later joined his son and the extended family, while also facing a round of police interviews. For Jake, it was clearly a win-win situation despite the personal stress that the kidnapping of his son brought with it. Jerome was released unharmed, and Jake claimed to have never paid a cent for the demanded ransom. The *Chicago Tribune* summarized the events on April 21 after Jerome was finally freed:

> Jerome's return was the end of one phase of one of Chicago's most sensational kidnapping cases. For the last eight days the search for him had been conducted by police

and by gangsters engaged by Factor to intercede with the kidnappers. Indications have been for several days that Factor, through the offices of his hired hoodlums, Murray Humphreys and Sam Hunt, had established contact with the kidnappers and had made arrangements for Jerome's release. The boy's return and his reluctance to give [police] Capt. [Daniel] Gilbert any details of his abduction were considered indicative that the release was made possible through a private deal.

Several suspects were interviewed by detectives, but no one was ever charged or convicted of the crime. It was suspected that members of the Roger Touhy gang, a keen rival of the Capone outfit, may have been behind the kidnapping of Jerome. Once that group realized that Jake Factor had aligned himself with Humphreys et al, they may have decided to quickly retreat from their final ransom demands to avoid future gangland retribution. There was also speculation that Jake the Barber arranged the kidnapping of Jerome (with Jerome's willing participation) in an effort to delay Jake's own appearance before the Supreme Court. If one was willing to subscribe to the latter theory, then perhaps it would be feasible for Jake to utilize the same type of feigned process again in the future to suit his own needs.

Therefore, it was not surprising when Jake himself was kidnapped late in the evening of June 30, 1933 outside of a night club called The Dells in Morton Grove, Illinois, a suburb of Chicago. Newspapers across the country quickly gobbled up information from the Associated Press on the incident to share with their readers:

> Factor, habitué of gaming tables—the story runs that he has pocketed one million from his play in recent weeks—was pounced on by two auto loads of kidnappers bristling with guns. From a car behind, Mrs. Factor and Mrs. Al Epstein, hysterical, watched their husbands dragged from the automobile young Jerome Factor was driving. Jerome was sent on his way. Epstein was put out some distance away.

Once again, details of the kidnapping and the ransom demands were murky. Apparently, Jake's family remitted some type of ransom, and on July 12, Jake was released unharmed. Yet suspicions regarding the temerity of the kidnapping began to surface, beginning with Jake's appearance when released. Although he sported an unkempt beard, he still wore the same clothes that he had on when he was snatched outside The Dells casino. Although slightly wrinkled, his suit was immaculate, as were his shirt and collar. Detectives also noted that his hands were clean, and aside from a slight weight loss, Factor appeared to be in remarkably good shape after his twelve-day ordeal. Author John Tuohy has suggested in his book (page 140) that Jake's abduction might have been pure fantasy considering that the Supreme Court had not been receptive to Factor's defense arguments during the recent hearing:

> Perhaps while discussing his limited options with his attorneys, Factor may have mentioned the delay in the hearing brought about by Jerome's kidnapping. If he, Jake, were kidnapped and then returned safely and his kidnappers were captured, then the ensuing trial would delay his hearings long enough for the statute of limitations against him to run out. It wasn't a sure thing but unless drastic measures were taken his deportation to a jail cell in England was.

And so, as the story goes, a plot was hatched with Humphreys and mob boss Frank Nitti that would facilitate the disappearance of Jake for a few days, followed by his miraculous return, and then the blame for it all would be placed on rival gangster Roger Touhy and his cohorts. This deception was intended to clear the way for Jake to avoid the dreaded deportation to England, while also ridding the Capone organization of its nagging rival Touhy. Years later, this exact scenario was proven to be feasible, and shortly after the release of the suave Factor in July of 1933, he began to complete his part of the bargain by identifying the Touhy gang members as his kidnappers to anyone who would listen…and the police were listening. If they could hang a kidnapping conviction on Touhy, it would clear another crafty criminal off the streets of the Chicago area. One party that was very interested in Factor's story was the British government, which went on the offensive even before Factor was released. It became clear that the English authorities were not buying Factor's situation at all as stated in *The Evening Times* (July 12):

> Charging that the recent kidnapping of John (Jake the Barber) Factor is a hoax and that Factor is in hiding, Lewis Bernays, British Consul at Chicago has demanded

the missing man's arrest. Bernays further asserted that the "kidnapping" of Factor's son, Jerome, a few months ago, was a prelude frameup to make Factor's disappearance look legitimate

It was rumored that Jake Factor, using outcast members of the Touhy gang to do the dirty work, spent up to $70,000 of his own funds for his faux kidnapping. Despite his very proper appearance after his release, no one seemed to question that Factor had indeed been kidnapped. Suspicion was placed on Touhy, although the Touhy gang was already being blamed for a kidnapping in St. Paul, Minnesota on June 15, 1933. In this instance, William Hamm, Jr., who was the president of the popular Hamm's Brewing Company was grabbed off the streets during the middle of the day. After a large ransom of $100,000 was paid, Hamm was released unharmed on June 19. As part of the overall plan, it made sense for the Capone gang to "leak" information to the press placing blame for the Factor kidnapping on the Touhy outfit. In fact, it was so effective that newspapers (United Press) across the country were already linking Touhy with the crime:

> From underworld sources came information today that five desperadoes who kidnapped William Hamm participated in the abduction of John (Jake the Barber) Factor. The United Press' informant declared that the five Hamm kidnappers were seen on Chicago's northwest side a week ago, two days before Factor was abducted.

It was believed that an old adversary of Touhy's, police Captain Daniel "Tubbo" Gilbert, working in conjunction with the Capone group, was largely responsible for the trumped-up charges against Touhy in St. Paul. Gilbert was the key investigator in the Jerome Factor kidnapping who was also a powerful union organizer on the side who clashed in the past with Touhy over "protection" fees for Touhy's beer trucks. Through his various enterprises on both sides of the law (including personal gambling successes), Gilbert was known as the "richest cop in America." His intent in the aftermath of the Hamm kidnapping was to exert his influence with the objective of pinning the crime on Touhy and his cohorts. This was likely a "favor" for the Capone group and the initial attempt to legally push Touhy out of business. Although Touhy was quickly arrested and placed on trial for the Hamm kidnapping, the proceedings ended quickly without a conviction.

In an interview for this book, local St. Paul crime historian Michelle Myers Berg provided additional insight into the Hamm kidnapping and the ensuing Touhy trial. Ms. Berg stated:

> Privately, those trying the Hamm kidnapping case knew that Roger Touhy was not really their man. Publicly, the jury agreed. After 19 hours of deliberation that resulted in complete public uproar, the jury acquitted Touhy of any involvement in the Hamm's kidnapping. The Feds were confounded! Ironically, they would have had to look no further than across the table to see the person who was largely responsible for the kidnapping and who profited the most from the Hamm's $100,000 ransom. That person was none other than former chief of police, Tom Brown. Brown had rapidly become a concierge for criminals making their way in St. Paul. He had happily facilitated some of the Barker-Karpis gangs' biggest hits after getting out of prison. The boys who did the dirty work (and were eyeballs deep in transporting Hamm across state lines and taking other sustained risks) each only received $7,800 for their work, Brown got $25,000. One quarter of the ransom.

> So, when Dan "Tubbo" Gilbert, detective to the Illinois prosecutor (and a Capone operative) suggested that it was a "kidnapping by Roger Touhy" (and not Brown and the Barker Karpis Gang), this proved to be irresistible for Brown. He was happy to do what he could to build up Tubbo's myth.

> It wasn't until much later . . . after the trial, and after they had already made Tom Brown Head of the new Kidnapping Division . . . that the St. Paul police realized just who it was that was truly responsible. And by then, what did it matter? They had no evidence to convict. And Touhy? Sent to prison for kidnapping someone else entirely: Jake Factor.

LIKED KIDNAPPERS EVEN LESS THAN SWINDLERS

After side-stepping one false accusation and trial in St. Paul, Touhy was eventually arrested for the Jake Factor kidnapping in Chicago, based primarily on the accusations of Factor himself. Despite flimsy evidence, the Touhy gang was placed on trial, with the first proceedings ending in a mistrial. On the second go-around, again ripe with conflicting and erroneous testimony by Jake and others, Touhy was convicted and sentenced to 99 years in prison. Meanwhile, Jake Factor was detained by the local jurisdiction as a material witness, which protected him from extradition and eventually allowed him to legally wiggle free of that ominous future. Since Factor was not extradited within the mandated 60 days, he was free to pursue his life's dreams (and enjoy his ill-gotten money) under a writ of habeas corpus. As for Touhy, he was destined to spend the rest of his life in prison for a crime he claimed he never committed!

Touhy and three others were convicted of the Factor kidnapping on February 22, 1934. This was followed by numerous appeals on Touhy's behalf due to the inconsistencies of the testimony, all of which were unsuccessful as Touhy was incarcerated at the notorious Stateville Correctional Center in Crest Hill, Illinois.

In his autobiography, **The Stolen Years**, written years later while he was still in prison, Touhy insisted (page 96) that he had actually been asked to help in the Factor kidnapping right after it occurred in 1933:

> On the morning of July first [1933], a knock on the door awakened me…a Chicago police lieutenant was calling. Jake the Barber Factor had been kidnapped…He said that, well, since I was widely acquainted out in this section of the county, that I might want to help. The reputation of Jake the Barber didn't smell like any hyacinth to me. I had read in the papers that he was wanted for swindling widows, clergymen, and other unfortunate chumps in England. The British crown was also trying its damnedest to extradite Jake back to England. Since I liked kidnappers even less than I did swindlers, I told the lieutenant I'd see what information I could pick up.

After experiencing a brief taste of freedom following a successful 1942 escape from Stateville, Touhy was captured, returned to the prison, and continued his efforts to secure his freedom based upon the irregularities of the trial. Ultimately, the story behind Factor's supposed kidnapping began to unravel. In 1954, Federal Judge John P. Barnes agreed with Touhy and declared the kidnapping of Factor to be a hoax as reported by the Associated Press on August 10, 1954:

JOE ZIEMBA

> Judge Barnes ruled that Touhy had no part in the alleged
> kidnapping, which he said was a hoax engineered by Factor
> to forestall extradition to England to face prosecution for a
> confidence game charge. Judge Barnes, in granting Touhy
> a writ of habeas corpus, said the one-time beer baron's
> conviction was procured by perjured testimony. Touhy's
> lawyers contended that Al Capone's old crime syndicate
> got Factor to frame Touhy so Capone could seize various
> labor unions dominated by Touhy.

Unfortunately for Touhy, disagreements between the various judicial branches of government voided his release in 1954, but he was eventually freed on parole in November of 1959 after serving over 25 years for a crime that he likely did not commit. Around the same time, Touhy's aforementioned autobiography **The Stolen Years** was published despite efforts by the Chicago underworld to prevent its wide distribution. There was a pragmatic fear that Touhy would unleash scores of business "secrets" and identify specific names in his book. On another level, Jake Factor—still sticking to his original claim that he was kidnapped by Touhy over two decades before--initiated litigation against Touhy and his publisher for passages in the book that he considered libelous. That suit was dismissed in 1964.

Touhy's life of freedom after years of incarceration was short, however. On December 16, 1959 Touhy and his bodyguard (Walter Miller) were ambushed as they were about to visit Touhy's sister at 125 N. Lotus in Chicago. Two assailants, both brandishing shotguns, blasted the two men from short range, hitting Touhy in both legs while Miller was hit three times. Miller and Touhy were rushed to area hospitals where Miller eventually recovered from his wounds. Touhy, however, expired in the emergency room at the now shuttered St. Anne's Hospital in Chicago. Ironically, one of the medical attendees working with the injured Touhy at St. Anne's was Dr. George E. Bryar, father of Sharon Eichinger, one of the current archivists at Morgan Park Academy. Dr. Bryar consented to share some of his thoughts for this book regarding that fateful night for Roger Touhy.

At the time, Dr. Bryar was a third-year medical student at the University of Illinois Medical School who was working part-time as an orderly at St. Anne's with the responsibility of addressing the needs of patients coming in to the emergency room at the hospital. Dr. Bryar recalled that evening as follows:

There were no licensed physicians in the ER that night. It was staffed by orderlies, medical students, student nurses, and a registered nurse with a licensed doctor on call. Roger Touhy was brought to the hospital in a squad roll (paddy wagon) and the emergency room quickly filled with police and reporters, but no one interfered with the treatment Touhy was receiving. He was essentially dead when he arrived, and he never said anything. We put a pressure cuff on him and started an IV, but he was moribund (in the process of dying). Unfortunately, there was no hope for Mr. Touhy. He passed away due to loss of blood from his wounds.

The next day, Dr. Bryar was requested to attend the formal coroner's inquest at Cook County Hospital morgue in Chicago along with a student nurse who was also on duty when Roger Touhy was brought in for treatment. Dr. Bryar recalls being seated between the student nurse on his right and another gentleman on his left who turned out to be none other than Jake "The Barber" Factor! About twenty years later, Dr. Bryar recalled a final connection with Jake The Barber:

> Around 1990, I met one of the Chicago policemen (Bobby Lewis) who took Roger from the site of the shooting to St. Anne's. He was at the City of Hope in California in the final stages of cancer. We had a long and pleasant conversation. As I left the hospital, I noticed a picture of Jake "The Barber" Factor on the wall of one of the corridors. It was a plaque honoring his significant donation to the City of Hope. How ironic!"

No one was ever arrested for the assassination of Roger Touhy.

MY DREAM HAS FINALLY COME TRUE!

Indeed, in his later years, Jake Factor became quite the philanthropist after moving to Los Angeles, but his road to respectability had a few bumps in it. While Factor was able to circumvent extradition back to England, he was finally convicted of fraud in Cedar Rapids, Iowa on November 17, 1942. Factor was then paroled after serving six years of a ten-year sentence. He became active (with the Chicago mob organization) in the early growth days of Las Vegas, becoming the figurehead manager and part owner of the Stardust Hotel in 1955 and later sold his interest in the facility in the early 1960s. By then, Factor had accrued an interest in politics, financially supporting John F. Kennedy to the tune of $20,000 during Kennedy's 1960 presidential campaign, while also donating $25,000 to a fund headed by Mrs. Eleanor Roosevelt that was established to help free over 1,200 rebel soldiers held prisoner in communist Cuba. All of this positive financial assistance likely influenced President Kennedy's decision to grant Factor a full pardon for his past misdeeds on Christmas Day of 1962. The pardon (for the mail fraud conviction) was received just in time to avoid another extradition effort for Factor by the U.S. Immigration Department, according to the *Chicago Tribune* on December 26th:

> The pardon was regarded as knocking the legs from under the deportation case and was hailed by Factor in Palm Springs, CA, with a statement to a *Chicago Tribune* reporter: "This is the best Christmas possible. All my worries are over. I expect the deportation proceedings will be automatically cancelled."

In his later years (Factor died on January 23, 1984 at the age of 91), Factor eased into the roles of investor, philanthropist and humanitarian, particularly in impoverished neighborhoods where he freely donated thousands of dollars to a variety of causes, including the building of churches, hospitals, and parks to benefit the inner city. His most impressive effort was the contribution of $1 million to construct a youth center in the Watts neighborhood of Los Angeles. When Factor passed away, California Governor Edmund G. Brown and Los Angeles Mayor Tom Bradley were among the mourners. *The Los Angeles Times* published an extensive obituary outlining the magnificent honors and achievements compiled by Factor during his lifetime, including a recollection of Factor finally becoming a U.S. citizen (he was born in Poland) after receiving the pardon from President Kennedy:

> When he was granted citizenship after the demise of efforts to deport him, Factor said, "My dream has finally come true!" Then U.S. District Judge Leon R. Yankwich, who swore in Factor as a citizen in Los Angeles said, "I take great joy in administering this oath. For 20 years this man has led an exemplary life. He has paid for the delinquencies of his youth. I welcome him as a fellow citizen."

IT HAS A RATHER FASCINATING HISTORY

An intensely private man, Jerome Factor recovered from the trauma of his youthful kidnapping and became very prominent in the insurance industry with early offices at 434 South Wabash in the Chicago downtown area. He poured his professional efforts into the financial world and later became a successful venture capitalist. Married with two children, Jerome maintained an 18-room residence situated on 2.5 acres (with a 250-ft. private beach) on Lake Michigan in Highland Park, Illinois and also spent time at a 6,200-sq. ft. house in Beverly Hills, California that featured a 2,500-sq. ft. master suite. However, Jerome appeared to favor his stunning residence in Palm Springs, California. As recently as 2016, Factor was mentioned in an on-line article ("Palm Springs Factor Estate") that discussed the potential sale of his palatial home (5,471 sq. ft.) in Palm Springs:

> This mid-century modern house on the 13th fairway of the Canyon Country Club Golf Course, is pure a mid-century style and sells with all of its furnishings and art work. It also has a rather fascinating history. The estate was built for venture capitalist Jerome Factor in 1969, cousin to makeup magnate Max Factor and the son of John Factor, proprietor of the Stardust Resort and Casino in Las Vegas. Possibly learned from his convicted gangster father, Jerome was big on privacy which might explain the windowless front elevation and the extension of the 14-foot house wall enclosing the pool.

While in Palm Springs, Jerome mingled easily with socialites, politicians, and starlets, and served as president of the prestigious Canyon Country Club where he enjoyed golf and organizing specific club events such as the annual Bill Demerast Golf Classic, which raised millions for youth programs.

Jerome Factor passed away on May 15, 1998 in Chicago at the age of 84. No one was ever convicted in conjunction with his kidnapping in 1933.

EXTRA POINT

Over the long history of the Morgan Park Military Academy football program, the students were always expected to cheer long and loud for their team on the gridiron. When Jerome Factor was a cheerleader back in 1929, he probably grabbed a large megaphone to lead the crowd through some of the typical "cheers" for the time, such as the following called "Yea Team, One, Two, Three:"

Yea team, one, two, three
Yea, team
Yea, team
Rah, Rah, Rah, Rah, Rah
Rah, Rah
Yea, team!

By 1953, the cheers became a bit more familiar:

One, two, three, four
Who are we for?
Morgan Park, Morgan Park
Yea, Morgan Park

Former Academy football player Jerome Factor (left) was kidnapped (and released safely) in 1933 in a case that was never solved. He is shown here in 1934 with his father, John "Jake the Barber" Factor and Jake's wife, Rella Cohen Factor. (Photo from the collection of the author)

CHAPTER 14

The Elastic Plan and the Beauty Queen

"Cadets poured onto the field in a blue-gray wave and carried the team to the showers on jubilant shoulders."
—The Academy News, 1933

As the Great Depression slithered into the 1930s, Morgan Park Academy braced for anticipated enrollment and funding challenges. Initially, the impact of the financial distress on the school was very soft. There was little change in enrollment numbers in 1930 and thus limited hope that the Academy would not be drastically affected by the financial chaos engulfing the country. With little or no endowment and no public support, Morgan Park Military Academy relied almost entirely on tuition to survive at that time. Without student registration fees the future of the Academy would be in peril.

Not enough credit for the Academy's survival has been given to Superintendent Harry D. Abells, a protégé of Amos Alonzo Stagg at the University of Chicago (class of 1897) where he was a member, and captain, of Stagg's baseball squad and also played basketball. After a year of graduate school, Abells was hired as a chemistry instructor at the Academy in 1898, eventually being named principal in 1907. In 1918, he became superintendent of the school where he served until 1945 when he was named superintendent emeritus.

Abells' love for the Academy was unquestioned, but aside from his emotional attachment to the school, Abells brought a tough business acumen to his role. As the economic threats evolving from the Depression became more apparent, Abells developed what today we might call a long-range strategic plan. Instead of reacting to the potential crippling results of the Depression after they occurred, Abells asserted a pro-active approach well before any business calamities were evident.

Fully understanding that the economy was rocked negatively by the Great Depression as never before, Abells evaluated means to counteract the certain loss of revenue from fewer students being enrolled in his elite private school. With less cash on hand, and perhaps fearful to spend it, parents could always weather this economic travesty by enrolling their sons in nearby public schools. At first, the enrollment figures remained strong. For the 1930-31 school year, enrollment in the Upper (high) school was 257 compared to 258 just a year before. The Lower (grade) school dropped from 100 to 78 (total of 335). While these lower numbers were not significant at the time, Abells noted other signs of concern. For example, attendance at Camp Traverse in Michigan during the summer of 1930 (aside from the football camp) dwindled to just 11 attendees resulting in a loss of $1,286 for the school. There was some discussion regarding the possible closing of Camp Traverse, at least on a temporary basis, but Abells decided to keep the facility open in 1931, provided that at least 15 students were enrolled.

CHANGING A PLUMP AND LAZY GUY

Meanwhile, the 1930 football season opened to great anticipation despite a very difficult schedule. About 30 athletes attended the annual pre-season session at Camp Traverse, where Coach Floyd Fleming eased the candidates into playing condition over a two-week period, as outlined by *The Academy News* on August 13:

> During the first day of camp, the boys go on hikes. This begins the process of changing a plump and lazy guy into a quick and heavy-set player. The second day is devoted to passing, catching, and charging. On the third day commences the backfield practice. From then on, every day they have real football. By the looks of the material we should have a crack team this year. Everybody that knows anything about the Academy team will take a stand that this year's team will be a team of teams.

The excitement over the new season was doused in early season losses to Michigan City (Indiana) High School (19-0) and Elgin Academy (also 19-0) sandwiched around a 19-7 win at Milwaukee (Wisconsin) University High School. The Academy rebounded to finish with a 5-3 mark for the 1930 season but completed a disappointing 2-2 slate in the conference. One of the highlights was the season-ending home game against undefeated Howe (Indiana) Military Academy on November 22. Due to the economic turmoil engulfing the country, the administration decided to stage a charity contest to benefit the Morgan Park Military Academy Welfare Fund. All proceeds would be distributed to the less fortunate in the area. Earlier in the month, a student-based "Social Welfare Association" called the Guardians had been established to help organize charitable efforts on campus. One of the first projects was for all students to contribute towards a fund destined to assist three families through the tough winter months from November through March. Next on the agenda was an effort to convince the Academy administration to utilize a football game as a charitable event. This would indeed take some convincing since the school was now including football team fees and gate receipts as part of its annual budget. However, the determined planning was about to become reality, as stated in *The Academy News* on November 19, 1930:

> After many days of hard trying and ceaseless ringing of telephones a committee of the faculty and the Guardians finally managed to arrange a charity football game, the receipts of which are to go toward helping the M.P.M.A. Welfare Fund. Col. Abells, Mr. (Hugh) Price, and Capt. Mahon have all cooperated and through their efforts bleachers to seat a capacity crowd have been borrowed from Thornton Township High School. The Guardians, working with Mr. Price are planning to make the day a big success. Mr. Joseph A. Rutkowski has kindly offered to furnish all necessary canvasses to fence in the football field and stands. Mr. Zechman will furnish all necessary lumber; Mr. Heitmann volunteered to furnish a truck for transporting the stands; Mr. Haas has printed posters advertising this game.

Football games were still played behind the then (and current) gymnasium on the south side of the Academy campus. There was no permanent seating, just a few temporary stands, the balconies on the rear of the gymnasium, and then seating/standing on the ground around the field. With the large homecoming crowd looking on, the Academy emerged from its battle with Howe Military Academy with a 13-6 victory. It would mark the conclusion of the three-year careers of stalwarts such as Guy "Sinny" Sinclair, the oft-injured, but elusive quarterback, and sturdy lineman James Carl Hansen, Jr., whose last name will be remembered forever on campus since Hansen Hall was named after his father (J.C. Hansen), the deceased (1927) former vice-president of the school's Board of Trustees.

WE MUST DO SOME WISE THINKING

Meanwhile, Abells and his staff continued to monitor enrollment and recruitment efforts throughout the 1930-31 school year. At that time, the school devoted a significant part of its budget to student recruitment. In his monthly report to the Board of Trustees on February 7, 1931, Abells wrote, "We are confident that to secure boys for 1931, under conditions which will probably be harder than those of last year, we must do some wise thinking and follow this up with energetic action." Abells encouraged a more aggressive (and on-going) campaign to recruit new students and began hinting at reductions in expenditures at the school.

Each April the Board would recommend which faculty members would be re-appointed for the following school year. At its April 13, 1930 meeting, the Board compiled such a list of 19 administrators and instructors for the 1931-32 academic year with one glaring omission: Coach Floyd Fleming was not on the list.

Instead, Fleming was one of four teachers on the list whose faculty retention would be finalized at an upcoming meeting. In Fleming's case, his future status at the Academy was apparently "subject to success in enrolling boys for camp," according to the Board minutes from the April 13 meeting. Fleming was still in charge of Camp Traverse but was on his own in terms of camp staff unless enrollment increased. For example, if enrollment reached a certain number (e.g. 15), another adult supervisor would be added to the staff. Fortunately, for Fleming (and the Academy), Camp Traverse showed a small profit for the season and Fleming was retained on staff, albeit with a portion ($800) of his annual salary now being derived from his duties as director of Camp Traverse.

By July of 1931, Abells was becoming more pragmatic in his evaluation of the Academy's financial future. He established a faculty committee to review all expenses and to make recommendations for possible reductions by stating:

> I am not pessimistic. On the other hand, I believe we shall all feel more secure and better in spirit if in this particular year we approach the situation with wide open eyes and good judgement with the co-operation of everybody. Consequently, I am making this recommendation for a committee.

As the 1931-32 school year opened, the overall enrollment dipped significantly, this time to 282 students, down from 335 from the previous year. The tight-fisted accounting department eased up on its usual insistence of prompt payments, allowing parents the entire semester to remit tuition and costs to the Academy, instead of the previous mandate for full payment at the start of each semester. As a sign of the difficult times, the Academy was even forced to reduce the hourly wage of the school painter from $1.25 an hour to 75 cents per hour. The painter was glad to have the work and the school took advantage of this particular savings element by assigning the worker to paint Alumni Hall, a faculty house, and the school infirmary! In truth, the drop in enrollment numbers also lowered the Academy's finances from additional sources beyond the basic room/board fee itself. The Academy required multiple uniforms for each student, and also benefited from student spending on campus from the school post exchange (store), the barber shop, and from sports participation fees, all of which resulted in less income for the Academy due to fewer enrolled students. Abells did implement the work of an internal committee to study costs and possible recommendations "for a general reorganization of the departments within the school," according to the Board minutes from November 9, 1931. At the same meeting, Abells was pleased with a report on the reduced costs relevant to the thrice daily meals served in the dining room. It was reported to the Board that the total number of individual meals served since the beginning of the school year totaled 865, with the average cost lowered to 15 cents for the food for each meal!

The Academy fielded a competent, but not overpowering, squad for the 1931 season. Philip Graver was named captain and the team faced another tough schedule, including the renewal of the rivalry with Lake Forest Academy (a 13-0 loss) which had been discontinued in 1919. Only seven games were scheduled (the Howe Military game was cancelled), most likely due to the departmental cuts that Abells recommended, and the Academy was just 1-2 when it traveled to Beaver Dam, Wisconsin on October 16 for a match with Wayland Academy. This was a significant date in the history of Academy football since it was the first night game ever played by the school. Although the Academy was confident of a victory after knocking off Wayland the past three years, the contest ended in a scoreless tie, prompting the 1932 **Skirmisher** to blame the lights:

> The first game the Morgan Parkers played under the bright lights turned out as a whole, unfavorably. The main noticeable effect of the lights was to cause a difficulty in judging the descent of the ball. The Warriors had some difficulty in getting used to the floodlights and the "ghost" [white] ball, and when they finally did settle down to their stride, it was too late to enable them to score on a strong Wayland team.

Coach Fleming offered a realistic assessment of the result in *The Academy News* on October 21:

> Both teams played high class football. It was hard fought. But because of our consistent gaining ground and their failing to gain, we feel we have lost and the Wayland team acted as if a tie game were a victory.

After a week off from competition, the Academy entertained the St. Alban's Saints from Sycamore, Illinois whose players were feeling the wrath of their unhappy coach Caddy Johnson. In a game preview from *The Daily Chronicle* in DeKalb, Illinois, readers were provided with some insight on the St. Alban's squad's reason for apprehension:

> The mere name of Morgan Park is bad enough to mention at the Saints' gates but this year it is worse. Morgan Park and Wayland played a scoreless tie, and when Coach Johnson recalls that Wayland slammed the Saints all over the lot here a few weeks ago to the tune of 27-0—ah, me. However, the local mentor is clever and he has found a good axe to hold over their heads. Last Saturday he told the squad before going on the field that it would be their last stand if they lost, and all subsequent games would be cancelled. The result was a victory. Will they fear "no more

games" again this week is a very important query that Mr. Johnson would like some bright youth to answer.

Phil Graver tallied twice, and added four extra points, as the Academy scuttled the Saints 34-0, who did manage to complete their season despite the threats of Coach Johnson. A 13-13 tie with Elgin Academy deadlocked the Warriors' record at 2-2-2 moving into the final game of the season against Northwestern Academy. As in 1930, the administration designated the last game on the schedule as a charity event, with all proceeds being donated to the local United Charities office, which *The Academy News* noted, "dispenses around eight-thousand dollars per week to support over nine-thousand needy families."

As they had since the football program was established back in 1894, the home games for the Academy were staged behind the current gymnasium on 112th Street. There had been some discussion of building a separate football facility on campus, but there seemed to be little hope during the Great Depression that this objective would become a reality. Yet, the thought of permanent seating for the football games, and the accompanying increased gate receipts, must have seemed attractive to Abells and his staff. The final game against Northwestern epitomized the need for a more dedicated football stadium as over 5,000 people attended the contest. However, due to seating restrictions, the game was played at nearby Ridge Park (96th and Longwood Drive) where temporary grandstands were constructed to accommodate the large crowd. Over $900 was raised, and the attendees were treated to a 12-0 Academy win, courtesy of two touchdowns by Graver.

With the team concluding its efforts with a 3-2-2 mark, some good news was received when three Morgan Park Military Academy players received "All State" recognition after the season. Both the *Chicago American* and the *Chicago Evening Post* named fullback Phil Graver, quarterback George Morgan, and tackle Floyd Haas as honorees. The 1932 **Skirmisher** aptly summarized the season by noting:

> This year M.P.M.A. has a record to be proud of: no conference games lost. Captain Fleming's hard work and long hours spent in coaching was in no small part responsible for the success of Captain Graver's team.

The tie games with Wayland and Elgin cost the Warriors the conference title, but the strong finish to the season managed to push another winning season onto Fleming's coaching accomplishments. But given the current financial dilemma, would Fleming even be around for the next football season?

PLAN AND STRIVE WITH ENTHUSIASM

In the wake of the continuing Great Depression, Abells proposed his most stringent recommendations to the Academy Board of Trustees on December 14, 1931. Abells' far-reaching plan called for strict cost-cutting, evaluation of staff personnel needs, and even rearranging priorities so that Abells himself would return to the classroom. Most importantly, he recommended a solid strategic plan that would prepare the Academy for survival based on less enrollment, rather than hoping for an immediate return to economic normalcy:

> Naturally, we are thinking about our attendance for next year. There is an old Roman saying which runs something like this: "Act as if you were going to die tomorrow; plan as though you were going to live forever." Practically all of our neighboring schools have lost 20 per cent in attendance this year. It is generally understood that we are most favored of any military school. In order to prepare for the loss which may be our lot this coming year, I believe we ought to make all arrangements to be able to carry on should we have a 20% reduction in attendance. Consequently, it seems to me the part of wisdom to act upon the basis of 240 [attendees], and then to plan and strive with enthusiasm and faith to have the same enrollment we have this year... everything in respect to what we have been doing at the Academy by every member of the faculty is absolutely open for study.

Abells left little doubt that he would do anything possible to keep the Academy functioning as a respected institution while maintaining fiscal responsibility to ensure the Academy's future. Typically, the Academy would offer its faculty members a somewhat competitive wage but would also provide room and board for the instructors and their spouses. Abells closed some of the Academy-owned residences and moved those individuals into the dormitories. He also froze salaries and slashed expenses by 23% for the 1932-33 school year while delaying the re-hiring of certain teachers until final enrollment figures were known for the new academic year, calling this his "elastic plan." In other words, the higher the enrollment, the more teachers that would be brought back for the school year. Nothing would be finalized regarding the faculty until enrollment numbers were firmly in hand just prior to the opening of the 1932 school year. The minutes of the School Management Committee on March 14, 1932 mentioned these plans and also stated that "Each teacher will be asked to indicate his willingness to cooperate with this plan. In case he feels he can do better elsewhere, he will receive the cordial support of the Academy in securing the position." Of course, in 1932, any job, educational or otherwise, would be difficult to pursue and secure.

After reducing costs across the board, Abells then created two additional revenue generating opportunities: a summer school in 1932 and a junior college in 1933. In a bit of a shock, the summer school would accept female students and the summer sessions would be operated in conjunction with the military academy, not necessarily as part of it. "The purpose, however, is to give as many members of the Academy faculty an opportunity to teach as is possible and at the same time secure the enrollment of pupils," stated Abells on April 11, 1932. The summer school filled the gap left when other local schools, both public and private, closed their summer sessions during the Depression. Morgan Park Junior College opened in 1933 to address that segment of the educational population on the south side of Chicago and maintained a presence on the Morgan Park Military Academy campus until the junior college closed in 1951. But during the Great Depression, the college would secure enough registration income to help keep both itself, and the Academy, above financial distress.

In an interesting development, Coach Fleming literally was placed in complete control of Camp Traverse for the summer of 1932. While the Academy still owned Camp Traverse, Fleming would be responsible for all camp expenses and his own compensation would be based on any profit that the camp might generate. This arrangement freed the Academy from any additional potential "loss" due to low camp enrollment, and certainly encouraged Fleming to actively recruit possible camp attendees to ensure that the summer would not prove to be financially devastating for himself personally. Fleming would need to find a minimum of ten students in order for the camp to remain open. However, the football camp would be scheduled as usual. On October 10, 1932, the Board minutes stated that "Camp Traverse had nine boys. The camp was conducted by Captain Fleming at no profit and no loss to the Academy." The Board approved the concept of a similar arrangement for 1933 where Fleming would be in control of the camp and pay the local taxes and insurance ($113) while also remitting $20 back to the Academy for each attendee after the first ten enrollments.

ICE SO THICK HOCKEY WOULD HAVE BEEN APPROPRIATE

Although enrollment at the Academy withered again for the 1932-33 school year, Coach Fleming was back on the faculty and ready for still another football season. Unfortunately, for Fleming and others, most faculty members were cut back to part-time status when the Upper School enrollment dipped to 189 students. In addition, the Academy closed the faculty houses and other buildings to reduce costs for rent and heating. The venerable Coach Fleming, and his wife, were now sharing dormitory space with most of his players!

Hobbled by a correlating (to enrollment) lack of players, and a wave of injuries, Fleming often found himself with less than 20 healthy players for the 1932 season. The result was a disappointing 2-6 record, with four defeats by shut outs to start the campaign. A pair of one-point losses to St. Albans (7-6) and Elgin Academy (13-12) extended the losing streak to six with the St. Albans defeat especially painful according to the local *Daily Chronicle* newspaper in De Kalb, Illinois on October 31:

> Everyman on the team was going like a prairie fire…In the third frame, the young soldiers got all steamed up and broke loose with a series of power plays that eventually carried the ball over for a touchdown, but their try for a point failed and that spelled defeat for them in large capital letters.

The losing skein was snapped at six when the team finished strong in its last two encounters, as cheerfully reported by the 1933 **Skirmisher:**

> Prepare for a shock—the heavies beat Northwestern! And a shut out at that, 20-0. There was snow on the field when we started, but the team got so hot that it disappeared—and it wasn't shoveled off. The subs got their first crack at conference playing—and you should hear them tell how they won that game. In celebration the whole team cleaned up on about the biggest meal in the annals (something like alleys) of history. About the only way we could properly

celebrate, though, was to go out and clean up on the Alumni, and we did, 14-0. But that Alumni game, boy, it was cold! Both teams went into the boiler room of Blake Hall to warm up between halves, and the ice on the field was so thick that hockey would have been much more appropriate.

Now living in a dorm and working on half-salary with little hope of being rehired for the next school year, Fleming was hit with more devastating news on February 5, 1933 when his beloved wife, Flora, passed away at nearby Little Company of Mary Hospital after a bout with cancer at the age of 48. Soon, Fleming would also learn that he had coached his last football game at Morgan Park Military Academy.

WILL COACH FOR $25 PER MONTH

Although Fleming was already assigned to manage Camp Traverse in 1933, the Board minutes from March 13, 1933 included the following cautionary language: "Captain Fleming is to consider that this summer's arrangement has no relation to his being a member of the faculty for 1933-34." While Camp Traverse continued to struggle with just eight enrollments, the new summer school proved to be quite successful, with 157 students participating in the eight-week session. With the junior college set to open in the fall, the future of the Academy appeared to be stable, despite the negative financial impact of the Great Depression. Abells' preparation for a worst-case scenario along with his plans for generating revenue through innovative new means, helped carry the Academy through the worst economic turbulence in this country's history. For Coach Fleming, however, his future at the Academy was already decided: Coach Fleming was not rehired for the new school year, ending a laudable 13-year coaching tenure for the three major sports at the Academy. At the time of his departure, Fleming was the all-time winningest football coach at the Academy with a record of 49-33-12. Although Fleming reappeared as a part-time faculty member in the early 1940s, he did not return to coaching at the Academy. Eventually, he drifted west and settled in Sequim, Washington where he married Jane Gatchet on August 15, 1962 and was an avid bridge player and instructor. Coach Floyd Fleming passed away on August 14, 1967 at the age of 76.

Perhaps his lofty salary prompted the downfall of Floyd Fleming. As noted previously, $800 of his annual salary was assigned to the Camp

Traverse budget. Whether that $800 was all or part of his income, it likely placed Fleming at the top of the compensation ladder at the Academy. With a total faculty budget of around $6,000 during the Depression for over 20 individuals, Fleming's share would appear to be abnormally high, even with his many years (13) of experience. This theory was collaborated somewhat when the Board of Trustees announced the hiring on September 11, 1933 of Fleming's replacement:

> Wade Woodworth, Northwestern University guard in 1930, and with experience coaching for the last two years at the University of Cincinnati, who has a wife, a two-year old girl and a baby, will be coach at the Academy for the living [room/board] for the family and $25 a month.

Woodworth was an exceptional find for the Academy. After his illustrious football career as an All-American lineman at Northwestern, Woodworth signed a contract to play pro football with the Green Bay Packers. However, his pact with the Packers included a clause that he could ease out of the agreement if he was to secure a coaching position. Woodworth did just that and spent two years at Cincinnati where he served as an assistant coach for the football, swimming, and track teams. But for $25 per month? Clearly, this was a cost-savings initiative for the Academy that just happened to land a very qualified candidate for the low-paying (albeit with room and board) position. Woodworth became available to the Academy when he announced his resignation from Cincinnati on July 24, 1933, to play professional football with the newly formed Cincinnati Reds of the National Football League. When that endeavor did not materialize, he was able to land on his feet at Morgan Park Military Academy with his growing family.

RED HAIR GLOWS LIKE THREE-ALARM FIRE

Aside from the football field, Woodworth was already a national celebrity in a completely different sport: speed boat racing. By the time he reached the Academy, Woodworth had already captured over 40 victories on water, most notably the 1931 "Albany to New York Marathon" in New York. And, he was also a national spokesman for Welch's Grape juice! But it was his prowess on the football field that separated Woodworth from others as a player. On November 21, 1935, he was named to the first unit of

Northwestern's all-time football squad, announced by *The Pittsburgh Press*, with a memorable description of both his appearance and his athletic skills:

> Wade Woodworth, a picturesque red-head, who chugged from town to practice on a rustic motorcycle and doubled as a traffic cop in the off season, was the showiest of all Northwestern guards. Red scorned a helmet. His flaming mop of hair shone like a beacon light in the scrimmage.

During his playing days at Northwestern, Woodworth captured the attention of sportswriters who were intrigued by the big (6'0", 200 lbs.) gentleman with the bright red hair, but without a helmet. His frisky personality was a natural attraction for wordsmiths in the press, such as *The Akron Beacon-Journal* on November 5, 1930:

> He has red hair, and it's not a quiet, retiring red either, but the kind that glows like a three-alarm fire. His disposition matches his hair. Woodworth, who is the Wildcats' right guard, disdains the use of a headgear, stockings, and much padding. Coach Dick Hanley is alarmed that before the season is over the young man will ask to play in a bathing suit. The red head is a hard, clean and peaceable player until he concludes an opponent is becoming too free with the use of hands or knees. Then he becomes real rough. His anger was aroused in the Minnesota game when an opposing lineman kept putting his knees into the quarterback's back. Elbowing his way into the Minnesota huddle, Woodworth grabbed the offender by the shoulder and growled: "I never believed you were a dirty player and don't yet. But use those knees once more and I'm going to start you on a ride!" After which there was continuous peace and quiet.

Woodworth went to work quickly with the team after his late hiring. With only about two weeks before the first game on September 30, he focused on evaluating talent, installing an offense, and physically preparing his club for a lengthy 11 game schedule, one that would include three battles within seven days during the season. Woodworth proved to be an inspiring and energetic coach, often personally demonstrating correct blocking and tackling techniques to the players. Enthusiasm for the team's prospects began to sneak on to the campus, especially after an opening 20-7 win over Calumet City (now Thornton Fractional North) High School in the opener. Captain (and fullback) Hal Carlson scored two touchdowns and was a battering ram on offense which *The Academy News* (October 13, 1933) described "As 100 per cent better than that displayed in the past few years."

More good news would follow as the Academy dispatched Pullman Tech (19-13), and Morton High School (6-0) with Carlson scoring the lone touchdown in the latter game. The next outing was a visit to the always tough Wayland Academy in Beaver Dam, Wisconsin. After coughing up a safety early in the contest, the Academy struggled to score until Jimmie Miller intercepted a wayward Wayland pass and returned it 40 yards for the winning score. Carlson blasted into the end zone for the extra point as the Academy escaped with a 7-2 victory. The *Wayland Greetings* (December 1933) indicated that the school (which had been undefeated) was not all that unhappy with the loss: "The final score was Morgan Park 7, Wayland 2. Of course, the boys were disappointed, but they had played a splendid game and the chances on a sloppy field, not any weakness in play, gave a score against them."

Although the Academy then suffered a pair of close losses to Lake Forest Academy (8-0) and Onarga Academy (2-0), the most thrilling game of the season took place when the team traveled to Culver (Indiana) Military Academy on November 18, a week after securing a 7-0 victory over Elgin Academy to end the two-game skid. The rivalry between the two service academies had been brewing over the past three decades, although the annual contest with Northwestern still seemed a larger event in the eyes of the Academy students.

CADETS POURED ONTO THE FIELD IN A BLUE-GRAY WAVE

A large group of Academy students and faculty made the long train trip to Culver, Indiana, a journey of about 100 miles east of the Academy. The Culver student newspaper took note of the incoming Morgan Park followers in an edition published the day of the game:

> A notice has just been received that Morgan Park is bringing this afternoon a group of sixty or more students in addition to their football team. Several Cadet Club men and several

members of the corps have been delegated to accompany these visitors.

The ensuing skirmish waged between the two polished military elevens was outstanding as the clubs battled deep into the fourth quarter without either team scoring a point. Then, with less than five minutes to play, Culver combined some shifty formations along with a solid running game to push across the first score and provide the hosts with a 6-0 advantage. It was at this point, as Culver prepared to cash in on the extra point kick, that defender Ed Schoening of the Academy burst through the line and blocked the kick keeping the Culver lead at 6-0. *The Academy News* on November 22 accurately described the last few minutes of the exciting contest:

> The prospects for "Chicago's own" looked black. Then Schoening blocked the try for point. Three minutes to play! Spectators began edging toward their cars. Suddenly a pass clicked, then another, and a third. Two desperate line smashes and Carlson was over. At least a tie. The lineup for the extra point. Carlson smashed that line one more time and the game was "in the bag." Faculty members hugged each other and pounded each other on the back. Cadets poured onto the field in a blue-gray wave and carried the team to the showers on jubilant shoulders. Three such minutes of play have not been seen before or since in a Morgan Park game!

The dramatic 7-6 win over Culver brought the Academy's 1933 record to 6-2 and two days later, on a rare Monday game, the Academy defeated St. Albans 20-6, with the versatile Carlson scoring all three touchdowns. Five days later, the Academy blasted Northwestern 52-12 in the presumed season finale. With that win, the Warriors moved to a sparkling 8-2 mark for the season in Coach Woodworth's first campaign. However, on Thanksgiving Day (November 30), the Academy accepted the opportunity to play powerful Tilden Tech High School of Chicago with just two days' notice after Tilden's scheduled game with St. Rita of the Chicago Catholic League was cancelled. The Tilden meeting was not even mentioned in the **Skirmisher**, while *The Academy News* described the event as a "post-season" game and noted only the final score, a 25-6 decision for Tilden Tech in a game played at the St. Rita stadium.

With the now final 8-3 record, Coach Woodworth was satisfied with his charges, especially with the way the team embraced a new coach and a new system with little time to prepare for the beginning of the season:

> Coach Wade "Red" Woodworth expressed himself as very pleased with the record made by his first prep school team when interviewed by *The Academy News* [December 7]. The coach's shock of flaming red hair bristled and his hair-trigger smile flashed when asked what he thought of the team's record for the year 1933. "When a green bunch starts 'cold' and plays the tough schedule that the Warriors did and rolls up the impressive total of 144 points to their opponents 81, you don't need to ask what I think of them," he said. "I wish I could give an emblem to everyone, for the loyalty of the squad has been one of the things that has made my job here very pleasant."

BLAZE OF GLORY, GASTRONOMICS, AND GARRULOUSNESS

With the successful season complete, Coach Woodworth and his club were honored at both a ritzy dance and then a banquet just prior to the Christmas break as noted in *The Academy News* on December 19:

> "Maurie" Kent, freshman coach at Northwestern University, will be the chief speaker in the festivities tonight when the big football banquet puts the final period to the eminently successful grid season of 1933. Following close on the heels of the football dance last Saturday night, the big feed will end the season in a blaze of glory, gastronomics, and garrulousness.

By this time, Woodworth was already deep into the basketball season, which would ultimately lead to a 9-9 finish, including capturing a second-place trophy at the Sycamore (Illinois) Tournament. Rumors floated around campus that Woodworth had been offered a coaching job at Northwestern University, and a collective sigh of relief was evident when the coach decided to remain at the Academy for at least one more year. He was truly revered by his players, and he planned a two-week summer cruise of the Great Lakes with some of the Cadets on his yacht "Circe." The administration appreciated his efforts as well, especially after Woodworth presented a safety-based idea to the Board on November 11, 1933. When noting that individual private cars had generally been used to transport the basketball, baseball, track, and rifle teams to various "away" events, Woodworth studied the issue and determined that 2,420 miles would be gobbled up on these athletic trips. As such, he proposed the following (from a document located in the Academy archives):

> The cost of taking 18 men in four cars figuring gas at 18 cents a gallon and each car averaging ten miles to the gallon would be about $180, counting oil, etc. This would not include break downs or accidents of which there is a possibility during the winter months when boys are driving. I will transport 23 boys any distance in a comfortable, modern, heated bus for 15 cents a mile, or $360 for 2,420 miles.

While Woodworth's idea would not likely save drastic amounts of money, it did seem to eliminate safety and mechanical concerns, since all participants would be safely transported in one bus, a significant advantage that would diminish the fear of one, or all, of the four autos not surviving a long trip during the 1933-34 school year. And, despite his rather limited salary, Woodworth and his family seemed to enjoy the campus atmosphere. When Woodworth secretly married Miss Lucille McCutcheon in 1931 during his last year as a student at Northwestern University, it seemed an ideal match between the swashbuckling football All-American and speed racer, and the petite, attractive blond co-ed. Years later, some of the Academy alumni fondly recalled the presence of the Woodworth family. In November of 2002, Richard Stillman (Class of 1934) told the *Academy Magazine* that:

> Woodworth married a Northwestern beauty queen and all the cadets hoped they would be assigned to the couple's mess hall table, and as a cadet officer I had the good fortune to sit at his table occasionally!

Stillman played football at the Academy and during World War II he earned his Ph.D., achieved the rank of Colonel, and served as secretary of the general staff under General George S. Patton. Later, he was the author of numerous books, both on Patton and other subjects, and was a professor of management at the University of New Orleans.

Another former student who remembered the Woodworths was Roy Schoenbrod (Class of 1936) who shared his recollections in the following article published in the *Academy Magazine* in May of 2001:

Roy also recalls being assigned to Capt. Wade Woodworth's table for 1933-34. Capt. Woodworth was the football coach and had been an All-American at Northwestern. He remembers his wife even better, however. "She was one of the most gorgeous women I ever saw," Roy said. "At lunch, once, as a prank, I unscrewed the top of the salt shaker. Mrs. Woodworth dumped it all over the table. She didn't say a word, but she must have known who did it. She calmly unscrewed the top of the pepper mill and dumped it all over my food!"

Ray Schoenbrod eventually received his degree in architecture at the University of Pennsylvania and later owned his own architectural company called Schoenbrod and Associates.

While the faculty and students of Morgan Park Military Academy were pleased that the Woodworths would be with them for at least another year, the young coach continued speed racing in the summer while also plotting his plans for the next football season. The school had recently approved the construction of a new football field on the north side of 111th Street, and the ambitious Father's Club at the Academy was deeply involved in a massive fund-raising campaign to support the project. The future indeed looked bright for the Morgan Park Academy football program and its energetic young coach.

Unfortunately, the 1934 season would prove to be a coach's worst nightmare…

EXTRA POINT

Football was always the primary sport of interest on the campus of Morgan Park Military Academy. Back in 1933, the Academy physician, Dr. Russell D. Robinson, prepared a list of health-related "hints" for the football players to follow during the season. This list differs greatly from the type of information that might be shared with today's modern player, but it does offer some amusing insight into sports medicine from over 80 years ago:

1. Do not smoke, as this makes a growing boy nervous and shortens his wind.
2. Do not over indulge in rich foods, such as pie, cake, candy and so forth, but eat plain, well-cooked wholesome foods, which build muscle.

3. Warm cooked cereal, such as oatmeal is recommended always for breakfast, rather than dry cold cereals.

4. 8-9 hours of sleep nightly.

5. Coffee limited to one cup daily for breakfast.

6. Do not neglect what seem to be minor injuries, as scratches, abrasions and cinder burns, but see that they are thoroughly cleaned out, and painted with tincture of iodine, and covered with a sterile dressing.

7. Be careful about throwing off your sweaters when hot and sweaty, as colds are readily contracted these chilly fall days.

8. "Athlete's Foot" is contagious and is usually acquired by going around gymnasiums and locker rooms barefooted. Always wear sandals or beach-clogs for this purpose.

9. Be careful as you can of your bodies in football games. Remember that you have to use them for many years to come and that every year many boys are badly hurt—see that you are not one of them.

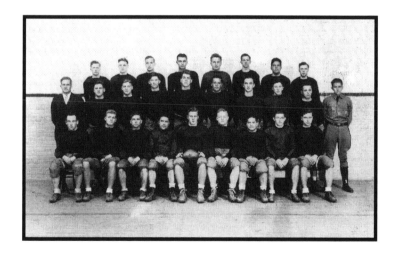

Coach Wade Woodworth (second row on left in tie) was an All-American lineman at Northwestern before he joined the Academy staff in 1933 following a coaching stint at the University of Cincinnati. His 1933 team finished 8-3. During the depression, Woodworth's salary at the Academy was a mere $25 per month, but with room and board included for his family. Woodworth eventually became the head football coach in his return to Cincinnati.

CHAPTER 15

Tragedy, Progress and the NFL

*"The fencing in of the field will keep the sidelines free
from some of the usual mob of spectators."*
—Academy News, October 16, 1934

Although Coach Woodworth may have been a bit pessimistic at the start of the 1934 football season with only three lettermen returning, the overall atmosphere on campus was positive as enrollment stabilized at 177 (for both Upper and Lower schools—six more than in 1933) and the new junior college opened. Surprisingly, the college also fielded a football team and Woodworth scheduled a scrimmage with the collegians on September 25 in preparation for the opening game at Pullman Tech on October 6. *The Academy News*, also published on October 6, contained a brief preview of the upcoming football season:

> The team is working and is being worked plenty hard by our renowned coach, "Red" Woodworth. They are getting in shape rapidly and are already anticipating the Culver game. Coach Woodworth said, "There are only three lettermen back with the squad this year and the team as a whole is pretty green and needs quite a bit of game and playing experience."

NO JOB TOO MENIAL, NO TASK TOO GREAT

That same issue of *The Academy News* published an update on the new football field being developed on the north side of 111th Street. Originally called Blake Field, the decision had been made earlier in the year to name the facility as "Abells Field" in honor of the long-time superintendent of the Academy, Harry D. Abells. Born in 1872 in Hatfield, Massachusetts, Abells arrived on campus in 1898 after graduating from the University of Chicago where he was an outstanding player and captain of the baseball team. At the Academy, Abells was initially hired as a physics and chemistry instructor, becoming school principal in 1907 and superintendent in 1918. He was instrumental in keeping the Academy open during the financial turmoil of 1914, and then worked diligently to help the Academy survive the Great Depression before becoming Superintendent Emeritus in 1945. His passion for the school was unquestioned, so the decision to name the new football field after Abells was a popular one. Perhaps the essence of Col. Abells was captured best in an article appearing in the April 1958 issue of the Academy *Alumni Bulletin*:

> He taught two classes in chemistry, took his turns at evening study hall, visited the infirmary two or three times each day to check on any illnesses that might have occurred. Once, to the horror of his commandant, he was seen lugging beds across the campus. They were needed in the infirmary and, to Col Abells, no job was too menial, no task too great. He never missed a teachers' meeting, a school dance, a cadet game or a meal from the dining room.

Work on transforming the open space of Abells Field into a playable gridiron had begun during the summer of 1934, supported largely by the newly established Fathers' Club. The dads raised $1,300 while members of the alumni chipped in with another $300 for the project. In addition, members of the Fathers' Club donated their own individual services, as reported in *The Academy News* (May 4, 1934):

> Abells Field! This addition to the Academy tradition and forward step in the development in the Academy's service to boys was brought about through the combined efforts of the recently formed Fathers' Club and the Alumni Association. Mr. J. Albert Robinson, father of cadet Robinson, is at present engaged in drawing up plans for

draining the field. As soon as the plans are complete Mr. Peter Fosco, father of cadet James Fosco, will move a body of men onto the field and put in the necessary drainage equipment. Mr. George Reed has agreed to do necessary grading of the field when the drainage is completed.

By the time the football season rolled around in October of 1934, the field was nearly complete, but not quite ready to be utilized for football action according to *The Academy News* (October 6, 1934):

> It has not yet been determined whether the field will be used this fall, due to the newly graded surface of the field. If the field is used, portable bleachers will be set up. Observing the games will be more enjoyable and the fencing in of the field will keep the sidelines free from some of the usual mob of spectators.

Meanwhile Coach Woodworth was working overtime to fashion a competitive team consisting primarily of players with little on-field experience. Only three lettermen returned, including fullback Fred Heitman, right tackle Charlie Orr, and halfback Dick Tomczak. The remainder of the starters such as quarterback Bruce Briney, right guard Russell Cannon, and left guard Waldemar Zinter were expected to learn on the job as the Academy team sought to equal, or better, the fine 8-3 record of 1933.

ZINTER BLOCKED A PUNT

Unfortunately, the visit to Pullman Tech on October 6 resulted in a sound defeat by the score of 18-0. About the only highlight for the Warriors was a blocked punt by surprisingly quick guard "Wally" Zinter in his first start for the Academy that was noted by the *Chicago Daily News* on October 7: "Zinter, a guard on the Academy eleven, blocked a punt during the game and at that time suffered only a nose bleed." Whether Zinter was hit in the face with the punted football, or perhaps kicked in the scramble to block the kick, he picked himself up and trotted to the sidelines for treatment of a bloody nose. After the game, he reported no other concerns and returned with the team to the Academy campus to rest and prepare for a military dress parade on Sunday. It was after the parade that Zinter began to complain about headaches and it was decided by the faculty to rush him to Evangelical Hospital in Chicago as a precaution. While in the hospital,

Zinter lapsed into a coma and never recovered. He died from his apparent football injuries on Tuesday, October 9, 1934. On October 10, the coroner investigated Zinter's death and the results were reported by the *Chicago Tribune*:

> A verdict of accidental death was returned by a coroner's jury investigating the death of Waldemar Carl Zinter, Jr., 17 years old, Morgan Park Military Academy football player. Zinter died Tuesday night in the Evangelical Hospital of blood poisoning, which developed after his nose was broken in a game last Saturday between the Academy team and the Pullman Technical High School.

Dr. George E. Bryar, father of current Academy archivist Sharon Eichinger, offered an explanation for Zinter's death, although Dr. Bryar cautioned that his interpretation is based only on a professional opinion without reviewing the original coroner's report:

> It is impossible to say how the boy died without the report of the coroner. In any case, here is my best guess. The nasal fracture resulted in a fracture of the base of the frontal skull (the cribiform plate). This caused a leak in the cerebrospinal fluid. Over the next few days, this became infected (a meningitis) which they called a "blood poisoning" in the news report (above). This would jive with death on Tuesday and the injury on Saturday. We did not have any antibiotics to treat meningitis in that era. It was usually fatal. All this, of course, is conjecture.

Face masks on football helmets were not required in 1934, meaning that Zinter may have escaped the Pullman Tech game unscathed with a modern helmet and/or access to modern antibiotics. As such, Zinter's death rocked the campus and the immediate world of high school football. The upcoming game with St. Albans was cancelled and the Board of Trustees seriously considered dropping the entire football program. No one would have questioned that decision if it had been implemented.

A wake for Zinter was held on Saturday, October 13 at his home (8458 South Ada in Chicago) prior to his burial in nearby Cedar Park Cemetery. *The Academy News* paid tribute to Zinter in its October 19 edition:

From the first day he began to make many friends and to make rapid progress in making himself indispensable to the corps of cadets. "Wally" was one of the best liked cadets on the campus. He was a friend of every cadet and was well liked by all of his instructors. Besides being an excellent student, for he had been proclaimed a proficient cadet, he had also made rapid progress in the military work. Last June he had been promoted to a cadet sergeant. He was also Guardian of the Morgan Park Spirit. "Wally" Zinter was more than capable of guarding this spirit.

FOOTBALL WOULD BE CONTINUED AT THE ACADEMY

In the same issue of *The Academy News*, it was announced that the football season would be resumed, albeit with the introduction of increased safety procedures:

> In a meeting Monday evening [October 15], presided over by Colonel Abells and attended by representatives of all branches of Academy life, it was decided that football would be continued at the Academy. In order that parents might feel more at ease, suggestions were made to protect football players in the future. Dr. C.C. MacLane, after fully explaining the causes of the accident, and giving a very complete summary of accidents in football, both college and high school, made the suggestion that a young and competent physician with a football background, thoroughly examine each football player before each game, and confer with the coach during the game in watching the physical condition of the boys. It was further suggested that an immediate consultation be held with Dr. Russell Robinson, academy physician, to receiving suggestions in achieving that end.

Although these medical "suggestions" seemed more precautionary than preventative, the large crowd participating in the meeting at Alumni Hall agreed to move forward with the remainder of the football schedule. This left Coach Woodworth with the daunting task of rallying a grieving group of shocked teenagers back into football condition, both mentally and physically. With just four days back on the practice field before traveling to powerful LaGrange High School, Woodworth embraced the challenge of preparing his already inexperienced club for a difficult adversary. As it was, the LaGrange contest was a foreshadowing of a very tough season. Falling behind early after an opening 90-yard kickoff return, the Warriors never recovered and dropped a 33-0 decision to the host team. The unrelenting ground attack of LaGrange even impressed the local *LaGrange Citizen* (October 25, 1934) which used word play to compare the prep halfbacks with the legendary All-American Red Grange from the University of Illinois:

> The long La "Grange" runs which thrilled the spectators throughout the game imply a certain amount of good blocking, and of that there was plenty in Saturday's game. In fact, the exceptional blocking performance of LaGrange occasioned the umpire to remark after the game to Coach Ollie Stenger, that it was some of the finest blocking he had ever seen in high school football.

After the game, a dejected Woodworth told *The Academy News*: "The team looked very good before the game with LaGrange but LaGrange showed a few things about football that they did not know." Yet somehow, Woodworth inspired his troops to not only score their first points of the season the following week (October 27) at Lake Forest Academy, but also defeat the hosts 12-6. It was a very special meeting of the two old rivals, who first met on the gridiron 40 years previously in 1894. It was also Homecoming at Lake Forest and several of the home school's alumni from that 1894 team were in attendance. When quarterback Bruce Briney plunged over for the winning touchdown, it marked the first time since 1910 that the Academy had defeated Lake Forest, although the teams had played only sporadically since that time.

GROUND PLANTED WITH QUICK-GROWING CROP OF OATS

Back on campus, the Academy Fathers' Club was pushing to prepare the new Abells Field for its debut for the Homecoming game against Elgin Academy on November 10. "A nine-foot fence now surrounds the field. The ground itself was planted with a quick-growing crop of oats earlier in the season and now boasts a luxurious green carpet. In fact, the oats will have to be cut before the Elgin game," reported *The Academy News* on November 2. The Academy hired a professional field announcer and sold verbal "advertisements" from local merchants to be read during the game. The large Homecoming crowd was now surrounded by a sturdy fence, thus preventing casual observers from entering the premises and resulting in a nice reward of $109.65 for the Academy from the gate receipts.

After stumbling to an 18-0 defeat at the hands of Onarga Academy on November 3, the Warriors inaugurated Abells Field on November 10 with a hard-fought 13-6 loss to Elgin Academy, the eventual conference champion. The defeat left the Academy with a 1-4 record entering the final game of the season, a Dad's Day event at Abells Field. A fired-up Woodworth squad made up for a season of sadness and frustration by pummeling Wayland Academy 28-6 in the finale behind four touchdowns from Bruce Briney. *The Academy News* (December 14) summarized the happy results as follows:

> Although their season might be called spotty, it ended splendidly with a good old-fashioned shellacking of the Wayland team for the delight of the on-looking Dad's Day spectators. With their dads looking on and the desperation of the whole season's defeats behind them, the Warriors rose up on their hind legs and smote the Waylanders where they lived and when the smoke of battle cleared away the score board registered M.P.M.A. 28, Visitors 6. The game was played on the freshly mowed oat field of the new Abells Field and ended a season of drubbings with a feeling of "we could do it when we really got our backs up."

During the off-season, the Fathers' Club began to improve Abells Field and by 1938 had added a field sprinkling system, new bleachers, shrubbery, track and jumping pits, and a new flag pole, among other items. But the biggest surprise during the winter after the 1934 season was the departure of Coach Woodworth. Woodworth had compiled a satisfactory 10-7 record during his two years as the Academy football coach and was extremely popular with the students. However, Woodworth, along with the other faculty members, had worked for a pittance ($25 per month, along with room and board) during the early days of the Great Depression. A job was a job during that time, but Woodworth was likely seeking more financial security for his growing family. He eventually returned to the University of Cincinnati where he was named head football coach midway through the 1937 season when head coach Russell Cohen resigned. After a 0-5 conclusion during the remainder of the season under his guidance, Woodworth returned to his previous position as line coach in 1938, remaining in that position until 1940. He also served as the freshmen basketball coach at Cincinnati, while continuing to compete in power boat racing for many years. Woodworth supplemented his coaching salary by owning a bus company serving private schools in Cincinnati, as well as operating the Cincinnati Play School. He passed away in Volusia, Florida on June 25, 1992 at the age of 86.

FORGET ALL THE FOOTBALL THAT YOU EVER KNEW

The search for Woodworth's replacement ended quickly when another noted football star, Claude T. Grigsby, was hired by the Academy in April of 1935. Grigsby had prepped at Tilden Tech High School in Chicago (winning nine letters in football, basketball, and swimming) before playing collegiate football at Georgetown University. In 1927, he was named an All-American and he participated in the prestigious East-West All-Star football game following the 1927 season. After graduation from Georgetown, Grigsby returned to the Chicago area and was employed as the Director of the Chicago Life Guard Training School while also becoming a noted football official, particularly in collegiate contests, such as the Big Ten Conference. As much as the students enjoyed the presence of Coach Woodworth, the arrival of Grigsby for his first meeting with the team on June 3 was awaited with great anticipation. In a brief interview with *The Academy News* (May 4, 1935), Grigsby outlined his plans, and challenges, directly to the players for the upcoming season:

> I am most anxious to get out to Morgan Park and see what material we have. We are going to work hard out there and I promise that you will get sick of scrimmaging, for that is all we will do for the hour or more we are on the field. My one request to you fellows is that you forget all the football that you ever knew for we are going to play a different game of ball than you are acquainted with. We are going to use a low defense, a thing that is used only in the East. Forget that you have hands for we will use our bodies. The Warner "wing-back" system will be used.

In 1935, total enrollment on campus increased slightly to 187, indicating that the Academy, although struggling, was still surviving the worst days of the Great Depression. The football camp at Camp Traverse had been discontinued with the departure of Coach Floyd Fleming, but Coach Grigsby invited candidates to participate in an "early" conditioning camp on campus the week before school actually opened in September of 1935. As usual, *The Academy News* (September 12) provided insight into the pre-season workouts:

> The football team has been hard at work a week before the opening of the Academy. This year, time has been spent in conditioning the candidates for the football squad. Coach Grigsby, who has been supervising the squad says "they are now in tip-top shape and could tear a lion apart." The spirit shown this year is, if possible, better than that shown in previous years and by all appearances MPMA will have a banner team.

Robert Reid, the center for the 1935 club, shared his memories of the conditioning camp with the *Academy Magazine* in October of 2002:

Our coach was Claude Grigsby and we did not see a football for at least the first week. He was determined to have us in the best condition possible and, as a result, the few injuries we had during the season were relatively minor.

Despite the optimism, Grigsby's first edition stumbled through a 3-6 season, failing to score in five of those contests. Off the field, the students were busy selling something new to raise money for the school: advance tickets to the home football games. Although the Academy was shut out in those first three contests against Blue Island (12-0), Pleasant View (13-0), and Pullman Tech (12-0), the receipts for ticket sales were impressive. Total receipts for the first three games (as reported by *The Academy News* on October 13) were $277.85. "As most everyone in the corps knows, one of our chief aims is to finish the payments on our fence that surrounds the Abells Athletic Field," stated the *News* adding: "Of course, the corps has just got started in this ticket selling business. When some real games come along, such as Lake Forest, Onarga, and Culver, Abells Field will take in some real money!"

The first victory of the season was achieved in the fourth game against Wayland Academy in Beaver Dam, Wisconsin against an unusual opponent. In a move that would be quickly prohibited today, Wayland proposed that the Academy play two quarters against the Wayland varsity, and two quarters against members of the Wayland alumni. The concept was accepted by the Academy, but neither of the Wayland squads provided stiff competition as Coach Grigsby picked up his first win with a 25-6 decision in this unique football confrontation. Two more wins against Lake Forest Academy (25-6) and Onarga Military Academy (14-8) evened the team's record at 3-3 for the season. Those last two victories seemed to solidify Grigsby's reputation as a tough, innovative coach, especially after quarterback Kenny Krichbaum scored on an 80-yard fake punt play against Lake Forest Academy. Even a guest alumni writer in *The Academy News* was smitten with Grigsby's efforts:

> Grigsby is a real coach. His success with the team this year is little short of amazing. He represents the epitome of Morgan Park ideals and sportsmanship. Some of his plays are a pleasure to behold and several of them have been clicking for touchdowns from mid-field. I am sold on his system and offer my congratulations.

NUMBING COLD AND GREASY FIELD

Unfortunately, the glow of the season diminished rapidly as the Warriors dropped their final three games to finish 3-6. The Homecoming loss (13-0) to Culver on November 16 was especially painful. In its preview of the game, the *Chicago Tribune* included a photo of co-captains Art and Richard Tomczak and reported that much more than just football would be on tap when the rival military schools met on Abells Field:

> More than 8,000 are expected to watch the contest. The Dads' Club of Morgan Park and several American Legion posts are aiding in the promotion of the game. The national championship drill team from the Beverly Hills post and the state championship band from the South Shore post will perform between halves.

Part of the allure of the Culver contest prompted *The Academy News* to once again impress its readers by publishing an edition of the school newspaper (including an action photo) less than two hours after the conclusion of the game on November 16. Henry Justin Smith, an Academy alumnus, author, historian, and Managing Editor of the *Chicago Daily*

News, was credited by *The Academy News* for his assistance in securing the rapid printing of the edition. The Culver game report was insightful, crisp, and descriptive:

> Fighting every minute of a cold, slippery, muddy sixty minutes of football against a fast and wily team from Culver, the Morgan Park cadets put on as good an exhibition of bull-dog tenacity as old grads of the Maroon and White could wish for this afternoon before the largest homecoming crowd in recent years. The final score was 13-0 in favor of the Indiana boys, but that does not begin to picture the spirit and suspense of a contest filled with suspense and scoring threats. Treacherous, slippery mud made the going uncertain at all times and made the suspense practically continuous. It is merely a coincidence that the score was not much larger on both sides, for fumbles without number were the order of the day.

The inconsistent season expired with a final 7-0 loss to Harrison Tech High School of Chicago, completing the 3-6 campaign. Following the completion of the schedule the team elected halfback Attilio "Tillie" Monaco as captain for the 1936 season, and much was expected of Monaco and Coach Grigsby in 1936. In particular, Grigsby was anxious to unleash the talents of fullback Owen Price, a multi-dimensional player who was a bruising runner as well as a gifted passer.

Although the Academy football club managed to turn things around in 1936, finishing with a 5-3-1 record, it was once again a frustrating experience with the team bouncing from impressive victories to surprising losses, especially near the end of the season. The Warriors started out by posting three straight shutouts in wins over Blue Island High School (6-0) and Elgin Academy (31-0) and a tie with Pullman Tech (0-0). The opener against Blue Island was sweet revenge after the Academy had dropped a 12-0 decision to the same club in 1935. But the *Blue Island Sun-Standard* (October 2) pointed to the dire playing conditions as the reason for the final outcome:

> The heavy Morgan Park Military Academy eleven took a wet and muddy game from Blue Island last Saturday by a score of 6-0. The Islanders looked rather well on their defense when they checked a strong Morgan Park drive in the first quarter. Blue Island staged an unexpected drive

in the second quarter when the boys used some nice teamwork. Ray Malatinka cooperated in the drive when he took the ball on a spinner and advanced almost to the goal line. With touchdown on the tip of their fingers the local gridders fumbled the wet and slippery pigskin and Morgan Park recovered on the one-yard line.

The defeat of perennial Midwest Conference champion Elgin Academy on October 10 set up an early season showdown with long-time rival Lake Forest Academy on October 17. By 1936, the conference included Morgan Park Military Academy, Lake Forest Academy, Elgin Academy, Wayland Academy, St. Albans, and Pleasant View Academy of Ottawa, Illinois. As the early part of the 1936 season evolved, it appeared that the Academy and Lake Forest would be the most formidable squads in the circuit. Lake Forest survived the showdown with a 7-0 advantage, but the Academy rebounded with three more wins over St. Albans (59-0), Onarga Military Academy (19-6) and Calumet High School of Chicago (12-0). After those impressive wins vaulted the Academy's record to 5-1-1, a complete reversal occurred in the final two encounters, a 34-0 drubbing from Culver and a 44-0 whipping courtesy of St. John's Military Academy. Despite the sudden late season reversal of fortunes, the final 5-3-1 mark was considered successful by the team, and the league coaches named center Frank Harrison, end Robert MacLane, and versatile back Owen Price to the all-conference honor squad.

However, even with the significant turnaround in 1936, Coach Claude Grigsby decided to pursue greener pastures and moved on from the Academy by accepting the head football coaching position at Marmion Military Academy in Aurora, Illinois. His assistant coach at Marmion was a youngster out of Notre Dame named George Ireland who would later coach Loyola University of Chicago to the national collegiate basketball championship in 1963. Later, Grigsby became the head football coach at St. Patrick High School (Chicago) in 1942. Throughout his career, Grigsby established himself as one of the most respected football officials in the country. He worked the most important high school games in Chicago (including the Prep Bowl) and was usually found on Saturdays overseeing key collegiate games. Grigsby ultimately made it to the National Football League as a referee where he worked from 1947-1951. In later years, he was employed in sales and also by the Chicago Park District. In 1953, Grigsby was elected to the Georgetown University Athletic Hall of Fame. He passed away in Chicago on May 19, 1965 at the age of 62.

AS THE FINAL GUN WENT OFF, PANDEMONIUM REIGNED

To replace Coach Grigsby, the Academy began a national search to identify a knowledgeable coach who could continue the successful football tradition. In the end, the search team found its ideal candidate right on campus in the person of Captain George Mahon. Following his graduation from Ohio Wesleyan in 1921, Mahon spent several years coaching in Ohio high schools before joining the Academy staff in 1926. He initially served as assistant football coach to Coach Floyd Fleming during Fleming's long tenure, but with adding the duties of head football coach in 1937, Mahon was now busy as football coach, basketball coach, baseball coach, head of the physical education department, dean of sophomores and full-time instructor! As a highly regarded athlete at Ohio Wesleyan (football, basketball, and baseball), Mahon was well-versed in coaching strategy but was also keen to uncover one missing element in the Academy's system that he was determined to address immediately: consistency. In an interview with *The Academy News* (June 10, 1937) shortly after his hiring as head grid coach, Mahon identified his goals and objectives:

> Starting next fall, I hope to have a closer coordinated system among heavies, lights, and bantamweights. This implies that the same plays, signals and same system will be used, which will enable a boy to move up or down from one squad to another.

Mahon's new "coordinated" system worked well in 1937 as the Academy finished with a 6-3 record. Included in those victories was a win (27-0) over a tough, new opponent, Lemont High School, from a far southwestern suburb of Chicago and an always satisfying triumph over Culver (25-7). Team Captain Albert Johnson, fresh off the injured list, scored twice for the Academy in the latter game, including an 80-yard interception return. *The Culver* (Indiana) *Citizen* provided a nicely descriptive account of the contest on November 17:

> Upsetting the dope in a decisive way the scrappy Morgan Park Military Academy football team soundly clipped the wings of the Culver Military Academy Flying Squadron Saturday afternoon in Chicago to the tune of 25-7, before a capacity Dad's Day crowd at the Chicago institution.

The 1937 **Skirmisher** dropped an illuminating account of the Academy's solid win in this burgeoning rivalry: "As the final gun went off, pandemonium reigned while the victorious home team and the cadet body cheered the event." An even stronger testament to the rivalry was published by the *Blue Island Sun* on November 18, which sought to capture the joyous campus reaction:

> Such rejoicing as comes only with great and decisive victories resounded through the Morgan Park Military Academy campus Saturday. The Warriors beat Culver. Culver, who in the past, has been M.P.M.A.'s most dreaded and most often successful foe. So welcome was this victory that the bell in Blake Hall's tower, silent for over ten years, was kept ringing for some time after the game. Alumni Hall, scene of the Dad's Day dinner, echoed with the lusty cheers and songs of victory…Culver had been beaten!

Under Mahon's command, the rivalry between Culver and Morgan Park Military Academy would reach its zenith in just two short years. But for now, the National Football League (NFL) was about to invade the Morgan Park Military Academy campus.

AGREE TO ALLOW CHICAGO CARDINALS TO USE ABELLS ATHLETIC FIELD

Coach George Mahon was rarely without a cigarette as he strolled through the Morgan Park Military Academy campus. On a hot summer day in 1938 he casually took a quick puff as he digested the news he had just received from Col. Abells. The Academy's fields and facilities were about to be turned over to the Chicago (now Arizona) Cardinals of the NFL for that team's pre-season training camp. Since the still new Morgan Park Junior College also fielded a football team, Mahon figured that things could get somewhat tight as all three teams competed for fields, showers, and meals during the late summer. While the decision to allow the professionals on campus had already been decided, Mahon had just one major fear: the overuse of Abells Field. The new facility had been the recipient of gradual improvements each year by the Fathers' Club and was now a welcome and pristine home for the Academy gridders. When packed for home games, as it usually was, Abells Field was also a definite home field advantage.

Quickly, Mahon retreated back to the administrative offices and entered his plea that the pros be allowed the run of the place—except for Abells Field. His request was evaluated but ultimately rejected. Abells Field had already been discussed in the negotiations between the Academy and the Cardinals, but there was some wiggle room. In the final contract language, the Cardinals primarily would be utilizing the south field behind the gymnasium for their daily workouts and the carefully cultivated landscape of Abells Field would be available for use only on a limited basis.

It was actually a great deal for the Academy to host the Cardinals in 1938. The empty dorms would be used (at a price, of course!), and the team would be served its meals each day in the empty dining hall, again for a price. Basically, it was another fiscal win for Abells, who was becoming adept at securing income from various sources such as summer school that had not been utilized before. But a pro football team on campus? Abells shrugged and knocked down some more paradigms; he would do what he could to ensure the survival of the Academy.

There was some resistance on the Board, but Abells was a master of persuasion and the contract with the Cardinals was signed prior to the team arriving on August 18, 1938. The club would be on campus until September 11 before the Academy opened for the school year and thus eliminating any concerns from Mahon about sharing facilities at the same time. According to the contract (found in the Academy archives), the school would allow the Chicago Cardinals "to use the south football field, the gymnasium, locker room and showers...on any day the team is on the premises except Sundays. The Academy understands that Kennedy Park is available to the Cardinals on Sundays." The agreement also included specific information regarding the financial terms of the partnership:

> It is further agreed that room and board for the players, numbering about fifty men, will be supplied by the Academy at the rate of $2.50 per day basis per man. It is further agreed to allow the party [Cardinals] to use Abells Athletic Field three times per week for scrimmage, it being understood by both parties that the field will not be in use more than one and a half hours at a time. The party agrees to reimburse...for any damages done to any property...by any one in connection with the Chicago Cardinals Football Club in any capacity.

With the agreement, Abells was able to generate approximately $3,000 more for the Academy's treasury and keep some school workers employed for a few weeks in the summer. The management of the Cardinals seemed pleased with the arrangement as well. After training in Duluth, Minnesota in 1939, the Cardinals returned to the Academy once again in 1940. In an interview with the author, the late fullback Mario "Motts" Tonelli described the 1940 Morgan Park Military Academy training camp existence for the Cardinals' players:

> We worked out twice each day. We started at 9:30 in the morning and went until lunch. Then we came back out at about 1:00 and practiced until 4:00 or 5:00. After dinner, we had a pep talk from the coach and then went over film or specific plays. At night we were just plain tired!

Once the Cardinals departed on September 11, 1938, Coach Mahon welcomed 32 players to his own training camp. Unfortunately, only three of the candidates were lettermen from the 1937 season. Surprisingly, Mahon and his new assistant, Henry Bollman (an all-conference center at Rice University), guided the boys to a sterling 5-2-2 record, a mark that elicited some sunny comments from the 1938 **Skirmisher**:

> When only three lettermen returned from last year's heavyweight football squad, Coaches Mahon and Bollman decided to make the best of the bad situation and consequently made no predictions as to what possibilities this team, which was to be the lightest and most inexperienced that had romped enemy territory for years, had. This was only the beginning of the story, however, because when a group of high spirited, well-conditioned boys want to play the game the best they know how, such difficulties are certain to be overcome.

Although undefeated (along with Onarga) in conference play, Onarga was awarded the title since the Academy finished with a pair of ties. Onarga's sole tie was a 0-0 deadlock with the Cadets. Overall, the toughest defeat was at the hands of Culver, a 14-12 setback in the annual slugfest with the Indiana military school. It wasn't due to any perceived lack of support, as the *Hammond Times* reported on November 2 prior to the contest at Culver:

> The entire corps of cadets of Morgan Park Military Academy will attend the annual game with Culver Military Academy at Culver, Indiana. The cadets will go to the game on a special train which has been chartered from the Pennsylvania Railroad by the Fathers' Club. In addition to the 250 cadets, it is expected that about 300 parents, Morgan Park fans and members of the alumni association will take the train.

After the Culver disappointment, the Academy ended the season on a high note by knocking off St. John's Military Academy 16-7 and new foe Marmion Military Academy 26-12 to wrap up the1938 schedule with a 5-2-2 finish. The guest speaker at the annual football banquet was halfback Jay Berwanger of the University of Chicago and the first winner of the Heisman trophy. Berwanger spoke to the players about teamwork, trust, and determination, but Coach Mahon likely never heard a word. He was already thinking about the 1939 season—and a rematch with Culver…

THE "LIGHTS" GAINED WHERE THE "HEAVIES" LOST

With Coach Mahon's system of coordinating the same instruction on all different team levels to ensure an overall knowledge of plays and expectations, players could easily be moved "up" or "down" as required to address positional or injury needs within the program. The co-captain of the 1938 lightweight squad, Richard Duchossois ('40), would likely have moved up to the heavyweight roster in 1939 until sustaining a season-ending injury as reported by the 1940 **Skirmisher**: "If an injury had not forced "Dutch" from playing football last year he probably would have gone up to heavyweights. As it happened the "lights" gained where the "heavies" lost, for "Dutch" came out and helped Lt. Gentleman with the lightweight backfield." Duchossois later attended Washington and Lee University before entering the service during World War II. Rising quickly through the ranks to become a captain and then a major, Duchossois saw action in five European campaigns winning two Bronze Stars and a Purple Heart after being shot in the side in September of 1944. Following his discharge in 1946, he returned to the Chicago area and began a magnificent business career and is now the Chairman Emeritus of The Duchossois Group, Inc. in Elmhurst, Illinois. The company is perhaps best known for its ownership positions in the Churchill Downs (Kentucky) and Arlington Park

(Illinois) race tracks, among its other interests. He is likely the most generous benefactor of Morgan Park Academy in the school's history and is also the namesake of the Richard L. Duchossois Integrity and Values Award at the Academy which is the highest honor that an alumnus of the school can receive. The 2016 winner of that award, Denny Cresap ('52) told the *Academy Magazine* about his admiration for Mr. Duchossois:

> Two years before I started at the Academy in 1948, Richard Duchossois set the gold standard of achievement for a Morgan Park Academy graduate when he returned from five European campaigns in WW II with two Bronze Stars and a Purple Heart. Richard was an inspiration to all of us back then and I would hope he continues to be an inspiration to graduates for as long as there is a Morgan Park Academy.

For his part, Mr. Duchossois, the former football, track, and boxing athlete at the Academy, has remained steadfast in his appreciation for the education he received at the school as he noted in an interview for this book:

> Morgan Park has been a major contributor to whatever success I may have had. It taught me discipline, loyalty, competition and that second place was never good enough. Without that background, I don't think that I could have had a successful career in five European campaigns. I learned the discipline, respect and loyalty when I was a buck private and I also learned that when you're an officer, how to respect and help the people that you command. I wouldn't have known this if it hadn't had been for my education at Morgan Park and the opportunity to participate in all their sports activities.

EXTRA POINT

In 2009, Morgan Park Academy established a "Walk of Fame" (now the Hall of Fame) to "honor former students, coaches, and teams who have represented MPA and MPMA through athletic excellence." The two earliest honorees, in terms of their graduating class, were Bernard "Bud" Reichel (Class of 1936) and Owen Price (1937). Both of these late athletes played on the football teams coached by Claude Grigsby.

Reichel was born in Ladysmith, Wisconsin in 1918 and became a three-sport standout at the Academy (football, basketball, and track), while also participating in the band, the drama club, and working for *The Academy News*. That publication described Reichel after the 1935 season as "Shifty, fast, and a hard hitter. Too bad he is a senior. He can play half or full positions with equal power." Meanwhile, the 1936 **Skirmisher** lauded Reichel as "a line smasher 'Bud' was the tops. When he hit his opponents they really knew they were hit!" Following graduation, Reichel attended Tulane University and later served in the U.S. Navy from 1944-1946. An entrepreneur, Reichel served in various business capacities throughout his career, including as president of Budd, Inc. a prominent vending machine company in Jacksonville, Florida. After divesting himself from Budd, Mr. Reichel became a general contractor, overseeing the construction of homes, apartments and commercial buildings, as well as numerous Shakey's Pizza Parlors. Reichel passed away on June 24, 1994 in Alachua, Florida. In 2015, his daughter, Betty Reichel, honored her father's experiences at the Academy by establishing the Bernard Kormann Reichel Global Scholarship for future Morgan Park Academy students. "Morgan Park was everything to my dad," she told the *Academy Magazine* in 2015. "It was his home."

While Owen Price was a gifted athlete at the Academy, his football career blossomed when he attended the Texas College of Mines (now The University of Texas at El Paso or UTEP). Price spent two years at the Academy, earning letters each year in football, basketball, baseball, and track, shattering the school discus record as a member of the track and field team. *The Academy News* praised Price after the 1935 season, noting that "Because he uses his head, keeps cool, and looks to see where a receiver is free, he is the best passer on the squad, and always plays heads-up football."

As he was at the Academy, Price was a triple threat in college, meaning he could hurt the opposition by running, passing or kicking, and he did all three very well in Texas. During his junior year (1940) at Texas, Price topped the Border Conference in rushing, punting, and scoring. He was also the finest punter in the United States, with a lofty 48.0 yards per kick average. If that number seems impressive, it certainly should be. Even though that mark was for one season, the highest collegiate career record for punting average belongs to Johnny Townsend of the University of Florida with an average of 46.27 from 2013-2017 according to *Sports Reference College Football*. The presence of Price in the backfield inspired fear among his opponents as noted in an article from *The Arizona Republic* on November 5, 1941 focusing on the Arizona State football team:

Coach Dixie Howell [of Arizona State] warned that Owen Price, Texas Mines' star back, would be the most dangerous man they have encountered. "The Miners haven't the all-around strength of the Arizona Wildcats," Howell said, "but I'm sure we're going to have to do a lot of scoring to offset Price's offensive work."

During his final season in 1941, Price led the nation in passing (based on total completions) for most of the season (eventually finishing second) and once again was the foremost punter in the country with a 45.0 average. Although he was named twice to the Little All-American honor squad and was drafted by the New York Giants in the 1942 NFL draft, Price opted to serve his country during the early stages of World War II. He was commissioned as a pilot with the Army Air Corps and participated in 240 missions over China, India and Burma, receiving eight flying medals for his extraordinary service. According to his biography in the Academy Hall of Fame, Price retired from the service as a "Lt. Colonel and Command Pilot" and "went on to a successful business career in sales and real estate. He passed away on November 24, 1970 at the age of 52." Price was named to the University of Texas at El Paso Football Hall of Fame, but he always seemed to remember his time at Morgan Park Military Academy, according to his son, Charles (from the Academy's web site):

> My late father, Owen Price, spoke many times about the great times he had playing sports for the Academy. The competition and camaraderie meant a lot to him. His teammates, excellent coaches and teachers were always special to him and he appreciated all that they did for him to help him be successful. Owen always believed that the lessons, discipline and teamwork that he learned playing for the Academy helped him greatly to achieve his success in athletics in college and later on as a U.S. Air Force pilot. Learning how to perform your very best consistently and sometimes sacrificing yourself for the good of the overall team or mission were qualities he frequently spoke of.

It should be noted that Owen Price was part of an illustrious family whose presence on the Academy campus began when his grandfather, Dr. Ira Price, was a German and French instructor in the 1880s. According to the family, Owen Price's father, Charles, attended the Academy, as did his four brothers, Ira, Glynn, Richard, and Laurence.

The Academy Heavyweight team scrimmages prior to the 1936 season with Art Johnson carrying the ball. Note that many players still were not wearing helmets at the time.

Coach Claude Grigsby was the Academy's head coach in 1935 and 1936. Grigsby (on the right) is pictured with the 1936 captain Attilio "Tillie" Monaco.

In an innovative publicity shot for the 1936 season, several members of the football team pose with one of the many cannons that were placed throughout the campus at that time. Standing from left: Louis Rathje and Mike Krichbaum. Standing on cannon: Art Johnson and Bob Clark. Seated on cannon (from left): Ed Cerny, Junior Harrison, Captain Tillie Monaco, Owen Price, Dick Grest, Howie Martin and Dan Roberts.

The captains of the 1938 Lightweight football team were (from left) Richard Duchossois and Edward Kelly.

CHAPTER 16

Game of the Century

"A miniature Army-Navy football spectacle is in prospect when Morgan Park Military Academy meets Culver."
—Chicago Daily News, 1939

No one could believe this...

Certainly, there were great expectations that the annual football collision between Morgan Park Military Academy and Culver Military Academy might be something special, but as each week of the 1939 season passed, the stakes seemed to get higher.

The game was held on Armistice Day, November 11 (now Veterans Day), a date obviously very important to both military schools. As they reached Abells Field the players were greeted by a massive crowd estimated at over 5,000. With limited seating on the meager bleachers on both sides of the gridiron, most of the spectators stood four or five deep along the fence surrounding the football field. The roars of the crowd and the competitive cheers from the cadets at both schools prior to the kick off filled the air between 111th and 112th Streets across from the Academy campus. Everyone anticipated a close battle, especially since both teams entered the contest undefeated, a rare occurrence in the long history between the two prestigious institutions. Morgan Park was aiming to reverse the narrow 14-12 setback it suffered a year ago, while Culver was hoping to avoid the 25-7 defeat it absorbed in 1937. And who could forget perhaps the greatest game in the history of the series, the 7-6 Morgan Park victory back in 1933, secured only by a miraculous blocked extra point kick late in the game? Since the series between the two academies began in 1899, there had been controversies, tight games, romps, and surprises, but nothing could compare with the atmosphere and excitement surrounding the 1939 contest.

Yet the preliminary genesis of the competitive football fire was probably stoked a bit earlier in the summer of 1939 by something called "The Spirit of Culver." As the name indicates, "The Spirit of Culver" was a Hollywood movie largely filmed at Culver starring former child star Jackie Cooper, along with Andy Devine, and Freddie Bartholomew set on the tranquil campus of Culver Military Academy in Culver, Indiana. According to promotional advertisements, the motion picture promised to demonstrate the virtual "spirit" of Culver Military Academy:

"Spirit of Culver"
To stir the soul!
"Spirit of Culver"
To gladden the heart!
"Spirit of Culver"
To quicken the pulse!
"Spirit of Culver"
Overwhelming praise from opening day capacity crowds!
"Spirit of Culver"

Released in March of 1939, the movie eventually opened in the Chicago area in late May and played throughout the summer, where the Morgan Park Military Academy football players no doubt viewed the film at one of the local theaters that carried the flick, such as the Beverly, Jackson Park, the Cosmo, and possibly the Marquette, the Highway, or the Colony. "The Spirit of Culver" was locked in competition for viewers that early summer from other popular movies including Shirley Temple's "The Little Princess," "Never Say Die" with Bob Hope, and "The Oklahoma Kid," starring James Cagney. If the movie exposure was not enough to propel Culver into the national spotlight, it certainly didn't hurt when **Life Magazine**, the country's pre-eminent weekly publication, published a seven-page article on the school in its June 19, 1939 issue. The Culver name, it seemed, was everywhere...

ALREADY PREPARING AMERICA'S LEADERS

Culver Military Academy, like Morgan Park Military Academy, was founded in the 19th century. According to the school's current web site:

The Culver Military Academy was founded in 1894 by St. Louis businessman Henry Harrison Culver, who was born on August 9, 1840. Forced to care for himself from age 15, he settled in St. Louis, Missouri where he joined his two brothers in forming the very successful Wrought Iron Range Company in 1870.

In 1883, his health faltered and he and his wife, Emily Jane, moved to Lake Maxinkuckee in northern Indiana. He built a home on the northeast corner of the lake and became interested in the life of Marshall County and the local community, then called Marmont. His first major investment on the lake, the Culver Park Hotel, opened on the north shore in 1889. It was unsuccessful financially and closed after two years.

In 1894, Mr. Culver converted the hotel into dormitories, classrooms, and support facilities and established the Culver Military Institute. By Thanksgiving of 1894, the school formally identified itself as the Culver Military Academy.

In 1932, the Culver family relinquished control of the school by surrendering "all property, funds, and other possessions" to The Culver Educational Foundation, a not-for-profit entity. In 1939, commandant of cadets, Charles F. McKinney '12, prepared a monograph which stressed the importance of leadership. "Today as never before, the world needs leaders, leaders in every phase of human endeavor. The question is, 'Shall we wait for them to be a gift for us, or shall we deliberately develop them?'" It was a rhetorical question. Culver was already preparing America's leaders. (History, 2012)

With a significant national recruiting effort, the more than 600 students enrolled at Culver in 1939 were from 42 states and nine foreign countries. The cadets at Morgan Park, numbering over 200 in 1939, were also from different geographical locations, but the majority originated in the Chicago area, especially the "day" students. The rosters of the 1939 football teams reflected that status as well with Culver sporting a combatants' list from 15 states (only three players from Indiana) while the

Academy group included 30 players from the Chicago area out of 33 in total with four states represented. The large difference between the size of the two schools (in terms of enrollment), and the obvious difference in geographical origins of the players would be a concern for modern high school athletic administrators but was never given a thought in 1939. Opponents were scheduled without regard to the size of the opposing school. Currently in Illinois, there are eight different classes of competition in football based on enrollment, with special factors included when considering the status of all-male institutions.

And so it was that the actual "build-up" for the November 11 clash began much earlier in the school year. At the Academy, the Board of Trustees was eyeing the "home" encounter as a possible fund-raising jackpot with the large crowd anticipated for the game. The Board was anxiously preparing to solicit funds for an on-site swimming pool and it appeared that a nice portion of that funding might be garnered in conjunction with the Culver game and the accompanying packed house. In October, the Board formed a committee headed by graduates Fred Herendeen and Saul Epton, to attract publicity for the Culver match. Both were well-known products of the Academy. Herendeen, who was mentioned prominently earlier in this book, was a Broadway composer, but also a former player and coach at the school. Epton graduated from the University of Michigan and the John Marshall Law School and later became an influential judge in the City of Chicago.

MUSTER ALL POSSIBLE MORGAN PARK MAN POWER

One of the committee's more entertaining efforts was the development of a flyer (sent to members of the alumni) that warned of the "Blitz Krieg from Culver," accompanied by an illustration showing a pair of tanks each emblazoned with the word "Culver" attacking the defensive "Morgan Park Trenches" military position. The message on the brochure was simple:

> The way these Culver guys will be pouring in will make it necessary for us to muster all possible Morgan Park man power to combat the onslaught. All classes are turning out to fill our trenches…we will present a united front that cannot be cracked—if YOU will fill that gap. They say it is "more blessed to give than to receive." Let's GIVE Culver the chance to show what good sports they can be when they lose—as they surely will if you will fill that gap.

As the excitement was building early in the school year, Coach Mahon needed to remind his players that a few games still were scheduled before the Culver clash. Mahon's crew opened its season on September 23, with a difficult 2-0 win over Marmion Military Academy with the only points being scored when the Academy pinned Marmion deep in its own territory late in the fourth quarter. Defensive end Jack Berkery then blocked the ensuing Marmion punt and both teams scrambled after the ball which bounced back wildly out of the end zone for a safety, providing a nerve-wracking opening 2-0 victory for the Warriors.

Coach Mahon's defense was solid the following week as well when the Academy blanked Morgan Park Junior College 13-0. Halfback Chuck Correll, who would later star in both football and basketball at Illinois Wesleyan University, scored the first touchdown, while fullback Buddy Weckel tallied the second TD on a scamper around the left side. Meanwhile, Culver opened its season on that same day (September 30) by edging Pullman Tech of Chicago, 12-0. A week later, Culver suffered a minor blemish when it was held to a 6-6 tie with powerful Shortridge High School of Indianapolis, Indiana, before bouncing back with a resounding 31-6 thumping of Marmion Military Academy, the same team that dropped a tight 2-0 decision to the Academy earlier in the season.

By the time the first snow fell in Chicago on October 18, the Academy had rolled over three more opponents, knocking off Lake Forest 19-7, Onarga Military Academy 6-0, and Pullman Tech 28-6. Correll scored three touchdowns in the Pullman game. The Warriors now boasted a stellar 5-0 record, while Culver advanced to 4-0-1 after defeating Memphis Tech of Tennessee 6-0. The table was being set...

By this point in the season, it was likely that amateur prognosticators were reviewing comparative scores and either moaning or groaning about the potential outcome when the big game rolled around on November 11. Naysayers pointed to the Academy's two-point victory over Marmion, the same team that was demolished by Culver 31-6. On the other hand, those in the optimistic camp noticed the Academy's 28-6 win over Pullman Tech while Culver struggled to a 12-0 advantage in its opener over that same opponent. All of which failed to impress Coach Mahon who encouraged his club to remain focused on the next two opponents lest the Culver encounter lose both its luster and its importance.

Next on the schedule for the Academy was long-time rival St. John's Military Academy. Mahon feared a letdown from his players after the early season successes, but was hopeful that the strong student support (as reported by the *Chicago Tribune* on October 26) would provide adequate incentive for the squad:

> The Morgan Park Military Academy football team, band, cadets and members of the Dads' Club, will travel to Delafield, Wisconsin Saturday for the game with St. John's Military Academy. More than 400 are expected to be in the party which leaves at 8:35 a.m. on a Milwaukee Road special train.

Mahon's fears were certainly unfounded as the Academy destroyed the hosts 24-0, much to the delight of the team's avid followers. Chuck Correll was once again in the limelight with a pair of touchdowns, while end John Moore returned an interception for the final accounting for one of his two scores. With just two weeks remaining before the showdown with Culver, the Academy gridders, behind co-captains Bill Richards (quarterback) and Irwin Martin (guard), prepared diligently for the next barrier to an undefeated season: Elgin Academy. As an added incentive, a victory over Elgin would allow the Academy to capture the Midwest Prep School Conference title. After traveling to Minneapolis, Minnesota the previous weekend, perhaps the Elgin Academy club was experiencing some emotional fatigue near the conclusion of a long season. The team suffered a sound 25-7 beating at the hands of the Shattuck (Minnesota) High School and offered little resistance when the Academy showed up for the November 4 game. As usual Correll was a standout, scoring three touchdowns, behind the expert blocking of linemen Walt Schissler and Irwin Martin as the Academy rolled to an easy 34-0 victory.

On that same day, Culver maintained its unbeaten campaign by downing St. Bede Academy 15-0. Academy scouts were impressed by the heroics, and speed, of Culver halfback Jim Kresl, who scored on two occasions, once on a 95-yard jaunt from scrimmage. The win pushed Culver's record to 5-0-1 while the mark for Morgan Park Military Academy stood at 7-0. The dream matchup between the two powerful military schools was about to take place!

Over in Culver, Indiana, preparations were being made, both on and off the field, for the trip to Morgan Park. The Culver student newspaper, *The Vedette*, reported in October that for the first time in several years, the cadet student body, along with the marching band, would be making the trip to Chicago for the game:

Col. W. E. Gregory also spoke [on October 6]. The Acting Superintendent asked the white-stripers [students] if they would be willing to pay their own expenses to see the Morgan Park game. They all heartily agreed. A band member then rose to his feet and asked if the musicians could go to the game. Col. Gregory then asked if the boys would pay a little extra for the band. They again all voted yes.

In addition to the plans to move a large contingent from Culver to Chicago, the Culver Radio Club acquired and installed a new phone transmitter that would allow the Radio Club to broadcast the action of the football game back to the citizens of Culver. No one, it seemed, wanted to miss a moment of the upcoming game.

MORGAN PARK IS ALWAYS GOOD

A week before the contest (November 5), the *Chicago Tribune* provided a glimpse of the hype surrounding the Academy homecoming match with Culver, the information no doubt supplied by the special publicity committee led by Fred Herendeen. In a striking coincidence, the highly anticipated football battle also would fall on Armistice Day, allowing the school to tie-in the football game with dramatic military activities that usually surrounded this important holiday:

> Saturday will be the occasion of the football contest between Morgan Park and Culver Military academies at Abells Field on the Morgan Park campus. It will be the academy's homecoming celebration. A special train will bring the faculty and cadets of Culver in time for the game and, accompanied by their school band, the cadets will march up 111th Street from the Rock Island Station.

> Between halves, the alumni of the Morgan Park Academy will present a memorial program in cooperation with the Beverly Hills post of the Legion. The alumni will be directed by George Truesdell of Park Ridge. Taps will be sounded, and a volley fired. Both Morgan Park and Culver are undefeated teams.

In the week before the contest, Culver coach Russ Oliver reported that his team was in good shape. According to *The Culver Citizen*:

> Cheered by their 13-0 victory over St. Bede's Academy at Culver last Saturday, Captain J.B. Thomas, rangy right end and scrappy Culver captain, and his teammates are taking Morgan Park in stride and are hard at work preparing for what will be their biggest test of the current season. The cadets are mindful of what happened to another Culver team year before last in Chicago. Doped to win by several touchdowns, the heavy cadet eleven came back after that game on the short end of a 25-7 count which wrecked their title hopes. Morgan Park is always good, and this year's team will be a tough one to beat. Culver realizes that, and a real battle is expected. The Culver cadets will be at top-form with practically every regular in fine shape. Coach Russ Oliver has six sparkling backs who can handle that ball in big league style and his line is improving with every game.

In the same article, *The Culver Citizen* eagerly added to the pre-game hyperbole with the game beginning to seem secondary to the excitement and pageantry:

> Undefeated records will be at stake Saturday afternoon when one of the oldest military prep rivalries in the country will be renewed. Culver Military Academy meets Morgan Park in a prep classic of the middle-west on the Morgan Park Field at 2:00 p.m. Both teams boast powerful lines with smooth running and clever backs to work behind them, and both teams will have their respective cadet corps in the stands to cheer them on. The Culver corps of 600 strong will leave Culver Saturday morning by special train, arriving in Chicago in time for a pre-game review and to lend a lusty cheer to the sixty minutes of football in store for the fans Saturday afternoon.

Of course, the Chicago metropolitan newspapers, such as the *Chicago Tribune*, added to the building anticipation on the Wednesday before the game:

287

They're making preparations for one of the biggest events of the season on Chicago's far south side Saturday afternoon. Morgan Park Military Academy's football team has won the Midwest Prep Conference championship. It will be homecoming day and Armistice Day. And the visitors will be the unbeaten Cadets of Culver Military Academy, renewing one of the oldest prep rivalries in the nation.

The thrills and color of an Army-Navy game will be seen in the contest between the two undefeated elevens. Cadet corps of both schools will parade with their bands between the halves.

On that same day (November 8), the *Chicago Daily News* chipped in with still another pre-game proclamation that perhaps captured the forthcoming football banquet most colorfully:

A miniature Army-Navy football spectacle is in prospect Saturday when Morgan Park Military Academy meets Culver. Morgan Park Cadets clinched the Midwest Prep School Conference championship by its 33-6 victory over Elgin Academy last week and vow to take Culver's scalp come Armistice Day. A trainload of Culver rooters, including the entire corps of cadets and the famous marching band, will invade the Morgan Park stronghold for the colorful clash. Russ Oliver, former nine-letter man at the University of Michigan, coaches the Culver eleven, and Captain George A. Mahon of Ohio Wesleyan directs the undefeated M. P. M. A. squad.

NEVER HAD A FOOTBALL IN HIS HANDS

In the days before the game, Coach Mahon continued to stress the defensive capabilities of his club, figuring that the easiest way to defeat Culver would be to stymie the visitors' offensive aspirations. In the previous seven victories, the Warriors had outscored their opponents 129 to 18. If the intent was to indeed stifle the Culver offense, Mahon and his assistant Henry Bollman would need to focus on the movements of both dangerous halfback Jim Kresl and the Culver captain, end J. B. Thomas. Meanwhile, the Culver defense would need to deal with a multitude of Morgan Park offensive threats, beginning with the talented halfback Charles Correll, quarterback Bill Richards, and fullback Bob Waggoner. Culver's defenders were capable as well, giving up only 19 points in their first six outings.

A special issue of Culver's student newspaper, *The Vedette*, was published on the day of the game (November 11) and probably served as ample reading material for the over 600 representatives from Culver who crammed into the special train heading to Chicago that morning. In an article sharing some insight into Culver's practice regimen for the week, *The Vedette* noted some key concerns for the visitors:

> Morgan Park this year is led by [Chuck] Correll, a back who has…figured in all MPMA victories so far this year. Correll's passes to a big end named Moore have netted consistent gains, and the line-up includes several other passers, so Morgan Park seems to have an excellent aerial attack. In an attempt to stop the Correll-to-Moore passing game, the team has been drilled to cover pass receivers on all possible plays. [Coaches] Jerry Whitney and Col. Hoge stressed the ability to beat the opposing line to the punch and knife through to await enemy ball carriers. The ends will play their own positions to stop all double reverses.

Little did the Culver newspaper, or its followers, realize that the player named Moore was an absolute football rookie, having never played the game before the 1939 season! His story was explained in the *Chicago Tribune* just after the Culver game:

> A senior who never had a football in his hands until this fall is one of the four-star players carrying the veteran Morgan Park Military Academy team to its most successful season this year. He is John Moore, a 180-pound end who, according to his coach, George Mahon, is "fast and tough and knows how to handle the ball." A natural athlete, John has been improving steadily from game to game and is using his ability at basketball to good advantage as a pass catcher. Recently, he scored two touchdowns against St. John's Academy.

During his gridiron apprenticeship, Moore received a great deal of personal instruction from assistant coach Henry Bollman, an unsung albeit critical part of the 1939 squad. Bollman was a two-year starter at center for Rice University in Texas and later served as the freshman football coach at Ohio State University before joining the Academy staff. His knowledge of the interior game, as well as his insightful training and positioning of untested players, proved to be extremely beneficial to the team. Now, as the hours slipped by and the kick-off loomed nearer, the Academy players quietly prepared themselves for the most important game of their young lives.

NEVER BEFORE HAS ABELLS FIELD SEEN SUCH A SPECTACULAR SIGHT

After weeks of planning, all was set for the arrival of the Culver corps and the ensuing parade and football game. Each specific item was scratched off the overall Academy staff list of "things to do," such as adding temporary bleachers, printing an expanded program, stocking the concession stand, and identifying time slots for each segment of the day's activities. Everything was certainly under control, except for the one intangible that the Academy bosses could not oversee: the timely arrival of the Culver train. For whatever reason, the train was late, impacting all of the events that were scheduled to follow, not the least of which was the highly anticipated football game! Crowds were already forming around the Rock Island station when the Culver team and supporters finally arrived several minutes late.

But the wait was worth it as the Culver group quickly disembarked the train and the band was hurriedly organized to lead the pack up the hill on 111th Street and then move a block further west to the entrance of Abells Field. And what a splendid sight it was! Observers lined both sides of 111th Street from the railroad station to the field, a distance of about a half mile. The Culver marching band paced the marchers up the hill with a variety of musical compositions, much to the delight of the cheering sidewalk crowds. Although the football teams would soon be slugging it out on the pristine Abells Field, the fans of both academies showered the students with warmth and cheers, much to the delight of *The Academy News*:

> Never before has Abells Field seen such a crowd and such a spectacular sight, both from the point of view of football and of marching boys. The game was delayed in starting because the Culver Corps arrived late and after marching on the field gave Culver cheers for their opponents. The Culver Corps was followed by the Morgan Park cadets, who tho fewer in number made up for quantity by quality.

The local cadets played Culver's Alma Mater while the Morgan Park boys stood at salute.

As the two bands concluded their performances and the fans anxiously sought prized seating in the already over-flowing bleachers, public address announcer Captain Jean L. Taylor of the home school introduced the starting lineups to the ear-splitting cheers of the assembled throng of football fans. For the Academy, the usual starters would be in place: Jack Berkery and John Moore at the ends; tackles Walter Schissler and Richard Kerns; guards Warren Guderyahn and Irwin Martin; center Spencer Stuart, along with the backfield of quarterback Bill Richards; halfbacks Dave Plitt and Chuck Correll; and fullback Bob Waggonner. Overall, the rosters were not large in terms of physical size by any means. Schissler was the largest man on the field at 210 lbs. (and the only player in the game over 200 lbs.), while Plitt was the smallest at 153 lbs. Culver's biggest man was right tackle Jim Berry (199 lbs.) from Sapulpa, Oklahoma meaning that Berry would be lining up against the Academy left tackle Schissler throughout the afternoon.

As the two squads of undefeated gladiators finally faced off with the opening kickoff, the hard-hitting Culver defense forced the first turnover on the play, when the Academy return man coughed up the pigskin at his own 20-yard line, providing Culver with excellent field position to start its first offensive drive. Casey Clements, a rugged fullback from Mankato, Minnesota, burst off tackle for eleven yards on the first Culver play, setting the visitors up nicely at the Academy 9-yard line. With that first down, Culver sent Clements and Kresl into the line four straight times without success. As a collective sigh of relief swept through the Academy bleachers, Coach Mahon's offense took over on downs and elected to punt the ball back to Culver immediately. This was a common tactic in the early days of football, and Mahon decided to have punter Warren Guderyahn boot the ball out from the shadows of his own goal posts in an effort to secure a more advantageous defensive field position. The strategy worked as Martin, Schissler and Kerns anchored a stingy Academy defensive effort that prevented Culver from initiating any type of offensive success. After multiple series by both clubs with little or no offensive spark by either team, the first quarter ended in a scoreless tie.

The second stanza, however, was a different story as the Academy began to win the battle in the trenches. Schissler was having an outstanding day blocking for the backfield and his efforts paid off early in the second quarter when fullback Howard Weckel followed Schissler through a big opening and raced 40 yards for the first score of the game. Although Schissler's extra point was off the mark, the legion of Academy fans howled in delight as the team grabbed the first advantage in the contest. Just a few minutes later, the Academy struck gold again as reserve halfback Simon Allen faked left, then cut back to his right and slipped through the line to start a 38-yard scamper to boost the Academy's advantage to 12-0. This time, Schissler's kick was true and Culver was suddenly down by a 13-0 count.

As the clock ran down at the end of the first half, Culver's fear of the Academy aerial attack was realized when Correll connected from mid-field with Berkery with a bullet of a pass that Berkery grabbed while sandwiched between two Culver defenders. As Berkery came down with the reception, he quickly evaded both defenders and won the foot race to the end zone, completing a 50-yard scoring play. Although Schissler erred on the extra point, the Academy wrapped up the first half with a solid 19-0 lead.

Before a crowd estimated at over 5,000 strong, the marching bands from both schools provided the halftime entertainment while the two teams rested at opposite ends of Abells Field during the break, sucking on orange slices and measured sips of water. Meanwhile, the student workers in the concession stands battled to keep pace with the demands of the crowds seeking hot dogs, popcorn, coffee, candy, or soft drinks during the intermission. Coach Mahon would later report that the refreshment profit for the day would exceed $600, a vast improvement over the $132 netted from the attendees at the Onarga game earlier in the season. On the field during the break, Coach Mahon stressed that the powerful Culver offense must be kept in check during the second half if the Academy hoped to retain its advantage. Players such as Kresl and Clements had the speed and the moves to score at any time for Culver, so Mahon reminded his charges that a total team effort would be needed to ensure a happy ending to the glorious day.

OUR GUYS THOUGHT I BROKE MY NECK!

As the second half wore on, it was evident the defenses of both teams would determine the final tally. Neither offense could generate any type of successful drive and the second half consisted primarily of three quick downs, followed by a punt, and three unsuccessful plays by the opposing club. Danny Maxson of Culver and Warren Guderyahn of the Academy were the punters called upon by their teams to salvage field position throughout the second half. Culver's best chance to score was thwarted by junior Ed Kelly.

Kelly was on the field when Culver defensive back Buddy Adams from Bartlesville, Oklahoma intercepted an errant Warrior pass on his own 15 and appeared to have a clear path to the end zone 85 yards away. However, Kelly was determined to preserve the shutout as he told *The Academy Magazine* many years later in 2001:

> I was all the way on the other side of the field, at about the Culver 15, but I turned and chased the runner down field and caught him at about our 25. As we fell together, two of his blockers tumbled on top of us. Some of our guys thought I had broken my neck, but thank God, I didn't. I was knocked out, however, and did suffer a concussion. But Culver didn't score!

No one managed to score in the third period, and under darkening skies due to the late start of the game, neither team relied on the passing attack in the fourth quarter. As the final seconds clicked away on the Abells Field circular clock, the Academy crowd erupted in a long and continuous roar of elation and success. Culver had been defeated 19-0! While the two combatant teams lined up to shake hands after the game, the marching bands took turns playing the school songs for their respective institutions.

Although post-game newspaper coverage of the game was brief, the *Chicago Tribune* summarized the afternoon concisely:

> Morgan Park Military Academy's football team, champions of the Midwest Conference, yesterday celebrated its Armistice Day homecoming by defeating Culver Military Academy, 19 to 0, in the renewal of one of the oldest prep rivalries in the central states. It was Morgan Park's eighth consecutive victory and Culver's first defeat of the season.

Over at Culver, the game report in *The Vedette* was somewhat subdued:

> After tussling with Morgan Park Military Academy, one of the best prep school teams ever seen in the Midwest Prep Conference, the heretofore undefeated "Flying Squadron" came out on the short end of a score of 19-0 last Saturday before a far from disheartened corps. Culver's team left an impression on patrons and alumni of one of the greatest-spirited and hardest fighting prep school outfits ever seen

in this territory. The corps is to be given a boat-load of thanks for its super support.

EVERYONE CONNECTED WITH THE ACADEMY WAS HAPPY!

Little did the players know at the time, but the Culver game would be remembered for years (and perhaps forever) as the greatest game in Academy football history. This distinction was achieved not only for the meeting between two undefeated teams, but also because the hard-fought win was grabbed from the Academy's staunchest rival in front of what was likely the largest crowd to witness a football game in the Academy's long existence. However, before the celebration for a successful season could begin, there was just one more road block: a final game against the competitive St. Bede Academy on November 18. Culver had defeated St. Bede 15-0 on November 4, but the Academy team was anxious to conclude its season unbeaten and unquestioned. The team did so by vanquishing St. Bede 13-7 behind the near flawless play of Correll who tallied one rushing touchdown, then tossed a long pass to set up the final score by halfback Dave Plitt. The perfect 9-0 season was now complete, with the Academy outscoring its adversaries 157-26 over the course of the campaign. In its final remarks concerning the 1939 season the 1940 **Skirmisher** yearbook praised both the players, and the coaches:

> This season made everyone connected with the Academy happy—and here is why. Moore's defensive work and [Merritt] Ranstead's receiving ability—Schissler's defensive-offensive work and super place kicking—Guderyhan's all-around work topped by his punting—Stuart's line backing—Martin the ever present "Little Gibraltar" of the line—Kerns' ability at sensing plays and breaking them up—Berkery's pass receiving and fine defensive work—Weckel's runs on reverses and his defensive work at halfback—Correll's everything and Richard's toughness, hard hitting and exceptionally clean playing along with his defensive work really stood out. And of course, the men responsible for all this: Captain Mahon and Lieutenant Bollman...the best squad seen in many years around old M.P.M.A. led by captains Bill Richards and Irwin Martin.

Many years later in 2000, Martin distinctly recalled his 1939 team in an article for the *Academy Magazine*, and noted the impact of the coaching staff:

> Coaches George Mahon and Henry Bollman deserve much of the credit for the perfect season, of course, but the individual honors abounded. Nine of the starting MPMA eleven had been selected for all-conference honors and never before in the history of the Midwest Prep Conference had so many members from one team been named to the all-conference first team. Chuck Correll was named to the all-state team by the *Southtown Economist*.

Martin was inducted into the Morgan Park Academy Hall of Fame in 1999 and recalled that his co-captain responsibility in 1939 (with Bill Richards) was "truly memorable." Martin joined the Army during World War II and ended up completing a 20-year stint in both active duty and the reserves, retiring as a Lieutenant Colonel on the General Staff at the Presidio in San Francisco, California. Martin enjoyed a successful business career following his time in the service and eventually owned a real estate brokerage firm in Arizona. But as part of his induction into the Academy Hall of Fame in 1999, Mr. Martin provided a moving remembrance that captured the "Spirit" of Morgan Park Military Academy:

> In looking back at my experiences, nothing contributed more to my life than those years at MPMA. I later found that the school was still a great part of me, and I missed many of my classmates. A small reunion was held in 1970, and it became evident that there was a guardian spirit in our class that was unlike anything we had heard of in other schools, both private and public. We, in effect, became Guardians of the Spirit of MPMA, and we have maintained it since the first gathering [in 1936]. The school has had a profound effect upon many, and its been my pleasure to help guard and maintain that spirit we first experienced.

H. Irwin Martin, captain of the undefeated 1939 football squad, and perhaps the greatest team in the history of the program, passed away in 2009 at the age of 87.

EXTRA POINT

For many years, Morgan Park Military Academy hosted a massive memorial service on Armistice Day each year. Because of the excitement and huge crowds attending the Culver-Morgan Park Military Academy game on November 11, 1939, the Armistice Day activities were moved one day later to November 12. The location of these annual tributes was always the same: a small stone monument that rested on a grassy island between a pair of paved streets. The monument remains in the same location to this day on the present Morgan Park Academy campus.

The *Chicago Tribune* reported on the 1939 Armistice Day plans and provided some insight into the impressive size and reach of this event which honored the sacrifices made by the participants in World War I:

> Fourteen patriotic groups in the Morgan Park and Beverly Hills community will hold memorial services next Sunday on and adjoining the campus of Morgan Park Military Academy. All will assemble at 2:45 o'clock in the afternoon at Memorial Boulder, 112th Street and Lothair Avenue, under the sponsorship of the Morgan Park Women's Club. Later, an outdoor speaking program on the campus of the academy will be followed by a full-dress parade by the cadets of both the Morgan Park High School and the military academy.
>
> Mrs. James Shirely, president of the Beverly Hills Auxiliary of the American Legion, will open the service by placing a wreath on the boulder. A commemorative address will be delivered by Mrs. Thomas Gifford, president of the 3rd District of the Illinois Federation of Women's Clubs, and taps will be sounded by members of the drill corps of the Beverly Hills Post of the Legion under the direction of Capt. Herbert St. Germain. The program on the campus of the academy will be under the chairmanship of Col. Haydn E. Jones, assistant superintendent. A concert will be presented by the high school band and the invocation will be read by the Rev. Charles Ross, pastor of the Methodist Episcopal Church. Edward Hayes, past national commander of the Legion, will be the principal speaker of the day. The combined cadets of the high school and the

military academy will conclude the program with a dress parade.

From all reports, the ambitious plans for the many Armistice Day ceremonies on November 12, 1939 were perfect, much like the 1939 Academy football team...

The coaching staff for the undefeated 1939 Morgan Park Military Academy squad was (from left): Alex Gentleman, George Mahon and Henry Bollman.

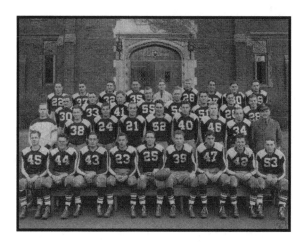

The 1939 club finished with an unblemished 9-0 record, including a 19-0 defeat of rival Culver Military Academy before over 5,000 fans at Abells Field.

CHAPTER 17

In the Shadow of War

*"Let it be understood that this is strictly a troop
movement and dates are not allowed."*
—The Academy News, October 24, 1940

In the summer of 1940, Coach George Mahon was still basking in the glow of the perfect 1939 season. He glanced at the clock on the wall in his Athletic Director's office and fired up another cigarette. As Coach Mahon leaned back in his chair, he glanced out the office window, stuck in the rear of the school gymnasium building, and watched the Chicago Cardinals from the NFL practice on the Academy's south field.

The ticking of the clock seemed unusually loud that day, as if the countdown to the upcoming season was battling to remind him of the upcoming rebuilding year. After all, Mahon's roster had been stripped of its entire starting lineup from the previous season. It would be difficult to even come close to the success of the championship 1939 squad. Perhaps as a prelude to the mass exodus of seniors, star halfback Chuck Correll had not even lasted until the end of the school year, opting to transfer to Morgan Park High School after the first semester to fulfill his graduation requirements.

The Chicago Cardinals, fresh off a cringe-inducing 1-10 season in 1939, were also in a full-blown rebuilding mode and had returned to the Academy in 1940 to launch their pre-season training endeavors under new mentor Jimmy Conzelman. The Academy welcomed the Cardinals, not only for the publicity earned whenever there was a newspaper article about the pros at Morgan Park, but also for the additional revenue the team brought to the campus treasury through the *per diem* charges for the use of the Academy facilities, including the dorm rooms and dining hall.

On the bright side, enrollment at the Academy was increasing in 1940, and it could be argued that the success of the 1939 football team and its accompanying publicity might be a profound factor in that significant increase. This upward trend continued and by early September of 1941, the Academy announced that enrollment was at an all-time high of 375 combined for the Upper (high school) and Lower (grade school) Schools.

In addition, Morgan Park Military Academy would be part of the revamped Midwest Prep Conference again, although the circuit would add teams and introduce new rules for conference members that some might view as restrictive. The new composition of the conference members would be an odd mix of private and military schools stretched out over three states as announced in the local media (Associated Press) on September 25, 1940:

> Meyer Morton, Chicago attorney and veteran western conference football official, has been named athletic commissioner for the conference, which has the following members: Onarga Military School, Onarga, Illinois; Morgan Park, Illinois, Military Academy; Elgin Military Academy, Illinois; St. John's Military Academy, Delafield, Wisconsin; Culver Military Academy, Culver, Indiana; Todd School, Woodstock, Illinois; Lake Forest Academy, Lake Forest, Illinois; Pullman Tech, Chicago, and Park School of Indianapolis, Indiana. Football and basketball championships will be awarded by the conference and will be determined on a percentage basis. Each member must play at least four conference football games and schedule at least six conference schools in basketball.

FROM THE EXHIBITION PUT ON SATURDAY IT LOOKS BAD

In terms of rebuilding his football team, Coach Mahon would face a tough challenge, especially with a daunting conference schedule. Still, Mahon was cautiously optimistic when asked about his prospects for 1940 by *The Academy News* (September 25): "Due to the fine showing we expect of our boys we know they will put on a good show throughout the year." While Coach Mahon might have been guilty of being a bit evasive in his positive outlook, assistant coach Henry Bollman's comments in *The Academy News* on October 9 following an opening 12-7 loss to the Alumni were not only tough, but probably pragmatic:

> There are seven teams in the conference and we should be about seventh. The reason for this is because we lack a good line and especially good guards and tackles. From the exhibition put on Saturday it looks bad, but eventually I hope we will develop our team into one of the best, and playing against our hardest enemies and come out, like we did last year, victorious.

The Warriors would face a reduced schedule in 1940 of just seven games, prompted by a new conference rule that did not allow any of the members to compete against a public school. (Note: Pullman Tech of Chicago was actually a private vocational school at the time, operating under funds bequeathed in his will by railroad magnate George Pullman, founder of the Pullman Palace Car Company.) Other schools, such as Marmion Military Academy, simply dropped out of conference membership consideration rather than eliminate traditional rivalries from public schools on its schedule.

With just five lettermen (and no starters) returning from the championship squad of 1939, it became quickly obvious that the team's major shortcoming in 1940 would be on offense. After being defeated by the Alumni 12-7 in that exhibition game, the Academy scored just once in three opening regular season losses to Loras Academy (14-0), Onarga (7-6), and Lake Forest Academy (27-0). Two key returnees in the backfield, Ed Kelly and Dick Engelman, brought some hope to the team's followers, but both were hindered by an inexperienced line. The Academy's only breakthrough in the 1940 win column occurred on October 19, when Elgin Academy fell 13-0 as Kelly generated a pair of touchdowns. Still, the annual rivalry game with Culver on November 2, was highly anticipated. Beginning on October 9, *The Academy News* published plans for the trip to Culver, and it was expected that all students would join the football players on this journey:

> Accompanying the Morgan Park team to Culver this year will be the entire corps, friends, parents, faculty, in fact anyone who has the price for a round trip ticket which includes lunch, train fare, game admission and trip back. The exact amount has not yet been set. The last time the

corps made the trip two years ago, it was two dollars. It will probably be the same this trip.

Two weeks later (on October 24), *The Academy News* issued an update for all potential cadet travelers with a not-so-subtle warning:

> First let it be understood that this is strictly a troop movement and dates are not allowed. Of course, if the favored one goes with your parents nothing can be done about it. Until the trip back, however, you will not be allowed to visit anyone. The cost of the trip will be $2.50, and every cadet will attend.

Despite the glow of a boisterous fan base behind them, the Warriors struggled once again on offense and dropped a 13-0 decision to the hosts. Two more lackluster defeats to St. John's (37-7) and Pullman Tech (21-7) closed out the disappointing season for Coach Mahon. Just a year after enjoying the richness of a successful 9-0 campaign, Mahon endured a devastating 1-6 mark in 1940.

If one could take a mirror to a full football season and then reflect it into the future, the results from the Academy's difficult 1940 schedule were largely identical in 1941. Displaying a tough defense, but hindered by a threadbare offense against virtually the same opponents as the previous season, the Academy stumbled once again in 1941 with a final 2-6 record. After scoring only 33 points throughout the entire 1940 season, the Academy could do little better in 1941, finishing with just a total of 37, while yielding a respectable 93 points over eight games (including 33 in a season-ending 33-0 loss to St. John's). Despite the lackluster results, halfback Orville "Bud" Hall and Nathaniel Skarin, a fearsome 221 lb. tackle, were both named to the all-conference team. Skarin was also named the most valuable player for the club as well. Later (in 2014), Skarin was named to the Morgan Park Academy Hall of Fame for his superlative efforts both on, and off, the field. As noted, he was the captain and MVP of the football team in 1941, along with being selected to the all-conference team at tackle. He repeated those all-conference accolades in basketball, and then closed out his Academy athletic career by batting .415 and .316 during his final two baseball seasons, both of which included conference championships.

AS A PEOPLE, WE LOVE PEACE

Yet points, wins, and losses were becoming increasingly irrelevant at a key military school in a country that was stubbornly resisting the urge to slide into the lurking global conflict that would be known as World War II. Although the United States had been uneasily balancing on a neutrality stance regarding the growing hostilities in Europe, there had been plenty of gloomy forecasts bouncing around the country focusing on the difficulty in remaining neutral for much longer. On November 9, 1941, Morgan Park Military Academy hosted a pre-Armistice Day observation with Illinois Governor Dwight H. Green as the keynote speaker. In his remarks, Governor Green urged the country to prepare itself for the war effort that was certainly to come in the future as reported by the Associated Press:

> Every ounce of force at the command of the American people must be mobilized in the fight to preserve the American way of life. As a people, we love peace. We do not seek conquest, nor do we desire anything that belongs to other nations. But we are determined to hold that which is ours against any aggressor force which would seek to despoil the liberty our forefathers bled to win for us.

And then on December 7, 1941, peace was no longer an option. The fear that the United States would be drawn into the war was realized with the surprise Japanese attack on Pearl Harbor in Hawaii. Years later in the May 2000 issue of the *Academy Magazine*, football player C.W. "Bill" Getz recalled the awful feeling when the students at the Academy learned of Pearl Harbor:

> Sunday, 7 December, 1941 started like any other Sunday. Quiet. My memory is cloudy as to when and how we first heard of the Pearl Harbor attack, but I would venture to say it was probably via radio in Hansen Hall later that day (the actual attack occurred at 12:55 p.m. Chicago time). My roommate, Jim Hume, was probably studying and may have had the radio on. To be sure, the news passed around campus very quickly, even for a Sunday, but my recollection is that it was later in the afternoon before we really got any details. Monday morning was a sober time. The entire cadet corps assembled in Blake Hall to listen to President Franklin Delano Roosevelt deliver a talk to a

joint session of Congress to recognize that a state of war existed between the Empire of Japan and the United States since the day before, and that it was a day that would live in infamy.

I remember clearly that scene in Blake Hall. There was an eerie silence before the President's speech. It was not the usual din of conversation one heard prior to any formal activity. Not that morning. I cannot speak for all the cadets, but I have no doubt that at least the seniors and juniors knew in their hearts and minds that what they were listening to would change their lives forever. When the President finished his speech, the radio played *The Star Spangled Banner*. On the very first note, and without any command, the entire cadet corps snapped to attention and stood there—rigid throughout the moving, melodious melody. It was one of those memorable moments of my life and, even today, I get goose bumps when I think about it. Duty, Honor, Country. That was the day those words took on a whole new meaning for the Class of 1942.

Indeed, the Class of 1942 witnessed significant changes in the lives of its members, as many chose to enlist quickly upon reaching their 18th birthdays, including the aforementioned Bill Getz. As for the Academy, the reaction to the outbreak of hostilities was not mentioned in the Board of Trustees meeting held on December 8, 1941. Instead, the main source of discussion seemed to be the unpaid bills left over from the summer training camp of the Chicago Cardinals professional football team. The board of Trustees instructed one of its members to "get in touch with Mr. [team owner Charles] Bidwill and push for a settlement of the account." However, in subsequent meetings in early 1942, the Board moved quickly to shorten the academic school year and to reduce the daily schedule from eight to six periods in order "to give more opportunity for military instruction in the theoretical work." Cadets such as Bill Getz took advantage of the revised schedule to complete their requirements and thus enter the service sooner than anticipated:

I enlisted as an aviation cadet in the United States Army on May 5, 1942, shortly after my eighteenth birthday, the required minimum age. The Academy graduated some of us early because of the war. I flew two combat tours with the Eighth Air Force out of England, as did my classmates and friends. I was a captain and on my way home before I was old enough to vote or drink.

176 GRADUATES OF MORGAN PARK MILITARY ACADEMY NOW IN ACTIVE SERVICE

Getz was typical of the enthusiastic reaction to the country's war needs by the Morgan Park Military Academy cadets and alumni. By April of 1942, the *Chicago Tribune* reported that 176 members of the Academy alumni, including 112 officers, had already entered the service, an extraordinary number for such a small school:

> A total of 176 graduates of Morgan Park Military Academy are now in active service in the country's armed forces. Of this number, four are lieutenant colonels; two majors; eight captains; 16 first lieutenants; seven naval officers. Two of its graduates have been listed as casualties. Morgan Park's military men are seeing service in all parts of the globe.

By the time the 1942-43 school year began in September, enrollment at the Academy had increased to 388 total students and the school welcomed a new football coach. George Mahon had suffered through an unknown illness during the previous year and elected to step away from the football program while remaining active in numerous other administrative areas, including serving as the school's athletic director. Mahon wrapped up his six-year head coaching stint with a sterling 23-17-2 record. Although he decided to not return to his head coaching position, he did serve as a respected assistant coach at times throughout the next two decades.

Joining the staff in 1942 was veteran grid coach Maurice Bugbee, formerly of Aurora (Illinois) College. While at Aurora, Bugbee compiled a 6-13-3 record while leading the football team from 1939 through 1941. In 1942, Bugbee did his best to formulate a competitive football squad at the Academy, albeit one that was vastly inexperienced on the offensive side. During an opening four game sequence, the Academy tallied just a single touchdown while dropping three of those initial contests. Injuries contributed to that early dry spell as valuable halfback Bud Hall was sidelined with a broken rib while receiver Jim McHugh was knocked out for the season with a broken collar bone. The loss of Hall, even for a short period of time, was disastrous. Just a junior, Hall was already an all-conference player with dazzling speed and shifty moves when he carried the ball. It was anticipated that Hall would handle most of the passing assignments in 1942 and would take on the role of punter as well. A tough, stubborn individual from the south side of Chicago, Hall had already made his mark as the primary pitcher on the baseball squad while also snaring the Academy's heavyweight boxing title.

Yet even with Hall's talented presence, the Academy gridders failed to mount much offensive excitement during the season. One of the highlights of the tough schedule was a rugged 6-0 victory over Pullman Tech on November 7. With time running out and the two clubs deadlocked in a 0-0 tie, Hall wrestled a wayward pass from halfback Jack Parchman away from a pair of Pullman defenders and sped 30 yards for the only score of the game. Following a depressing 47-14 loss to the conference champs from St. John's Military Academy, the Warriors pulled off their biggest offensive effort in the season finale on November 21, a 20-0 win over Lake Forest Academy as documented in the 1943 **Skirmisher**:

> This game was a real tribute to the MPMA spirit and fight. After being badly beaten the week before, they had enough determination and fight to play their best game of the season and to rout Lake Forest by a 20-0 score. Frank Major, Jack Parchman, and Bud Hall played really fine football to give the Warriors this victory in their last game of the year.

With the victory over Lake Forest, Bugbee's crew managed to finish with a 3-6 mark, but the coach wasn't around much longer to plan for the 1943 campaign. According to the Board minutes from February 15, 1943, "Lt. Bugbee has applied for a commission in the U.S. Naval Aviation Corps and may be called for service any day now." Indeed, Bugbee did depart for the military with his head coaching position being filled by Jim Marberry, a 1942 graduate of Carbondale Teachers College (now Southern Illinois University). George Mahon concluded his brief football "retirement" and returned to the team as Marberry's assistant. Bugbee received his commission in the Naval Reserve, and after training at Dartmouth and Princeton Universities, he served in Europe on an LST (Landing Ship, Tank) vessel. After the war, Bugbee moved to California and secured a position as a Los

Angeles County probation officer. He became Executive Director of the Boys' Clubs of Long Beach, California in 1947 and remained in that position until his death in 1975 at the age of 61.

IF WE'RE GOING TO GO, NOW'S THE TIME

During the War, the Academy monitored the heroics of its graduates in the service and *The Academy News* published regular updates on these alumni, with both the good news---and the sad. Through the course of World War II, 45 graduates of Morgan Park Military Academy lost their lives, a staggering number for one institution. Many were former football players, but all were remembered—and honored—when the school dedicated an impressive memorial to its own servicemen on November 14, 1943. By this time, over 500 Academy grads were now in the armed forces according to the *Southtown Economist*:

> Mounted between white columns in a replica of the south arcade of Mt. Vernon, a plaque bearing the names of more than 500 Morgan Park Military Academy alumni serving in the armed forces was dedicated Sunday in services at the Academy, 2153 W. 111th Street. The roll of honor and façade are the gift of Ald. John J. Duffy. Cong. Fred A. Busbey made the dedication. Names of nine former cadets who have died in service were inscribed on the honor roll in gold while two additional memorial trees were planted and added to the memorial archway of trees dedicated to alumni killed in the present war.

In September of 1943, the *Chicago Tribune* published an article on the specific heroics of Academy graduate Phil Falk in the final days of the battle for Guadalcanal in the Pacific:

> How two Chicago marines sought to save one another when they were in tight spots was told today by Pvt. Joseph T. Kinane, whose buddy, Pvt. Philip A. Falk, was killed in action beside him in the final cleanup of Guadalcanal. The way Kinane tells it his outfit, one of the most experienced in the Solomons warfare, moved down a hill to establish a contact line between two platoons. A corporal and three men were in his squad and a burst of fire from the Japs

concealed in a natural trench in the edge of the woods at the foot of the hill checked them. The corporal was wounded and the others were driven to cover.

Kinane and a comrade tried to wiggle up to the corporal, but were stopped by machine gun fire only five feet away in a coral depression. A hand grenade exploded almost in the face of Kinane's comrade, who leaped to his feet and made his way back up the hill, while Kinane covered him with gunfire. A fourth man went for help, but hours after none had come. It was then that Kinane saw his buddy, Falk, sitting on the hill, covering another marine, and he yelled to him to get help from a machine gun post on the hilltop. Falk misunderstood and thinking Kinane was wounded, rushed down the hill to his help. But they couldn't reach the corporal who lay only ten feet from the Jap line with an enemy machine gun only 50 feet away. "If we're going to go, now's the time," said Falk and turned over to get more ammunition from his belt. At that moment he was shot through the heart. However, his devotion helped Kinane battle his way out. He took ammunition from his comrade's belt to cover his retreat. Later, on the hilltop, Kinane learned help had not come. The machine gun post there had been under mortar fire and was knocked out. However, they gathered a bunch of fresh marines, went back, cleaned out the nest of Japs, and brought back Falk's body for burial in a marine graveyard.

As the war moved slowly forward, more and more stories of heroic Academy graduates like Falk reached the campus and were shared with the current cadets who grasped the information and made their own preparations for their inevitable participation in the global conflict.

CLASSROOMS CONVERTED INTO DORMITORY SLEEPING ROOMS

Enrollment for the 1943-44 school year increased to 417 for the combined upper and lower schools, and new gridiron mentor Jim Marberry scratched out a schedule that included some new opponents in Lockport (Illinois) High School and Chicago Vocational High School. Marberry had plenty of talent to work with, including the return of a healthy Bud Hall and versatile Captain Jack Parchman. However, those students returning for the new school year were soon informed of some significant changes on campus as reported in *The Academy News* on September 13, 1943:

> To accommodate the large enrollment this year some of the classrooms on the first floor of Hansen Hall have been converted into dormitory sleeping rooms for cadets. Former classrooms 113 and 118 will thus accommodate eight more boarding students. This will necessitate new arrangements for classroom space.

In addition, Col. Abells announced other internal changes intended to move the Academy into a more militaristic environment, including the following new regulations:

- Special privileges for athletes discontinued.
- Special permits for students to leave campus for family events were abolished.
- Any "home" time allowed (under extraordinary circumstances) will be made up during vacations.
- Civilian clothes will no longer be allowed on campus.
- Finally, normal military uniform requirements will be strictly enforced.

THE BALL SNAPPED BACK, THE TOE CAME DOWN

Back on the football field, Coach Marberry instituted some changes as well, implementing the fashionable single wing offense along with the Notre Dame "T' formation. Both offenses had become popular with major college teams and Marberry drilled the essentials of each offensive strategy into his team during long, grueling practices. For the first time since 1939, there was considerable optimism for a successful season. The 1944 **Skirmisher** reported on the successful opening month of the 1943 season: "Because we started the season with a new coach and with nine previous lettermen, our hopes ran high for a championship team. Mowing down three consecutive teams made the prospects even brighter"

Bud Hall sparked the Academy in an opening 39-6 rout of Lemont High School by scoring two touchdowns and adding a pair of extra points. In an unusual statistic for the game, six touchdowns by the Academy were called back due to penalties! A few days later, Hall's field goal provided all of the points that the Warriors would need in a 3-0 win over Roosevelt Military Academy. On October 16, Hall was the hero again, as he tallied twice and kicked an extra point to eclipse Onarga Military Academy 13-12. The outcome was still in question late in the game with Onarga trailing 13-12 as energetically described by *The Academy News* on November 1:

> In the last couple of minutes Onarga's team got its back up and went plunging over for a second touchdown while the stands chanted "Hold that line!" You might have heard a pin drop when the lineup for the extra point came but no one would have paid any attention to it anyhow for all eyes were glued to that ball which might tie up the ball game. The ball snapped back, the toe came down, BUT a red sweater crashed through and the kick was blocked. Whew!

The strong finish to the Onarga game left the Warriors with some confidence, along with a perfect 3-0 record to start the season. But then the injury bug invaded the team as recounted by the 1944 **Skirmisher**:

> At this time five of the lettermen were injured or taken ill, one of whom was Jack Parchman, captain of the team. With these accidents, everyone's hopes for the long-awaited champion team faded…many of these boys did not return to the lineup for the remainder of the season.

The perfect record for the year exploded on October 23 when Lockport High School picked apart the Academy defense to the tune of four touchdown passes on its way to an easy 33-0 victory. The following week, Bud Hall's score pushed the Academy ahead 7-0 against Chicago Vocational High School, but the visitors scored twice in the final period to edge the Academy 13-7. The team rebounded for a tight 7-0 win over Pullman Tech before concluding the season with a 33-0 loss at St. John's Military Academy.

After scoring 39 points in its opening win over Lemont, the Academy offense could muster only 30 points during the remainder (six games) of the season, but still eked out a winning 4-3 record, in what turned out to be Coach Marberry's only season at the Academy. It should be noted that the MVP of the squad, Orville "Bud" Hall, went on to play football at the University of Illinois.

As the war effort intensified all over the globe, by mid-1944 over 600 graduates of Morgan Park Military Academy were now on active duty. Unfortunately, the number of alumni lost in the conflict was also increasing. In March of 1944, it was learned that Richard Engelman, a 1941 graduate of the Academy and a member of the undefeated 1939 football team was killed in action in Bougainville (Papua New Guinea). He was, at the time, the twelfth member of the Morgan Park Military Academy to lose his life in combat. *The Academy News* continued to provide a somber, but proud, series of updates on school alumni who were serving in the war. For example, students were informed that former football captain Mike Kirchbaum twice received the silver star for gallantry in combat and that he participated "in the original invasion of Africa, the jump to Sicily, the Salerno bloody business, and the Anzio amphibious operation."

SIGNED A PROFESSIONAL CONTRACT FOR $110 PER GAME

With the 1944 football season approaching, the Academy turned to one of its own to lead the struggling program. During the 1943 campaign, Lt. Joe Ziemba led the Lower School squad to a 5-1 record. Based on this accomplishment, and his previous experience as an exceptional player and coach, Ziemba was offered the position of head varsity football coach. A graduate of St. Benedict's College in Atchison, Kansas, Ziemba was named to several All-American teams during his senior year. At the time, the school was aptly named the "Notre Dame of the West" since so many players from the Chicago area played for either Notre Dame or St. Benedict's. Although St. Benedict's was considered a "small" school back in the 1930s and 1940s, it played institutions that would now be considered "major" colleges, such as New Mexico State, Creighton, and Wichita State. He was drafted by the Chicago Cardinals of the National Football League in 1940 and signed a professional contract for the lofty wage of $110 per game. However, to demonstrate the difference between the lucrative world of pro football today and the struggling circuit of the early 1940s, pro football players were required by some teams at that time to provide their own shoes and shoulder pads!

During the Cardinals' 1940 training camp at Morgan Park Military Academy, Ziemba reinjured a knee that had initially been injured in college. While waiting for a diagnosis at nearby Little Company of Mary Hospital, Ziemba decided that the anticipated knee surgery would likely do more harm than good (players were not paid if injured) and reluctantly bid farewell to his pro football career. Ironically, at the time, pro football players needed a second job to make ends meet and playing pro football would certainly hinder the career goals of any former player seeking to enter the coaching field. Ziemba returned to Kansas and joined the football coaching staff at Rockhurst College in Kansas City before eventually being hired by the Academy in 1942.

In the interest of full disclosure, Coach Ziemba is the father of the author. While there is no denying that his career at Morgan Park Military Academy was a major influence on the development of this book, it would also be difficult to avoid his significant contributions to the Academy football program. His fingerprints were simply all over the program for nearly two decades and the numerous interviews and conversations conducted with former cadets from that era usually returned to discussions about the coach. So, while no special treatment will be afforded Coach Ziemba, his story will be shared, along with those of his many players and students.

With the able George Mahon returning as assistant coach in 1944, the Academy prepared for a rugged schedule that included a couple of tough suburban schools as well as the return of powerful Marmion Military Academy. With few returnees, Coach Ziemba relied on the quick feet of diminutive sophomore quarterback Bernard "Buddy" O'Brien to generate some offense for the Academy. However, the offense was nowhere in sight during the first game of the season, a 32-0 drubbing at the hands of Argo High School in southwest suburban Summit, Illinois. The club then ran off three straight victories over Roosevelt Military Academy (6-2), Onarga Military Academy (32-0), and Lockport High School (20-7). That mini winning streak then turned into a three-game losing streak with losses against Marmion Military Academy (51-0), Pullman Tech (19-12), and St. John's Military Academy (38-13). A season-ending 19-13 win over Chicago Vocational High School salvaged a 4-4 record in Ziemba's rookie campaign. Receiver Flem "Flipper" Flott snared 12 touchdown passes (most from O'Brien) to share team MVP honors along with guard Bill Sharp. Perhaps the highlight of the season was the annual banquet which was transformed from more of an internal celebration to an extravaganza. Instead of student speakers or local business dignitaries, the keynote speakers included Coach Lynn Waldorf of Northwestern University, pro football pioneer (and later head coach of the Chicago Bears) Paddy Driscoll, and Ted Fisher, the sports editor of the *Chicago Herald-American*.

CAPTURED FOURTEEN GERMANS WITHOUT FIRING A SHOT

Somber war news continued to impact the campus as 1944 rolled into 1945. Although there was a general sense that the tide was turning, and the war might conclude soon, the number of Morgan Park Military Academy participants continued to grow. Records in the current Academy archives indicate that ultimately 875 cadets and staff members served in the armed forces during World War II, of which 49 gave their lives. In December of 1944, it was learned that former football player Howard Martin ('37) had perished in the Pacific Theater. Martin had enlisted in June of 1941 and soon thereafter was assigned to duty in the Philippines. Unfortunately, he was captured by Japanese forces in early 1942 and endured the horrendous Bataan Death March, where the U.S. prisoners were marched approximately 60 miles without adequate food or water under the blistering sun. Those that survived the march were imprisoned in the Philippines and later crammed into deplorable ships headed for further incarceration in Japan. The ship carrying Lt. Howard Martin was attacked and sunk by unknowing U.S. forces in December of 1944.

In November of 1999, Barry Kritzberg of the Academy staff wrote a wonderful article in the *Academy Magazine* on the individuals lost in the war. Utilizing forgotten correspondence and dusty Academy records, Kritzberg expertly pieced together the personal stories of those who were lost. One of the more unique remembrances concerned Lt. Donald W. Yarrow:

> Lt. Donald W. Yarrow ('42), wounded in 1944, returned to combat and was killed crossing the Rhine for "the great drive deep into Germany" on March 23, 1945. He was 20 years old. His obituary, in the *Chicago American*, told how Lt. Yarrow once captured fourteen Germans without firing a shot. He couldn't have fired a shot, however, for he was out of ammunition. It was only after taking the prisoners to the stockade that he realized that he had no bullets in his carbine.

117 SENIOR OFFICER CADETS WERE EXPELLED

Meanwhile, back on campus, the administration needed to quell its own student rebellion, and to this day, no one seems to know what prompted this bold activity by the cadets! Basically, there was apparently still some student unrest as the result of stricter regulations put in place in 1943, including the discontinuation of weekend or family emergency leaves, or "passes." There was also some disappointment expressed by the cadets regarding the food in the mess hall. Whatever the reason, the boarding students on campus unleashed a series of pranks in Hansen Hall in January of 1945 that certainly caught the attention of the administration. The Chicago newspapers quickly jumped on the situation and turned the juvenile pranks into local headlines. As the *Herald-American* reported:

> As the climax to a series of disturbances, 117 senior officer cadets were expelled today [January 17] from Morgan Park Military Academy. Trouble began Sunday [January 15] night when pranksters pulled the fuse on the master control and threw three-story Hansen hall into darkness at the study hour. Yesterday, Cols. Harry D. Abells and Haydn E. Jones met with cadet representatives to hear complaints. The seniors asked for later hours on Saturday night, and passes on Friday nights for students with satisfactory grades.
>
> Again, last night fuses were pulled and the cadets milled the corridors until lights came on again. The disciplinary action was ordered today. Parents of Chicago cadets were notified to come and take their boys home. Out-ot-town cadets were being put on trains for their homes. A spokesman for the school said: "We have not yet determined our action as to the cadets. They will stay home until such time as the Academy determines, on the basis of individual cases, what is to be done with them."

Clearly, the situation was embarrassing to the school and the administration swiftly moved to rectify things. After all, the loss of 117 students would have a serious financial impact on the Academy's bottom line for the remainder of the 1945 school year, as well as in ensuing years. In a follow-up article on January 18, the *Chicago Tribune* stated that "all but a few [expelled students] would be reinstated and the whole matter cleared up by the end of the week." At the February Board meeting, the minutes reflected (from an unknown person) that "We [the Academy administration] had a most unusual cadet disorder…Just what the real cause for the outbreak, I cannot say, but the cadets reported that it was primarily started as a prank and then developed into seriousness and they took this opportunity to endeavor to force the Academy authorities to give them privileges which they had two years ago."

The topic of the student rebellion popped up over 40 years later when members of the football teams from the late 1940s gathered on campus for a reunion in May of 1999. In an article in the *Academy Magazine* (date unknown), former student John Perlberg remembered that "I was excused from exams, sent home, expelled for participating in the revolt. I have no idea what it was all about, but it was a great rebellion." In the end, after some boisterous discussions with both the students and their parents, all of the cadets were welcomed back on campus except for six who withdrew voluntarily and one cadet who was actually expelled on a permanent basis.

MORGAN PARK IN THE SOUTH SUBURBAN LEAGUE?

If the news of the student rebellion was not enough excitement on campus during the winter months of 1945, there was also some interesting discussion behind the scenes regarding the Academy's successful athletic programs. The Academy had been quietly distancing itself from the Midwest Prep Conference and its stifling scheduling requirements. Recently, the Academy had begun scheduling public schools in the area in an effort to entertain stronger competition than was afforded by playing only private schools as mandated by the Midwest Conference. Then, in early 1945, the Academy was apparently offered the opportunity to become a member of the prestigious South Suburban Conference (consisting of all public schools) which would be a huge step "up" in competitive athletics for the school. In a letter to key administrators and Coach Ziemba on February 25, 1945, Col. Abells outlined this possible new conference affiliation:

> On this snowy morning Capt. Mahon and I are visiting
> about several matters. He brought up the two-year-old
> problem of the Academy joining some athletic league.
> All things considered, he asks the recommendation that
> we apply for membership in the South Suburban League
> composed of Blue Island, Calumet City, Kankakee, Argo,
> Lockport, [and] Bloom (Chicago Heights). This would
> not affect our scheduled games with Pullman, Onarga,
> Roosevelt and the others. Please consider this and give
> us your straw votes. Capt. Mahon knows all the men. He
> has been over the matter with our cadets, with the fathers,

with the private school league and with the Midwest Association, including Mr. Willis of the Illinois High School Association. We need to get action. The South Suburban League meets next Monday.

On paper, the mere suggestion that a small private school such as Morgan Park Military Academy would even be considered as the competitive equal of the large public schools in the South Suburban Conference seems frivolous at best. However, the Academy had historically taken on the foremost schools in the area, no matter what the size. And in 1943 and 1944 the Academy had already scheduled teams such as Lockport, Argo, and Lemont, and was certainly competitive in these contests. Another positive reason for joining a local conference would be the reduction of travel costs as well as an increase in gate receipts from home games. For example, the potential rivalry with Blue Island High School, located roughly three miles south of the Academy, would seem attractive as fans from both schools might find it convenient to attend games at either school in any sport.

For reasons unknown, the Academy did not join the South Suburban League in 1945, despite the intriguing aspects of the potential partnership. Instead of joining ranks with schools such as Bloom, Thornton, and Blue Island, the Academy opted to help create a new league composed strictly of private schools. The announcement was made by the Associated Press in late May of 1945:

> A new high school athletic circuit, to be known as the North Central Conference, was organized at a meeting at Morgan Park Military Academy Monday night [May 28], with Capt. George Mahon of Morgan Park named president. The four schools in the circuit are Morgan Park, Pullman Tech, Onarga Military Academy and Roosevelt of Aledo, Illinois.

Another big change for the football program was the creation of a summer "pre-season" training camp (the Camp Traverse, Michigan camp days were long gone by now) for the team arranged by Coach Ziemba. The costs would be absorbed by a student fee as well as the Academy Fathers Club. Lake Geneva, Wisconsin was selected as the location for the camp. Ziemba and Mahon would oversee the training camp along with two new coaches: Gene Rodie and Gene Marshall. Rodie was a star athlete at Illinois State

Normal University (now Illinois State University) where he was the captain of the baseball team and also an assistant coach. Later he coached football and baseball in Niles, Michigan. Since 1942, Rodie had been assigned as an instructor at the Naval Air Technical Training Center at Navy Pier in Chicago. Gene Marshall arrived at the Academy after graduating from Northern Illinois State Teachers College (now Northern Illinois University) and then coaching basketball, baseball, and swimming at Northwestern Military Academy. With George Mahon returning as the assistant coach, the Academy now employed four experienced coaches focusing on the football program in 1945.

By the time the pre-season training camp began in Lake Geneva, the horror of World War II had concluded with the Japanese surrender on August 14 (followed by a formal ceremony on September 2 aboard the USS Missouri in Tokyo Bay, Japan). Germany had surrendered previously on May 7, 1945 and the country, as well as the Academy, struggled to return to normalcy.

TOO MUCH MOISTURE

With a solid group of returnees, including Buddy O'Brien, Captain Dick Allen, and gifted receiver/back Ted Heitschmidt, the coaches looked forward to a challenging, and hopefully, successful season in 1945. The championship of the newly created North Central Conference was certainly a viable goal, but strong opponents from the public-school sector loomed throughout the schedule. On September 21, the *Chicago Tribune* provided some insight on the expectations for the Academy team in 1945:

> Morgan Park Military Academy, a member of the newly formed North Central prep conference, opens its schedule tomorrow against Crete in Morgan Park. Coach Joe Ziemba has 14 lettermen returning, including a veteran in every spot, and reports the team's condition is excellent.

The season began on September 22 against another new suburban opponent, Crete High School (now Crete-Monee). Despite a heavy downpour later described by the 1946 **Skirmisher** as "too much moisture," the Academy rolled to an 18-0 victory. The elation of that opening win was marred a week later when Argo prevailed 20-0, despite an excellent two-way performance by Dick Allen. Since the Academy administration had been a strong proponent of the formation of the new North Central Conference, there was also an eagerness among the players to distinguish themselves in the first year of the four-team circuit. As such, the games against its conference foes were considered crucial for the Academy gridders. Beginning with a 31-0 swamping of Roosevelt on October 6, the Warriors captured all three of the inaugural North Central Conference games to capture the first league crown with an undefeated 3-0 record. Onarga fell 34-6 on October 13 while the Academy escaped with a hard-fought 7-6 win over Pullman Tech on November 3. Close losses to non-conference adversaries Lockport 7-6 and Marmion Military Academy (13-7) helped to even the final Academy mark at 4-4 for the season. The 1946 **Skirmisher** summarized the team's successful run at the conference championship:

> With the season highlighted by the winning of the North Central Conference championship, the Corps may look back and observe that the "Warriors" won four out of eight games. Injuries among the first "Eleven" were light, but rather costly in the tough games which were lost. This year's coaching staff was comprised of Major Mahon, athletic director; Captain Ziemba, head coach ably assisted by Gene Rodie. During the fall at Lake Geneva, Lt. Marshall likewise assisted in the coaching of the heavies. The team's successes on the gridiron were mostly responsible by the coaching staff, especially Captain Ziemba, who worked hard developing the team that won a championship. This year's team selected Dick Allen as the most valuable player of the 1945 season.

The conference championship, along with improved showings against strong suburban public schools in 1945 marked the beginning of a new era in the history of the Academy football program. With exceptional players such as O'Brien and Heitschmidt returning in 1946, the Warriors were about to prove that they could play with anyone, whether they be solid private school teams or fearsome public-school opponents. As the War ended, the Academy continued to enjoy high enrollment figures, along with winning sports programs, and the school was about to enter its own "golden age."

EXTRA POINT

As noted previously in this chapter, Morgan Park Academy proudly sent approximately 875 graduates and staff into the service during World War II. Many did not return, but *The Academy News* and later staff, such as Barry Kritzberg, did an extraordinary job of keeping the stories of these heroic individuals current both during the war and long after it ended. In the March 23, 1945 issue of *The Academy News*, the paper reported on the visit of one of its "wounded warriors" and told of the difficult challenges he faced in the early days of the war, only to survive, prevail, and return home with an inspirational outlook on life. His story is repeated here, but note the wonderful message that concludes this brief biography from 1945:

> Lieut. Walter Hinkle returned to the Academy March 16, after he had been liberated from Bilibid prison camp at Manila on the Island of Luzon. Lieut. Hinkle was liberated when the advancing American armies broke through the Jap defense of Manila. He arrived home March 8, aboard a transport plane. Walter lost his leg in infantry combat on the island of Panay in the Philippines 11 days after Pearl Harbor.
>
> While in the Philippines, Lieut. Hinkle required a wooden leg that was fashioned for him by an American officer. This leg has a particular importance to Lieut. Hinkle, for you see, it contained a 250,000-word diary in which he recorded all his hardships and hopes during his imprisonment. He has not been allowed to disclose the information contained on the scraps of paper upon which his diary was written. Before Lieut. Hinkle was shipped overseas he was a private sociologist at the state penitentiary in Jackson, Michigan. Lieut. Hinkle was a member of the class of '36. He spoke to the corps on March 16.
>
> He told the cadets that they should appreciate America for all that it is and that such things as the laughter of children in the streets, the sound of the street cars and cars blowing their horns are things to be remembered and are the things that make America what it is.

In a rare action photo surviving from 1944, Academy punter Koren boots one away during a 20-7 win over Lockport High School.

CHAPTER 18

The Golden Age of MPMA Football

*"Immediately after the game, the entire first team rushed
to the tower in Blake Hall and, according to tradition,
rang the bell, for the first time in seven years."*
—MPMA Skirmisher Yearbook, 1947

After the conclusion of World War II, the United States enjoyed a booming economy, marked by an uptick in jobs, an expanding housing market, and a generous jump in the growth of the auto industry. The country had rebounded from the most horrific global conflict in history and now, with millions of service men and women returning home to rebuild their lives, it was time to partake in the opportunities that were available. This era is generally recognized as the "Golden Age" of American history, a term denoting a time of great happiness, success and achievement.

Parallel to the country's pleasing economic growth, the Morgan Park Military Academy football squad experienced its own "Golden Age" of success. From 1946 through 1949, the Academy's gridders lost just four games while competing against new and emerging opponents from the rapidly growing south and southwestern suburbs of Chicago. With a robust roster of 40 players in 1946, including returning three-year quarterback Buddy O'Brien, Coach Ziemba wasted little time in preparing his troops by bringing the crew to Lake Geneva, Wisconsin on September 3 for the now annual football training camp. Two chartered buses transported the

Academy contingent north to its headquarters at the Lake Geneva Hotel. Practices started immediately under the watchful eyes of coaches Ziemba, Mahon, Rodie, and Marshall. The schedule for the duration of the week-long camp was as follows:

7:00 am	Rise and breakfast
9:00-10:45	Practice
11:00-12:00	Swimming
12:00-1:00 pm	Lunch
1:30-3:30	Practice
3:30-5:30	Swimming and rest
6:00	Dinner
7:00	Team meetings

With nearly four hours of physical practice time, along with team meetings each day in Lake Geneva, the coaches hoped to prepare the experienced team for a challenging schedule. *The Academy News* reported on September 24:

> With Major Mahon and Lt. Marshall coaching the line and Capt. Ziemba and Lt. Rodie guiding the backs, the team gradually took on some of the polish that makes a winning team. With hard, clean playing and a spirited backing from the Corps of Cadets it is possible to foretell a most successful season.

Cadet Richard Dabbert was a member of the 1946 team and vividly recalled the 1946 football season preparations in the May 2002 edition of the *Academy Magazine*:

> As a senior, I went out for football again and was content to gather splinters on the bench. I remember spending a week practicing at Lake Geneva before the season started. The cost for participants was $25.

The tone of the season would be set within an approximate 24-hour period when Ziemba scheduled an unprecedented opening weekend: two games in two days! On Friday, September 20, 1946, the Warriors entertained visiting Luther Institute (now Luther North) of Chicago in the first game of the new season and grabbed an easy 19-0 win according to *The Academy News* on September 24:

The first team of the M.P.M.A. squad played about six minutes of the first quarter, during which their right end, Red Williford, crossed Luther's goal line twice. Ted Heitschmidt converted once for the extra point. With the Cadets in the lead 13-0 at the end of the first period, Coach Ziemba sent in his able second team. Coach Ziemba kept his first team on the bench for the remainder of the game and managed to send in everyone on the entire varsity squad. The reason for the benching of the first team was to prevent any possible injury in the first game of the season that would handicap the squad throughout the rest of the schedule.

The second game of the year followed just hours later as the Academy welcomed Crete High School from the far southern suburbs. With his regulars still fresh after seeing limited action the previous day against Luther, Ziemba unleashed his potent offense with Co-Captain Don Kreger scoring three times from his backfield position in a 48-0 romp over the visitors.

INNOVATION STIRS CADET ENTHUSIASM

With the two-day football extravaganza now complete, Academy students and fans still took notice of another huge change during the games: the advent of female cheerleaders representing the Academy. In that very busy issue published on September 24, *The Academy News* provided the details behind this stunning development at the all-boys school under the headline "Innovation Stirs Cadet Enthusiasm":

Last September 13 when Major Mahon made an announcement in chapel soliciting cadets for positions as cheerleaders, not many were interested until the Major announced that it was probable that there would also be girl cheerleaders this year. Then the interest of the cadets quickened. Arrangements were made to secure girl cheerleaders from the Beverly area. Most of them will come from the Junior College, from Morgan Park High School, and from Calumet High School. The cheerleaders, will this year, receive expert tutelage and will hold several practice sessions to improve their techniques.

With the cheerleading issue thus happily solved (and placed under the guidance of Ruth Rodie, the wife of Coach Rodie), the football team turned its attention to suburban power Argo High School which had outscored the Academy 77-0 in the three previous meetings between the two schools. The 1946 edition of the Warriors would surely be tested by the imposing Argo squad. However, on September 28, the two clubs would batter each other defensively and walk away with a scoreless tie. While the Academy failed to secure the victory, it proved that it could be competitive with one of the strongest of the suburban public schools. Now 2-0-1, the Academy made quick work of fellow private schools Roosevelt Military Academy and Onarga Military Academy during the next two weeks. On October 5, the Warriors routed Roosevelt 45-0 and then blasted Onarga 24-6 a week later. Quarterback Buddy O'Brien passed for one score in the Roosevelt contest and ran for another to highlight the easy victory while Williford tallied twice to pace the victors in the Onarga clash. After building up a 24-0 advantage after the third quarter, Coach Ziemba cleared the bench and Onarga managed to score the first touchdown against the Academy in five games.

The Roosevelt triumph prompted *The Academy News* to begin speculating on the possible gridiron accolades that the 1946 team might very well achieve during the remainder of the season. In its October 11 issue, the student newspaper noted:

> By this time most people are looking to the Academy to win a second consecutive conference championship and beat St. Johns for the first time in six years. Don't misunderstand this, however, for the games remaining are by no means easy.

Expectations increased after a 12-0 victory over Lockport High School on October 19 as Don Kreger provided both scores on runs of 35 and 64 yards respectively and then exploded when the Academy drubbed Roosevelt High School of Chicago 38-0 in a game that was scheduled when both teams were faced with a mid-season open date on their schedules. Now sporting a 6-0-1 record for the season, the Warriors were primed for their final two showdowns, one against Pullman Tech for league championship honors, and the other a visit from St. John's Military Academy--the Academy's most potent rival.

But first, Coach Ziemba planned another major test for his feisty group of athletes: a scrimmage game against Chicago Catholic League power De LaSalle High School. The two clubs met on October 29 in an "unofficial" contest that would be played under regular game conditions, except for kickoffs being banned for the day. After falling behind 13-0, the Academy rallied to score three times late in the contest to secure a 19-13 win that was immediately forgotten…

The trip to Pullman Tech on Saturday, November 2 was a short one, just a little over three miles straight east on 111th Street. However, expectations were large as the two undefeated conference foes met with the North Central Prep Conference title up for grabs. An errant Academy fumble on the opening kick turned the ball over to Pullman Tech, and on the second play from scrimmage, Pullman halfback Nick Adducci raced 35 yards for the first—and only—score of the game. The stunning 6-0 defeat was the first for the Warriors of the season and the game marked only the second time that an opponent scored against the stringent Academy defense. While the loss to Pullman was disheartening, the key to a successful season would rest with the ability to snap the recent football hex held over the Academy by St. John's which had not been upended by the Warriors since the undefeated 1939 season. Prior to the big game, David Condon of the *Chicago Tribune* provided some insight into the importance of the contest:

> Cadets at Morgan Park Military Academy have 300 pounds of roast beef and 100 pies lined up to celebrate a big weekend party with their dads. To further assure a momentous celebration, the Cadets have promised a football triumph over their perennial rivals, St. John's Military Academy of Delafield, Wisconsin, tomorrow afternoon. The battle with the Wisconsin invaders will close one of Morgan Park's most successful campaigns. Last week the Warriors lost their chance for an undefeated season when Pullman Tech won 6-0, in the contest to settle the North Central Prep Conference championship, but this upset is expected to gear the Cadets to an all-out drive in their finale.

With the prediction of victory still fresh, the Warriors backed up their confident pre-game boast by scoring quickly in the first quarter when Buddy O'Brien nailed Red Williford with a touchdown pass. In the second period, halfback Don Kreger broke loose and raced 85 yards for a second score, providing the Academy with a 13-0 halftime advantage. With the end of the seven-year hex against St. John's in sight, O'Brien and Williford connected again for a third period touchdown pushing the Academy lead to 20-0. For the remainder of the contest, the tough Academy defense took over and frustrated the vaunted ground attack of the visitors, resulting in a final score of 20-0. It was a perfect end to an almost perfect season, as the Academy concluded its schedule with a respectable 7-1-1 record, while outscoring its opponents 206-12. Therefore, it was easy for the 1947 **Skirmisher** to reflect back on the accomplishments of the successful 1946 team, including the critical St. John's game:

> Immediately after the game the entire first team rushed to the tower in Blake Hall and, according to tradition, rang the bell, for the first time in seven years. As the bell tolled a victory over St. John's everyone present realized that this was the climax of one of the most successful football seasons in the annals of the Academy.

At the annual football banquet Don Kreger and Karion Fitzpatrick were acknowledged as the co-captains of the team, while Kreger, Fitzpatrick, Williford, O'Brien and guard Art Jicha were named to the all-conference team. Kreger, who gained 834 yards in only 101 carries, was named the Most Valuable Player for the season. Williford topped the club in scoring with 49 points (Kreger had 48) while quarterback Buddy O'Brien ended his career with 22 touchdown passes, an impressive number in the days before the forward pass became the main offensive weapon for most teams. In 2010, O'Brien was named to the Morgan Park Academy Athletic Hall of Fame after earning ten varsity letters during his time at the Academy. O'Brien was also named all-conference in basketball and selected as the school's best "All-Around Athlete" in 1947. He later went on to play baseball for the University of Notre Dame.

HOPES FOR SUCCESSFUL SEASON ALMOST CRUSHED

The lone loss to Pullman Tech in 1946 served to provide the proper incentive for returning players in 1947. Many of the athletes received ample playing time the previous year due to Coach Ziemba's generous use of reserves in "blow-out" games. Still, very few actual starters returned, and the offense was placed in the hands of quarterback Ted Heitschmidt, a 6'3" returnee who shared time with Buddy O'Brien the previous season and also saw some time at the end position. Heitschmidt was also a fire-balling right-handed pitcher on the baseball team and the football coaches worked with him before the season to lighten up on the speed of his deliveries to his receivers. Heitschmidt was big, fast, and durable. Off the field, the Academy decided to drop its affiliation with the North Central Prep Conference and compete as an independent in 1947.

In 1946 the pre-season week in Lake Geneva, Wisconsin was followed by a "double-header" where the Academy once again entertained two different opponents on successive days. On September 19, visiting St. Charles High School fell to the Warriors 13-0, while on September 20, the Academy blasted Crete High School 33-0.

While the 1947 edition of the Morgan Park Military Academy football squad looked strong in its two opening contests, the overall experience factor for the team was limited and the last thing that Ziemba could afford would be injuries to key players, but that was exactly what happened according to the 1947 **Skirmisher** yearbook:

> The groundwork for the season was laid at Lake Geneva, where the Warriors held their pre-school opening practices. Optimism among the players ran high, despite the lack of experience on the part of many of the first stringers. Hopes for a successful season were almost crushed before the first game, when Allen Carlson, regular halfback, injured his knee and was lost for the season. A few days later, Captain Pete Pratt, left end, suffered a shoulder injury, and was also lost for the season. Halfback Chuck Fidler was lost for the season following the first game. Don Wilkin, who had never played end, replaced Pratt. Ken Nelson moved from fullback to halfback to replace Carlson, and Gene Kosciolek, fourth string fullback of the 1946 team, took over the fullback duties.

Fortunately, the coaching staff had two weeks off between games after the Crete contest and worked to patch together a workable offensive unit for the Warriors after the unseemly spate of serious injuries. With most of the starters inexperienced at the start of the season as well, one could not predict exactly how the Warriors would react when many of the younger players would be under competitive fire for the first time against Howe Military Academy on October 4. Surprisingly, the Warriors eased past Howe 21-0 to remain undefeated at 3-0 and *The Academy News* (October 10) heaped praise on the new starting quarterback:

> Much of the credit should go to Ted Heitschmidt whose leadership, passing and running were sensational...In the

third quarter, Heitschmidt scored the Warriors' second touchdown on a sensational 45-yard run. He also made his second conversion making the score 14-0. Kenny Nelson scored the last touchdown for the Academy, taking a 35-yard pass from Ted and running 25 yards to score. Ted kicked the extra point to make the score 21-0. The second team then entered the game and held Howe scoreless. The Academy's line was sensational and completely out charged Howe's heavier line. It would be hard to name any one player, as each one was outstanding.

Nelson, the fullback turned halfback due to team injuries, was the star once again the following week when the Academy dismissed Roosevelt Military Academy 33-6. Nelson scored three times during the first half on runs of 45, 5, and 40 yards to push the Warriors ahead 20-0 at the break. The triumph over Roosevelt left the team with a perfect 4-0 record at the midway point of the 1947 season.

WARRIORS JUST KEEP ROLLING ALONG

A trip to unbeaten Lockport High School on October 18 provided the only stumble during the season as the two clubs battled to a 7-7 tie. Heitschmidt scored all seven points for the Academy in the contest as the Warriors dropped to a 4-0-1 for the year. Following the Lockport game, the *Chicago Daily News* raised the level of recognition for the Academy football team by marveling at the success of the team despite the rash of crucial injuries to key starters:

> No matter what happens at Morgan Park Military Academy, the football Warriors just keep rolling along and it's going to take a real upset to stop them short of their goal of an undefeated season. The south side school, which always turns up plenty of good grid prospects among its 300 cadets, is campaigning as an independent this fall... but the Warriors are finding the new opposition so much like the old that they're undefeated in five games with only a 7-7 tie with likewise unbeaten Lockport to mar their record.

The loss of three regulars would be more than enough to wreck many a team. But not Morgan Park Military. The Warriors go right on winning. They'll try for No. 5 tomorrow against Onarga Military Academy, loser of only one of five games. Powerful Pullman Tech comes in for a November 1 homecoming date and M.P.M.A. closes with St. John's Military Academy at Delafield, Wisconsin. The air-minded Warriors depend heavily upon the passing combination of quarterback Ted Heitschmidt to end Tom Tiernan. With Chuck Fidler gone, the brunt of the running attack is carried by right halfback Ken Nelson, 160-pound runner. He has raced for six touchdowns in four games. The Warrior line is one of the heftiest in the area with Len Baldassari, 6-0, 230 pounds, and Bob McGuire, 5-11, 180 pounds at tackles; "Rufe" Wasick, 6-1, 190, and Dan Tuffs, 5-11, 175 at guards; Dave Daisley, 5-10, 180 at center, and Harry Pratt, 6-2, 200 at end. And if you think that combination coached by Capt. Joe Ziemba isn't tough, think this over—the Warriors whipped St. Charles 13-0 and Crete 33-0 in games played on consecutive days.

However, that deadlock with Lockport was quickly forgotten as the Academy blew past Onarga (18-0), Pullman Tech (13-0), and St John's Military Academy (12-6) to finish the season with an undefeated 7-0-1 record. Emerging halfback Lenny Wolniak paced the Warriors over Pullman Tech with a pair of touchdowns to avenge the lone defeat suffered in 1946, while Wolniak and Tiernan scored the touchdowns in the season finale at St. John's. It was the first undefeated season for the Academy since 1939 and the ninth such mark in school history. Once again, the Academy piled up an impressive point difference throughout the year, outscoring its opponents 150-19. Heitschmidt was named the Most Valuable Player after his spectacular season, which included rushing for an average of 10.6 yards each time he touched the ball, while Wolniak (643 yards) and Nelson (472 yards) topped the overall rushing attack.

But the biggest honor in Heitschmidt's athletic career was still two years away. After a brief stint at the University of Michigan as a pitcher, Heitschmidt eventually signed with the major league baseball New York Giants. Heitschmidt was considered a "bonus baby" after receiving a monetary "bonus" in the form of $20,000 when he joined the Giants in 1949. This was a phenomenal amount of money at the time, especially for a young athlete who was still just 18 years old, and the news of his signing was documented in sports pages across the country. His career was stymied by injuries after playing in the Giants' minor league system in the early 1950s. A highlight of Heitschmidt's brief tenure in the professional ranks was a "one hitter" he tossed while a member of the Trenton Giants in New Jersey.

As a final tribute to the undefeated squad of 1947 the entire team was inducted into the inaugural Morgan Park Academy "Hall of Fame" in 2010. End Tom Tiernan was also elected to the Hall of Fame in 2012, based not only on his efforts for the football and track squads, but also for being named to the second team of the "All State" basketball honor squad selected by the *Champaign* (Illinois) *News-Gazette* in 1948.

EXTENSIVE BUILDING AND RENOVATION PLANS

As the post-war economy continued to boom across America, the Academy announced plans for a massive new building program in the spring of 1948 as reported in the *Chicago Tribune* on March 21:

> Extensive building and renovation plans, costing $925,000, have been announced for 75-year-old Morgan Park Military Academy. The proposed program—building of a combination armory, swimming pool, and auditorium; infirmary, scholastic hall, lower school, and gymnasium improvements, and remodeling of Blake Hall—is expected to begin in the fall. Underway is a campaign drive in which patrons and friends of the school are being asked to purchase "packaged" living memorials or contribute to the general fund.

> Teams equipped with kits containing brochures outlining the project, are canvassing assigned communities, calling on those interested in the welfare of the school and cadets. Col. Harry D. Abells, superintendent emeritus, who retired recently after 50 years of service, is assisting in the improvement program.

In a testament to the positive and supportive efforts of the Academy alumni and friends, over 75 people volunteered to personally call on individuals and businesses in an eager attempt to secure funding for the

Academy's latest project. Ironically, Col. Abells, who almost single-hand-edly saved the school from closure in 1908, remained a central figure in another major fund-raising effort forty years later. Although the ambitious program unfolded as planned (by July of 1948, over $125,000 had already been collected) and various improvements were implemented to the structures on campus, the construction of the new buildings, including the long-awaited swimming pool, was never undertaken.

CAPT. ZIEMBA'S STORY HOUR

As the Academy's golden age of football continued into 1948, it was simply becoming a reign of terror for opposing teams. Despite adding new and challenging teams to the schedule (Joliet Catholic High School appeared in 1948), the Warriors managed to continue their domination of both public and private schools. The pre-season prognosis was a bit unsettling as the Academy returned a host of talented men in the backfield, but only one experienced starter on the line. However, the 1949 **Skirmisher** yearbook accurately described the stable of fleet runners as a "'dream backfield' composed of Bill Giannos, Len Wolniak, Chuck Fidler, Leo Drelles, Bob Kaak, and Bud Hunt." The 1947 Chicago Cardinals, champions of the National Football League, had originally coined the phrase "Dream Backfield" when the Cards became the first professional club to start four former collegiate All-Americans in the backfield. Football aficionados on the south side of Chicago will fondly recall that quartet of runners: Charley Trippi (Georgia), Pat Harder (Wisconsin), Marshall Goldberg (Pittsburgh), and Paul Chrisman (Missouri). Goldberg later switched to defense and was replaced by another skilled runner, Elmer Angsman of Notre Dame.

But before the prep version of the "Dream Backfield" could be unleashed on unsuspecting opponents, the team gathered in Lake Geneva, Wisconsin once more for the now traditional pre-season training camp. The players met on campus on August 30 for initial drills, and then departed for a week-long stay at the Hotel Geneva on September 7. Most of the funding for the trip was provided by the ever-influential "Football Committee" of the Fathers Club, and members of the club were invited to visit their sons during the training camp. Not so ironically, key members of the Academy administration also made the trip, much to the "delight" of the football team members. "When we went to the pre-season camp at Lake Geneva, we stayed at a nice hotel and all of the players intended to cut loose," remembered halfback Cal Bouma, "but Coach Ziemba and the

Dads really sat on us!" If the players were dismayed by the grueling five hours of practice each day, or by the ever-present visibility of their parents and teachers, they failed to show it. The Lake Geneva trip certainly might be construed as a "reward" for the undefeated season of 1947, but it also served as a challenging physical regimen as well as a team "bonding" experience. Coach Ziemba demanded perfection on the field, but also slyly revealed a subtle sense of humor during team gatherings as noted by *The Academy News* on October 1:

> After supper at 6:00 pm the fun began for the tired but eager Warriors. One of the most enjoyable periods of the day was Capt. Ziemba's story hour when certain restricted information from highly personal letters was read for the edification of wayward athletes in order to keep them on the straight and narrow.

Usually picking on an easily identifiable trait (e.g. snoring) of one of the players, Ziemba would carefully invent, and "read" a letter from one of that player's loved ones that accentuated the specific trait much to the delight of that player's teammates. As the team howled in laughter, the "serious" letter might then wander into another "story" regarding a certain player or players that had everything to do with entertaining the players and nothing to do with the truth. The coach believed in humor as a method for uniting the players and molding them into an effective team, feeling that a team that could laugh together could certainly play together. "He expected you to produce but he had a good sense of humor and was a great kidder," said Bouma. "He basically took a bunch of ordinary players and made them into a heckuva team," added Bouma. "We played much bigger schools and did manage to win most of our games."

One of the members of the Academy "Dream Backfield" was halfback Bill Giannos, who turned out to be the Warriors' most visible ball carrier during the 1948 season and quickly discovered the kinship among his teammates. Giannos was from Evanston, Illinois and spent his first two years of high school at Evanston Township. He transferred to Morgan Park Military Academy for his final two years and immediately reported for football practice in the fall of 1948. Years later, he recalled in an *Academy Magazine* article (May 2006) that although he was a member of the football team at Evanston and was acclimated to the game and its rigors, Coach Ziemba was "something else. He was tough and knew his football. He worked us hard and could motivate a guy by a tap on the helmet or a look.

Fortunately, the guys on our team really had the guts, and we worked hard and played hard."

MAYBE IT WAS THE WEATHER

Despite the lack of a "finished" line, the Academy traveled to St. Charles High School for the season opener with high hopes for a solid season. The leadership of veterans like Giannos and Len Wolniak was expected to pay dividends until the very green front line gained much needed experience during the early part of the schedule. Among the aspiring linemen who would play a pivotal role during the season were Fritz Koberna, Lloyd George, Russ Beckman, John Buechner, and Dick Gruenwald. Unfortunately, the first encounter of the season resulted in a 13-7 St. Charles win, as the victors punched across a touchdown late in the game to erase a 7-6 Academy lead. Giannos and Chuck Fidler paced a rushing attack (Fidler tallied the lone score on a 12-yard run) that was chased all over the field by the St. Charles defenders but failed to dent the goal line after the first period. However, the Warriors brushed aside that initial defeat and prepared for the invasion of Joliet Catholic the following week. While not as strong a foe as it would become in later years (Joliet Catholic has won an unsurpassed 13 state football titles in Illinois), the visitors brought a big and talented squad to Morgan Park for the second game of the season. *The Academy News* documented the results of the contest in its October 1 edition:

> Maybe it was the weather; it might have been the field; perhaps it was the home crowd; but mostly it was the greatly improved line play that caused the Morgan Park Warriors to revenge last week's defeat by beating Joliet Catholic High School 6-0 on the local field. Fine line work on behalf of fighting Fred Koberna and Lloyd George and the brilliant ball handling by Lennie Wolniak brought the crowd to their feet time and time again during the game. Halfway through the third period Wolniak broke loose, this time for 62 yards…Butch Kaak carried over from [the two] to pay dirt. The line was able to hold the Joliet backfield to no sizable gain in the fourth period and the gun ended a 6-0 encounter, the Cadets' first victory over a new opponent. Capt. Joe Ziemba, coach, had maintained an almost 100 percent [attendance] record at practice, demonstrating that the players are anxious to learn…

The tight win over Joliet Catholic prompted the Warriors to reel off four more wins in succession, by defeating Howe Military Academy (29-7), Roosevelt Military Academy (19-0), Lockport High School (27-7) and Onarga Military Academy (31-6). By this time, Giannos was clearly the offensive spark for the team, scoring three touchdowns against Howe, rushing for 181 yards and a touchdown versus Roosevelt, and adding another score in the Lockport contest.

An important part of the football program at the Academy in the 1940s was the "Father's Club" which was quite visible in terms of fund-raising and volunteering where needed, whether it be for field maintenance or securing pledges for monetary donations to the school. Each year, one game on the football schedule was designated as "Dads Day" and it became as popular as the traditional "Homecoming" at other high schools. It was a well-financed and respected event on the Academy calendar since it afforded the school—and its students—the opportunity to formally recognize the work of the fathers throughout the year, with one of those significant contributions being the pre-season football training camp in Lake Geneva, Wisconsin. In 1948, the "Dads Day" celebration was slated for October 9, with Roosevelt Military Academy providing the gridiron varsity opposition, while the fresh-soph team would entertain Blue Island High School. Following the second game, the guests would assemble for dinner, according to the *Chicago Tribune*:

> It will be Dads Day Saturday on the Morgan Park Military Academy campus. The annual celebration when fathers visit their cadet sons will be highlighted with a football game and banquet. Fathers and faculty will meet for an informal session after the football game. About 700 guests are expected to attend the banquet in the gymnasium, Louis George, in charge of arrangements, said. Members of the Mothers Club will help in serving the guests. There will be entertainment and community singing with music throughout the dinner. Ernest E. Colwell, president of the University of Chicago, will speak on "Discipline and Your Future."

I WANTED TO THANK THE FOOTBALL TEAM

During that five-game winning streak, more rumors began swirling regarding the recruitment of the Academy into still another major prep conference as reported in the *Chicago Daily Herald*:

> As the season nears its close all schools plan for their 1949 schedules. Arlington, Leyden, and Niles are scouting around to line up schools for a new conference. We have little idea of who they might have in mind but possibilities from this point might be Belvidere, DeKalb, Marmion Military Academy, Morgan Park Military Academy, Hinsdale, Downers Grove...and Kankakee.

While it was unlikely that the Academy would have ventured to jump into such a conference solidified by large public schools mainly from the northern and western Chicago suburbs, most leagues at the time focused on their football opportunities, so it was intriguing that the tiny Academy (in terms of enrollment) was considered the competitive "equal" of these much larger institutions. As it was, the 1948 season was nearly concluded with just two games remaining for the 5-1 Warriors. On October 30, the Academy saw its five-game winning skein snapped in a 14-12 heartbreaking loss to local rival Pullman Tech. *The Academy News* provided the disappointing details (date unknown):

> Warriors supporters were shocked by the turn of the events as Pullman came from behind to defeat the favored MPMA team, 14-12. Just before the first quarter ended, Bill Giannos ran 45 yards to the Pullman 11. Len Wolniak drove to the one-yard line as the second quarter started. Giannos carried over for the touchdown. A placement failed. The third quarter featured a steady drive by the Warriors to the Pullman 16-yard line. Giannos went around end for 12 yards, Wolniak ripped off three more yards over tackle. Giannos scored again from the one-yard line...but the extra point failed.

With the Academy seemingly safely ahead 12-0 entering the final period, the squad was surprised by a determined Pullman club that managed to score twice, and added both extra points, to stun the Academy 14-12. With an off-day the following week, Coach Ziemba and the team participated in an intra-squad game on Friday, November 5 to benefit the local "Community Fund." While no score was recorded, the contest pitted the seniors against the underclassmen and provided a sneak peek into the future for the Academy football team since the majority of the starting linemen were juniors. The team then completed its 1948 campaign the following week by walloping the Glenwood School from Glenwood, Illinois 45-0 as Giannos tallied on runs of 53, 62, and 42 yards. Overall, the team finished with a 6-2 mark in 1948, paced by the fabulous running of Giannos, who rushed for 847 yards on just 79 carries for a scintillating 10.7 rushing average. Wolniak carried the ball 109 times for a solid 696 yards and a 6.4 yard per carry average. Giannos, who also scored 74 points, was selected as the Most Valuable Player by his team and both Giannos and Wolniak were also named to the first team of the All-Independent honor squad selected by the *Herald-American*. Finally, Giannos was elected to the Academy Hall of Fame in 2010 for his accomplishments not only in football, but also for wrestling and track. During his Academy years, his work as an artist was encouraged and he eventually became the editorial art director for the *Star Magazine* published by the *Kansas City Star*. In 2005, he donated a bronze sculpture of a football player/wrestler to Morgan Park Academy. As he told the *Academy Magazine*, "I wanted to thank the football team, and the sculpture is my way of saying thanks, teammates!"

TULEY HAS NEARLY TEN TIMES THE STUDENTS

Perhaps one of the key reasons why the Academy was continually pursued to participate in larger conferences might be because the football team never avoided scheduling tough competition from "bigger" schools. This fearless intent was captured by the *Suburbanite Economist* (now the *Daily Southtown*) on September 7 in a pre-season article regarding the Academy's rigid schedule for 1949, although the scheduling may have been promoted by the Academy's decision to avoid a conference affiliation again in 1949:

> Morgan Park Military Academy is preparing for a stiff football schedule and has already held a number of practices. Captain Joe Ziemba, former Mt. Carmel and Chicago Cardinal grid star, will again coach the team. The Cadets have added four "big schools" to their schedule this year including South Shore and Tuley of the [Chicago] Public League, Niles of the Suburban circuit and Blue Island of the South Suburban. There are 260 high school

boys in MPMA, Tuley has nearly ten times that many students. The other three new Warrior opponents are well over 1,000. The Warriors have won 20 games, lost three and tied one the past three years. "Our line should be very good with three regulars and five other lettermen back," says the former Mt. Carmel gridder. "But the backfield is a big question mark." A squad of 45, including freshmen, is in its second week of morning practice. Much work needs to be done before the first game with South Shore September 16 at Eckersall Stadium.

In an effort to provide his smallish grid team with an advantage against the larger schools on the schedule, Coach Ziemba unveiled a "platoon" system prior to the 1949 season. Due to the early rules of the game, and later the tradition of the sport, most football players were on the field whether their team was on offense or defense. It was expected that individuals would stay on the field for each minute of the game unless there was a rare substitution due to inefficiency or injury. According to the rules of the time, if a player left the field for whatever reason, he was not allowed to re-enter the game during the same period. Around 1941, the rules were changed on the collegiate level to allow unlimited substitution, primarily due to the apparent lack of acceptable talented players during the war years. Despite the significance of the rules change, not many college teams considered the "platoon" option of utilizing separate units on offense and defense. There was even less attraction at the prep school level where the lack of experienced players and coaches was more visible. Certainly, teams were now free to substitute individual players more often, but few elected to substitute entire offensive and defensive units during a contest. However, the Academy football team of 1949 jumped right into the "platoon" system as a means of remaining competitive on the football field. Legendary University of Michigan coach Fritz Crisler (once an assistant at the University of Chicago under Amos Alonzo Stagg) was probably the first mainstream coach to embrace the platoon system when he did so in 1945. In an interview with *Sports Illustrated* magazine on February 3, 1964, Crisler recalled the circumstances that led to this significant change in the rules:

> He [Crisler] sat down at his desk, leaned forward and rested his elbows on it. "Now," he said, "about the substitution rule. Let's go back and review the circumstances that

made platooning possible. World War II had created a tremendous drain on manpower, and in the 1941 meeting of the Football Rules Committee many people felt that football schedules should be scrapped entirely. But the services urged that the colleges continue all athletic programs as best they could, pointing to their importance in conditioning the boys who would eventually be called up and to the morale and leadership factors involved."

"With this directive from the services, the Rules Committee met to ponder the question—the staggering question—of how we were to continue with our ranks so depleted. Since the problem was obviously a matter of depth...I came to the conclusion that the answer might be found in a relaxation of the substitution rule. The rule at the time said that if a boy started a quarter and was taken out he could not return to the game during the same quarter. So, if you had only a limited number of men, a narrow bench, and you had to make substitutions for reasons of injury or fatigue, and one thing and another, you might very well run out of men altogether. But if a boy—with a minor injury or the wind knocked out of him—could be taken out and returned as soon as he was able to play again, why, that would be most helpful. The Rules Committee found the answer in three little words. Instead of having the rule say that a substitute could enter the game only once in a quarter, the committee approved a rule permitting a substitute to enter the game 'at any time.' Just those three little words...I don't think anybody at the 1941 meeting of the Rules Committee visualized platooning as it was later developed."

The first opponent to experience the wonders of the Warriors' platoon system was South Shore High School of the Chicago Public League. As Coach Ziemba rotated players with every change of possession, the Academy was able to stay close to South Shore throughout the game and eventually pushed over the winning touchdown late in the game on a Bob Kaak scoring toss to receiver George Michale resulting in a 7-0 victory. A visit to Joliet Catholic the following week resulted in a 19-7 Academy triumph, as halfback Cal Bouma ravaged the Joliet defense for 214 yards on just 22 carries. Bouma scored once on a five-yard scamper, while quarterback Bob Kaak tallied on a one-yard plunge. The final score also involved Kaak, as he unfurled a 40-yard scoring toss to Michale. The Academy next sailed past Howe Military Academy 13-0 as Michale scored on another pass from Kaak and sophomore fullback Frank Burd added a four-yard touchdown, and then the Warriors ripped Roosevelt Military Academy 43-6 with Michale and Burd once again finishing scoring drives.

WINNING HAS BECOME THE HABIT

Now 4-0, the 1949 Warriors were proving to be a tough defensive challenge for opposing teams, racking up 89 points and allowing just 13 in those first four outings. Some of the linemen responsible for this success were captain Russ Beckman, centers Jerry Voss and Pete Cappas, guards John Buechner and John Leventis, tackles Beckman and Jack Lucido and ends George Michale and Don Neri. However, hopes for another undefeated season were dashed when the Academy traveled to distant Niles, Illinois to take on the local high school. Down 13-0 at the half, the Academy rallied in the third period according to the *Arlington Heights Herald* on October 21:

> The Nile gridmen downed a highly noted Morgan Park Military Academy eleven 20-12 under the lights of the Niles field…Morgan Park came back with renewed spirit after the half and scored on a 15-yard pass from Bob Kaak, quarterback, to George Michale, end, after Morgan Park had recovered a Trojan fumble on the 20-yard line. The Cadets failed to make the extra point. Morgan Park scored again in the final period when Michale caught a two-yard pass from Kaak in the end zone. The Cadets missed a chance to tie the score when they failed again to make the extra point.

Trailing 13-12 late in the game, the Warriors allowed the final score after an extended Niles scoring drive that left the hosts with a 20-12 victory. The Academy bounced back to flatten Tuley High School of Chicago 25-7 to improve to 5-1 with just two games remaining on the schedule. In an unidentified newspaper article found in the Academy archives, one Chicago outlet summarized the recent success of the Academy football program:

Winning has become the habit at Morgan Park Military Academy since Joe Ziemba became coach six years ago. The Warriors have won 23 games, lost three and tied one in the last three seasons. This fall they have won five and lost one. Morgan Park will seek its sixth victory Saturday against Pullman Tech and will close its season November 5 against Blue Island. Ziemba also played on undefeated football teams. In 1933 he was tackle on the Mount Carmel High School squad which went through its schedule without a loss and he was a member of the 1937 St. Benedict's college eleven which was unbeaten. The 1949 Morgan Park team is sparked by the passing combination of Bob Kaak, quarterback, to George Michale, 6-foot, 3-inch, 205-pound end, and the running of Cal Bouma, a 6-foot, 170-pound halfback.

The game against Pullman Tech on October 29 would be bittersweet since it was announced earlier in 1949 that this would be the final game in a rivalry that stretched back to 1920, when the Academy won the first game in the long-running gridiron feud 14-0. Over the years, the competition between the two neighboring schools was surprisingly close. Entering the 1949 season, the Academy had grabbed 11 victories, while Pullman Tech had captured 10 wins. One game, in 1936, ended in a scoreless tie. However, declining finances pushed the administration of the Pullman Free School of Manual Training (Pullman Tech) to close the doors of the institute effective at the conclusion of the 1949-50 school year. Ironically, the game against the Warriors would be the last one ever played by Pullman Tech as it concluded its final season.

That proud history was ended with a 38-0 thumping by the Academy. Bouma scored three times to pace the rout while Jim White added two more touchdowns as the Academy moved to 6-1 on the season. With state football playoffs not yet in existence, and with no conference crown to pursue, the Cadets of Morgan Park Military Academy hosted the Blue Island High School Cardinals on November 5 in the final contest on the 1949 schedule. Basically, playing for pride against the much larger member of the South Suburban League, the Academy scratched out an exciting 7-6 victorious outcome, with the details captured by the *Blue Island Sun Standard*:

> The Cadets scored their touchdown on the seventh play of the second half. The leading ground gainer of the day,

the Academy right halfback Bouma, went over from the one-yard line. The Cadets succeeded in scoring the all-important extra point on a desperation pass from Geno Cantele to Bouma. During the first three quarters the Cadets' rushing game proved too much for the Cards as Cantele and Bouma gained a total of 140 yards. In the fourth quarter, however, the Redbirds dominated the play as they fought back trying to pull the contest out of the fire. With only minutes to play, the Cards completed two passes for a net game of 31 yards. Moore dashed from the Academy 14-yard line for the score. The fateful kick for the extra point was blocked.

For his efforts in the Blue Island game, Bouma was selected as the Chicago area "Prep Back of the Week" by the *Chicago Herald American*. With the narrow victory, the Academy celebrated the laudable 7-1 season record that completed a superlative 27-4-1 ledger during the "Golden Age" of Morgan Park Military Academy football from 1946-49. Further individual accolades were received in the post season when Bouma, Michale, and tackle Jack Lucido were chosen for the first team of the "All Non-Conference" honor squad by the *Chicago Daily News*.

In particular, the victory over Blue Island was especially satisfying to one local eighth grade student who dreamed of playing football one day at the Academy. Pete Voss would later recall: "When we beat Blue Island 7-6, it might have been the greatest win in school history. No one could believe that a little school from the south side could beat a big school like that!"

EXTRA POINT

Perhaps no one has done more to preserve the history of Morgan Park Military Academy than former Academy senior faculty member and archivist Barry Kritzberg. In May of 1999, Kritzberg helped organize a reunion of the Academy classes from 1947, 1948, and 1949, which would have included many of the players from the school's "Golden Age" of football. The following is excerpted from an *Academy Magazine* (November 1999) article that Kritzberg authored about that day, including former students commenting on the school, proms, discipline, the dining hall, and of course, their football coach:

I went to a reunion of virtual strangers, you see, where I had quite a time. I enjoyed the stories, the quips, and the jokes. There was a cheerful note of irreverence in it all, and yet one could tell that they loved the old place and all it meant to them…One of those who did have him [Coach Ziemba] as a teacher interjected, that Ziemba was "an expert at tossing erasers at the heads of inattentive cadets in his civics classes." That prompted Butch McGuire ('48) to say that it was books, not erasers, that were thrown at him. "I could also expel gas at will, and for that skill, I was made to sit on the window sill, with the window open, for the rest of the year. But, he was a wonderful guy and a great coach."

And then they were off, telling story after story, in a free-wheeling session of tales told out of school that lasted well into the evening hours…John Steinhart ('47), a retired geophysicist who taught for thirty years at the University of Wisconsin, told a tale on himself: "The prom was the night before graduation. I can't remember my prom date, but I do remember that she wasn't my first choice and I probably wasn't hers. I do remember that we went to the Indiana Dunes afterwards, where we drank all night. I remember that I had to be back at MPMA in the morning to deliver the valedictorian address, but I don't remember giving it at all."

"I wasn't the valedictorian of my class," Butch McGuire [owner of the popular Butch McGuire's restaurant in Chicago] said, "and if it wasn't for one other student, I would have been at the bottom of my class. I had the distinction of doing study halls even through my senior year." Tom Tiernan ('48) noted that MPMA taught him one very important lesson: "Eat everything, or you'd starve. Every Friday night we had baked beans and cottage cheese. I still eat it; no one understands!"

Prior to the 1949 season, Coach Joe Ziemba (right) discusses strategy with (from left): George Michale, Bob Kaak, Russ Beckman and John Beuchner. The 1949 club ended its season with a 7-1 record, completing a successful four-year run with a 27-4-1 mark.

In 1948, Morgan Park Military Academy posted a 6-2 record, counting Joliet Catholic and Lockport among its conquests.

CHAPTER 19

Cinderella Loses Her Slipper

"We were great, then we were lousy."
—Academy Football Coach Richard Boya, 1955

Before he became the United States Ambassador to Portugal, as well as one of the most successful real estate developers in the country, Al Hoffman Jr. ('52) was a cadet at Morgan Park Military Academy who really desired to play football. "I wanted to play very badly, even though I was not the biggest person on campus," recalled Hoffman. "I was maybe 110 pounds, but I went up to Coach Ziemba and told him I wanted to play football. He looked at me for a few seconds, then just picked me up and hung me on the coat rack by my belt. Then he left me there! A few minutes later, he came back, put me back on the ground, and simply said, 'Try wrestling.'"

While Cadet Hoffman never contended for a playing position on the Academy football team, he did manage a successful wrestling experience while in high school. "Even at 110 pounds, I was not fast or agile enough to be a wide receiver. So, I did choose wrestling thanks to his advice. I was able to get my letter and even wrestled at West Point even though quite frankly, I hated wrestling. Again, the drive to succeed is what kept me going." As a senior at the Academy, Hoffman finally connected with the football team when he served as the team manager. "I loved carrying the equipment for the team members. In this small way, I felt as if I were 'and I was' an accepted member of the team. All the players were simply a great group of guys whom I admired very much."

During his years at the Academy, Ambassador Hoffman also participated in the sports of tennis, bowling, and softball, while joining the rifle team, the Debate Club, the Grenadiers, *The Academy News* staff, and the class play. In other words, it was a very healthy high school experience for the future United States Military Academy (West Point) graduate, all of which helped prepare him for his future endeavors: "As a member of the ROTC, I always had in the back of my mind, a desire to be a pilot in the Air Force. This desire drove me to maintain the high standards necessary for success in my career as an Air Force Officer from West Point." During his time in the Air Force, Hoffman piloted F-100 fighter jets, before graduating from the Harvard Business School and initiating his own very successful business career. The *Washington Post* once (June 25, 2002) identified Hoffman as "the most influential developer in a state [Florida] crowded with influential developers" and he eventually served as the United States Ambassador to Portugal from 2005-2007.

Despite these numerous accomplishments, Ambassador Hoffman, who still attends Academy events, looks back fondly at the influence of his high school years, especially the athletic program: "MPMA expressed the highest standards of sportsmanlike conduct. I was very much aware of this and tried to emulate and personify those standards even though I was not qualified to become a football player. Cadets at MPMA always took their time there seriously but still kept time aside to put their sense of humor on display and have fun. Quite simply, that was our purpose and mission."

HEAVY SEARCH FOR TALENT

Perhaps the football squad in 1950 could have used the talents of Cadet Hoffman, as the team lost 25 members due to graduation from the formidable 1949 edition which finished with that sparkling 7-1 record. The schedule was extremely difficult as well since most of the smaller, private schools disappeared with the exception of Howe Military Academy. One unique aspect of the schedule was the return of Culver Military Academy, which had not played Morgan Park Military Academy since 1942. The season-ending meeting of the two powerful military schools would prove to be one of the most exciting matches in recent history.

Coach Ziemba, along with new varsity assistant Gene Rodie, welcomed 29 players (out of the high school enrollment of 154) to the opening of training camp. Unlike previous years, the players were not afforded the opportunity of the Lake Geneva training excursion. Instead, the pre-season festivities would be held right on campus. While optimism generally is evident at the beginning of any athletic season, the coaches were restrained in their preliminary evaluations, especially with talented runner Frank Burd being the only starter returning from the previous season. "There's no way we can get around it," said Ziemba in an interview with the *Chicago Daily News* on September 20. "We'll have to work hard and develop the material available." That material included 18 inexperienced gridders fresh up from the frosh-soph squad. The *Daily News* offered further insight into the Academy's questionable 1950 prospects:

> Like many of the Chicagoland prep teams that created outstanding records last year, there is a heavy search for talent going on at Morgan Park Military Academy this year in order to fill gaping holes left by graduation last spring. And that's just what head grid tutor Captain Joe Ziemba and his assistant, Gene Rodie, are concentrating on at the Academy. Wholesale graduation robbed the Warriors of all but one returning regular, halfback Frank Burd, although seven lettermen are back in the fold.
>
> Coach Ziemba is starting his seventh season at the helm of Warrior grid destinies and his record displays an imposing array of victories over the past four years. His teams have won 27 contests while dropping four and tieing two. Last year's record was one of Ziemba's most brilliant as his eleven copped seven wins against one defeat.

After reviewing the results of the team's opening encounter, one might surmise that the talk of the lack of talent and the lack of experience was premature. After all, the Warriors easily knocked off South Shore High School of Chicago 25-19. Backfield star Frank Burd led the way by scoring on a 56-yard run and then again by returning an interception 55 yards in the final period. His running mate, Gino Cantele, added another touchdown. Unfortunately, the offense then faltered in shut-out losses to Niles (15-0) and Argo (12-0) before the Cadets rebounded to slam Waller High School of Chicago 27-7 in front of a capacity Dad's Day crowd at the Academy. This event was one of the highlights each season on campus as captured by the *Southtown Economist* (October 18):

> The varsity easily defeated Waller High School 27-7. Dads and Cadets lined up for retreat formation and marched

to the gymnasium where a committee of "Mothers of the Cadet Corps" served the evening banquet. Principle speaker of the evening was Harold O. McLain, president Railroads Ice Company. Musical entertainment by Jane and Carl Rupp was enjoyed by all. The Waller victory convinced Coach Joe Ziemba that his cadet eleven is on their way to another impressive season. The Academy team journeys to Howe, Indiana, next Saturday.

Even more impressive than the dinner entertainment was the earlier on-field performance of Frank Burd. He scored twice in the first quarter on runs of 19 and 22 yards, and totaled 189 yards on just 18 carries, outdistancing the entire Waller team which managed just 110 yards combined from both rushing and passing efforts. The Academy maintained its momentum the following week as it dispatched Howe Military Academy 26-6 with little trouble. "Coach Joe Ziemba's Warriors displayed an improved brand of football and had little difficulty in winning from their Indiana rivals" reported the *Southtown Economist* on October 25.

FUMBLES BECAME A DANGEROUS THREAT

Sadly, the Howe victory would prove to be the final victory etched into the 1950 record book by the Academy. Joliet Catholic prevailed 26-6 on October 28, followed a week later by a 35-12 loss in forlorn conditions at Blue Island High School as reported on November 9 by the *Blue Island Sun-Standard*:

> The loyal fans who came to witness the game were treated to quite a contest, although they were forced to brave a bitter wind, beating rain, hail, and chilling temperatures. In the last ten minutes of the game neither team was able to gain consistently because of a heavy shower of rain and hail. Footing became insecure, and fumbles became a dangerous threat.

Now saddled with a somewhat disappointing 3-4 record, the Academy team nonetheless eagerly awaited its final adversary of the year, Culver Military Academy. Although the rivalry began back in 1899 when Culver scratched out an 18-6 win, the intermittent series was discontinued after the 1942 season, probably due to the war effort. Both schools had enjoyed exceptional success on the football field and their pitched battles on the gridiron always attracted media and fan attention. Perhaps the most spirited edition of the rivalry occurred in 1939 when Morgan Park capped an undefeated campaign by scuttling the Culver invaders 19-0. Culver captured wins in the next three seasons (1940-1942) before the competition between the two respected prep schools was suspended. Although the teams had not met during the "Golden Age" of Academy football, both the players and coaches were well aware of the important bragging rights that were associated with both present and past encounters. The ghosts of the legendary 1939 battle still drifted through the halls of the Academy via the proudly displayed trophies and photos from championship teams of years gone by.

To add to the significance of the 1950 skirmish with Culver, the Academy also designated the game as being the annual "Homecoming" date. Ironically, just as in 1939, the date of the game fell on November 11, now Veterans Day but still identified as Armistice Day back in 1950. With the combined corps of cadets from both schools present during halftime, the Academy planned to honor the memories of the students from both institutions who had lost their lives in the service.

Culver jumped out to a 12-0 lead in the first quarter on a pair of touchdowns by Chuck Parks before Frank Burd countered with an Academy score in the second stanza. The score remained 12-6 until late in the game as the two punishing defenses straightened up and refused to budge, not allowing either offense to touch the end zone.

When all appeared lost late in the contest, the Academy mounted, and sustained, a long scoring drive culminating in a Gino Cantele score with only two seconds remaining in the contest. As both sides of the stadium held their collective breaths, the Academy extra point attempt failed, leaving the final score at 12-12. Due to the tie game result, a coin flip determined that the Warriors would retain possession of the "Brass Bonnet" trophy that would reside in the hands of the winners for the next year. The bonnet was actually a "battered, but gold-plated WWII helmet" according to *The Academy News* that would be presented to the winner of the Culver-Morgan Park game each fall. The contest in 1950 marked the first time that the "Brass Bonnet" surfaced as the symbol for victory in the renewed rivalry between the two military schools.

The literal "last second" touchdown against Culver allowed the Academy to finish with a 3-4-1 mark for the season, a tough response to the recent four full years of football success. In summary, the 1951 **Skirmisher** yearbook stated:

Despite the average record compiled, the coaches were well satisfied with the showing of the team, since all of the opponents, with the exception of Howe Military Academy, were schools with enrollments far larger than that of the Academy.

Burd and Cantele performed exceptionally well for the Warriors throughout the season with Burd being named the MVP after picking up 838 yards on the ground in 124 attempts (6.8 average per carry) while topping the club with 55 points. Cantele gobbled up 412 yards rushing on 65 carries (6.3 average) and added 24 points. In addition, Burd and tackle Walter Elsner were both selected to the "All-Independent" honor team picked by both the *Chicago Daily News* and the *Chicago Herald-American*. Cantele, at just 5'9" and about 170 pounds, was a diminutive athlete who captained both the football and track teams at the Academy while also starring in baseball and basketball. For his all-around sporting achievements in four sports while at the Academy, Cantele was selected for the school's Athletic Hall of Fame in 2014.

One of the off-field highlights of the 1950 season was when Coach Ziemba was invited to be the only speaker representing a high school at the annual Kiwanis Sports Program dinner held at the Hotel Sherman in downtown Chicago on September 28, 1950. Ziemba shared the dais with an incredible group of legendary athletes including football's Red Grange, baseball's Rogers Hornsby, Olympic hero Jesse Owens, boxer Tony Zale and golfer Chick Evans. It was an extraordinary honor for the Academy instructor who was recognized for the dominating success of his teams on the local gridirons over the past few seasons.

Meanwhile, with Burd due back in 1951, along with numerous lettermen, it was hoped that the 1951 season would return the Academy football team to its preferred position of gridiron prominence. Sadly, it was not meant to be…

WARRIORS HAD A DISASTROUS SEASON

The off-season brought some physical changes to the Academy as several buildings were remodeled to accommodate the growing student population which hit a total enrolment of 373 students (for both upper and lower schools) during the 1951-52 school year. The *Chicago Tribune* noted the structural changes:

> Improvements include conversion of the former chapel-study hall into a little theater, relocation of science laboratories, renovation of science equipment, larger quarters for the music department, and relocation of military headquarters. Military activities will be located in Alumni Hall, with space for offices, classrooms, rifle range and armory.

What the article failed to mention was probably the biggest reason for the numerous changes: the closing of Morgan Park Junior College. Founded in 1933 by the Academy administration in a brilliant move to offset the economic downside of the depression, as well as to offer an affordable local college education option, the junior college closed its doors at the conclusion of the 1951 school year, as reported earlier in the year on January 31 by the *Southtown Economist*:

> Decision to close the school was taken after careful deliberation, it was said. Factors which prompted the decision of the trustees were listed by the trustees as follows: "Declining enrollments, certainty of military service for large segments of the male population of junior college age, increasing costs of operation, and many other influencing factors."

The closing of the junior college, which utilized classroom and facility space on the Academy campus, nudged the administration to quickly remodel the space previously used by the college. This allowed the Academy to "expand" within its own tight community and to offer additional opportunities—and more space for doing so—without initiating any new construction. New emphasis was placed on musical endeavors, theater, and equestrian activities.

Apparently, the loss of the junior college did not deter large numbers of aspiring players for the Academy football team from eagerly reporting for the opening of the 1951 season according to the *Blue Island Sun-Standard* in its preview on August 30:

> Over 60 candidates reported to Coach Joe Ziemba. With preliminary physical exams and conditioning exercise completed, the squad will stage the first game-condition scrimmage on Saturday morning, September 1.

Aside from Captain Frank Burd, seven other lettermen returned, along with 22 newcomers from the frosh-soph squad, and numerous other returning varsity hopefuls with limited experience from the previous season. Indeed, things looked good for the Warriors when they opened up the 1951 season on September 15 with a date against Bowen High School of the Chicago Public League. Bowen was a huge school in the teeming south side of Chicago with an enrollment that once stretched to over 4,600 students. After the two clubs battled to a scoreless tie through three quarters at Eckersall Stadium, defender Bill Krizenecky created some hope for the Academy when he intercepted a pass on the Bowen 40-yard line with less than five minutes to play. Shifting over to the offensive side, fullback Krizenecky and Burd pushed the ball down to the Bowen 13. From there, quarterback Frank Casey tallied the winning touchdown on a crafty reverse, leaving the Cadets with a 6-0 margin that stood up for the final score in the victory. Unfortunately, the tight win over Bowen would prove to be the highlight of the season as the shocked Academy eleven proceeded to lose its final eight games in 1951 to finish with a surprising 1-8 mark for the season.

Certainly, no excuses were offered by the coaches and players, and no one blamed the rugged schedule, which included Joliet Catholic, Argo High School, Reavis High School, and Niles Township. In fact, none of the smaller private schools that appeared in previous years were encountered on the 1951 schedule. The Academy had collided with similar "large" foes in the past, so the schedule was not considered either unfair or intimidating. Playing much larger schools was the new normal for Morgan Park Military Academy so there was no room on campus for hiding behind that convenient alibi. Instead, in its post-season synopsis, the annual **Skirmisher** yearbook simply defined the season as "disastrous":

> The 1951 Warriors, captained by Frank Burd, and coached by Captains Ziemba and Rodie, had a disastrous season in compiling only one win against eight losses. The season was particularly heart-breaking in that the worst defeat was only a three-touchdown margin suffered at the hands of Culver. The Warriors dropped four contests by the margin of a touchdown or less.

In an interview for this book, Frank Burd noted that the Academy never hesitated when facing a much larger school on the gridiron:

It was a great pleasure to play larger schools, for we were competitive with them, and to beat them was very satisfying. Our first game in 1950 was against the highly touted South Shore High School team which had gotten impressive coverage in the *Tribune*. We won 25-19. We also gave Argo a good game that season and they too had gotten good press. As long as our small school could put enough good players on the field, size of the student body didn't matter. For years the small MPMA was very successful. No doubt Coach Ziemba was a critical part of that.

So how bad was the final record in 1951? It matched the 1940 team as being the closest an Academy squad had approached a winless season since Coach Otho Ling finished with a 0-2-1 mark during the flu-interrupted year of 1918. And, it was the first single win campaign since the 1940 club wrapped up a 1-6 record following the undefeated 1939 championship season. Tough, close losses to South Shore (6-0), Niles (14-12), Waller High School (20-14), and South Suburban Conference champion Blue Island (7-0) dominated the frustrating season for the Academy. In particular, the Niles defeat stung when the victors pushed over the winning score with just 49 seconds left in the contest.

At the conclusion of the season, the team was treated to another auspicious football banquet on campus. The guest speaker was recently retired, but future Pro Football Hall of Fame quarterback, Sid Luckman of the Chicago Bears, who followed an impressive array of pro football-related guest speakers in previous years such as Charley Trippi and Marshall Goldberg, stars of the Chicago Cardinals. "Coach Ziemba had connections so that he was able to get great pro football players to attend our banquets," recalled Frank Fonsino ('59). "It was a great opportunity for us on the Academy teams to meet and talk with these well-known professional players." At the banquet itself, running back Frank Burd, a three-year starter, was once again named as the team's Most Valuable Player, a rare repeat at the high school level. Burd topped the team in rushing and was named to the honorable mention squad on both the All-Chicago Area and the All-State honor squads.

Following the football season, Burd zipped over to the gym where he was the second leading scorer on the Academy's 1951-1952 basketball squad, and then graduated early in 1952 before enrolling at the University of Michigan in time for spring football practice (Burd would transfer later that year to the United States Military Academy). He still feels that his experience at the Academy adequately prepared him for the rigors of college football:

> I left MPMA very comfortable with the game of football and fully prepared for both Michigan (where I played in Spring practice having graduated in February) and West Point which I entered in July. The Michigan coaches were among the nicest men imaginable and the West Point coaches among the most serious in demeanor as well as purpose. The key in my view is being comfortable with the game itself and coach Ziemba contributed much to that. My confidence about going to play at a first-rate football school was probably rooted in my respect for Coach Ziemba. After our Argo game, Frank Casey, who later captained the Knox College team, overheard two scouts from a small college ask to see me and Coach Ziemba said no, that I was going to a big school. I was quite ignorant of such things, but Coach Ziemba was not. I believed in his judgement. We always felt well prepared for a game. If he thought I should play at a big school, I was convinced I could. The Michigan spring practice, a few months after my February graduation from MPMA was an absolutely wonderful and satisfying experience. Incidentally, I was quite proud of the game I had when we (Army), upset Michigan in their stadium my third year at West Point. I should add that it was easy to believe in Coach Ziemba, because he seemed to be a gentle and kind, if enormous, man.

THINK CLEARLY, SEEK EXCELLENCE

Fast forward a few decades and we find the now Dr. Frank Burd back on the Academy campus. After a long, successful career in the military, education, and business fields, Burd delivered an inspiring commencement address to the Academy's 2017 graduation class. Drawing from his own experiences at both the Academy, and his own personal life, Dr. Burd praised the students for their accomplishments and left them with a positive, pragmatic message: "Stay cool, open-eyed, be sure of yourself, think clearly, seek excellence, work hard, and aim at the good." Following his graduation at the Academy in 1952, Burd played football at the United States Military Academy (West Point) and averaged 5.9 yards per carry as a fullback during his senior year for the ferocious Army ground attack. Burd became an intelligence officer with the Thirteenth Air Force from 1956-1960 and later completed his Ph.D. (in political science) from the University of Chicago. He was a faculty member at the University of Maryland, Baltimore County for 34 years, serving as the chair of the Department of Political Science. In 2018, Dr. Burd was still serving as the president of the Baltimore Council on Foreign Affairs, a post he has held since 1980.

But in 1952, the talented and familiar figure of Frank Burd would finally be missing from the Morgan Park Military Academy football team. While quarterback John Gislason and veteran tackle William Westenberger would captain the team, rumors were once again swirling regarding the prospect of the independent Academy team joining one of the powerful suburban conferences. Long-time sports editor and columnist John E. Meyers of the *Chicago Heights Star* newspaper suggested on April 18, 1952 that the traditional South Suburban League, which had been around since 1927, divest itself of some of its current members and re-name itself "The Big Eight." Any previous members of that revered circuit that were now "homeless" could then establish a new conference as outlined by Meyers:

> Let us start with the South Suburban, which we recommend junk that name and under our set-up adopt the label the Big Eight. Under this plan, the South Suburban would retain Bloom, Thornton and Blue Island only from its present membership. But ...available and fairly close by would be Joliet, East Aurora, West Aurora and Elgin. To fill out an eight-team loop, we suggest that LaGrange detach from the West Suburban and join the South Suburban. For those cut loose by reforming the South Suburban and for unattached schools, we suggest a new league. Ex-South Suburban schools proposed as members are Lockport, Argo and Thornton Fractional. Unattached schools the league could embrace are Reavis of Oak Lawn, Joliet Catholic and Morgan Park Military Academy. A seventh member would be Rich Township, which will be in business as a four-year high in 1953. As the eighth member we suggest Bradley, now of the Kankakee Valley.

While a new league would actually be initiated in the south suburbs in the next year, the Academy would not be a part of it as the South Suburban league maintained its membership and a host of newer high schools such as Oak Lawn, Reavis, Bremen and Carl Sandburg began planning for a future conference affiliation. The Academy continued to schedule any and all public schools in the area and added new opponents when familiar foes were unavailable. "Many of the bigger schools simply wouldn't schedule MPMA," said Jerry Bowden ('57). New to the 1952 Academy schedule were Oak Lawn High School and Hammond Clark (Indiana) High School.

As the school year began, Coach Ziemba added the responsibilities of Athletic Director for the Academy while his predecessor in the athletic director post, Major George Mahon, was promoted to the position of Principal and Director of Enrollments for the upper school. The number of students under Mahon's tutelage increased again with total enrollment jumping to 404 (Upper and Lower schools combined) in early 1953.

BUY JUNIOR A HOT-ROD

By 1952, renewed calls for improving the safety of football players were being heard around the country. While face masks were not yet required, subtle changes were made to help preserve the human body from the risk of injury. One significant move was to restore the "fair catch" in 1951. This would protect the receiver of a punt from being unmercifully mowed down by the onslaught of oncoming defenders while that receiver was waiting not only to catch the ball, but also to initiate a "return" of some type. Teams with educated kickers who could extend the height of a punt could utilize this skill to pounce at full speed on the receiver once his hands touched the ball, often resulting in a lost fumble, as well as possible injury to the receiver. With this rule change, the receiver simply needed to signal (via an elevated wave of his arm) that he was not intending to return the kick. Later in 1952, the fathers of football clamped down on unnecessary roughness in the game by suspending any player who was inclined to utilize his locked hands, elbows, or forearms to strike his opponent.

In Chicago, as in other locations, the safety of high school football players continued to be a concern. Jerome Holtzman, the eminent writer for the *Chicago Sun-Times* (and later elected to the Baseball Hall of Fame for his contributions, including "inventing" the "save" statistic in major league baseball), provided his own insight into the prep safety discussion as a young writer for the *Chicago Sun-Times*:

> Should you allow your boy to play high school football?
> That question seems to be a perplexing one for parents
> these days, so perhaps the following figures gathered by the

National Safety Council will be of some help. The council reports that there was one high school football fatality last year for every 100,000 participants. In contrast, 28 of every 100,000 boys of high school age were killed in auto accidents in 1951. Thus, the fatality risk is 28 times greater riding around in an auto.

Doug Mills, the University of Illinois athletic director, said in Chicago recently that he has spoken to many troubled parents who don't want their boys to go out for the high school football team because they might get hurt. "Yet these same parents," Mills explained, "turn right around and buy junior a hot-rod. It doesn't make sense."

The Academy was on the forefront of the safety issue and began using the new plastic helmets in an effort to provide additional safety features for the players. However, the initial results were not terribly encouraging. One player recalled that the first time he wore the plastic headgear in a game, he survived a head-to-head collision only to realize that "my helmet simply broke in half!" Later improvements by the manufacturer would strengthen the helmets, but players still went into battle without any facial protection. As such, football players were usually identified by black eyes, fat lips and bruised cheekbones during the season.

OUR OFFENSE WAS WAY AHEAD OF ITS TIME

With another ambitious schedule facing the Academy in 1952, the team employed a version of the "T" formation on offense where the quarterback lined up directly behind the center, with the other three backs situated horizontally behind the quarterback, thus forming the "T" configuration. This formation was extremely popular at all levels of football in the 1950s since it was designed to mystify the defense in a variety of ways. With the quarterback securing the snap of the ball directly from the center, he could either throw the ball, hand it off to one of his backs, or retain possession of the pigskin himself. If the hand-off was to one of the backfield men, the runner could follow his own backfield blockers, as well as the linemen, to the designated "hole" in the line. Since the receiving back was usually situated about five yards behind the quarterback, he could accept the hand-off at full speed and hit the assigned hole quickly. The quarterback also had the "option" of running parallel to his backfield mates and then either keeping the ball himself or lateraling the football to one of his trailing runners similar to what is now known as the "option" play. In the Academy version of this favored formation, Coach Ziemba spread the field a bit more and utilized the strengths of his running backs, especially the quarterback (John Gislason). "Our offense was way ahead of its time," said Pete Voss, starting center from 1951-1953. "Coach Ziemba knew more about football than anyone and he did things no one else did. He could have been a big-time college coach. I played football my freshman year at Michigan State, and the coaches there had nothing on Big Joe. The coaches there told me things about being a center that Coach Ziemba had told me in high school!" The Academy's "spread" offense focused on running the ball, but also allowed Gislason the option of throwing the sphere as well. The key was to confuse the defense, even to the point of using an unbalanced line to challenge the defenders.

The Warriors did rebound slightly from the ugly 1951 results by compiling a 3-4-2 mark in 1952. In the opening outing on September 20 against Oak Lawn High School, the offense looked superb as quarterback Gislason scored twice in a 28-7 romp over the visitors. Gislason tallied from the 2 and the 23, while halfback Al Gilbert and fullback Bill Craske also added touchdowns. Kicker Julian Zedeno, a student from Ecuador, was true on all four extra point attempts to ensure the final margin. Once again, larger schools dominated the schedule with losses being administered by Joliet Catholic (26-13), Hammond Clark (21-0), and Blue Island (35-6). Perhaps the toughest setback was a 29-0 spanking by Culver.

In the annual battle for the "Brass Bonnett" trophy, Culver broke open a tight game by blasting the Cadets for 20 points in the fourth quarter to secure the victory. The difficult loss blemished the yearly Homecoming festivities, which in 1952 honored the Academy graduates from the class of 1902. Prior to the game on October 11 the Culver Academy *Vedette* newspaper warned of the Warriors' challenging offense:

> Morgan Park's team won one, tied one, and lost one. They sometimes use a highly tricky split formation, six men on one side of the field and five on the other. This wide spread and their excellent passing team, quarterback John Gislason and end Tom Keating has quite an air-minded club.

However, in the Culver game, it was the winners that provided the aerial fireworks, Culver unleashed 24 passes (completing 15) in a passing attack seldom experienced at the time at the high school level. Then struggling along with a 1-3-1 mark late in the season, the Academy managed to even its 1952 record, all in just one weekend! On Friday, October 24, the Warriors traveled to Oak Lawn for the second meeting of the year with Oak Lawn High School, resulting in an overwhelming 54-13 win—the most points scored in one game since a 59-0 thumping over St. Alban's in 1936. Then on Saturday, October 25, the Academy prevailed at Glenwood School 34-0, evening the team's slate at 3-3-1. After the success of this unusual "double header," the Warriors moved down the street for a battle with always strong Blue Island High School. The two lopsided victories the week before apparently grabbed the attention of the *Blue Island Sun-Standard*:

> Community High's Cardinals, who are experiencing a rough season, face their neighborhood foes when they take on Morgan Park Military Academy in a non-conference game. From the scores it may be assumed that the Cadets have an offense that should measure up…On offense the Cadets boast a better than average quarterback in John Gislason. Gislason can pass, does a good job at calling the signals and is the type of quarterback who can run with the ball adding a lot to the deceptive T-formation along with a unique spread formation. This game means nothing to either team as far as a title goes, but the rivalry between the neighborhood rivals should produce an interesting game for local fans.

Despite the pre-game hype, the vaunted Academy offense disappeared for the evening and the Warriors dropped a 35-6 decision to Blue Island. The only bright spot was a nice 43-yard completion from Gislason to end Harry Karzas, followed by Gislason's eight-yard sprint for the only Academy touchdown. The season then concluded with a scoreless tie game with Reavis High School, leaving the Cadets with that 3-4-2 finish. Lineman Bill Westenberger was selected as the MVP for the 1952 season while the versatile Pete Voss was elected as the captain for the 1953 squad.

CHICAGO'S OWN MILITARY ACADEMY

In a sense it seemed the 1953 Academy football team was back in a conference, although the school certainly did not join a circuit that year. Rather, the team played a schedule that was top heavy with members of the sparkling new Southwest Suburban Conference, which was formed in 1953 with members including Bremen High School, Oak Lawn High School, Reavis High School, Rich Township High School, and Carl Sandburg High School. With only five original members, the league needed another common opponent and the Academy was anointed for that responsibility, scheduling each of those foes with the exception of Carl Sandburg. It was a pattern that would repeat over the next few years as the Academy and its larger public-school opponents became very well acquainted. "We filled out the open dates for the teams in the Southwest Conference," noted Jerry Bowden ('57). It appears that the Academy had expressed interest in joining the new league, according to an article in the *Chicago Heights Star* on September 25, 1953:

> The Academy attempted to gain entrance in the new Southwest Suburban Conference, but fell short in its desires, settling for a whitewashing of Oak Lawn in '52 in addition to a scoreless deadlock with Reavis. Morgan Park's two victims are presently considered the teams to beat in league play this year.

In other words, if the Academy was indeed refuted in its bid for conference membership, the author appeared to indicate that the Warriors were well equipped to handle any adversaries from the emerging circuit on the field of play. "We really didn't think about the size of the school, we just played who we were scheduled," said Art Canfield ('56).

The opening contest on September 26, 1953 against Rich Township (since divided into Rich East, Rich South, and Rich Central High Schools) proved to be a football fan's delight as reported by the *Star* newspaper:

> Rich Rockets stayed within reach of the more experienced Morgan Park Military Academy football team for more than three quarters before succumbing to the Cadets murderous ground attack. The final score of the high-scoring, see-saw battle on the military academy gridiron was 38-26. Bobbie Freed led the winner's attack with two touchdowns and an overall gain of 180 yards from scrimmage. Freed and his Cadet mates were far the superior of the spirited, but inexperienced Rockets. It took little more than one play for the hosts to surge to an early 7-0 lead. Freed returned Jerry Jonas' kickoff from the 12 to the 29 and raced 71 yards on the following play to count the first touchdown of the

season. Richie Dina converted, and Coach Greg Sloan and his young squad were confronted with a deficit after only a little more than a minute gone.

Thanks to the expert coverage of south suburban schools by the *Star* newspaper, readers could enjoy intimate coverage of the prep school athletic events, including accurate statistics. Following the Rich Township encounter, the Star published extensive statistical information, indicating that the Academy rushing game churned out 325 yards, but attempted (and completed) just one pass for 27 yards. Meanwhile, the Rockets picked up 104 yards on the ground and managed another 86 through the air. In total, the Warriors amassed 17 first downs to just five for the visitors.

As the football season progressed, work continued on campus with some new construction initiatives. George Truesdell, a member of the 1914 football team under Coach Fred Herendeen, was now the vice president of the school's Board of Trustees and was also chairman of buildings and grounds. Under Truesdell's leadership, funding was generated to update the rather archaic gymnasium as announced on January 1, 1953 by the *Blue Island Sun-Standard*:

> The building now under construction is the first phase of a plan to completely modernize the old gymnasium. Built in 1894, the old gym has been outgrown and is inadequate for present demands. The first phase of construction will be a three-story addition which includes two spacious locker-shower rooms, a large wrestling-general exercise room, commodious storage for sports and athletic equipment, and an enlarged boiler and heating plant to supply all four buildings on the south campus. George W. Truesdell, MPMA '15, vice president of the board of trustees raised the first shovel of dirt while others joined in the ceremony. It was a great day for "Chicago's Own Military Academy."

Other plans (which failed to materialize) included a regulation size swimming pool and a separate basketball facility. Both were to be constructed as soon as funds were available with the new basketball structure to be built on the fields south of the current gymnasium, and the swimming pool to also be situated south of the present gym. The revitalized gymnasium building was eventually dedicated in May of 1954 at the cost of $115,000 in what was the first "new" construction at the Academy in 25 years. (Note: the gym was built in 1901, not 1894 as indicated in the above citation. However, it was the second gymnasium constructed on that site.) In the spring of 1954, enrollment at the Academy swelled to 412 students on both levels, seeming to indicate a continued bright future for the institution. The ambitious construction projects were planned to address the needs of an anticipated growing student population.

SECOND VICTORY IN TWO DAYS

In week two of the 1953 football season, the Academy slipped past Oak Lawn 20-6 behind Freed's three touchdowns on runs of 5, 55, and 72 yards. The Warriors collected 301 yards (all on the ground) while limiting Oak Lawn to 120 yards for the contest. The win set up a highly anticipated match with keen rival Culver Military Academy the following week. With both teams undefeated (2-0) thus far in the early season, excitement was brewing on campus where a victory over Culver had not been experienced since 1939. Sadly, that streak continued as Culver edged the Warriors 13-6. In late October, the Academy once again knocked off two different foes on consecutive days, vanquishing Oak Lawn 12-0 as Al Gilbert tallied both touchdowns on October 23 and then trouncing newly opened Bremen High School on October 24, as reported in the *Chicago Tribune*:

> Halfback Al Gilbert scored four touchdowns to lead Morgan Park Military Academy to its second victory in two days, a 46 to 6 conquest of Bremen, IL in Morgan Park yesterday. The homecoming crowd saw Gilbert go over on plunges of 1 and 9 yards, a 57-yard punt return, and a 40-yard end run.

The twin victories moved the Academy club to 4-2 on the year, but a pair of ties with returning foe St. John's Military Academy (6-6) and newcomer Maryville Academy (0-0) followed by a season-ending loss to Reavis (21-6) left the Academy with a final 4-3-2 mark. Gilbert and Freed scored 17 of the team's 22 touchdowns behind ends Ron Loomis, Gerry Krivsky, and Chuck Fischer; tackles Gene Frigo, Jim Stokes, and Jerry Zaccari, along with two-way guards Fred Pipin, George Mahon, and Bob Viscount. Fullback Ken Noorlag and quarterbacks Rich Dina and Roger Peterson joined Gilbert and Freed in the backfield.

Center/linebacker Pete Voss was named the MVP for the season and noted: "The 1953 team was the last good one for Coach Ziemba."

He carried on the school's football tradition and put together a successful team from a very small student population. He made the game fun and addressed the players by reversing the spelling of our names and made the game interesting." George Mahon, a guard on that team added: "I remember the way he would call out the starting lineup at practice. Ssov (Voss) at center, Noham (Mahon) and Nipip (Pipin) at guards, Galroon (Noorlag) at fullback, Simool (Loomis) at end and so on."

Indeed, if one reviewed the statistics from the games played solely with members of the Southwest Suburban Conference (Oak Lawn, Bremen, Reavis, Rich Township) in 1953, the Academy finished with a 4-1 record, with two of those wins coming at the expense of Oak Lawn. The sole loss in the games against the conference contenders would seem to indicate that the Academy football team would have been in the running for the conference title—if the school had been accepted as a member of the Southwest Suburban Conference earlier in the year.

As the coaching staff of Joe Ziemba and Leland Dickinson prepared for the 1954 season, they would do so with only four returning starters: fullback Ron Loomis, tackle Fred Pipin, halfback Ken Noorlag, and end Chuck Fischer. But the biggest loss would be center Pete Voss, not only for his playing ability, but also for his leadership skills. In 2018, Voss was elected to the Academy's "Athletic Hall of Fame" as a most deserving individual, especially for a neighborhood kid who grew up at 112th and Lothair just steps away from the Academy campus.

While attending the Academy, Voss sampled just about everything available to an energetic student on campus. Whether it was serving as captain of the football team or taking on the lead role in the senior class play, Voss was at the forefront in his endeavors. As an athlete, few individuals can match his versatility—and prominence—as a three-sport star. Voss was brought up to the varsity football team as a sophomore (unusual at the time) and earned a letter all three years. As the center on the club, Voss rarely found himself in the headlines, but he consistently paved the way for the backfield with his effective blocking schemes. He was so prominent at his position (playing both offense and as a linebacker on defense) that Voss was elected both the captain and the Most Valuable Player of the football team in his senior year—a rare honor for an interior lineman.

Following the conclusion of the football season, Voss exerted his leadership and skills on the wrestling mat where he also lettered for three years and was undefeated in dual meet matches during his senior year. He finished in fourth place in the state sectional tournament and advanced to the quarterfinals of the state tournament. Once again, he received the distinct honor of being named the Most Valuable Player on the MPMA wrestling squad in his senior year. Without taking a break, Voss was also a valuable contributor to the baseball team. After being named the MVP and captain of the frosh-soph team in 1952, he went on to grab two more letters during his final two seasons on the varsity.

With Voss departing to Michigan State, the 1954 version of the Academy gridiron team jumped into a competitive schedule beginning with Lemont High School on September 17. Lemont was the four-time defending champion of the Northeast Conference and Coach Bill Ryan, then at the beginning of a successful 42-year career at Lemont, was anxious for his season to start when interviewed on September 25 by the *Southtown Economist* prior to the season opener:

> Coach Bill Ryan will unveil his 1954 edition of Lemont Township High School's football juggernaut Friday afternoon when they meet Morgan Park Military Academy. The squad has been working out for the past three weeks in preparation for its defense of their four-time Northeast Conference title. "Barring injuries, we look forward to a winning season," the youthful mentor contended. "The boys, however, are lacking in experience and the team does not have much depth. The bright note is the Braves' hard-running backfield combined with the team's all-around speed."

In response to the imposing Lemont offensive threat, the Academy bundled a tidy offense along with a stubborn defense to escape with a 13-6 decision in the opener. It was the first of four wins for the Warriors that season including Carl Sandburg (13-2), Bowen (6-0), and Maryville Academy (8-6). In each of the wins, the Academy relied on that stringent defense since the offense was unable to tally more than 13 points in any one game. The result was a somewhat disappointing 4-5 record described by the 1955 **Skirmisher** yearbook:

> The MPMA Varsity compiled a record of four wins and five losses against very rugged competition. The Warriors fielded a better-than-average defensive unit, but never during the season were they able to put together a steady offensive drive. The Warriors are faced with a tremendous rebuilding job in 1955 with the loss of fifteen seniors.

Ken Noorlag, who raced 80 yards for the only score in the win over Bowen of the Chicago Public League, and scored the lone touchdown against Maryville, topped the Academy in scoring with 25 points while Fullback Ron Loomis was named the team's MVP. Linemen Jerry Krivsky and Warren Rusgis were tabbed to help lead the rebuilding efforts in 1955 as team co-captains. But first, all of the players were faced with a major adjustment to both the football team and its program administration...

CADETS GET NEW GRID STAFF

Although the transition had been discussed behind the scenes for some time, the news greeted the returning players in August that Coach Joe Ziemba had decided to relinquish his football coaching duties prior to the 1955 season. Aside from a full teaching workload and his duties as athletic director, Ziemba was also now responsible for the creation of a school intramural program as announced in the August 28 issue of the *Southtown Economist* under the headline of "Cadets Get New Grid Staff":

> The football hopefuls at Morgan Park Military Academy will operate under the leadership of a new coaching staff during the 1955 season. Capt. Joe Ziemba, veteran of 12 years coaching at the school, will devote his time to the directorship of all inter-scholastic athletics and a program of intramural sports. Lt. Richard N. Boya, Jr., former head coach at Wayland Academy, Beaver Dam, Wisconsin, will assume charge of the varsity football team. He comes to the Academy with an excellent record as a player and coach. Headed by Cadet Jerry Krivsky and Warren Rusgis, co-captains of the 1955 team, all returning football players will meet coach Boya at the first practice...Approximately 75 prospective members of the squad are expected to be present.

In 1955, the still-growing Southwest Suburban Conference added its seventh member with nearby Evergreen Park High School (Lincoln-Way High School in New Lenox, Illinois had joined the circuit in 1954). Still with an "uneven" number of members, the conference teams once again utilized the Academy to help complete their schedules. As such, the Academy encountered five of the Southwest Suburban clubs during the year, but only succeeded in prevailing over Evergreen Park (20-6) on the way to finishing with a difficult 1-8 record. Despite the record, the **Skirmisher** noted that "the Warriors displayed superb courage in maintaining high spirits throughout each game."

The ponderous losing streak to Culver continued in 1955 with a 27-7 setback as Charles Scruggs scored the only touchdown for the Academy prompting Coach Boya to tell *The Academy News*: "We were great, then we were lousy, we have to be more consistent." In the lone win of the season over Evergreen Park (20-6), Scruggs scored on a one-yard plunge while junior halfback Ed Madsen added two more touchdowns. Madsen paced the team with 30 points as was named the captain for the 1956 season while Scruggs walked off with the MVP trophy for the 1955 campaign.

More uncertainty faced the football hopefuls in 1956 as Coach Boya departed after just one season (resigning on February 6, 1956). He eventually returned to Wayland Academy as football coach and public relations director before moving back to his alma mater of Lawrence University as vice president for development and external affairs. In 1987, Richard Boya was named director of development for the University of Wisconsin, Division of Intercollegiate Athletics. He also held other positions in the fund-raising area, including director of special gifts and requests at the College of St. Thomas in St. Paul, Minnesota. In 2012, Boya was honored by Lawrence University with the "Presidential Award" for his work in the institution's giving and planning programs.

Back on campus, a no-nonsense import from the state of Michigan, Al Bloomer, was brought in to direct the football efforts in 1956. Bloomer favored the split-T formation and implemented that style at all levels of the gridiron program. Bloomer was an Eastern Michigan grad who toiled three years on the line for the Eastern football team. He had gained experience prior to arriving at the Academy during coaching stops as an assistant at Armada (Michigan) High School and as the head coach at Linden (Michigan) High School where he compiled a 14-4 record.

Although total enrollment had slipped slightly from 412 in March of 1954 to 400 in March of 1956, all seemed well at the little campus on 111th Street. Or was it?

EXTRA POINT

Academy football coach Joe Ziemba was a big man (6'4", 230 pounds). A former All-American football player at St. Benedict's College in Kansas, he also loved to bowl and could toss a bowling ball straight down the alley as if it was a lightweight softball. In the November 2001 issue of *The Academy Magazine*, alumnus Pearson Williams, Jr. recalled, "The cadets went bowling off campus and it was there that Coach Ziemba acquired a distinctive reputation. Legend has it that the powerful Ziemba whipped one ball down the alley and sent a hapless pin-boy out on a stretcher. A week later, another pin-boy saw Ziemba enter the bowling alley and announced: 'I know about him; I quit!'"

Yet when the affable coach moved away from the sidelines in 1955, he never moved very far away from the memories of his players. At a reunion of the class of 1955, George Mahon, a member of that class who literally grew up on the campus since his father was a long-time instructor and coach, shared some thoughts on the vaunted football squad and its respected coach:

> I remember as a boy the glory days on the athletic field of the late 30s and 40s. Admittedly these memories were formed through rose colored glasses for as a young boy, I saw the cadets as larger than life heroes. While we had no undefeated teams during the early 50s it must be recognized that by then we were playing Chicago and suburban high schools that had enrollments far in excess of our own. We were never embarrassed. I attribute our success in part to the qualities we absorbed because of the military aspect of our experience, but largely due to the quality of the coaching we received. All the coaches were dedicated men, but I remember in particular Joe Ziemba. I recall a football game during our junior year when we were playing one of the western suburban schools. I played guard, but not first string, but was used to shuttle in plays. I happened to be in on a play where we scored a touchdown, and the referee looked at me at the completion of the play and said "you have a very well-coached team." An extraordinary comment from a referee, right there on the field. And he was correct. Joe was an extraordinary coach, and extraordinary in other ways. A big, quiet and essentially gentle man, who always exhorted us to be our best, and instilled both enthusiasm and pride, and did it with constant encouragement and a sense of humor. Joe was a true teacher who left a deep impression on many of us.

Coach Ziemba eventually left the Academy in 1959 after compiling an overall record of 50-36-7, which remains as the most football coaching wins in school history. He joined the coaching staff at Blue Island High School briefly and taught at that school until suffering a fatal stroke in February of 1973 at the age of 54. Frank Burd ('52) added a final comment for this book regarding his former coach at Morgan Park Military Academy:

> I would just repeat my earlier observation that Coach Ziemba's steady and quiet confidence probably had much to do with an attitude of confidence in his players so that they could simply play the game, do their best, and not be excessively worried. I might also add that I never heard a player criticize Coach Ziemba. My point is that he created an attitude and a framework for approaching playing football which even though playing at a higher level was a challenge, the difference was not with the game or how one approached it, but simply that there were more good players on the field. Football at MPMA was certainly a pleasure and it gave me my very closest high school friends. It has never occurred to me to be anything but grateful for the experience with Coach Ziemba.

The 1950 team (Frank Burd is the ball carrier) prepares for its opening game against South Shore High School of Chicago, which was won by the Warriors 25-19.

The crowded Morgan Park Military Academy sideline is shown from an undated photo from the early 1950s at Abells Field. Coach Ziemba is standing to the left.

Captain Pete Voss (#49) discusses the upcoming 1953 season with (from left); Coach Joe Ziemba, quarterback Rich Dina (#40) and Coach Leland Dickinson.

CHAPTER 20

Apple Boys and the Book of Knowledge

---

*"We took a little abuse wearing those uniforms. They called
us "Apple Boys" because we were part of the corps."*
—Richard Vitkus, Class of 1957

Ed Madsen leaned back in the front booth of the Weits Cafe in downtown Morris, Illinois. While a stroke a few years ago robbed Madsen of the mobility that helped him become the co-MVP of the 1956 MPMA football team, it could not wrestle away the wonderful memories from that time.

Memories come freely to Madsen, and he is honest and proud when sharing them...

"Playing football at Morgan Park Military Academy was an honor," he said. "I enjoyed every bit of it and I really liked the discipline...so much so that I couldn't wait for the next season to get started!" Madsen traces his football success to his freshman year when he decided that "I really wanted to get involved and I was determined to be not only a football player, but also be very good at what I did." He started out as a lineman but found himself in danger of losing his starting job the next season. "Some young freshman was beating me out and as a result, my dad, who wasn't really a football fan, gave me a hard time. However, the coaches gave me the chance to return punts in my sophomore year. I ran one all the way back in practice and the coach told me to do it again . . . so I did. They then moved me up to varsity to return punts. It made my Dad very happy since I carried the ball." Madsen saw regular playing time in the backfield his junior year and topped the team in scoring, which pleased the entire family. "My grandfather came to every game and convinced my dad to come as well. Soon, they were all football fans!" added Madsen.

Under Coach Al Bloomer, the 1956 football squad hoped to use the "split T" formation to open up the offense, score a great deal of points, and keep consistent pressure on the opponent's defense. The points came easily in the debut of the new offense on September 15 against Maryville Academy, but the Academy's defense was just as porous, allowing Maryville to use some big plays to prevail 27-21. Madsen scored once and quarterback Walt Fricke added a pair of touchdowns for the Academy, which out-gained the victors 294 to 183 in total yardage. The following week, the results were similar as Rich Township edged the Academy 16-6, despite allowing the Warriors a significant advantage in total yardage. The Rockets utilized a single wing attack which emphasized the versatility of halfback Bruce Pradin, who passed for 105 yards and rushed for 58 more. The *Chicago Heights Star* devoted much of its first page in the sports section on September 25 to the game, including several photos used to accompany the extensive coverage of the contest:

> Nearly 1,000 fans were on hand for the Rockets' home opener and their first game on the new Rich High field. The turf, incidentally, was in surprisingly good shape for a new field. Outweighed nearly 25 pounds to the man in the line, the Rockets, nevertheless, produced an encouraging reversal of their dismal defensive showing a week earlier… Activity centered around mid-field for most of the third and fourth periods until midway through the fourth quarter [with Rich ahead 14-6]. After Pradin had picked up five off tackle, he again found Gary Elliott with a pass and the diminutive halfback cut to the sidelines and ran 38 yards to the Cadet seven before Ed Madsen dragged him down.

> In making the tackle, Madsen suffered a severely bruised chest and play was halted for 15 minutes while officials hunted fruitlessly for a stretcher. Play was finally moved to the other end of the field while Madsen awaited the arrival of an ambulance. During the delay, the Rockets offense cooled and four running plays by Pradin were able to advance the ball only to the one-yard line.

A late safety by Rich Township nailed the defeat by a 16-6 count, but the injury remains vivid to Madsen to this day; "I caught the guy and made the tackle near the goal line but hurt my ribs pretty badly and they stopped the game." The reason for the delay (no available medical personnel or even a stretcher) has been readily corrected over the years in an effort to preserve the safety of the players, but it remains a painful memory for Madsen. With Madsen out of action the following week, the Warriors still managed to crank up the yardage machine and sneak past Hyde Park High School of Chicago 13-6 for Coach Bloomer's first Academy win. Rich Vitkus tallied all 13 points in the Warriors' victory. Madsen returned for the annual battle with Culver, in which the Indiana invaders prevailed 27-7 to drop the Academy to 1-3 on the season. The Warriors managed to split their final four contests to finish with a 3-5 mark. The highlight was a two-game winning streak at the expense of Carl Sandburg High School (9-6) and Elmwood Park High School (33-7). In the Sandburg game, Bloomer's club failed to attempt a single pass, but rather relied on a powerful running game (245 yards) to subdue the Eagles. With the Academy ahead late in the third quarter, the hosts scored on a 51-yard run. However, the effort to equal the score on the extra point attempt was silenced by lineman Chris Ellis, according to the *Blue Island Sun Standard* on October 25: "Jim Vos's try for the extra point was foiled as 260-pound MPMA tackle Chris Ellis securely enveloped him at the line of scrimmage."

Fricke and Madsen were named the co-MVPs for the season as Fricke topped all scorers with 42 points while Madsen and Vitkus earned 21 each. Promising and imposing lineman Chris Ellis was selected as the captain for the 1957 squad.

His selection as captain of the 1957 football team was simply another solid attribute to the remarkable career of Ellis at the Academy. On February 7, 1957, the *Chicago Tribune* published a feature article on Ellis, who was just as impressive as a heavyweight wrestler as he was an offensive lineman during his Academy career:

> How would you feel if you were 16 years old and Alexander-like, almost found yourself without any more opponents to conquer? We say "almost" because Chris Ellis of the Morgan Park Military Academy wrestling squad hasn't, as yet, met every heavyweight competing in the Chicago area, but the 14 he has met this season all have been on the losing end of the judges' decision.

Ellis, 6-foot 2 inch, 270-pound junior who is still growing…will have a chance to extend his unbeaten string to 15 today when he leads his teammates against visiting Mount Carmel in a return match. Should Morgan Park gain the team victory, it would give the Cadets coached by Jack Gifford, former Purdue wrestling star, a 27-6 record for the last two seasons. Should Ellis go into the state meet unbeaten, he is bound to be a prime target for equally as determined title seekers. But Ellis isn't afraid. After subduing 14 rivals from throughout the Chicago area, he has good reason not to be.

Ellis would indeed advance to the Illinois High School Association wrestling finals at the conclusion of the 1957 season, where he dropped a tight 1-0 decision to Hugh Wilson of Fenton High School in the opening round. By the time he graduated in 1958, Ellis was named captain of both the football and wrestling teams and was also the MVP for both sports. In addition, he was elected president of the student council as well as the lettermen's club and also found time to star in the senior class play "The Caine Mutiny Court Martial." For these exemplary achievements, Ellis was inducted into the Academy's Athletic Hall of Fame in 2014.

I TOLD HIM I MADE A BIG MISTAKE!

As the 1956-1957 school year progressed, the Academy administration monitored the overall enrollment and noted a slight decrease in attendees from two years previously. Although that number (400) was not drastically different than the 1954 totals of 410, there was some advance evidence that indicated the enrollment could dip even further during the next semester beginning in early 1957. Of more pertinent interest to the Board was an auditor's report for the 1955-1956 school year which resulted in a deficit of $10,712. Again, this was not a startling number, but the Board minutes from October 15, 1956 reported that the auditor predicted "a greater deficit during the current year." Meanwhile, it was business as usual for the Academy as the administration reviewed pragmatic methods to reduce expenses while still maintaining a lofty level of enrollment.

Since its beginning the Academy had positioned itself to offer a quality education that was available to all students. During this time, the school was still not integrated, although it was readily accepting students from foreign countries, prompting some minor language barriers on the campus. "We had a lot of Latin students," remarked Frank Fonsino ('59). "Military men in those countries would send their children here to learn the military life." Art Gaetano ('59) added: "As freshmen, we couldn't always understand these students, but it worked out."

Rich Vitkus ('57), one of the stars of the 1956 football team, shared his recollection of the changing student clientele of the Academy: "One thing I remember was at the start of the school year, limos would pull up and drop off the sons of Latin American leaders. We had mob kids and dictators' kids, but it was no big deal to us. There were regular kids, wealthy kids, and some who just needed some discipline."

The students from the various backgrounds would ultimately mesh at the Academy, primarily because of the common academic requirements and unbending discipline rules that were dutifully enforced. Parents seemed to be receptive to the rugged demands of the school, while others decided simply to send their sons to a private institution, rather than a public school. "My parents were concerned with the public-school education," said Mike Luetgert ('58) when explaining why he enrolled at the Academy. Others, such as Art Gaetano, were provided with a certain parental "push" when the time arrived to select a high school. "I was not the best citizen growing up," said Gaetano. "My dad was a doctor and he threatened to send me to boarding school. I saw an ad for the Academy in a magazine and decided I wanted to go there. However, after the first week, I told him I made a big mistake!" Gaetano had quickly discovered the challenging life of a freshman, or plebe, at a strict military school. "First you went through plebeship your first year. We had to walk on a certain side of the sidewalk. Then we shined the seniors' shoes, but it worked out. It toughened us [plebes] up and bonded us."

The Academy was, after all, a military school and cadets who attended in the 1940s and 1950s delight in telling tales of the "misery" of that particular student way of life. During the first year of high school, the Academy freshmen/plebes were scorned by the upperclassmen. Harry Klein ('56) related that "When I was a plebe, when we walked down the hallway if a senior came by and thought we did not give him enough room to pass by, he would smash you into the wall. We also were expected to make the beds for the senior boarding students, so we were basically private servants for them. One senior was a little out of his mind and would intentionally hurt plebes. A bunch of us got together and straightened that out!"

Classroom time was equally strict and demanding according to Klein: "I was born in Cuba and spoke Spanish, but this school was so tough that

I almost flunked Spanish!" Because classroom discipline was so much different then, it was not unusual for instructors to utilize a more "hands-on" approach to education. For example, if a student happened to doze off during a particular class, the instructor might enlist unusual means to remind the student that sleeping in class was generally considered to be a very bad idea. Jim McClure was a member of the class of 1935 and shared his thoughts on the Academy's stringent discipline in the January 2008 issue of the *Academy Magazine*:

> At that time [1930s], our classes were usually small, and the legendary Captain Francis Gray would toss an eraser with remarkable accuracy at any dolt in our seven-student college algebra class who was inattentive...Should any weary cadet rest his eyes or lower his head for a moment, there would be a resounding *thwack!* or *thud!* as a heavy book would hit the back of a dozing head. An elegant variation was slamming down a desk top with a very distinctive, compelling noise!

YOU DON'T KNOW, YOU DON'T CARE

Many of the Academy graduates from the 1940s and 1950s interviewed for this book related similar stories, indicating that the disciplinary methods were certainly consistent throughout the decades. The aforementioned Captain Gray was a math instructor at the Academy from 1917-1960 and was a feared disciplinarian, if not a favorite, of students throughout the years. His influence on the campus during his lengthy tenure was so significant that prolific author (and former Academy football player) James Vesely wrote a book in 2006 called **Cadet Gray: Stories of Morgan Park Military Academy**. The summary of the book from its Amazon product page encapsulates the rich career of Captain Gray so accurately described in Vesely's book:

> Early morning formations and close-order drill, Saturday afternoon football games and the pure hell of being a plebe. Spit-shined shoes and polished brass, flying flags and fluttering guidons. Sunday parades, full-dress balls, and the never-ending grind of studies. The joy of cars and girls and dreams of youth. And above all, the exciting, confusing, always uncertain adventure of growing up and coming

of age. Sixteen heartwarming, often humorous stories that cover four decades of ritual, custom, and tradition at Morgan Park Military Academy, seen through the eyes of one legendary instructor Capt. Francis S. Gray. For more than forty years, his common sense and stubborn insistence on academic excellence helped generations of cadets through awkward adolescence and into young manhood.

Captain Gray was certainly a common denominator for many graduates of Morgan Park Military Academy. He was there, it seems, forever. Gray was a forceful instructor who, despite his experience (i.e. his age), usually found different means to reach different students who were struggling with math. Ed Jerabek from the class of '56, simply recalls, "His class was very hard." If a student was perceived as not doing his best in the classroom, or perhaps guilty of not paying attention "an eraser would be thrown at your head," smiled Frank Fonsino ('59). "He also had a favorite expression," according to Fonsino: "You don't know, you don't care, and you don't give a damn!"

Yet aside from his gruff exterior, Gray was always ready to share his own time freely to help a student improve, whether it was in the classroom or on the athletic field. Tom Tiernan ('48) told the *Academy Magazine* (May 2000) about his own experiences with Captain Gray:

> I avoided Captain Gray's classes like the plague. He seemed like a mean S.O.B. One night while I was trying to sneak out, I saw Captain Gray strolling up to get his evening newspaper. I hid behind the stand. Captain Gray got his paper, tucked it under his arm, and said, almost complacently. "That'll be twenty demerits, Tiernan," and walked off without another word. But I'll tell you one thing few people know: Captain Gray, even at his advanced age, could still shoot free throws—underhanded, mind you—with the best of them. I did not shoot free throws very well, at all, and after one game in my junior year, Gray, who was not my coach—came up to me and cryptically said, "Tiernan, gym, 5 a.m. tomorrow." I thought I had done something wrong, but he got me in that gym before sunrise to teach me how to shoot free throws. I made 86 percent of my shots during my senior year, thanks to Captain Gray.

The personal tutelage of Captain Gray paid immediate dividends for Tiernan as he was, as noted previously, selected to the second team of the all-state basketball squad his senior year (1948) at the Academy and later played varsity hoops for three years at the University of Michigan.

George A. Mahon ('55), the son of the Academy's legendary coach and athletic director, also attended the Academy and provided the following comments about Gray at an alumni reunion (undated) in the 1990s:

> Francis Gray taught mathematics. We never referred to him as anything except Captain Gray for he was too imposing a figure to engender anything so frivolous or disrespectful as a nickname. His focus was to get us to think. And if he ever suspected us of not thinking, we were at great risk of being the object of his considerable displeasure, which could be withering.

Gray was a staunch supporter of Academy athletics and was usually present at any sporting event on campus. Ed Jerabek was also a member of the Academy track team (running the 100-yard dash) and remembered a time when he received some subtle assistance from Captain Gray: "We would always see him at track meets and one time he threw his hat out as a target for me." Ed Madsen noted that Gray played college football and was one who encouraged toughness in the Academy players: "He told us that 'I used to play football with a piece of newspaper for a helmet!' While he was tough on grades, he loved football and since I was the captain of the team my senior year, I received passing grades in his class!"

Captain Francis Stewart Gray, who was both beloved and feared for decades at the Academy, passed away on March 14, 1965 at the age of 82. His wife, Anna, who lived with Captain Gray on the Academy campus for most of their adult lives, died in November of 1983 at 92.

A COUPLE OF SKIRMISHES ON THE BUS

Attendance at the Academy was divided between boarding students and day students. In other words, one was not required to "live" on campus in order to attend Morgan Park Military Academy. So, while some went home each night, all were faced with the same stringent requirements, both from the academic and military sides of the school. John Peterson ('56), the MVP of the 1955-1956 basketball team, was one of the day students but indicated that there was no relief from the Academy's scholastic expectations: "Even though I was a day student and lived close by, I still didn't get home until around 7:00 p.m." One of the dangers lurking during the daily commute to the Academy for day students was the on-going "discussions" regarding the students' uniforms, which needed to be worn during the transit. "I was a day student," said Frank Fonsino, "and other kids would tease you. There were a couple of skirmishes on the city buses." Richard Vitkus explained further: "We took a little abuse wearing those uniforms on the bus. We were called "Apple Boys" because we were part of the *corps.*" Eventually, such treatment would need to be thoughtfully discussed and reconciled such as when Fonsino noted, with a certain amount of pride: "Two of us were on the bus one day and three guys in front started to tease us. Classmate Bob Jerit just got up, went up there, and started pummeling them. He then came back, sat down, and said 'the problem is over.'"

Pete Voss ('55) lived close enough to the school to walk there every day. He still marvels at the various extracurricular outlets available to the students:

> One of the interesting aspects of the Academy was that for a smaller school we had the same activities as the bigger schools, so students had a great deal of opportunities along with the military responsibilities. Even if you were not involved in sports there were many things to do that certainly took up your time. For example, the yearbook and the student newspaper were really well done.

Aside from the discipline, sports, and academics, the Academy also helped to assist its students on the social level as well. "There were four big dances per year," said Jim Bowden ('56). The "day" students would often help find dates for the boarding students, but all were given the opportunity to identify a dance partner from one of the local schools in the neighborhood. With the Academy's lofty reputation, it was not unusual for the dates (and their families) to have high hopes as well. But that was not always the case. "I got fixed up with this girl who lived in a mansion in Beverly," remarked Frank Fonsino. "When I came to the door to pick her up her Mother asked if I was part of the Fasano family. I said, 'No, my Dad was a steel worker.' She just looked at me and then said 'Just make sure my daughter is home on time.'"

I WASN'T EVEN SHAVING YET!

As a strict military school, the Academy staff was consistently forging unquestioned discipline. Classroom methods used then to ensure attentiveness and to minimize any student disruption might be considered abhorrent in today's educational system—and rightly so. Instructors at the Academy freely administered whacks on the backs of heads or whipped erasers (back when chalkboards were in use!) in the direction of any offending party. At the center of the disciplinary system throughout the years was the demerit system. Demerits could be issued for a variety of reasons, such as improperly shined shoes, tardiness, slouching in formation or not being clean-shaven. For example, Frank Fonsino ('59) complained that he once received a demerit for not shaving correctly and "I wasn't even shaving yet!" Jim Bowden ('56) explained: "You knew what the rules were, and they didn't change. You tried to stay within the rules to avoid demerits since you needed only seven and then you were restricted to your room for the whole weekend. I did push it to the limits and they were watching you, but I adjusted to it." Cal Bouma ('50) recalled that guilty students who reached the demerit "limit" could expect a rough weekend: "Guys had to tote their rifle and run with a backpack filled with bricks when they messed up! You could only get so many demerits and you would be walking all weekend!" Frank Caravette ('55) added: "I didn't mind the discipline. I was a day student but appreciated it. The discipline helped us in life."

In fact, without fail, all of the former students interviewed for this book embraced the discipline and acknowledged that the high school experience at Morgan Park Military Academy was both rewarding and memorable. Ed Jerabek ('56) stated that, "I needed discipline coming from 26th and Pulaski in Chicago. If I stuck around there, I wouldn't have friends like the ones that I still have from the Academy. The last thing I wanted to do was be a boarder at the Academy—but I loved it." Frank Fonsino added: "I had no intentions on going to school here, but my father asked me how I would like to go to MPMA. I never heard about it, but my grandmother knew another kid in the neighborhood who went to the Academy in the 1930s and then became a dentist. My father suggested I go for a semester to try it, but I never left the Academy and my grandmother probably said, "Maybe something good will come of this kid!" Jerry Bowden ('57) simply noted, "Despite all of the discipline, I had absolutely no regrets in attending the Academy."

And yet, there was another type of individual discipline in the classroom of football coach Joe Ziemba that rivaled the methods of Captain Gray. "He was a big man," said Cal Bouma. "You had to pay attention otherwise you would have an eraser coming your way! He was so big that he could just pick you up and shake you!" Pete Voss remembered that "If guys were goofing around in class, he just threw their briefcases right out the window. He was a comical, caring good guy in class, but was definitely different on the football field. However, everybody did everything they could to get in his class." Orlando Caravette ('58) was one of those good-natured students who once fell prey to the comfortable surroundings of old Blake Hall on the campus: "It was so hot in Blake Hall that one time I was dozing off, so he [Ziemba] just picked me up and threw me out the window. Fortunately, the room was on the first floor! All of the kids had a good laugh that time, but I never fell asleep in that class again!" Art Gaetano ('59) still has some fond memories of what Coach Ziemba called the "Book of Knowledge": "He had this very big book in his classroom that he called the "Book of Knowledge," said Gaetano. "If you weren't doing your work properly, he would take that book, open it in the middle, and place it on your head. He would then slap the book together so that you would 'absorb' the book's knowledge!" Brian Donnelly added: "If you weren't a 'victim' of Coach Ziemba, you weren't cool!" "If he didn't pick on you," said Ed Madsen "You knew he didn't like you!"

COVERED WITH PIGEON DROPPINGS

One of the best student pranks on the Academy campus occurred sometime during the night of April 29, 1910, when an unknown person or persons climbed the 120-foot Morgan Park village water tower and "painted the numerals of the senior class of Morgan Park Academy," reported the *Chicago Tribune*. So, there it was—the bright, white number '10--painted in large features on the side of the water tower. To help identify the perpetrator, the Academy faculty called a student assembly and (assuming that students only owned one pair of shoes) examined the bottoms of each student's shoes. This quickly led to the identification of one David Coleman from Los Angeles, California, as being the only student with the proverbial "paint on his feet." Coleman was suspended briefly from school and there is no evidence that he ever resumed his passion for large artistic landscapes! But one of the Academy students from the 1950s proudly equaled that prank. As Ed Jerabek stated: "Brian Donnelly once got in trouble for climbing the tower in Blake Hall and ringing the bell. He came down covered with pigeon droppings, so he was easy to identify!"

AN OMEN OF THINGS TO COME

There were other pranks on campus throughout the years, but not all were committed by students. On March 18, 1957, a sudden storm with ferocious winds blew through the campus and destroyed the Morgan Park Military Academy "Roll of Honor," a stately façade with eight columns that was designed to replicate the south side of George Washington's Mount Vernon residence in Virginia. The "Roll of Honor" (dedicated November 14, 1943) contained the names (at that time) of the over 500 Academy alumni and staff serving in the WWII military. Unfortunately, the damage by the weather "prankster" was too severe and it was decided to not rebuild the structure. Later, the names were listed on memorial plaques located near the present Jones Bowl on the campus. But perhaps this unsolicited attack by Mother Nature on the most cherished military location on the grounds was an omen of things to come.

While still boasting of a strong enrollment in early 1957, the Board of Trustees noted that this figure had slipped to 369 in March of 1957, down from 400 a year previously. That number would drop still further (to 339) in September of 1957. In addition, the bothersome financial deficits were of concern as well. In May of 1957, both Superintendent Clarence Jordan (who had served as Superintendent since 1950) and Assistant Superintendent Eugene Farmer announced their resignations, although Farmer was coaxed back to the Academy with the new role of Acting Superintendent for the next (1957-1958) school year. He signed his new contract on June 9, 1957 securing his appointment until July 31, 1958. Jordan, a profoundly experienced school administrator who also had served as the Superintendent of schools in the Illinois communities of Waukegan and Joliet, moved to Florida and joined the faculty of the University of Orlando Junior College. By August of 1958, he was named as the Dean of Students, a position he maintained until 1963, before concluding his academic career as a professor of sociology until 1971. Colonel Jordan, a true American hero who served in both world wars, passed away on May 8, 1979 in Orange, Florida at the age of 81.

During the summer of 1957, the Board apparently began evaluating the future of the school, including the possibility of initiating an abrupt change to the very structure of Morgan Park Military Academy. At the Board meeting on June 24, 1957, it was "suggested that directors give some thought as to the long-term relationship of military affairs in the Academy activities. Full discussion was postponed until more definite suggestions were available," stated the minutes from that meeting. There is no clear evidence from the records of these meetings as to when the topic of demilitarization was first approached, but the possibility was evidently discussed at length by the Board during the ensuing months. With Colonel Farmer being retained on just a one-year contract, there was likely some preparation being made for securing a more permanent leader for the Academy—but in what capacity?

THE CADETS WEAR ARMY BLUE

As usual, football grabbed center stage as the 1957-1958 academic year began in September. Coach Al Bloomer, an Air Force veteran, returned as the head coach, assisted by Willis "Bill" Earle, a recent graduate of Eastern Michigan University. For now, Bloomer's intent leading into the 1957 season was to reverse the 3-5 mark from the year before. The Warriors routed Maryville Academy 20-0 in the opener as Bob Haven returned an intercepted pass 32 yards for a touchdown and Orlando Caravette added a pair of extra points. John Duzansky and Paul Djikas also tallied rushing scores for the Warriors. The following week (September 21), the Academy celebrated its 85th Anniversary and welcomed back the Class of 1907 according to the *Chicago Tribune on* September 19:

> Morgan Park Military Academy alumni will return tomorrow to commemorate the academy's 85th year as an elementary school and college preparatory school. The Cadets, now as in 1873, wear army blue, but to the jubilee class of 1907 the uniforms and the sound of marching boots will not be familiar, because from 1892 to 1915 the academy was a co-educational preparatory school for the University of Chicago. The Academy's 400 cadets will participate in the campus decoration contest Saturday preceding the football game against Luther South High School.

While the venerable *Chicago Tribune* erred in its reporting on the date of the infamous split from the University of Chicago (which was 1907), the report was true in its depiction of the vibrant military aspect of the Academy in 1957. However, the enrollment rolls in September of 1957 had slipped to a total of 339 (not 400) for both the Upper and Lower Schools. But this issue did not affect the football team on that fine, sunny afternoon of September 21. Buoyed by a supportive crowd of alumni and friends, the

Academy eased past Luther South High School 13-6 to move to 2-0 on the young season. The following week, the Warriors tied Reavis High School 7-7 to remain undefeated (2-0-1) through the first month of the season.

RULES HAD TO BE SET UP

Around this time (September 26), the *Arlington Heights* (Illinois) *Herald* published an editorial hinting at the advantages of private schools (over public schools) especially on the athletic field. This discussion was becoming evident on a more regular basis as private schools in Illinois appeared to have an upper hand in athletic competition since they could enroll students from any geographical area, while public schools could accept only students from their own districts. In order to address possible "raiding" of athletes by either private or public schools, a rather strict transfer rule was in effect in 1957 that prohibited an athlete from participating in sports for a period of one year if that athlete transferred from one high school to another. "To some persons it may not seem right but the reasons for this policy are very sound," wrote the *Herald*. "Rules had to be set up for…the protection of the public schools in the matter of transfer of students particularly after students established themselves as good athletes." Obviously, there was a genuine fear that the private schools would pluck away elite athletes from the public schools, and so the rule was enacted by the Illinois High School Athletic Association. It remains a point of contention to this day, although transfer eligibility rules generally are now based on finances, parental divorces, and physical family "moves." As such, an athlete does have the opportunity to play immediately for his or her new school under certain circumstances.

But the concern in 1957 was the apparent "free" movement of athletes between schools, with public schools warily watching student overtures from their private brethren. Among the key private school destinations identified by the *Herald* were Marmion Military Academy, Joliet Catholic, Nazareth Academy, Onarga Military Academy, and—Morgan Park Military Academy. Certainly, the Academy was open to students from all over the globe, but there was never any evidence that students were recruited based on their athletic ability. Still, the intent of the aforementioned editorial was obvious: private schools could utilize their open enrollment policy to attract student athletes from any location, thus implying that the private school could advantageously stockpile athletes. As such, stringent eligibility rules regarding transfer students were welcomed by most prep outposts in 1957. Perhaps the thinly veiled reactive fear of competing with private schools was the reason for the gradual change in the Academy's football schedule. Once top-heavy with public school opponents, the future 1958 football schedule would include just three public institutions.

WE GOT MURDERED BY CULVER

As the Warriors embarked on the long bus ride to Culver Military Academy on October 5, it was with hope that the end of the long losing streak to Culver might be ending. The Academy had last defeated Culver in 1939, and after a long break in the series, managed a 12-12 tie in 1950. But since that deadlock, Culver had rolled off six straight victories, limiting the Cadets to a mere three touchdowns during that stretch. "We got murdered by Culver on a regular basis," moaned Orlando Caravette ('58). In 1957, that negative skein continued as Culver strolled past the Academy 37-6 to end the losers' brief flirtation with an undefeated season. The *Culver Citizen* reported:

> Culver Military Academy's football team scored three first quarter touchdowns and then exhibited plenty of offensive and defensive power to go on to a 37-6 victory over Morgan Park Military Academy before a large Dad's Day crowd here last Saturday. For Morgan Park, the play of Paul Djikas, pint-sized quarterback, was outstanding.

The disappointment at Culver was followed with three more defeats against Oak Lawn (21-0), Carl Sandburg (30-13), and Elmwood Park (14-2). The once promising season groaned to a close on November 1 when the Academy (now 2-4-1) hosted Lemont High School. After a scoreless first half, both Duzansky and Djikas scored on short runs (Caravette converted both extra points)to pace the Warriors to a 14-0 advantage to wrap up the 1957 season with a 3-4-1 record. The victors piled up an astonishing 385 yards on the ground during the Lemont game. The impressive rushing attack, led by Bob Haven, John Duzansky, Paul Djikas, Mike Luetgert, Dan Lenzi, Bob Rosi, and Willie Wirth managed to out-gain the opposition on the ground by over 300 yards during the season, despite the overall losing record. Of course, running behind the powerful Chris Ellis (the team MVP), ensured that the backfield enjoyed some superlative blocking throughout the year. On defense, tackle Chuck Cleary made things difficult for opposing rushers. Djikas and Tom Ponzo were elected captains for the 1958 squad, which would be in need of a new head coach after Al Bloomer departed. Coach Bloomer secured a new coaching position (over 74 other candidates) at Ludington High School in Michigan. He coached at Ludington for three seasons before retiring from the game but remained at the school as an English instructor. After his coaching responsibilities ended, Bloomer was a basketball referee and a baseball umpire, while remaining active in Ludington on the local bowling and golf circuits. Coach Bloomer passed away at the age of 86 on June 11, 2012 in Ludington.

AN INTIMATE, ALBEIT RAMSHACKLE ATMOSPHERE

Cadets attending Morgan Park Military Academy (especially boarding students) faced a daily schedule that accounted for just about every minute of their time. When students did manage to roam the neighborhood, they could visit a drug store/pharmacy near the Rock island Railroad tracks east of the school or stroll down 111th Street to the west to stop by the Swank Roller Rink at the southeast corner of 111th and Western. Other popular businesses of interest to the students were Hoff's Record store and Hunssinger's Bakery, both near the Academy campus. But what about the coaches? Did they also have a favorite place to wind down and discuss the day's events in a private locale? It would be imprudent for the coaches to visit a local watering hole where a wayward parent or an inquiring administrator might not look fondly if faculty members were enjoying themselves in a public facility. Instead, the coaches regularly visited a local establishment on Western Avenue called DiCola's Seafood. Founded in 1933, the business is still a popular local destination in the Beverly/Morgan Park neighborhood of Chicago. Back in the 1950s, the Academy coaches could stop by DiCola's to pick up some fresh seafood for dinner, but they were also welcome to visit a quiet room in the rear of the store that offered privacy as well as adult beverages! DiCola's did not have a bar (nor a bartender) but did offer a secluded place where folks from the neighborhood could stop by for refreshments. Chuck DiCola, the grandson of the original owner, and whose father Anthony later owned the business, recalled the unique arrangement:

> This was an area at the back of the store (before entering the "true" back room/work area) that was out of most customers' line of sight that contained a large circular wine-bottle display, long past its original intent. Its top's

circumference was about 5 feet or so and, at counter-top height, served as a makeshift bar top.

A group of neighborhood customer/friends would find the time, beginning in early afternoons, to drop by and imbibe in the intimate, albeit ramshackle atmosphere. It was self-serve all the way, with the guys finding their own beers, pouring their own shots, standing around, swapping stories, and then settling up at the cash register at the front of the store by simply reporting their intake (the "honor system"). My dad loved the action and never seemed to mind the imprecision of the whole thing, but I do remember that he would sometimes pour less expensive bourbon into bottles with more expensive labels and wonder how it was that the same guys would claim "spider" privileges (if the last liquor in the bottle filled a shot glass to the brim, it was a freebie).

I remember a football-related happening in the back-room bar area. It featured Chicago Bears great (and one of the NFL's toughest guys) Ed Sprinkle. (My dad was an avowed Chicago Cardinals fan, but he was buddies with some of the Bears who lived in the neighborhood.) One day, when I was sitting near the "bar" peeling shrimp and lapping up the conversation, Sprinkle came in and, during his stay, tore a Chicago phone book in half. I expected him to then bend a steel bar or bite off a snake's head, but that was the only feat of strength he performed that day!

ELIMINATE THE MILITARY ASPECT OF THE ACADEMY

While normal life continued in the neighborhood at DiCola's and other locations in the spring of 1958, rampant rumors regarding the future direction of the Academy were swirling about the campus. Based upon the sliding enrollment and a concern that academic standards were simply not strong enough, the Board of Trustees embarked on a "rehabilitation" program intended to strengthen the Academy in all phases of its role as an elite preparatory school. The minutes of the March 24, 1958 Board of Trustees meeting were precise and to the point in revealing a startling announcement: "The Board and headmaster will work out the implementation to eliminate the military aspect of the Academy." The minutes also revealed that the Board had been in negotiations with Mr. Frederic B. Withington,

Jr. to assume the restructured position of Headmaster of the Academy. A job offer was forwarded to Mr. Withington and he accepted the proposal via a letter dated March 28, 1958: "My wife and I are looking forward to living in and joining the community of Morgan Park Academy." The word "Military" had already been omitted in Withington's correspondence but this was merely the start of the demilitarization process.

For the Board of Trustees, the worst was yet to come...

EXTRA POINT

One of the most comforting aspects of student life at Morgan Park Military Academy was the lifetime friendships that were initiated among the students. "The Academy was small, so you knew everybody as well as what they did," said Ed Madsen. "There were no cliques," added Jim Bowden. "Everyone got along. We were all in the same boat." Jack Peterson recalled that "Ed Jerabek and I started here in the sixth grade and the friendships we accumulated during that time have lasted over 60 years. I can still say anything to these guys and we're still close." Madsen was well-known for his 1957 white Thunderbird sports car that he parked off campus but proudly shared with his classmates. Many of the former Cadets fondly remember their participation in what was considered an "illegal" campus activity: a fraternity. Harry Klein and Ed Jerabek (both of the class of 1956) were the co-founders of an organization called the Zetas. "Fraternities were not sanctioned at the Academy," noted Jerabek, "but there were four or five on campus. Harry and I decided to start our own and we caught some trouble. But, it built up over time." Ed Madsen stated that "The guys from the Zetas all loved going to the Academy. If we had the chance to do it all over, we'd still go there again."

The original members of the Zetas met while attending the Academy's Lower School, according to Jerabek, who documented the group's early days in a personal article entitled "The Story of the Zetas." The formal creation of the organization took place when Jerabek, Klein and their friends were freshmen in the Upper (High) School wrote Jerabek:

> Many of the upperclassmen who were members of off campus fraternities would look for possible pledges among the freshman class. As the year rolled on there were signs of a breakup of our own small group. Some were being asked

to join fraternities and while some of us were interested, others weren't. Rather than risk the breakup of our own group, Harry and I met one day to discuss the idea of starting our own fraternity and staying together. First, we had to check with the other guys to see if they were in favor of the idea, and secondly, if they were willing to endure the pressure that would be in store from the upperclassmen who were pushing them to join their fraternities.

The name "Zeta" was suggested by a member based on the fifteenth letter of the Greek alphabet. "Years later," Jerabek said, "I looked up zeta in a dictionary and laughed to myself as I read the definition. Zeta represented the sixth letter of the Greek alphabet, and not the fifteenth as all of us thought. If I find out which of our brothers was guilty of this long-ago blunder, he may get stuck with XV demerits!" Through their high school years, the Zetas excelled in athletics at the Academy, enjoyed weekend road trips together, and visited the A&W root beer stand on Western Avenue before or after an evening of drag racing down 87th Street. In 2018, the Zetas continue their regular reunions and Jerabek revealed that the Zeta fraternity was still active on the Morgan Park Academy campus at least through 1975. "It's evident that later Zeta brothers had more class than its founders did—by changing the fraternity's name to Zeta Chi Delta!"

Halfback Ed Madsen was the co-MVP of the 1956 Academy team that finished 3-5 under Coach Al Bloomer.

A packed house at Abells Field in 1957 supports the Warriors during a 3-4-1 campaign. Coaches Al Bloomer and Bill Earle are standing on the left.

CHAPTER 21

Bugles Are Silent: End of an Era

"Parents blast Morgan Park Military cut."
—Chicago Tribune, 1958

April 5, 1958

People were crammed everywhere in the little meeting room on the second floor of Blake Hall. Some were sitting, some were standing, but all appeared to be angry. The warm spring day (61⁰) certainly did not help matters as the congested room quickly became hot and muggy. Facing the audience from the front of the room were members of the Academy's Board of Trustees along with recently hired school Headmaster Frederic B. Withington. Although Withington was not scheduled to officially start his new job until July 1, he was asked by the Board to participate in this meeting and hopefully take advantage of the opportunity to meet students, faculty, and parents, and to explain his plans for the upcoming school year. Unfortunately, the anticipated cordial discussion and atmosphere quickly disintegrated. Withington was clearly on the hot seat...

When word of the possible significant changes to the Academy's structure and curriculum leaked out in late March, alumni and parents reacted immediately. A parent group was quickly formed with the objective to secure more specific information about the rumored transition away from the military affiliation, but also to seek clarification regarding speculation concerning the curriculum. Above all, the parents were displeased that their input had not been requested, nor considered, during previous board deliberations on these pertinent topics. Basically, the parents claimed they had not been informed of any possible changes to the Academy. The speed with which the parents and alumni organized was rapid. A letter was prepared by the parents' group in early April and mailed to over 600 parents and an initial meeting was held with the trustees prior to the April 5 discussion.

Parental satisfaction was elusive in that initial meeting, prompting the second discussion to be scheduled on April 5. "Prior to the April [5] meeting a group of 175 parents had met with the trustees and made a resolution, unanimously adopted by those in attendance, that the present character of the school be retained," wrote the *Southtown Economist* on April 16. "The trustees indicated that they would not withdraw from their present position." The prospect of voicing their concerns at the next meeting encouraged more than 200 parents and alumni to show up in Blake Hall on April 5 in an effort to ease the stalemate with the trustees. Apparently, both sides expressed their viewpoints, but no viable solution was reached. Instead, the gap between the two groups appeared to intensify. Withington received the brunt of the often-unfriendly inquiries, but solidly defended the board's position.

On April 16, 1958 under the headline "Parents in Arms Over MPMA Plans" the *Southtown Economist* reported that:

> Parents of Morgan Park Military Academy last week adopted a resolution calling upon the school's board of trustees to reverse their stand in plans to "de-militarize" the school within the next few years. A mass assembly of more than 200 parents, who met with the new headmaster of the school, Frederic B. Withington, Jr. and the board of trustees April 5, voted unanimously to form a group to protest the proposed changes in the academy's curriculum. The 17-man board of trustees has been presented with a resolution asking that they reverse their stand, but whether any action has been or will be taken by the board is not known.

The parents' group further charged (as reported in the same article) "that meetings with the trustees and Withington, who has been retained to implement these changes, had failed to clarify the reasons why certain changes are being made and left questions of paramount importance unanswered."

On April 22, the Board of Trustees fired off a single-spaced two-page letter to "Friends of Morgan Park Military Academy" that officially addressed current issues facing the Academy: primarily a drop in the annual enrollment and a slippage in academic preparation for the students. Although slight adjustments to the financial operation had been effective since 1956, the academic issue was now of greater importance according to the letter: "Obviously the magnitude of this effort to have the Academy among the leading secondary schools in the rapidly changing educational character of the United States is nothing that the trustees assumed without great thought and a very sober recognition of the long-term responsibility they had undertaken." Among the academic areas of focus for the Board were to ensure that Academy scholastic standards were equal to the mandates of most colleges and universities, as well as to be cautious of accepting students into the Academy who experienced academic difficulties at other schools. Perhaps the one item of greatest concern to current students and parents was the status of the military program at the Academy, and the Board discussed this issue as well: "There will be no change in the military program during the 1958-59 school term. As soon as possible, and before enrollment starts for the 1959-60 term, the parents and public will be informed in detail of any changes that will be made."

At the Board meeting less than a week later on April 28, further plans for the future were outlined in the minutes:

> There was an extended discussion relating to the rehabilitation program now in progress. Mr. Withington expressed his thoughts on the many facets of the problem. The consensus of this discussion was the change in the school character is unequivocal in that it will be a military school during the 1958-59 term, with every effort extended to make the military program outstandingly successful. Beginning with the 1959-60 term, it will be a non-military school regardless of what military phases may be retained. Enrollment fees will be refunded at the request of parents up to August 1, 1958.

THE ONLY CONSTANT IS CHANGE

Prior to these meetings, the Board of Trustees had adopted the term "rehabilitation program" to both identify and describe the proposed changes at Morgan Park Military Academy. If the board could be accused of neglecting parental and alumni input in its important deliberations, it must also be credited with having the courage to even address such massive changes in what would surely become a very hostile environment. And, if the board was certain of the need to implement such rigorous and dramatic alterations to the very proud fabric of the Academy, it did so fearlessly, but not flawlessly. Predictably, the animosity towards the Board, and Withington, became a verbal bloodbath, with wounds that continue to exist some sixty years later. Ultimately, the Board of Trustees would discontinue the military affiliation of the Academy permanently after the 1958-1959 school year. It was a decision that surprised many of the "military" alumni, such as Bob Dudley ('54): "I was shocked and disappointed. A tradition wiped out in a moment's notice. My thoughts returned to the academy graduates who served their country and those who never returned." Mike Luetgert ('58) added: "It was disappointing; the end of a tradition." Frank Fonsino ('59) recalled his initial reaction:

> I, like most others, was very disappointed when the military was dropped. When that kind of thing happens, a part of you is "lost" as well. Some still refuse to support the Academy because of it. Because the school's enrollment had been dropping for a number of years, I guess the Trustees didn't think that they had much choice. Military schools were losing popularity across the country. It was a realistic decision. I didn't like it, but as a philosopher [Heraclitus] once said "the only constant is change."

For new Headmaster Withington, his baptism at the Academy was indeed one of fire, and one that he likely did not anticipate. Born in Hawaii, and a graduate of Harvard University, Withington was the Principal of the prestigious Upper School of the Sidwell Friends School in Washington, D.C., when he was recruited for the Academy position in March of 1958. Although he was affiliated with a Quaker educational institute, Withington was a verified WWII hero. As a bomber pilot during the conflict, Withington was twice shot down, once over Poland and once over Yugoslavia where he eluded enemy forces for over four weeks before returning to his own lines. For his efforts, Withington was awarded the Air Medal, the Distinguished Flying Cross, and the Purple Heart. Reportedly, Withington was selected as the Academy Headmaster from a list of over 220 candidates. In 1992, Withington authored a recollection (published in the *Academy Magazine* in November of 2004) of his years (1958-1966) at the Academy and reflected on the reasoning for his move to Chicago: "We saw it as a big step up professionally and the financial compensation offered would rescue us from our almost bankrupt family status in Washington. Little did I know what I was in for!"

The stiff opposition to the demilitarization continued throughout the spring of 1958 when the unsatisfied parent organization (now called the "Combined Parents of the Academy") demanded the resignation of Withington and the entire Board of Trustees according to the *South End Reporter* on May 21:

> Some 100 parents of cadets attending Morgan Park Military Academy, during a mass meeting held at the school May 17, adopted a resolution calling upon the 17-man Board of Trustees and the new Headmaster Frederic B. Withington, Jr., to resign. The parents group, aroused by the trustees' decision to "demilitarize" the school by September 1959, report that if the trustees and headmaster fail to resign within 10 days from May 17, the situation will be taken into court. The parents, it was said, feel that the resignation of the new headmaster and trustees is imperative and that they "be replaced by a board that was not a closed corporation but one elected by all interested parties including parents, faculty, alumni, and business and professional people."

In addition to the parents, a bevy of prominent alumni members stepped forward to urge the Board to reconsider its decision, according to the *Southtown Economist*:

> Among the distinguished alumni of the Academy are top military brass, government officials, industrialists, financiers and educators who say that the military training they received at the Academy contributed to their success. Through their association the alumni pointed out that demilitarization of the Academy is inadvisable at a time when the nation's security and military strength is of utmost importance.

In an earlier response on April 23, the Board strongly supported Withington and stressed that the improvement of the school's academic structure would not be an "overnight" accomplishment as noted in the *Southtown Economist*:

The trustees said the scholastic standing of the Academy has greatly improved since the tightening up of requirements in 1956. However, they pointed out, "the magnitude of this effort to have the Academy among the leading secondary schools in the rapidly changing educational character of the United States is…a long-term responsibility."

Meanwhile, the Combined Parents of the Academy group released the results of its own poll that surveyed 829 families in the immediate area and surrounding suburbs. The poll requested input as to whether these families supported the demilitarization of the school. The results, according to a *Southtown Economist* interview with Mothers' Club President Mrs. Barbara Rosi, "turned up only 25 [families] who would enroll their children in a non-military school." In other words, noted Mrs. Rosi, 93% of those surveyed did not favor the planned demilitarization. As the range war between parents and the trustees waged on through the end of the school year, neither side was budging from its position. The Board of Trustees re-elected six of its current members on May 19, while the parents enlisted the aid of two attorneys to evaluate possible legal action against the Board. On June 4, the *Southtown Economist* stated that 224 supporters from around the country had signed petitions seeking the ouster of the Board members. Mrs. Rosi explained that "the reaction of these signers is an overwhelming repudiation of the Morgan Park Military Academy Board of Trustees and a vote of no confidence in the board as it is presently constituted."

In August of 1958, the Board announced that the name of the school would be changed to Morgan Park Academy prior to the 1959-1960 school opening. Certainly, the great risk in all of this turmoil was the chance that the Academy would lose a significant number of both present and future enrollees as the result of the demilitarization. Again, there was a disparity on both sides as Mrs. Rosi claimed that at least 100 students would not return to the Academy for the 1958-1959 academic year while Withington told the *Southtown Economist* on August 3 that the numbers would be slightly less than the previous year:

> Withington also stated that only eight students have resigned from the school during the last two months, and that he expected no more than 20 less students than last year's enrollment of 340 when school convenes in the Fall.

In reality, both sides were erroneous on the enrollment issue as a total of 265 students were in place as of October of 1958. The huge drop in total tuition revenue forced the Board to evaluate the possible sale of some of its real estate holdings (including Abells Field) as well as secure a short-term loan with a local bank. One of the more obvious changes to student life on campus was the allowance of "civilian" garb on certain occasions and Cadets were now required to procure only two military uniforms (instead of three). In addition, non-military faculty members were no longer required to wear uniforms. Overall, the threatened litigation against the Board was not initiated and the outcry aimed at the trustees seemed to diminish once the school year began. As such, at the October 27 meeting of the Board, Trustee George Wiegel reported that "the relations between the Academy and formerly disgruntled parents and alumni seemed to be improving to a most encouraging extent." Although the tempestuous and often acrimonious verbal battle between the two groups appeared to lessen (but not disappear), Withington and the Board of Trustees plowed ahead with their strategic plan for the Academy.

However, as 68% of the faculty from the 1957-1958 ranks returned for the new academic year, there was one noticeable missing instructor: George Mahon. The beloved former coach and athletic director departed the campus to accept a "position in California" according to the Board minutes on August 11. Mahon, who had been with the school for over three decades and was the coach of the unbeaten 1939 football team, eventually retired and passed away in July of 1965 at the age of 65 in San Bernardino, California.

MIGHT BEAT CULVER

With coaches now ready to patrol the sidelines during games dressed in sport coats and business suits instead of military uniforms, the 1958 edition of the Academy football team gathered for pre-season practice under the tutelage of new head coach Willis "Bill" Earle. Returning to the coaching ranks after a few seasons was Athletic Director (and long-time head football coach) Joe Ziemba, who joined the staff as Earle's assistant, along with Harold Krainock. Ziemba returned to the football fold despite being tasked with the new assignment to totally revise the school's internal physical education structure for the new school year as part of the school's educational realignment in 1958, according to *The Academy News*:

Under the direction of Joseph Ziemba, head of the physical education department, the Academy will offer an afternoon sports program for all students. Every boy will be expected to participate in regular periods of physical education for one or two hours at least four afternoons a week in a sport of his choice each season. All regular varsity sports and teams will continue. It is the aim of this extended physical education program to provide leadership development for all boys and to improve their physical condition.

Notwithstanding the decreased school enrollment, the football squad welcomed 29 prospects on August 25 including several key players from the previous season. Coach Earle was optimistic about the upcoming schedule (and the final one as Morgan Park Military Academy) as explained by *The Academy News* in a lengthy interview on August 20:

Coach Earle thinks this year's squad "Might beat Culver. At least with 12 returning lettermen we could have one of the best varsity teams in years. We'll also have five other boys who were members of last year's team." He looks to Chuck Cleary, last year's defensive tackle to play offensively as well this year and fill a big gap in the line. And he hopes Ken Powell, a new team member, can hold down the other tackle post. "Our best hope lies in the return of co-captain and quarterback Paul Djikas who is the key man on the field and directs our split-T with belly series. Djikas will be supported by returning letterman Dan Lenzi at fullback. Former letter winners Bob Haven at right half and Willie Wirth at left halfback complete the backfield." Coach Earle intends to use the two-platoon system if team strength and depth permit.

It should be noted that two cousins were playing football for the Academy in 1958 and both shared the same name of Paul Djikas, with one identified as P.L. ('59), while the other Paul was known as P.J. ('61). Paul Louis (P.L.) Djikas was the returning quarterback in 1958 but was also the school's MVP in both basketball and baseball the preceding year. In addition, Djikas was honored with the Superior Cadet Award during his junior term and elected as President of the Guardians (the liaison between the students and the school administration) during his senior year. As such, Djikas was a smart,

---

experienced anchor for the 1958 backfield which combined the quickness of Wirth, Rosi, Haven and Ron Matray with the power of fullback Lenzi. The first test for this dangerous backfield was slated for September 13 at Maryville Academy. The Warriors had first begun playing Maryville in 1953 (a 0-0 tie) and the two schools were usually evenly matched on the gridiron. However, the students from each institution largely represented completely different socio-economic backgrounds. While the Academy offered educational opportunities to families with the financial means to afford a top-flight private school, Maryville offered solace to children simply needing a "home." The *Chicago Tribune* (September 28, 1958) shared a glimpse behind the history and accomplishments of Maryville Academy:

> Maryville Academy, Des Plaines, the home of 750 dependent children, will hold an open house Sunday with guided tours of the buildings and grounds. Children who live at Maryville, sometimes called the "City of Youth," are mostly from broken homes, with only a small number classified as orphans. None of them, according to the Very Rev. Msgr. George Halpin, superintendent of the institution, is adoptable. The children live in halls, or dormitories, each accommodating 30-36 youngsters. Since it was organized [in 1882], the institution has been responsible for the education of more than 20,000 children between the ages of 3 and 18.

In other words, the football players at Maryville, despite being from a completely different economic universe than their opponents, were extremely tough, and that unique toughness was evident on the field in the season opener. The two clubs battled fiercely throughout the first half with Dan Lenzi's 12-yard run around right end accounting for the only Academy points as Maryville grabbed a 7-6 halftime lead. Midway through the fourth quarter, Maryville tallied on a 30-yard touchdown pass to expand the lead to 13-6 (the final score as well) at which point *The Academy News* noted:

> Morgan Park, now enraged at the many frustrations, gathered its attack and drove impressively downfield, but they were stopped inches from the goal line by the final gun. As Coach Willis Earle pointed out, the game was lost by Morgan Park mistakes. "Sloppy playing cost us the game. We lost the ball three times on fumbles." The many

spectators from the Academy, however, were able to catch glimpses of a Morgan Park team which, although fumbling away its chances on Saturday, gave promise of generating into a formidable attacking team.

INCISIVE TIMING AND ASSURED PRECISION

That anticipated "promise" for the 1958 team burst out in a big way the following week when the Warriors toppled Luther South High School 27-7 for the first victory of Coach Earle's Academy career. Unlike the previous week, the Academy did not lose a single fumble and out-gained the hosts 206 yards to 59 yards on the ground. All of which impressed the student reporters from *The Academy News* on October 3:

> Showing an amazing improvement over its fumbling performance against Maryville, the Warriors ran and passed with such incisive timing and assured precision that Luther South was completely outclassed. Indeed, it was only in the dying moments of the fourth quarter that the home team was able to muster a scoring march against Morgan's reserves. Offensively and defensively the Morgan Park varsity realized the potential that sputtered and coughed against Maryville with a consistent verve and fierceness in play execution. Coach Earle commented after the game that "this week every lineman and every back earned 'lineman of the week' and 'back of the week.' The team really played as if they meant it." Great credit must be given to Coaches Earle, Krainock and Ziemba, who took the disorganized team of a week ago and tinkered it into the fine, confident club that won over Luther South.

Elusive halfback Willie Wirth initiated the scoring feast for the Academy when he eased into the end zone from the one-yard line in the first stanza. Ron Matray later scored on a four-yard romp to push the Academy ahead 13-0 at the half. Later in the third quarter, P. L. Djikas scored, as described artfully by *The Academy News*: "Djikas, who operated skillfully all afternoon in his running of the split-T option, sliced over from the eight after a beautiful piece of deceptive ball-handling." Wirth added the final tally in the fourth quarter on an eight-yard scamper to move the final score to 27-7.

LISTENING TO ELVIS

The October 3 issue of *The Academy News* also provided an amusing update on the school's new "mandatory" after-school physical education program instituted by Coach Ziemba:

> Perhaps the biggest improvement has been the elimination of the "barracks dweller." Formerly, this ignoble individual stealthily entered his room at 3:30 pm never to see daylight till the next morn. His recreation consisted of listening to Elvis and other activities of this caliber. This activity was periodically interrupted by a trip to the "weeder" [student smoking room]. This routine went on with monotonous regularity throughout the school year. Fresh air was looked upon with medieval superstition as something to be avoided lest a tragic illness would fall upon the "barracks dweller." The result of the activity (?) was a pallid, feeble individual hardly to be considered a representative American boy. Results of the present program are producing results at this early stage. The "barracks dweller" possesses a tinge of color in his cheek. He bounces up the barrack steps two at a time. He has discovered physical education can be rewarding after all.

With 62 of the 167 Academy high school pupils playing football on some level, the physical education program offered the non-football students the opportunity to participate in some active sports programs such as softball, tennis, and track almost every afternoon. Meanwhile, the football team continued to grind through the 1958 schedule and welcomed the first home game of the season on September 27 against Luther North High School. Once again, Wirth was the hero as he sprinted around the right end for the only touchdown of the game with just 34 seconds remaining. Wirth then added the extra point as the Academy survived with a 7-0 victory.

OFFICIATING WORSE THAN BAD

Next up for the Cadets would be the final meeting ever with Culver Military Academy, a rivalry that began in 1899. Culver had dominated the series in recent years, collecting seven straight victories since the memorable 12-12 tie in 1950. The outcome in 1958 was no different, as powerful Culver remained undefeated (3-0) with an easy 20-0 win over the Academy. Still, there was some controversy as veteran Culver head coach Russ Oliver complained loudly about the officiating in the contest. Oliver told *The Culver Citizen* on October 8: "I expected the officiating to be bad up there, but it was worse than bad." At the top of Oliver's list of concerns were three touchdowns that were called back due to penalties. In addition, Oliver bemoaned the fact that his club was punished with 130 yards in penalties, compared to Morgan Park's 45 yards. Still, three touchdown receptions by Culver end Don Houder was more than enough to secure the victory as the once majestic rivalry between the two prep school football behemoths quietly slipped away.

With the final year of the football program for Morgan Park Military Academy now half over (the school did, however, continue the football program following the demilitarization), the Cadets' record stood at 2-2 as the team prepared for the final stretch of this historic season. Next in line was a game against Parker High School of Chicago in which the Academy trailed 6-0 in the third quarter. At that time, Bob Rosi provided the needed spark as he broke through the Parker defense and raced 60 yards to the opponent's ten-yard line. From there, Willie Wirth pushed across the tying touchdown. P. L. Djikas added the extra point and the Warriors emerged with a tight 7-6 victory. On October 18, the Academy entertained another new opponent in Lincoln-Way High School of New Lenox, Illinois. The visiting Knights were members of the Southwest Suburban Conference and the school district now includes Lincoln-Way Central, Lincoln-Way East, and Lincoln-Way West (Lincoln-Way North was closed in 2016). East has captured two state football titles (2005 and 2017) while Central grabbed the 1997 Illinois championship. But back in 1958, Lincoln-Way was no match for Morgan Park Academy as the Cadets smothered their guests 18-6 to move to 4-2 on the season, the most wins for the team since 1954.

The last home game in the history of the Morgan Park Military Academy football program took place on October 25, 1958 when the Warriors were stomped by Notre Dame High School from Niles, Illinois 27-7. This left one final contest for MPMA., an afternoon game at Lemont High School on Saturday, November 1 at Lemont High School. Entering the matchup with a 4-3 mark, the Academy hoped to snatch that important fifth win to ensure the school's best football finish of the decade. With a nice kickoff temperature of 56 degrees, the post-Halloween crowd settled in for what promised to be a competitive game. It was perfect football weather for early November with no precipitation, and little wind, in the forecast. Although both teams had difficulty in moving the ball early in the game, Lemont quarterback Tom Hoinacki connected with a 32-yard completion to end Smith Campbell that brought the ball down to the Academy ten-yard line. From there Lemont Captain Bob Kowalski scooted around right end for the first score of the game. After the extra point failed, the Warriors managed to deadlock the game at 6-6 at the half. The Academy added a pair of touchdowns in the third period as reported on November 6 by the local newspaper, *The Lemonter*:

> The invaders struck quickly for two TDs in the third period, assuming what appeared to be an insurmountable 18-6 margin. Like good infantrymen, the Cadets stayed on the ground for their scoring forays.

Lemont bounced back to narrow the gap to 18-12 on a long touchdown pass as the action moved into the final quarter of the final football game for Morgan Park Military Academy. The ensuing action was picked up by *The Lemonter*:

> Holding a precarious 18-12 lead, Morgan Park soon rectified the uneasy situation when they sent their star left half, [Willie] Wirth, over his own left tackle on a 68-yard scoring jaunt. Late in the fourth frame our boys moved back into contention by virtue of another 50-yard overall pass and run play. With a little over a minute left to play, Kowalski's on-side kick was recovered by Lemont on the Cadet 48. A pass was good to their 39, but three subsequent aerials went incomplete as the game ended [with the Academy prevailing 24-18].

As the game, and the season, ended Morgan Park Military Academy completed the campaign with a solid 5-3 record, the best the team had achieved since the 1949 club finished 7-1. Willie Wirth, the speedy 125 lb. halfback, paced the team in rushing (605 yards; 6.1 average), and in points (44). For these accomplishments, Wirth was also selected as the MVP of the 1958 team, the final Cadet to secure this honor. Djikas, Rosi, Matray,

Haven, and Lenzi all accumulated significant yardage during the year and Lenzi and durable lineman Chuck Cleary were named as the co-captains for the 1959 season.

Willie Wirth's exciting 68-yard scoring run against Lemont would prove to be the final touchdown in the long, respected football history of Morgan Park Military Academy, and the last victory to complete a superb 306-179-35 ledger from 1893 through the 1958 season.

On January 2, 1959, the Illinois Secretary of State officially changed the corporate name of the school to Morgan Park Academy...

EXTRA POINT

Amid the outcry over the possible demilitarization of Morgan Park Military Academy in the spring of 1958, the passing of the man most responsible for the success of the Academy in the 20th Century was barely noticed. On March 2, 1958, Col. Harry Delmont Abells died in North Bennington, Vermont. Abells joined the Academy faculty in 1898 (as a Chemistry teacher) before being named the school's principal in 1907. In 1916, he became the Superintendent and held that position until becoming superintendent emeritus in 1945. He eventually "fully" retired in 1951. Although his many contributions to the school have been listed earlier in this book, probably his most significant accomplishments were leading the school through its divorce with the University of Chicago in 1907 and overcoming its nearly catastrophic financial challenges in 1914. He also pushed for the construction, and completion, of Hansen Hall and Alumni Hall in the 1920s, two buildings which still claim an important role on the Academy campus. Later, during the Great Depression, Abells helped the Academy to survive once again when he started Morgan Park Junior College as well as a summer school for all students in the area, including females! In 1929, the **Skirmisher** yearbook described Abells as "A man who is fair, who can be strict without unnecessary harshness, and who can be a real teacher and still a good friend..."

It was therefore somewhat ironic that shortly after the loss of Col. Abells, new Headmaster Frederic Withington, Jr. was hired by the Board of Trustees in late March of 1958. Withington was immediately cast into the board-created turmoil of demilitarization and represented the "face" of the Academy during those difficult times. Withington left the Academy in 1966 to become the Head of Friends Academy on Long Island, New York. During his eight years at Morgan Park Academy, Withington helped to rebuild the enrollment that dropped significantly during the uproar over the demilitarization, eliminated the boarding school option, and changed the now irrelevant school protocol so that women were now admitted as students. As Withington noted in his *Academy Magazine* memoir:

> It should be noted that the pioneering Morgan Park Academy was the very first private independent secondary school in modern times to both "demilitarize," become co-educational, and discontinue boarding. These patterns, especially becoming co-educational, later became common in many private and independent schools.

Withington also oversaw the controversial sale of some Academy land and helped direct the school during some challenging financial times in the early 1960s. However, he was unable to convince the Board of Trustees to integrate the school, a status that was not resolved until the 1966-67 school year began. He remained at Friends Academy for 22 years before retiring. Frederic B. Withington, Jr. passed away on September 29, 1993 at the age of 71.

The 1958 squad was the final team to play under the Morgan Park Military Academy name. Coach Bill Earle led the club to a final 5-3 record, including big wins over Lincoln-Way and Lemont. Players, coaches, and managers of that historic unit are as follows. Bottom row (from left): Murdock, Bouramas, Solano. Second row: Wirth, Barton, Castellanos, Blitz, Chouvalis, Amadio, Smith. Third row: Gifford, Woodsworth, Glesener, Karstrom, Karas, Savich, Rosi. Fourth row: Coach Krainock, Krysti, P.J. Djikas, Matray, P.L. Djikas, Ferris, Lenzi, Coach Earle, Coach Ziemba. Fifth row: Gaetano, Sappenfield, Timmons, Ponzo, Cleary, Lang, Abbott, Schloesser.

EPILOGUE

Back to the Future

"Morgan Park Academy is building a future as bright as our storied history."
—Head of School Mercedes Z. Sheppard, 2018

Michael "Mick" McClure ('60) clearly remembers the first football game he witnessed at Morgan Park Military Academy: "In 1953, MPMA hosted St. John's Military Academy at Abells Field and I took the bus from 90th and Vincennes up to the Academy because my brother attended St John's and I thought he might be at the game." McClure, who later became the Executive Vice President of the Houston Oilers/Tennessee Titans of the National Football League, was also part of the group of Academy students who participated in the academic transition in 1959-1960. After spending three years at St. John's Military Academy, McClure transferred to Morgan Park Academy for the beginning of his senior year in the fall of 1959, was a member of the football team, and was later inducted into the Academy Hall of Fame in 1996. Following graduation from DePauw University, his phenomenal career included stops as Director of Public Relations and Marketing for the Chicago Bulls of the National Basketball Association from 1973-79; Vice President of Marketing and Media Relations for the Houston Oilers 1979-81; Senior Vice President of Marketing and Broadcasting for the Chicago White Sox major league baseball team from 1981-89; and as Executive Vice President of the Houston Oilers/Tennessee Titans from 1989-1999. He is one of the very few individuals who worked in an executive level position for teams in three different major professional sports leagues.

Much was different on campus in 1959 when McClure entered the Academy, especially in regard to the student dress code. Gone were the mandatory military uniforms replaced by the new student "uniform" of a school blazer, a white shirt and tie. Meanwhile, the first female students were admitted to the Academy's Lower School (11 girls entered the high school in 1960). On the football field, Coach Bill Earle departed the Academy after one season and was hired as the head coach at Holy Name High School in Escanaba, Michigan. During his four years at Holy Name, Earle compiled an impressive 25-4-2 record, including the team being voted as the Michigan Upper Peninsula champions in 1962 when Earle led the squad to a 7-1 mark before leaving to accept a similar position at nearby Munising High School. Coach Willis "Bill" Earle passed away on October 8, 2009 at the age of 80 in Indiantown, Florida.

Morgan Park Academy enrollment dipped again for the opening of school in September of 1959 with a total of 218 students, but only 134 of those were registered for the Upper School. "1959 was a challenging year for the academy and especially in sports," recalled McClure. "Enrollment declined after demilitarization and we ended up with about 130 boys. One of several reasons for my transfer as a senior was to participate in football. I had started on the St. John's Military Academy freshman and sophomore teams, and then played very little as a junior on the varsity. When I visited MPA, Jim Draper was not only the football coach, but also the principal. He was very enthusiastic about the team and told me he thought I could be a valuable member of the team. That was music to my ears and I dedicated myself to being in good shape when fall training camp began."

Coach James Battles Draper had joined the Academy staff in August of 1958 after serving as the head of the English Department at Germantown Academy in Philadelphia, Pennsylvania. Draper was a World War II veteran and a graduate of Bowdoin College in Brunswick, Maine where he was a member of the football, track, and hockey teams. In addition to his duties at Morgan Park Academy as Assistant Headmaster, Upper School Principal, and English instructor, Draper added the responsibilities of head football coach for the 1959 season. Although this book concluded its coverage of the venerable Morgan Park Military Academy football program after the 1958 season, the Academy produced some very successful teams over the next two decades until the program ended in 1978. In fact, the Academy won 95 games, lost only 44, and tied four contests from 1959 through 1978. We hope that someday, this story may be told as well.

HOW COULD TINY LITTLE MPA BE IN THE GAME?

But in 1959, Coach Draper was responsible for continuing the tradition in the first year of the non-military scenario, and he did so with a group of about 30 players that finished the year with a 3-3-1 record. Here is McClure recalling the capabilities of his new teammates and their willingness, and determination, to pursue excellence on the football field:

> Almost everybody played both ways. We were strong across the front line with junior Wayne Michalak at center, seniors Paul Djikas and Ed Karas at guards, seniors Chuck Cleary and Dan Lenzi at tackles, and senior Lloyd Krysti and myself at ends. Our quarterback was Bob Lloyd, a lanky junior with a strong arm. Halfbacks were junior Bill Springer and senior speedster Ron Matray. Our fullback was senior Ricky Castellanos. We had a huge 260-pound senior, Rich Schloesser, who played both offensive and defensive tackle. Coach Draper would use the 215lb. Lenzi at fullback for his short yardage blocking and running and put Schloesser in at Lenzi's tackle position. I would estimate those 12 played the vast majority of the snaps. Cleary was a big-time talent. Tall, strong and mean. Matray was a long-range threat from anywhere on the field. Our offensive line averaged about 200 pounds with Michalak, Djikas, Krysti and I between 170 and 180, Karas at 185, Lenzi or Schloesser at 215 or 260 and Cleary at 230.

By far the most memorable game of the season was the final contest at Notre Dame High School of Niles, Illinois. The heavily favored Dons were a bit surprised when the spunky Academy squad refused to yield and trailed at halftime by a thin margin of 13-7. "They had about 1,000 students and had five teams running signal drills in warmups on a wet, rainy night in the northwest suburbs," remembered McClure. "We had one team running signal drills. They had more than one thousand fans in their stands and I doubt we had more than fifty. We surprised the hell out of them early and went off the field at halftime trailing 13-7. The priests on the sidelines were shaking their heads. How could tiny little MPA be in the game after the first 24 minutes? As you would expect their depth and superior talent prevailed in the second half and we lost 31-13 but won a huge moral victory."

McClure was aware of the controversial changes made at the Academy when he enrolled in the summer of 1959, but was a proud part of the students who experienced the myriad of changes in that critical first year (1959-1960) after the full demilitarization of the school:

> I had many friends at Morgan Park and I knew the decision to demilitarize was unpopular with alumni and some students had elected to transfer because of the change. Once the school year began those who had stayed and the few, like myself, who had enrolled as new students in 1959 all pulled together and set the tone for the future. Headmaster Ted Withington and Principal Jim Draper were outstanding educators and quality men. They built the foundation for the coed, private school that has not only survived, but thrived in the coming decades.

More changes followed the football program in 1960 when Morgan Park Academy elected to join the Private School League. As Headmaster Withington noted in his memoir:

> By the middle 1950s, Morgan Park Military Academy (because of the dwindling enrollment) had become less successful in athletics. In the fall of 1960, we were admitted, in some sports, to the Private School League of Chicago which included North Shore Country Day School, The Latin School of Chicago, The Harvard School, The University of Chicago Laboratory School and Francis Parker. All had strong academic reputations and their acceptance of us helped publicly confirm our new status as one of the leading schools of the area.

Venerable Blake Hall was closed in December of 1959 (and burned down in a suspicious fire in 1962), and most of the military-related artifacts on campus were gone by the end of the 1959-1960 academic year. The **Skirmisher** yearbook was now called the **Oasis** and Withington noted "The transition from military to a solid college preparatory day school was completed by 1961." James B. Draper coached the Academy football team to a 4-4 record in 1960 before departing in 1962 to become the Headmaster of the Pebble Hill School in Syracuse, New York. Following the 1964-1965 school year, "boarding" at the school was no longer an option as all students were now "day" students.

Withington and the Board addressed another red-hot issue in the early 1960s when the Academy sold Abells Field. In his memoir, Withington explained that the land was sold primarily because it was a safety hazard:

> The main athletic field of Morgan Park Academy was located on the north side of 111th Street. This had for many years proved to be a hazard since students and faculty were constantly crossing this heavily trafficked road. The school did have a second field on the south end of the campus next to the gymnasium. Some members of the Board saw the sale of this main football field as an opportunity to pay off the debt, of something like $300,000, that had been accumulated during the transition. They felt that the school could operate just as well without it and the dangers to students crossing 111th Street were worrisome.

Although Withington opposed the sale of the valuable property (it finally sold for $325,000), he ultimately supported the Board's decision. The Board minutes from the December 2, 1963 meeting revealed the real necessity for selling the revered football field: "It became clear, however, that the huge deficit could be eliminated only by heroic decisions, and so Abells Field was sold for $325,000 and field athletic activities were removed to a rebuilt South Field." However, the local community quickly became outraged when it was learned that the land that was once Abells Field would be developed into high rise apartment buildings in the prime residential neighborhood. Withington recalled the tense situation as well as the solution:

> Originally, I believe, the developer wanted to build a twelve-story high density apartment building. Eventually that was scaled back to meet objections of the community and the developer proposed putting up two story "condominiums," something no one had heard of at the time. Eventually this scaled down version of the development of the field was approved by the city of Chicago and the apartments went up. I didn't think they looked too bad, but I was sad to see the field gone.

Aside from Withington himself, there was general sadness among the many alumni football players who had proudly represented the Academy since Abells Field was opened in 1934. "I was sad when they sold Abells

Field after playing so many games there," said Cal Bouma ('50). "I was also disappointed when the football/track property was sold," added Frank Fonsino ('59). "I'm sure that it was sold for financial reasons as well."

With football games now moved to the south end of the campus, the Academy still managed to remain competitive on the gridiron behind some exceptional coaches. In 1962, a local graduate of Morgan Park High School by the name of Charles "Mac" Lewis joined the staff as head coach and immediately grabbed the championship of the Private School League with an overall 6-1 mark. This was the first football championship for the school since it became Morgan Park Academy. Lewis, who was also a star lineman at the University of Iowa and played one year for the Chicago Cardinals in the NFL, went on to compile a 21-9 record during his four years as coach at the Academy. As a member of the Cardinals, he was one of the biggest players (6' 6", 305 lbs.) in the pro circuit.

But the most prominent football mentor in the post military days was coach Warren Jones. After serving as line coach at St. Viator High School, Jones moved over to Morgan Park Academy in 1967 and created a superb record over the next nine seasons while also serving as the school's basketball coach, baseball coach, and athletic director. Jones came to the Academy with an enviable list of football accomplishments, including serving as head coach for Gordon Tech in the Chicago Catholic League for seven years, along with stints at St. Mel and St. Rita in Chicago, as well as at St. Agnes in Kansas City.

Perhaps his most admirable season was the 6-1 record that the Academy fashioned in 1972 when the team finished the season with only 12 players. His powerhouse squad of 1971 easily captured the conference championship while dominating its opponents, scoring 402 points in an 8-0 season while allowing just six. Overall, Jones rolled up an impressive 50-13-2 record in his nine years as the head football coach (including three undefeated seasons), equaling Coach Ziemba for most wins in Academy gridiron history, although Jones accomplished the feat in far fewer games. For his coaching prowess and success, Jones was inducted into the Morgan Park Academy Athletic "Hall of Fame" in 2013. When Jones announced his retirement from football coaching after the 1975 season, columnist Bernie Lynch of the *Southend Reporter* shared a glowing summary of the successful career of Coach Jones on January 8, 1976:

> When and where have you ever found an unusual situation
> of a man so dedicated to sports to head a school's almost
> completed coaching task and serve as the athletic director?

Morgan Park Academy has been gifted during the past nine years to have Warren Jones in its midst as the head football, basketball and baseball coach combined and enjoying success in each sport…guiding the Warriors to five Independent Football League titles in nine seasons at the South Side school. In his 25 banner seasons of grid coaching, Jones has been the inspiring, guiding factor behind a 131-38-4 record. In addition, the all-around athletic leader has had five baseball and four basketball title-winning teams at MPA.

Following the coaching departure of Jones from the football field in 1975, the Academy struggled through three more seasons before finishing 0-3 in 1978. Due to a lack of participation, the proud and lengthy run of the Academy football team ended. In the final game played by the school, the very last touchdown in school history was scored via a pass reception by freshman Jonathan Turk in a season-ending 34-8 loss to North Shore Academy on October 14, 1978. The decision to discontinue the football program had been announced at the September 12, 1978 Board meeting with a simple explanation: "This is the last year that football will be played as a varsity sport at MPA; it will be replaced by a soccer program next year." Later, at the November 14, 1978 Board meeting, a more specific declaration regarding the reasoning for terminating the gridiron team was noted:

Football was discontinued due to the lack of student interest, the expense and the number of injuries. The discontinuance of the football program, the role of the athletic programs and the impact on school spirit were discussed by several of the trustees. There was a clear consensus of opinion that the decision to eliminate the football program was the correct decision. There was also concern that this not have an adverse effect on the overall school program.

Today, Morgan Park Academy is thriving and offers a variety of athletic opportunities for both male and female students, according to Assistant Head of School Vincent Hermosilla:

From the long success of our football program to our position as the first high school to play James Naismith's new game of basketball, athletics has a rich history at Morgan Park

Academy, and one that continues today. Physical education and sports teams are an integral part of the MPA experience, with daily P.E. classes for students through ninth grade and a robust array of interscholastic teams that regularly challenge for postseason championships. In recent years, graduates have gone on to success at the college level in basketball, baseball, softball, soccer, tennis, and golf. Most important, the Warriors bring discipline, determination, and good sportsmanship to each competition and learn teamwork and leadership along the way.

And Morgan Park Academy has positioned itself well for the future with demanding academic requirements that have produced enviable results, such as a consistent record of having 100% of its graduates accepted into colleges and universities of their choice. Head of School Mercedes Z. Sheppard continues to focus on the future academic success of the students, but with an eye on the past:

Much about Morgan Park Academy has changed over the course of a century and a half, but as we approach our 150th anniversary, we remain true to the mission, vision, and values that have been the bedrock of an Academy education for generations of students. MPA graduates are confident young adults, original thinkers, and creative problem solvers who are ready to change the world through leadership and service--which has been true through the decades, even as those concepts have evolved with the world around us. With robust enrollment numbers and passionate engagement from parents, alumni, and friends, Morgan Park Academy is building a future as bright as our storied history.

As the laurels from the decades of football dominance have slowly retreated into the shadows of the historic Morgan Park Academy, the school itself refuses to allow that exemplary gridiron experience to be forgotten or discarded. With prominent displays of football success evident throughout the campus, and the annual enthusiastic consideration of worthy teams and individuals for the Academy's Athletic Hall of Fame, there is a firm grasp on the importance of the past gridiron deeds and triumphs. While the ghosts of football past are not visible, they remain on the stately campus. Students can still wander across the plush, green landscape where legends such as Amos Alonzo Stagg and Albert Benbrook once strolled. The ancient gym, which once housed legendary collegiate coaches such as Jesse Harper and Wallace Wade when they were students, continues to serve its original purpose on the south end of the campus as it has since 1901.

Behind the gym, the same rugged practice field still hosts a myriad of Academy athletic teams. Opponents are likely unaware of the historical significance of that very sacred ground where the top prep school football teams in the Midwest first met in combat almost 125 years ago. Perhaps they can hear, ever so faintly, the exuberant words of encouragement from coaches such as Fleming, Mahon, and Ziemba, or the muffled steps of a precise cadet marching unit preparing for a weekend parade. Maybe they can decipher the sad sounds of "taps" being played patiently and slowly in memory of the hundreds of former cadets who defended their country in time of war and many of whom paid with the ultimate sacrifice. The shouts and cheers charging from the forgotten balconies hanging from the back of the gym during big games have slipped away, as have the grunts and groans of hundreds of long-gone players toiling in the heat of pre-season football practices. The proud history of a place like Morgan Park Military Academy can be both overwhelming and intimidating, but it's there.

Just listen...

Abells Field sits empty shortly before it was developed into condominiums in the early 1960s. Built in 1934, the sale of the Abells Field property did help alleviate some of the school's financial challenges following the demilitarization of the Academy in 1959.

"I went to grade school and I went to college, but the only real memories of school that I have are of Morgan Park Military Academy and Morgan Park Academy. I remember every brick in every building. I remember every teacher and officer, and I remember every coach. It made gentlemen out of us…It seems that the most mystical and wonderful things occurred after going to one or both of the Academies. We see the school we loved, and the times we had. We see things that may no longer be there except in our minds, like the old Blake Hall with its cannons, or the old music room, or we see old friends as they were. With me it's some of my friends that are not with us… except at the Academy."

—Charles Cleary '60

APPENDIX

Morgan Park Military Academy
Yearly Football Results
1893-1958

The opponents, scores, and dates for each football game played by Morgan Park Military Academy from 1893-1958 were compiled by utilizing a variety of resources. Primary sources were (when available) school yearbooks, student newspapers, area newspapers, and an Academy binder containing hand-written schedules and scores by coaches throughout the years. However, often these materials did not agree on the final scores or dates of specific games. In those instances, numerous newspapers (with game reports) were consulted to ensure the scoring accuracy of those contests. The playing dates of games were rarely included in the Academy resources, so the exact dates of games were rescued from newspaper articles. The coaches for each year were identified using the same procedures as noted above. In the event that two coaches are included below, the first name is that of the Head Coach. In the early years of the program, the players often competed without a coach and that is indicated by the lack of a coach's name under each of those seasons.

Finally, during the years when there was no military affiliation for the school (Morgan Park Academy), the team is noted as "MPA" below. Otherwise, the acronym "MPMA" will be listed. Other abbreviations include: high school (H.S.); military academy (M.A.); athletic association (A.A.); athletic club (A.C.); junior college (J.C.); and, exhibition (EXH).

1893 Season
1-0

November 4	MPA	14	Lake Front Academy		12

1894 Season
4-3

October 20	MPA	4	Englewood YMCA		12
October 27	MPA	12	Lake Forest University (2nd team)		6
October 3	MPA	22	Morgan Park Village		0
November 7	MPA	12	Sisson and Smith Academy		0
November 10	MPA	6	Lake Forest Academy		18
November 17	MPA	6	University of Chicago (2nd team)		8
November 20	MPA	6	Englewood H.S.		0

1895 Season
6-2
Coach H.W. Dickinson

September 14	MPA	28	Auburn Park A.C.		0
September 18	MPA	0	Englewood H.S.		6
October 12	MPA	10	Blue Island YMCA		4
October 26	MPA	58	Northwestern Academy		0
November 2	MPA	34	Lake Forest University (2nd team)		0
November 9	MPA	6	Lake Forest Academy		0
November 16	MPA	16	Lake Forest Academy		4
November 23	MPA	0	Gibson A.C.		4

1896 Season
10-0

September 12	MPA	24	Auburn Park A.C.		0
September 16	MPA	12	Blue Island H.S.		6
October 7	MPA	14	Hyde Park H.S.		0
October 17	MPA	10	St. Charles H.S.		6
October 21	MPA	12	University of Chicago (2nd team)		0
November 4	MPA	10	Chicago Theological Seminary		0
November 7	MPA	10	Englewood H. S.		0
November 11	MPA	14	YMCA Training School		0
November 14	MPA	16	Austin Village		6
November 21	MPA	22	Armour Institute		0

1897 Season
4-2

October 9	MPA	0	Eggleston A.A.		8
October 19	MPA	0	University of Chicago		30

October 30	MPA	28	Lake Forest Academy	0
November 6	MPA	17	Northwestern Academy	0
November 10	MPA	6	University of Chicago Scrubs	0
November 20	MPA	21	Lewis Institute	0

1898 Season
4-1
Coaches F.R. Nichols and Harry Abells

October 8	MPA	45	Auburn Park A.C.	5
October 22	MPA	5	Lewis Institute	6
November 5	MPA	21	Armour Institute	0
November 16	MPA	18	University of Chicago (2nd team)	6
November 19	MPA	29	Lake Forest Academy	0

1899 Season
5-2
Coach F. R. Nichols

October 7	MPA	50	South Side Academy	0
October 14	MPA	0	University of Chicago (2nd team)	5
October 21	MPA	38	Central YMCA Training School	0
October 28	MPA	6	Lake Forest Academy	5
November 4	MPA	31	Northwestern Academy	2
November 11	MPA	22	Northwestern College	2
November 18	MPA	6	Culver M.A.	18

1900 Season
7-4-2
Coach Jonathan Webb

September 29	MPA	0	Morgan Park Town Team	0
October 6	MPA	5	Austin H.S.	11
October 13	MPA	0	St. Charles Athletics	5
October 17	MPA	57	YMCA Secretarial Institute	0
October 20	MPA	5	University of Chicago Scrubs	6
October 24	MPA	5	Bennett Medical College	5
October 27	MPA	12	Armour Institute	5
November 1	MPA	17	St. Ignatius College	0
November 3	MPA	24	Northwestern College	0
November 7	MPA	11	St. Vincent College	5
November 10	MPA	5	Lake Forest Academy	11
November 17	MPA	17	South Side Academy	12
November 24	MPA	24	Northwestern Academy	0

1901 Season
11-0-1
Coach Reuben M. Strong

September 25	MPA	15	Lake View H.S.	6
September 28	MPA	14	Normal Park A.A.	0
October 2	MPA	65	Austin H.S.	5
October 9	MPA	28	St. Viator College	0
October 16	MPA	29	Chicago Eclectic College	0
October 19	MPA	39	Armour Academy	0
October 26	MPA	11	East Aurora H.S.	0
November 2	MPA	28	Northwestern Academy	0
November 9	MPA	38	Lake Forest Academy	0
November 12	MPA	17	Chicago Dental College	5
November 23	MPA	0	University School of Cleveland	0
November 27	MPA	16	South Side Academy	0

1902 Season
8-3
Coaches August Holste and Fred Lowenthal

September 27	MPA	11	Morgan Park A.C.	0
October 8	MPA	12	Chicago Manual H.S.	0
October 11	MPA	10	University of Chicago Scrubs	5
October 15	MPA	24	Calumet H.S.	0
October 18	MPA	0	Northwestern College	11
October 25	MPA	10	Northwestern Academy	5
November 1	MPA	17	South Side Academy	18
November 5	MPA	35	Elgin Academy	0
November 8	MPA	10	Lake Forest Academy	11
November 12	MPA	11	Englewood H.S.	0
November 15	MPA	16	Armour Academy	5

1903 Season
2-3-3
Coaches John T. Lister and A.A. Stagg

September 23	MPA	26	Thornton H.S.	0
October 7	MPA	0	Englewood H.S.	0
October 22	MPA	0	St. Ignatius College	22
October 28	MPA	0	University of Chicago Scrubs	0
October 31	MPA	6	Hyde Park H.S.	0
November 7	MPA	6	Northwestern Academy	10
November 14	MPA	0	University H.S.	0
November 21	MPA	0	University School of Cleveland	16

1904 Season
6-0-2
Coaches Floyd Harper and John T. Lister

September 25	MPA	64	Thornton H.S.	0
September 28	MPA	5	Englewood H.S.	5
October 5	MPA	10	Hyde Park H.S.	0
October 8	MPA	0	Northwestern College	0
October 29	MPA	17	University of Chicago Frosh	0
November 3	MPA	41	Armour Academy	0
November 5	MPA	30	University School of Cleveland	0
November 18	MPA	57	University H.S.	0

1905 Season
8-2-1
Coach John T. Lister

September 23	MPA	33	Lake View H.S.	0
September 30	MPA	33	R.T. Crane H.S.	0
October 4	MPA	53	Englewood H.S.	0
October 7	MPA	10	Lake Forest College	0
October 14	MPA	6	Benton Harbor H.S.	10
October 21	MPA	51	Culver M.A.	5
October 28	MPA	0	St. John's M.A.	0
November 1	MPA	45	Elgin Academy	0
November 4	MPA	18	Northwestern Academy	6
November 11	MPA	4	University of Chicago Frosh	6
November 25	MPA	27	University School of Cleveland	0

1906 Season
9-0
Coach David Oberg

September 22	MPA	17	Thornton H.S.	0
September 26	MPA	24	Bloom H.S.	0
October 6	MPA	6	Elgin Academy	0
October 18	MPA	27	St. Ignatius College	0
October 20	MPA	18	Rockford H.S.	0
October 27	MPA	12	University School of Cleveland	0
November 3	MPA	27	Wendell Phillips H.S.	0
November 10	MPA	18	Culver M.A.	6
November 17	MPA	11	Lake Forest Academy	6

1907 Season
9-0

September 25	MPA	24	Morgan Park H.S.	0
October 2	MPA	4	University of Chicago Scrubs (EXH)	0

October 6	MPA	34	Bloom H.S.	0
October 9	MPA	67	Englewood H.S.	4
October 12	MPA	92	U.S. Cavalry (Fort Sheridan)	0
October 19	MPA	58	Chicago Veterinary College	0
November 2	MPA	10	Culver M.A.	5
November 9	MPA	24	St. John's M.A.	6
November 16	MPA	58	Lake Forest Academy	4
November 23	MPA	12	Grand Prairie Seminary	0

1908 Season
7-1
Coaches David Oberg and A.A. Stagg

October 3	MPA	53	Morgan Park Village	0
October 8	MPA	24	St. Ignatius College	0
October 16	MPA	12	Alumni	6
October 24	MPA	10	St. Viator College	0
October 28	MPA	5	Thornton H.S.	0
November 7	MPA	10	Culver M.A.	39
November 14	MPA	16	Grand Prairie Seminary	0
November 21	MPA	78	Evanston Academy	0

1909 Season
6-1
Coaches John Anderson and A.A. Stagg

October 2	MPA	45	Morgan Park Village	0
October 9	MPA	52	Chicago Veterinary College	0
October 16	MPA	52	Thornton H.S.	0
October 23	MPA	2	Culver M.A.	8
October 30	MPA	54	St. Viator College	0
November 13	MPA	52	Evanston Academy	0
November 20	MPA	90	Lake Forest Academy	0

1910 Season
6-0-1
Coaches John Anderson and A.A. Stagg

October 1	MPA	5	Morgan Park Village Team	0
October 8	MPA	9	St. Viator College	0
October 22	MPA	9	Oak Park H.S.	6
November 5	MPA	47	Chicago Veterinary College	0
November 14	MPA	25	Lake Forest Academy	0
November 19	MPA	0	Culver M.A.	0
November 26	MPA	6	Hinsdale H.S.	0

1911 Season
3-3
Coach John Anderson

September 30	MPA	18	Morgan Park H.S.	0
October 7	MPA	0	Stingers A.C.	15
October 21	MPA	22	Racine College	0
October 29	MPA	28	St. Viator College	0
November 11	MPA	6	Evanston Academy	10
November 18	MPA	0	Culver M.A.	32

1912 Season
2-4
Coach John Anderson

September 28	MPA	6	Morgan Park H.S.	0
October 8	MPA	19	University H.S.	7
October 21	MPA	0	Stingers A.C.	10
October 26	MPA	0	Rockford H.S.	33
November 9	MPA	6	Evanston Academy	14
November 23	MPA	0	Culver M.A.	54

1913 Season
Coach John Anderson
3-2-1

September 27	MPA	0	Morgan Park H.S.	0
October 4	MPA	41	Northwestern M.A.	6
October 11	MPA	0	University H.S.	32
November 1	MPA	12	Evanston Academy	19
November 5	MPA	70	Chicago Tech College	7
November 9	MPA	67	Marshall H.S.	0

1914 Season
4-4
Coaches Fred Herendeen and Roy Stephenson

October 3	MPA	9	Morgan Park H.S.	20
October 7	MPA	39	Lake H.S.	7
October 10	MPA	13	University H.S.	14
October 17	MPA	59	Deerfield H.S.	0
October 30	MPA	6	Lake Forest Academy	13
November 7	MPA	16	Loyola Academy	0
November 14	MPA	26	Northwestern M.A.	21
November 21	MPA	13	Culver M.A.	32

1915 Season
3-2
Coach David Stewart

October 2	MPA	18	Parker H.S.	3
October 9	MPA	0	LaGrange H.S.	55
October 23	MPA	9	Evanston Academy	67
November 13	MPA	31	Northwestern M.A.	7
November 20	MPA	7	Racine College	0

1916 Season
6-2
Coach David Stewart

September 30	MPA	38	Alumni	6
October 7	MPA	9	Lane Tech H.S.	0
October 14	MPA	12	Hyde Park H.S.	7
October 21	MPA	0	Keewatin Academy	12
October 30	MPA	31	University H.S.	7
November 4	MPA	0	Culver M.A.	32
November 18	MPA	40	Morgan Park H.S.	6
November 25	MPA	21	Northwestern M.A.	0

1917 Season
6-1
Coach Harry Schulte

October 6	MPA	41	Austin H.S.	0
October 17	MPA	33	Englewood H.S.	0
October 20	MPA	33	St. Rita College	7
October 25	MPA	13	St. Ignatius Academy	0
November 3	MPA	19	Morgan Park H.S.	7
November 10	MPA	24	Northwestern M.A.	13
November 17	MPA	14	Culver M.A.	47

1918 Season
0-2-1
Coach Otho Ling

October 5	MPMA	0	Morgan Park H.S.	0
November 2	MPMA	0	Lake Forest Academy	41
November 16	MPMA	0	Northwestern M. A.	6

1919 Season
7-4
Coach John Anderson

| September 27 | MPMA | 7 | Alumni | 19 |

October 4	MPMA	0	Lake View H.S.	12
October 8	MPMA	6	YMCA College	0
October 11	MPMA	13	Elgin Academy	0
October 15	MPMA	20	St. Rita College	0
October 18	MPMA	0	Lake Forest Academy	53
October 25	MPMA	57	St. Charles H.S.	7
November 1	MPMA	0	Bloom H.S.	32
November 8	MPMA	12	Northwestern M.A.	0
November 15	MPMA	7	St. Alban's Academy	0
November 22	MPMA	13	Morgan Park H.S.	0

1920 Season
5-1
Coach Floyd Fleming

September 8	MPMA	79	Blue Island H.S.	0
October 16	MPMA	6	Elgin Academy	0
October 30	MPMA	20	St. Alban's Academy	6
November 6	MPMA	14	Pullman Tech H.S.	0
November 13	MPMA	45	De LaSalle H.S.	0
November 20	MPMA	14	Northwestern M.A.	19

1921 Season
2-2-1
Coach Floyd Fleming

October 8	MPMA	0	Lindbloom H.S.	20
October 15	MPMA	0	St. Ignatius Academy	0
November 5	MPMA	20	St. Alban's Academy	13
November 12	MPMA	6	Elgin Academy	14
November 19	MPMA	40	Northwestern M.A.	0

1922 Season
3-2-3
Coaches Floyd Fleming

September 30	MPMA	0	De LaSalle H.S.	20
October 7	MPMA	7	St. Rita H.S.	7
October 14	MPMA	0	Lindbloom H.S.	35
October 21	MPMA	3	Loyola Academy	3
October 28	MPMA	25	St. Alban's Academy	7
November 4	MPMA	37	Pullman Tech H.S.	0
November 18	MPMA	7	Elgin Academy	0
November 25	MPMA	0	Northwestern M.A.	0

1923 Season
4-1-1
Coach Floyd Fleming

September 30	MPMA	0	St. Ignatius Academy	0
October 6	MPMA	0	Tilden H.S.	9
October 20	MPMA	31	Fenger H.S.	0
November 3	MPMA	41	St. Alban's Academy	0
November 17	MPMA	14	Elgin J.C.	7
November 24	MPMA	19	Northwestern M.A.	0

1924 Season
3-4-1
Coach Floyd Fleming

September 27	MPMA	6	Michigan City H.S.	6
October 1	MPMA	32	University H.S.	6
October 4	MPMA	0	Pullman Tech H.S.	13
October 25	MPMA	6	Danville H.S.	20
November 1	MPMA	14	St. Alban's Academy	6
November 8	MPMA	6	Bloom H.S.	16
November 15	MPMA	7	Elgin J.C.	25
November 22	MPMA	23	Northwestern M.A.	0

1925 Season
6-0
Coach Floyd Fleming

September 26	MPMA	7	Michigan City H.S.	0
October 10	MPMA	13	Pullman Tech H.S.	0
October 24	MPMA	34	Elmhurst Academy	0
October 31	MPMA	48	Latin H.S.	0
November 7	MPMA	30	St. Alban's Academy	0
November 21	MPMA	21	Northwestern M.A.	7

1926 Season
5-1-1
Coach Floyd Fleming

October 9	MPMA	20	Pullman Tech H.S.	6
October 16	MPMA	28	Onarga M.A.	0
October 23	MPMA	63	Elmhurst Academy	0
October 30	MPMA	0	Wayland Academy	7
November 6	MPMA	33	Howe M.A.	0
November 13	MPMA	0	St. Alban's Academy	0
November 20	MPMA	20	Northwestern M.A.	0

1927 Season
2-3-1
Coach Floyd Fleming and George Mahon

October 8	MPMA	7	Onarga M.A.	7
October 15	MPMA	12	Elgin Academy	27
October 29	MPMA	18	Howe M.A.	6
November 5	MPMA	6	Northwestern M.A.	19
November 12	MPMA	0	Wayland Academy	26
November 19	MPMA	20	St. Alban's Academy	6

1928 Season
4-4-1
Coach Floyd Fleming and George Mahon

October 3	MPMA	0	St. Aquinas Academy	0
October 6	MPMA	6	Mt. Carmel H.S.	13
October 13	MPMA	14	Wayland Academy	0
October 20	MPMA	0	Onarga M.A.	6
October 27	MPMA	25	Elgin Academy	0
November 3	MPMA	44	Northwestern M.A.	0
November 10	MPMA	7	Missouri M.A.	19
November 17	MPMA	24	Howe M.A.	0
November 24	MPMA	19	St. Alban's Academy	25

1929 Season
5-4-1
Coaches Floyd Fleming and George Mahon

September 28	MPMA	6	Loyola Academy	13
October 5	MPMA	7	Calumet H.S.	8
October 12	MPMA	13	Milwaukee University H.S.	7
October 19	MPMA	0	Onarga M.A.	0
October 26	MPMA	20	Chicago Harvard School	0
November 2	MPMA	10	Wayland Academy	0
November 9	MPMA	34	Northwestern M.A.	0
November 16	MPMA	0	Howe M.A.	18
November 23	MPMA	26	St. Alban's Academy	13
November 27	MPMA	0	Elgin Academy	6

1930 Season
5-3
Coaches Floyd Fleming and George Mahon

September 27	MPMA	0	Michigan City H.S.	19
October 4	MPMA	19	Milwaukee University H.S.	7
October 11	MPMA	0	Elgin Academy	19
October 18	MPMA	14	Wayland Academy	7

October 25	MPMA	6	Northwestern M.A.	0
November 1	MPMA	13	Onarga M.A.	6
November 15	MPMA	7	St. Alban's Academy	27
November 22	MPMA	13	Howe M.A.	6

1931 Season
3-2-2
Coach Floyd Fleming

September 26	MPMA	0	Michigan City H.S.	18
October 3	MPMA	0	Lake Forest Academy	13
October 10	MPMA	12	Onarga M.A.	0
October 16	MPMA	0	Wayland Academy	0
October 31	MPMA	34	St. Alban's Academy	0
November 7	MPMA	13	Elgin Academy	13
November 14	MPMA	12	Northwestern M.A.	0

1932 Season
2-6
Coach Floyd Fleming

October 1	MPMA	0	Pullman Tech H.S.	13
October 8	MPMA	0	Wayland Academy	3
October 15	MPMA	0	Onarga M.A.	26
October 22	MPMA	0	Lake Forest Academy	28
October 29	MPMA	6	St. Alban's Academy	7
November 5	MPMA	12	Elgin Academy	13
November 12	MPMA	20	Northwestern M.A.	0
November 19	MPMA	14	Alumni	0

1933 Season
8-3
Coach Wade Woodworth

September 30	MPMA	20	Calumet City H.S.	7
October 7	MPMA	19	Pullman Tech H.S.	13
October 14	MPMA	6	Morton H.S.	0
October 21	MPMA	7	Wayland Academy	2
October 28	MPMA	0	Lake Forest Academy	8
November 4	MPMA	0	Onarga M.A.	2
November 17	MPMA	7	Elgin Academy	0
November 18	MPMA	7	Culver M.A.	6
November 20	MPMA	20	St. Alban's Academy	6
November 25	MPMA	52	Northwestern M.A.	12
November 30	MPMA	6	Tilden H.S.	25

1934 Season
2-4
Coach Wade Woodworth

October 6	MPMA	0	Pullman Tech H.S.	18
October 20	MPMA	0	LaGrange H.S.	33
October 27	MPMA	12	Lake Forest Academy	6
November 3	MPMA	0	Onarga M.A.	18
November 10	MPMA	6	Elgin Academy	13
November 17	MPMA	28	Wayland Academy	6

1935 Season
3-6
Coach Claude Grigsby

September 28	MPMA	0	Blue Island H.S.	12
October 5	MPMA	0	Pleasant View Academy	13
October 12	MPMA	0	Pullman Tech H.S.	12
October 19	MPMA	20	Wayland Academy	6
October 26	MPMA	25	Lake Forest Academy	6
November 2	MPMA	14	Onarga M.A.	8
November 9	MPMA	6	Elgin Academy	20
November 16	MPMA	0	Culver M.A.	13
November 23	MPMA	0	Harrison H.S.	7

1936 Season
5-3-1
Coach Claude Grigsby

September 28	MPMA	6	Blue Island H.S.	0
October 3	MPMA	0	Pullman Tech H.S.	0
October 10	MPMA	31	Elgin Academy	0
October 17	MPMA	0	Lake Forest Academy	7
October 24	MPMA	59	St. Alban's Academy	0
October 31	MPMA	19	Onarga M.A.	6
November 7	MPMA	12	Calumet H.S.	0
November 14	MPMA	0	Culver M.A.	34
November 21	MPMA	0	St. John's M.A.	44

1937 Season
6-3
Coaches George Mahon and Henry Bollman

September 25	MPMA	6	Morgan Park J.C.	0
October 2	MPMA	6	Pullman Tech H.S.	9
October 9	MPMA	6	Elgin Academy	0
October 16	MPMA	12	Lake Forest Academy	13
October 23	MPMA	13	Howe M.A.	0

October 30	MPMA	13	Onarga M.A.	0
November 6	MPMA	27	Lemont H.S.	0
November 13	MPMA	25	Culver M.A.	7
November 20	MPMA	7	St. John's M.A.	20

1938 Season
5-2-2
Coaches: George Mahon and Henry Bollman

September 24	MPMA	7	Morgan Park J.C.	0
October 1	MPMA	0	Pullman Tech H.S.	27
October 8	MPMA	0	Lake Forest Academy	0
October 15	MPMA	7	Elgin Academy	0
October 22	MPMA	31	Howe M.A.	0
October 29	MPMA	0	Onarga M.A.	0
November 5	MPMA	12	Culver M.A.	14
November 12	MPMA	16	St. John's M.A.	7
November 19	MPMA	26	Marmion M.A.	12

1939 Season
Coaches: George Mahon and Henry Bollman
9-0

September 23	MPMA	2	Marmion M.A.	0
September 30	MPMA	13	Morgan Park J.C.	0
October 7	MPMA	19	Lake Forest Academy	7
October 14	MPMA	6	Onarga M.A.	0
October 21	MPMA	28	Pullman Tech H.S.	6
October 28	MPMA	24	St. John's M.A.	0
November 4	MPMA	33	Elgin Academy	6
November 11	MPMA	19	Culver M.A.	0
November 18	MPMA	13	St. Bede Academy	7

1940 Season
1-6
Coaches George Mahon and Henry Bollman

September 21	MPMA	0	Alumni(EXH)	13
September 28	MPMA	0	Loras Academy	14
October 5	MPMA	6	Onarga M.A.	7
October 12	MPMA	0	Lake Forest Academy	27
October 19	MPMA	13	Elgin Academy	0
November 2	MPMA	0	Culver M.A.	13
November 9	MPMA	7	St. John's M.A.	37
November 16	MPMA	7	Pullman Tech H.S.	21

1941 Season
2-6
Coaches George Mahon and Henry Bollman

September 20	MPMA	6	Alumni (EXH)	0
September 27	MPMA	0	Loras	7
October 4	MPMA	7	Lake Forest Academy	13
October 11	MPMA	6	Roosevelt M.A.	8
October 6	MPMA	0	Onarga M.A.	13
October 18	MPMA	18	Elgin Academy	13
October 25	MPMA	0	Culver M.A.	6
November 1	MPMA	6	Pullman Tech H.S.	0
November 15	MPMA	0	St. John's M.A.	33

1942 Season
3-6
Coach Maurice Bugbee

September 26	MPMA	0	Argo H.S.	25
October 3	MPMA	0	Marmion M.A.	6
October 10	MPMA	0	Roosevelt M.A.	9
October 17	MPMA	6	Onarga M.A.	0
October 24	MPMA	14	Elgin Academy	17
October 31	MPMA	0	Culver M.A.	13
November 7	MPMA	6	Pullman Tech H.S.	0
November 14	MPMA	13	St. John's M.A.	47
November 21	MPMA	20	Lake Forest Academy	0

1943 Season
4-3
Coaches James Marberry and George Mahon

October 5	MPMA	39	Lemont H.S.	6
October 9	MPMA	3	Roosevelt M.A.	0
October 16	MPMA	13	Onarga M.A.	12
October 23	MPMA	0	Lockport H.S.	33
October 30	MPMA	7	Chicago Vocational H.S.	13
November 6	MPMA	7	Pullman Tech H.S.	0
November 13	MPMA	0	St. John's M.A.	33

1944 Season
4-4
Coaches Joe Ziemba and George Mahon

September 23	MPMA	0	Argo H.S.	32
October 7	MPMA	6	Roosevelt M.A.	2
October 14	MPMA	34	Onarga M.A.	0
October 21	MPMA	20	Lockport H.S.	7

October 28	MPMA	0	Marmion M.A.	51
November 4	MPMA	12	Pullman Tech H.S.	19
November 11	MPMA	13	St. John's M.A.	38
November 18	MPMA	18	Chicago Vocational H.S.	12

1945 Season
4-4
Coaches Joe Ziemba and Gene Rodie

September 22	MPMA	18	Crete H.S.	0
September 29	MPMA	0	Argo H.S.	20
October 6	MPMA	31	Roosevelt M.A.	6
October 13	MPMA	34	Onarga M.A.	6
October 20	MPMA	6	Lockport H.S.	7
October 27	MPMA	6	Marmion M.A.	13
November 3	MPMA	7	Pullman Tech H.S.	6
November 10	MPMA	13	St. John's M.A.	27

1946 Season
7-1-1
Coaches Joe Ziemba and George Mahon

September 20	MPMA	19	Luther Institute H.S.	0
September 21	MPMA	48	Crete H.S.	0
September 28	MPMA	0	Argo H.S.	0
October 5	MPMA	45	Roosevelt M.A.	0
October 12	MPMA	24	Onarga M.A.	6
October 19	MPMA	12	Lockport H.S.	0
October 26	MPMA	38	Roosevelt M.A.	0
October 29	MPMA	19	De LaSalle (EXH)	13
November 2	MPMA	0	Pullman Tech H.S.	6
November 9	MPMA	20	St. John's M.A.	0

1947 Season
7-0-1
Coaches Joe Ziemba and George Mahon

September 19	MPMA	13	St. Charles H.S.	0
September 20	MPMA	33	Crete H.S.	0
October 4	MPMA	21	Howe M.A.	0
October 11	MPMA	33	Roosevelt M.A.	6
October 18	MPMA	7	Lockport H.S.	7
October 25	MPMA	18	Onarga M.A.	0
November 1	MPMA	13	Pullman Tech H.S.	0
November 8	MPMA	12	St. John's M.A.	6

1948 Season
6-2
Coaches Joe Ziemba and George Mahon

September 18	MPMA	7	St. Charles H.S.	13
September 25	MPMA	6	Joliet Catholic H.S.	0
October 2	MPMA	29	Howe M.A.	7
October 9	MPMA	19	Roosevelt M.A.	0
October 16	MPMA	27	Lockport H.S.	7
October 23	MPMA	31	Onarga M.A.	6
October 30	MPMA	12	Pullman Tech H.S.	14
November 13	MPMA	45	Glenwood School	0

1949 Season
7-1
Coaches Joe Ziemba and George Mahon

September 16	MPMA	7	South Shore H.S.	0
September 24	MPMA	19	Joliet Catholic H.S.	7
October 1	MPMA	13	Howe M.A.	0
October 8	MPMA	43	Roosevelt M.A.	6
October 14	MPMA	12	Niles H.S.	20
October 22	MPMA	25	Tuley H.S.	7
October 29	MPMA	38	Pullman Tech H.S.	0
November 5	MPMA	7	Blue Island H.S.	6

1950 Season
3-4-1
Coaches Joe Ziemba and Gene Rodie

September 15	MPMA	25	South Shore H.S.	19
September 22	MPMA	0	Niles H.S.	15
October 6	MPMA	0	Argo H.S.	12
October 14	MPMA	27	Waller H.S.	7
October 21	MPMA	26	Howe M.A.	6
October 28	MPMA	6	Joliet Catholic H.S.	26
November 3	MPMA	12	Blue Island H.S.	35
November 11	MPMA	12	Culver M.A.	12

1951 Season
1-8
Coaches Joe Ziemba and Gene Rodie

September 14	MPMA	6	Bowen H.S.	0
September 21	MPMA	0	South Shore H.S.	6
September 27	MPMA	0	Joliet Catholic H.S.	13
October 6	MPMA	7	Argo H.S.	19
October 13	MPMA	0	Culver M.A.	18

October 19	MPMA	12	Niles H.S.	14
October 27	MPMA	14	Waller H.S.	20
November 3	MPMA	0	Blue Island H.S.	7
November 9	MPMA	7	Reavis H.S.	19

1952 Season
3-4-2
Coaches Joe Ziemba and Gene Rodie

September 20	MPMA	28	Oak Lawn H.S.	7
September 27	MPMA	13	Joliet Catholic H.S.	26
October 3	MPMA	7	Lockport H.S.	7
October 11	MPMA	0	Culver M.A.	29
October 18	MPMA	0	Hammond Clark H.S.	21
October 24	MPMA	54	Oak Lawn H.S.	13
October 25	MPMA	34	Glenwood School	0
October 31	MPMA	6	Blue Island H.S.	35
November 8	MPMA	0	Reavis H.S.	0

1953 Season
4-3-2
Coaches Joe Ziemba and Leland Dickinson

September 26	MPMA	38	Rich Township H.S.	26
October 3	MPMA	20	Oak Lawn H.S.	6
October 10	MPMA	7	Culver M.A.	13
October 17	MPMA	6	Hammond Clark H.S.	14
October 23	MPMA	12	Oak Lawn H.S.	0
October 24	MPMA	46	Bremen H.S.	6
October 31	MPMA	6	St. John's M.A.	6
November 7	MPMA	0	Maryville Academy	0
November 13	MPMA	6	Reavis H.S.	21

1954 Season
4-5
Coaches Joe Ziemba and Leland Dickinson

September 17	MPMA	13	Lemont H.S.	6
September 24	MPMA	6	Rich Township H.S.	13
October 1	MPMA	6	Oak Lawn H.S.	13
October 9	MPMA	0	Culver M.A.	32
October 16	MPMA	13	Carl Sandburg H.S.	2
October 21	MPMA	6	Bowen H.S.	0
October 30	MPMA	0	St. John's M.A.	41
November 6	MPMA	8	Maryville Academy	6
November 13	MPMA	6	Reavis H.S.	19

1955 Season
1-8
Coaches Richard Boya and Jack Gifford

September 17	MPMA	13	Lemont H.S.	14
September 24	MPMA	0	Maryville Academy	18
October 1	MPMA	12	Rich Township H.S.	14
October 8	MPMA	7	Culver M.A.	27
October 15	MPMA	20	Evergreen Park H.S.	6
October 22	MPMA	7	Oak Lawn H.S.	20
October 29	MPMA	6	Carl Sandburg H.S.	14
November 5	MPMA	7	St. John's M.A.	15
November 12	MPMA	0	Reavis H.S.	19

1956 Season
3-5
Coaches Al Bloomer and Jack Gifford

September 15	MPMA	21	Maryville Academy	27
September 22	MPMA	6	Rich Township H.S.	16
September 28	MPMA	13	Hyde Park H.S.	6
October 6	MPMA	7	Culver M.A.	27
October 13	MPMA	0	Oak Lawn H.S.	32
October 20	MPMA	9	Carl Sandburg H.S.	6
October 27	MPMA	33	Elmwood Park H.S.	7
November 3	MPMA	19	St. John's M.A.	27

1957 Season
3-4-1
Coaches Al Bloomer and Bill Earle

September 14	MPMA	20	Maryville Academy	0
September 21	MPMA	13	Luther South H.S.	6
September 27	MPMA	7	Reavis H.S.	7
October 5	MPMA	6	Culver M.A.	37
October 11	MPMA	0	Oak Lawn H.S.	21
October 19	MPMA	13	Carl Sandburg H.S.	30
October 26	MPMA	2	Elmwood Park H.S.	14
November 1	MPMA	14	Lemont H.S.	0

1958 Season
5-3
Coaches Bill Earle and Joe Ziemba

September 13	MPMA	6	Maryville Academy	13
September 20	MPMA	27	Luther South H.S.	7
September 27	MPMA	7	Luther North H.S.	0
October 4	MPMA	0	Culver M.A.	20

October 10	MPMA	7	Parker H.S.		6
October 18	MPMA	18	Lincoln-Way H.S.		6
October 25	MPMA	7	Notre Dame H.S.		27
November 1	MPMA	24	Lemont H.S.		18

MORGAN PARK MILITARY ACADEMY
FOOTBALL COACHING RECORDS

COACH   WON-LOST-TIED
(No coach from 1893-1894)

H. W. Dickinson
1895   6-2
(No coach from 1896-1897)

F.R. Nichols
1898   4-1
1899   5-2
Career Total   9-3

Jonathan Webb
1900   7-4-2

Reuben Strong
1901   11-0-1

August Holste
1902   8-3

John T. Lister
1903   2-3-3
1905   7-2-1
Career Total   9-5-4

Floyd Harper
1904   6-0-2

David Oberg
1906   9-0
1908   7-1
Career Total   16-1
(No coach in 1907)

John Anderson
1909   6-1
1910   6-0-1
1911   3-3
1912   2-4
1913   3-2-1

1919   7-4
Career Total   27-14-2

Fred Herendeen
1914   4-4

David Stewart
1915   3-2
1916   6-2
Career Total   9-4

Harry Schulte
1917   6-1

Otho Ling
1918   0-2-1

Floyd Fleming
1920   5-1
1921   2-2-1
1922   3-2-3
1923   4-1-1
1924   3-4-1
1925   6-0
1926   5-1-1
1927   2-3-1
1928   4-4-1
1929   5-4-1
1930   5-3
1931   3-2-2
1932   2-6
Career Total   49-33-12

Wade Woodworth
1933   8-3
1934   2-4
Career Total   10-7

Claude Grisby		1946	7-1-1
1935	3-6
1936	5-3-1
Career Total	8-9-1

Claude Grisby
1935 — 3-6
1936 — 5-3-1
Career Total — 8-9-1

George Mahon
1937 — 6-3
1938 — 5-2-2
1939 — 9-0
1940 — 1-6
1941 — 2-6
Career Total — 23-17-2

Maurice Bugbee
1942 — 3-6

James Marberry
1943 — 4-3

Joe Ziemba
1944 — 4-4
1945 — 4-4

1946 — 7-1-1
1947 — 7-0-1
1948 — 6-2
1949 — 7-1
1950 — 3-4-1
1951 — 1-8
1952 — 3-4-2
1953 — 4-3-2
1954 — 4-5
Career Total — 50-36-7

Richard Boya
1955 — 1-8

Al Bloomer
1956 — 3-5
1957 — 3-4-1
Career Total — 6-9-1

Bill Earle
1958 — 5-3

MORGAN PARK MILITARY ACADEMY FOOTBALL ROSTERS

Rosters were compiled primarily through Academy yearbooks and newspapers, along with various metropolitan newspapers that covered the Academy football games. Generally, in these older publications, only last names are provided for players. As such, first initials are included here when two or more players have the same last name.

1894
Terpenny, Gustavson, Johnson, Bogert, Webb, Hale, Johnson, R.P., Dickie, Bell, Cleveland, Taylor.

1895
Bell, Dickson, Webb, Dewey, Green, Holste, Smith, Richards, Stevenson, Fulton, Ewing, De Lombre, Mc Alpine, Bogert, Johnson, Richards, Mann.

1896
De Lombre, Smith, Clark, Riley, Speed, McNabb, Ellsworth, Strauss, Riley, B., Morton, Mann, Stevenson, Wilcox, Murphy, Freeman, Walters.

1897
Smith, Boder, Stuart, Green, Harris, De Sombre, Rankin, Edwards, McNab, Ewing, Stephenson.

1898
Walker, Harper, Geddes, Eicher, Shryver, Dickson, McNab, Sittig, Horton, Nuckola, Smith, Brinton, Maloney.

1899
Freeman, Oberg, Dickinson, Paddock, Reniff, Preston, Schnur, Morgan, Ellsworth, Schryver, Nichols, Schroeder, Beckett, Lodge, Brinton, Pratt.

1900
Mefford, Middleton, Oberg, Berquist, Schnur, Cobb, Oliver, Miner, Wier, Paddock, Meech, Lodge, Mendenhall, Harper, Walters.

1901
Mefford, Newburn, Haight, Neville, Oberg, A. Lodge, W. Lodge, Flynn, Walters, Mendenhall, Schnur, Oliver, Cobb, Harper, Miner, McClure,

Stahl, McKessey, Marsh, McIntosh, Wheeler, Kerr, Miller, Eppert, Carroll, Bosley, Rexner, Kahn.

1902
Newburn, Oliver, Strauss, Haight, Simmons, Zeiss, McCaffery, Schober, Flynn, Miller, Cobb, Wrigley, Willis, Bennison, Oberg, McConoughy.

1903
A. Strauss, H. Strauss, Carter, Johnson, Stokey, Zeiss, Falk, Phillips, Brewer, Wrigley, Rixner, McKinley, Nicar, Smith, Garrett, Newburn, Donnelly.

1904
Wrigley, Garrett, Williamson, Baker, Chitwood, Falk, Benbrook, Donnelly, Thomas, Pearse, Stevens, Wallace, Leonard, Johnson, Berquist, Judy, Green, McKinley, Oughton.

1905
Stevens, Donnelly, Chamberlin, Ware, Palmer, Benbrook, Thomas, Deremer, Weldon, Wedow, Garrett, Falk, Baker, Freeze, Risser, Needham.

1906
McCarty, Patton, Spoons, Welch, Hill, Kenipley, Shastid, Needham, Beck, Tompkins, Beeman, Wedow, Robinson, Chamberlain, Risser, Bunker, Watts, Marshall, Weldon, Young.

1907
Frey, Gamman, Sauer, Prather, Gerend, Monroe, Stephenson, W. Robinson, Allen, A. Robinson, Devore, Berner, Stanley, Van Wilser, Vale, Thomas.

1908
Stephenson, Spoonts, Armstrong, R. Marr, Startzman, Frey, Smith, Radford, Berner, Kenfield, Robinson, Mills, Williams, Catron, W. Marr, Springgate, Cotter, Van Velzer.

1909
Kenfield, Reynolds, Hazlett, Wade, Herendeen, R. Marr, W. Marr, Radford, Couchman, Stephenson, Lockhart, Hubert, Nichols, Beckwith, Startzman, Pease.

1910
Herendeen, Westberg, Hazlett., Wade, Healy, Marr, Beckwith, Kenfield, Lanyon, Couchman,

Hubert, Wayte, Houghton, Schultze, Nichols, Dick, Wells, Shaw, Reinecke.

1911
Wade, Wayte, Schultze, Carson, Gebo, F., Coyle, Gunkel, Stevens, Erickson, Hazlett, Herendeen, Boyd, Sheperd, Wilce, Purdy, Brown, Kirkpatrick, Ruehl, McCausland, Anderson, Chalmers, Hunter, Upton, Francis, Herriott, Gebo, C., Drennan, Patrick.

1912
Anderson, Traynor, Parker, Kirkpatrick, Shepherd, Boyd, Wade, Brown, Carson, Muench, Houghton, Stevens, C., Stevens, E., Ruehl, Atwater, Herriott, Skeele Truesdell.

1913
Shepherd, Rattenbury, Parker, Truesdell, Cleveland, McFarlin, Stockhausen, Ruehl, Fisk, Fryer, Collins, Kepperling, Wagner, Pitts, J., Pitts, W., James.

1914
Stevens, Pitts, J., Tetzlaff, Truesdell, Pitts, W., Shepherd, McFarlin, Wagner, James, Fryer, Eissler, Muench, Coyle, Harvey, Flesher, Marhoefer.

1915
Fryer, Wagner, Curtis, A., Harvey, Hansen, Hullinger, Tetzlaff, A., Weess, Tetzlaff, G., Allen, Rattenbury, Hunter, Curtis, M.

1916
Tetzlaff, A., Jones, George, McDonald, Wirick, Hansen, M., Beedy, Tetzlaff, G., Hansen, E., Allen, Curtis, Nichols, Gorham, Meents.

1917
Wiring, Curtis, George, Hansen, Booth, Jones, Nichols, Gates, Moore, Truitt, Orr, Loeffler, Bullington, Olson, Blake, Rounseville, Iten, Thornton, Cottrell.

1918
Eidson, Taylor, Egbert, Hansen, Loeffler, Simpson, Iten, Dane, Gorham, Nichols, Sopkin, Frank, Walter, Mueller.

1919
Wolf, Kelly, Kings, Dyer, Walter, Rusnak, Neeley, Ferris, Paul, Iten, Cottrell, Sopkin, Gorham,

Simpson, Blake, Amsler, Godfrey, Nichols, Egbert, Frank.

1920

Arnold, Amsler, Blake, Gordon, Channon, Combs, Hamar, Horn, Kanter, Kreglow, O'Mara, Terman, Sopkin, Gorham, Herendeen, Wells, Clark, Ebert, Brassard, Wills, Crooks, Powell.

1921

Bear, Smith, Horn, Bouma, McManus, Mains, Kanter, McKinney, Farwell, Arnold, Pierce, Ambrose, Tackett, Clemmer, Sopkin, Terman, Schmitz, Vary, Crooks, Gorden, Schmitz.

1922

McKinney, Wheeler, Nelson, Reeser, Rittenhouse, Benko, Mains, Vary, Bouma, Hanson, Kracko, Bain, Soper, Clark, Holmes, Arnold, Annenberg, Clemmer, Null, Gear, Wilkins, Kelly, Binkley, Terman, Schmitz

1923

Droegemueller, Benko, Cass, Clark, Curtis, Garen, McAfee, Kelly, Nelson, Null, Ollier, Schmitz, Stevens, Stransky, Wickman, Wheeler, Frank, Rittenhouse, Arnold, Soper, Bain, Bates, Callahan, Drake, Hiller, Schnable, Sherwood, Cole, Stuart.

1924

Cass, Wiswell, Bain, Ollier, Stransky, Wrightsman, Stewart, Pond, Nelson, Garen, Cole, Miller, Beiles, Drake, Sullivan, Slayton, Arnold, Price, Wickman, Hart, Kelly, Mills, McAfee, Wortham, Palermo, Hathaway.

1925

Wrightsman, Goglin, Ollier, Horlock, Verbicka, Sullivan, Burdick, Sinclair, Arnold, Kelly, Schottler, Wortham, Cass, Korten, Hiller, Robinson.

1926

Korten, Drake, Hart, Brusa, Evans, Dare, Kiskaddon, Arnold, Wenger, Sinclair, Olson, Soper, Lutomski, Atwell, Richardson, Goglin, Booth, Kiddoo, Bood, Oster, Herring, Wagner, Carlson, Stuart, Lentz, Schnur, Hapeman, Bouma, Knauff, Bowman, Cabrera, Barber, Vogel, Schmidt, Qualkinbush.

1927

Bouma, Goglin, Klaus, Kiddoo, Wallace, Knauff, Atwell, Hodges, Cabrera, Brown, Lentz, Beinarauskis, Christie, Chapp, Carlson, Scanlon, Grundstrom, Maneely, Hansen, Wagner, Thomas, Schmidt, Cohen, Bergstrom, Qualkinbush, Schnur, Vogel, Nelson, Bood, Bell.

1928

Bouma, Cabrera, Orme, Klaus, Wortham, Sinclair, Wallace, Schnur, Collins, Bergstrom, Beinerauskas, P. Vogel, Bennett, Leatzow, Rosenberg, Hansen, Maneely, Ribbentrop, Wagner, Garen, Freeman, Novak, Miller, Scanlon, Loeffler, Qualkinbush, Wiegman, Larsen, Gauselin, Horst, Johannes, Bowman, Gundrum, Wagenseller, Goes, Wiegel, S. Vogel.

1929

Slama, Loeffler, R. Freeman, W. Freeman, Hutchins, Wiegel, Nelson, Willis, Tennyson, Wiegman, Hansen, Miller, Maneely, Bouma, Thrasher, Sinclair, Wagonseller, Feil, White, Richards, Hauert, Larsen, Allen, Kuss, Graver, Ribbentrop, W. Smith, Novak, Goes, Carlson, Feehery, Lowry, C. Smith, St. John, Norton, Clerk, Furmaniak, Vogel, Hesler, Fredenberger, Haas.

1930

Watkins, Kidder, Wagonseller, Freeman, Hansen, Ribbentrop, Sinclair, Graver, Nelson, Fischer, Leake, Norton, Keller, Caruso, Kozel, Furmaniak, Innes, Willis, Goes, Feil, Frank, Tennyson, King, Bennett, McRaith, McKague, Gilmore, Novak, Philipski, Rosicky, Swade, Vogel, Lavery, Lyman, Richards.

1931

Redmond, Kirn, Haas, McHugh, Carlson, Kornstein, Keller, See, Leake, Pontarelli, Norton, Smith, Slama, Psik, Brekke, Meadows, Wagenseller, Bennett, Jakubowski, Richards, Willis, Swade, Kozel, Graver, Morgan, Furmaniak, Boies, Scholler, Caruso.

1932

Barish, Dennis, Oberman, Mower, Bailen, Heitman, Carlson, Pontarelli, Tomczak, Pilkis, Keller, Meadows, Willis, Arcus, Brennan, Richards, Habich, Scholler, McHugh, Swade, Hokin, Vogl, Psik, Paulsen, Brekke.

1933

Slader, Tomczak, Zinter, Braatch, Mudra, Schuber, Saab, Maloy, Orr, Moehling, McClure, Stout, Schoening, Bailen, Barish, Haas, See, Blagetz, Schaps, Miller, Carlson, Heitman, Psik, Pilkis, Goes.

1934

A. Tomczak, R. Tomczak, Heitman, Orr, Schuber, Cannon, Howland, Brinker, Martin, Miles, Krueger, Meskis, Briney, J. Geneser, Leatzow, Do Mato, Carnes, Plitt, Maloy, Fosco, J. Moehling, E. Moehling, McClure, Mudra, Roberts, W. Geneser.

1935

Monaco, Roberts, Martin, Reichel, A. Tomczak, R. Tomczak, Schauer, Howland, K. Krichbaum, Dewey, Plitt, Schreyer, Moehling, Ritter, Miles, Howell, Price, Hillier, Noble, Geneser, Pallotto, Fosco, Johnson, Leatzow, Harrison, Rathje, Reid, Warden, MacLane, K. Krichbaum, Burny, Cerny.

1936

Krichbaum, Cerny, Harrison, Martin, Monaco, Grest, Rathje, Roberts, MacLane, Maxon, Baracree, Tobin, Clark, Price, O., Wehrheim, Raymond, Suthers, A. Johnson, Leatzow, McConnell, Van Dellen, Miller, Howell, Hillier, Ostrowski, G. Johnson, Burny, Hojnacki, Wax, Moore, Lane, Anderson, Price, I., Eagan, Castles, Morley.

1937

G. Johnson, G. Moore, Anderson, McConnell, A. Johnson, Leatzow, Suthers, Ostrowski, Duval, Duncan, J. Moore, Long, Kern, Mayhew, Trossman, Stuart, Van Dellen, Piper, Lane, Wynd, Shiplock, Glen, Bendinelli, Bacon, Morely, White, Plitt, Mackler, McClenathan, Devereaux.

1938

Fosco, Ranstead, Plitt, Bendinelli, Trossman, W. Stuart, Miller, Devereaux, Lane Shiplock, Berkery, Rinella, Allen, Richards, Sullivan, Tierney, Brooks, S. Stuart, Weckel, Kerns, Brown, Sexauer, Ault, Fisher, Flott, Kralovec, Corrigan, Heda, Waggoner, Wilson, Martin, Hurlbut.

1939

Berkery, Weckel, Fosco, Plitt, Martin, Richards, Ranstead, Allen, Kerns, Wynd, Guderyhan, Correll, Moore, Zientara, Stuart, Waggoner, Sexauer, McCarthy, Weber, Schissler, Skarin, Corrigan, Engleman, Burney, Kelly, Burke, Matlin, Taylor, Glasebrook, Hostetter, Sterner, Bohnett, Tibbles.

1940

Kelly, Burny, Weber, Skarin, McCarthy, Stebner, Engelman, Gardiner, Crowley, Stompanato, Grossberg, Booth, Washburne, O'Donnell, Froemke, Gilbert, Price, Stow, Parchman, L., Parchman, R., Kruger, Drury, Timpe, Hall, Forester, Spong, Hutchins, Baxter, Caley, Bohnett, Gans, Getz, Margraf, Forbes, Blew, Hunter, Glasebrook, Meyer, Byrne, Gemeinhardt, Deveney.

1941

Parchman, L., Parchman, R., Hall, O., Hall, C., Skarin, Blew, Gans, Stefanos, Booth, Badziong, Hutchins, Caley, Gemeinhardt, Gilbert, Crowley, Duchossois, Thrall, Kalafut, Major, Freund, French, Curme, O'Donnell, Froemke, Blazina, Splittstoesser, McHugh, Jaques, Doney, Barry, Garretson, Spence, Hintz, Fenton.

1942

Major, Hall, Parchman, McHugh, F., Gans, Blew, Barry, Doney, Blazina, Thrall, Everett, Cure, Koren, Whitney, Rubin, Prignano, Cox, Carter, Dodd, Schaudt, Leeming, Skarin, Frank, Marzullo, McHugh, J., Bacon, Sterba, Jacobs, Kopecky, Pardee, Gartleman.

1943

Dodd, Gilbert, Rubin, Doney, Bacon, Hall, Parchman, Thrall, Prignano, Schaudt, Cihak, Gartelman, Brittain, Coppin, Frank, Tonney, Christopherson, Limperis, Economos, Opitz, Tiernan, Sharp, Carter, LaPlante, Fischer, Flott, Rich, McHugh, Price, Rasmussen, Matherly, Eng, Olson, Marshall, Rogers.

1944

Kreger, Flott, Koren, Marshall, Skarin, Limperis, Gilbert, Smith, Williford, O'Brien, Berliner, Hammerstrom, Jicha, Largura, Barnes, Krumdick, Allen, Freberg, Hendricks, Economos, Tiernan, Bowyer, Galligan.

1945

Dabbert, Nelson, Hendren, Busbey, McGuire, Krumdick, R., Truesdell, Pronger, Walton, Shetler, Sunny, Simon, MacKimm, Mahon, Baldassari, Boyle, Gardner, Nightingale, Tuffs,

Meier, Pribanich, Aberson, Freberg, Pratt, Hendricks, Heitschmidt, Wasick, Williford, Bowyer, Kreger, Eden, Allen, Jicha, O'Brien, Tiernan, Fitzpatrick, Barnes, Milton, Carlson, Kling, MacDonald, Krumdick, V.

1946

Aberson, Adams, Andreasen, Baldassari, Busbey, Carlson, Caruso, Dabbert, Daisley, Eden, Fidler, Fitzpatrick, Gardner, Kusciolek, George, Gustafson, Heitschmidt, Howland, Hunt, Jicha, Kreger, Landon, Mahon, McCormack, McGuire, Meier, Milton, Nishkian, Nelson, K., Nelson, L., Nightingale, O'Brien, Peterson, Pratt, Pribanich, Schuldt, Tiernan, Vehmeyer, Williford, Wolniak.

1947

Kosciolek, Wolniak, Tuffs, Baldassari, Heitschmidt, Tiernan, Wasick, McGuire, Wilkin, Daisley, Nelson, K., Fidler, Nishkian, Gustafson, Beckman, Hraback, Landon, Nelson, L., Caruso, Drelles, Kaak, Howland, Lucido, Schuldt, Giannos, Alcock, Gruenwald, Koberna, Bennett, Liptak, Hilger, George, Hunt, Stark, Daly, Ditzler, Cass, Wolniak.

1948

Serventi, Paul, Voss, Ditzler, Mehan, Wiegel, Hofman, Koberna, Hunt, Drelles, Giannos, Wolniak, Gruenwald, George, Wilkin, Bouma, Beckman, Michale, Buechner, Hraback, Hilger, Wolff, Cappas, Forres, Lucido, Cantele, Elliott, DeGrandpre, Kaak, Neri, Buckley, Leventis, Fleming, Hartman, Fidler, MacKimm.

1949

Richards, Wiegel, Paul, Serventi, Hofman, Mehan, MacKimm, Maier, Michale, Kaak, Lucido, Leventis, Beckman, Buechner, Cappas, Forres, Hammond, Burd, Kahoun, Frank, Lovejoy, Elsner, Bouma, Krueger, DeGrandpre, Elliott, Voss, Nelson, White, Quist, Ruck, Hartman, Pitt, Cantele, Dargis.

1950

Hammond, Quist, Pitt, Cantele, Kahoun, Lovejoy, Dargis, Hirtz, Gamble, Heyna, Allen, Colby, Bauer, Melin, Jerit, Tierney, Larsen, Cresap, Jolly, Stutts, Berezny, Miniat, Elsner, Burd, Richard, Bort, Casey, Westenberger, Sweeney.

1951

Quist, Simi, Jolly, Sineni, R., Sineni, W., Zaferopulos, Voornas, Tipton, Sweeney, Poullman, Bandyk, Craske, Burd, Krizenecky, Leimnetzer, Helminski, Pepper, Cresap, Gapszewicz, Westenberger, Duffek, Gislason, Iglow, Jerit, Palotto, Mazik, Stutts, Casey, Kennedy, Tierney, Boyd, Lonergan, Dybalski, Gianacopoulos, Colby, Boex, Keating, Bauer, Karzas, Young, Larsen, Berezny.

1952

Martinez, Dina, Freed, Gilbert, Martinec, Zaferopulos, Mahon, Peterson, Riggs, McWhorter, Simi, Sineni, Leonard, Pepper, Darabaris, Craske, Larsen, Zedeno, Poullman, Eigelberner, Skontos, Voss, Mazik, Lonergan, Westenberger, Iglow, Karzas, Keating, Sadd, Dybalski, Brown, Gislason, Boyd, Criffield, Duffek.

1953

Manelli, Anderson, Peterson, Bingen, Kasotakis, Riggs, Markiewicz, Hodonos, Dina, Gear, Mahon, Freed, Gilbert, Viscount, Klein, Pipin, Taradash, Krivsky, Eigelberner, Hartman, Loomis, Rusgis, Jaffe, Stokes, Grundstrom, Frigo, Noorlag, Lang, MacDonald, Fischer, Voss, Zaccari.

1954

Faure, Klein, H., Kasotakis, Swank, Klein, H., Klein, K., Canfield, Scruggs, Martinec, DeGeorge, Rosi, P., Grice, Voss, Hodonos, Fischer, Pipin, Viscount, Manelli, Lavery, Zielinski, Gialamos, Martin, Herriott, Sergeant, Loomis, Lipe, Lasson, Cinotto, Krivsky, Grundstrom, Lang, Taradash, Noorlag, Gallagher, Fischer, MacDonald, Kasotakis, Rusgis, Frank.

1955

Klein, K., Scruggs, Blackmore, Bastis, Regan, Zielinski, Madsen, Ferris, Vesely, Krivsky, Fricke, Grice, Ellis, Hall, Canfield, Swank, Klein, K., Bowden, Bauer, Pappas, Rusgis, Cinotto, Vernon, Vitkus, Herriott, Gallagher, Sergeant, Frank, Hart, Hendricks, Swank, Lasson, Aitchison.

1956

Buol, Witt, Madsen, Mack, Johnson, Leatzow, Condos, Luetgert, Chrzanowski, Havle, Milonas, Stengele, Bowden, Vesely, Widen, Bastis, Lenzi, Hall, Aitchison, Fry, Ferris, Fricke, Vernon, Bauer, Selva, Kiskaddon, Vitkus, Pappas, Ellis, Rupp, Nieburger, Orr, Mateer, Ahearn, Cano.

1957

Matray, Wirth, Amadio, Ellis, Gaetano, Castellanos, Havle, Haven, Witt, Cano, Luetgert, Skonberg, Savich, Leatzow, Rosi, Blitz, Mack, Caravette, Lenzi, Ferris, Timmons, Duzansky, Lang, Ponzo, Cleary, Malysa, Bartush, Orr, Djikas, Marogol.

1958

Solano, Wirth, Barton, Castellanos, Blitz, Chouvalis, Amadio, Bouramas, Gifford, Woodworth, Glesener, Karstrom, Karas, Savich, Rosi, Krysti, Djikas, P.J., Djikas, P.L., Matray, Ferris, Lenzi, Gaetano, Sappenfield, Timmons, Ponzo, Cleary, Lang, Abbott, Schloesser, Haven.

OLD RIVALRIES: UPDATES ON MILITARY SCHOOLS AND OTHER EARLY OPPONENTS

Military schools, like boarding schools, are largely forgotten in the 21st century. Although a few of those institutions remain, public and private "day" high schools are much more prominent today. While not all of Morgan Park Military Academy's football opponents were military schools, many of the early prep rivals are now gone or have transitioned to meet the needs of the current high school students in their respective areas. The following summaries and updates of several of the Academy's former opponents were derived from newspaper accounts, school web sites, or other resources.

Bowen High School (Chicago, Illinois)
Founded in 1882, Bowen High School still exists on the south side of Chicago, but with an enrollment of under 400. Key alumni include drummer Gene Krupa, major league pitcher Eli Grba, recording star Joni James, and film director Andrew Davis.

Chicago Calumet High School (Chicago, Illinois)
Calumet opened its doors in 1889 as Calumet Township High School before becoming part of the Chicago Public

School system in 1900. Calumet High School was closed in 2006 and the campus is now known as the Perspectives Charter School--Calumet Campus.

Culver Military Academy (Culver, Indiana)
Culver Military Academy was established in 1894 as a military school for boys. Females were admitted in 1971 and the campus is now known as the Culver Academies which includes Culver Military Academy (CMA) for boys, Culver Girls Academy (CGA), and the Culver Summer Schools and Camps (CSSC). Its rich football tradition continues to this day. Included among the more prominent graduates are Bud Adams, owner of the Tennessee Titans of the National Football league; Frank Batten, founder of the Weather Channel; country music star Dierks Bentley; actor Hal Holbrook; Lamar Hunt, founder of the NFL's Kansas City Chiefs; Roger Penske, owner of the Penske Corporation; George Steinbrenner, former owner of New York Yankees; and comedian Jonathan Winters.

Elgin Academy (Elgin, Illinois)
Elgin Academy can trace its origins back to 1839 when it was chartered. The first campus building was opened in 1856. While the boarding school option was not offered after 1987, the school continues to thrive today as both a grade school and high school. One of its most visible alumni members is Jimmy John Liautaud, owner and founder of Jimmy John's Gourmet Sandwiches.

Englewood High School (Chicago, Illinois)
One of the earliest football rivals of the Academy was Englewood High School in Chicago which opened in 1873. While the school closed in 2008, the old Englewood building is utilized today for two separate schools: Urban Prep Academy (a public charter high school for boys) and TEAM Englewood (a public coed charter school). Englewood High School left us with some very well-known alumni such as Gwendolyn Brooks, a Pulitzer Prize winner and the Poet Laureate of Illinois; singer Gene Chandler («Duke of Earl"); playwright Lorraine Hansberry, author of **A Raisin in the Sun**; Robert Henry Lawrence, Jr., the first African American astronaut; and Robert W. Maxwell, a football player and coach after whom the Maxwell Football Club and the Maxwell Trophy are named.

Glenwood Academy (Glenwood, Illinois)
Originally founded as the Illinois Industrial Training School for Boys in Norwood Park, Illinois in 1887, the school moved to Glenwood, Illinois in 1890. One of the original supporters of the institution was Robert Todd Lincoln, son of President Abraham Lincoln. Today, Glenwood Academy is a boarding school for approximately 150 coeducational students in grades 3-8.

Howe Military Academy (Howe, Indiana)
Howe Military Academy continues to serve grades 7-12 on its campus in northeast Indiana. Howe is both private and coeducational. It was started in 1884 as Howe Grammar School before being named Howe Military Academy.

Lake Forest Academy (Lake Forest, Illinois)
Lake Forest Academy has flourished in recent years, especially after a merger with nearby Ferry Hall School in 1974 which allowed the combined institute to become coeducational. The Academy was founded in 1857 as a boy's prep school…and football still plays a major role in the school's extracurricular activities. There are many successful alumni of the merged schools including actress Jean Harlow; actor McLean Stevenson; James Aubrey one-time president of both CBS and MGM; Louis Upton, co-founder of the Whirlpool Corporation; and Charles H. Wacker, chairman of the Chicago Plan Commission (Wacker Drive in Chicago is named after him).

Maryville Academy (Des Plaines, Illinois)
Now in its 135th year (2018) Maryville Academy serves abused children at several locations, including its main campus in Des Plaines, Illinois. Rock musician Peter Townshend of The Who

has been a significant fund-raiser for Maryville in recent years. The school no longer offers boarding opportunities, or football, for its students.

Northwestern Military Academy (Lake Geneva, Wisconsin)

Northwestern Military Academy was founded in 1888 by Harlan Davidson, the former superintendent at Morgan Park Military Academy. The Academy's first location was in Highland Park, Illinois before moving to Lake Geneva, Wisconsin in 1915, becoming Northwestern Military and Naval Academy. It later merged with St. John's Military Academy (Delafield, WI) in 1995. Among its key alumni are actor Spencer Tracy and Major Art Wermuth, known as the "One-Man Army of Bataan" for his heroism during WW II.

Onarga Military Academy (Onarga, Illinois)

One of the oldest schools in the Midwest, Onarga began as Grand Prairie Seminary in 1863. By 1917, it had evolved into Onarga Military Academy until closing in 1972.

Pullman Tech High School (Chicago, Illinois)

Pullman Tech was virtually a neighborhood rival of the Academy football team since it was located a short drive east of Morgan Park. The school was opened in 1915 and closed in 1950. However, its building has been used since that time as Mendel Catholic High School, St. Martin de Porres, Unity Catholic, and Willibrord. It is now known as the Gwendolyn Brooks College Preparatory Academy in the Chicago Public School system.

Roosevelt Military Academy (Aledo, Illinois)

Roosevelt began in 1924 on the grounds of the vacant William and Vashti College in Aledo, Illinois. It closed in 1973.

South Shore High School (Chicago, Illinois)

South Shore opened in 1940 on the southeast side of Chicago. It is no longer in operation. Notable alumni include pro football coach Marv Levy, actor Mandy Patinkin, and financial advisor Suze Orman.

St. Alban's Academy (Sycamore, Illinois)

St. Alban's Academy began in 1890 as a boarding school for boys. Due to weak enrollment, it closed in 1938.

St. John's Military Academy (Delafield, Wisconsin)

St. John's Military Academy was founded in 1884 as a college preparatory school for boys. It merged with Northwestern Military Academy in 1995 and changed to its current name of St. John's Northwestern Military Academy. Beginning in 2018, St. John's will admit female students for the first time. It remains primarily a boarding school for grades 7-12. Its noted alumni include Daniel Gerber, founder of Gerber Foods; former Chicago Bear football player George Wilson (who also coached the Detroit Lions to the 1957 NFL championship); Martin Torrijos, former President of Panama; and Dan Rostenkowski, who served 36 years in the U.S. Congress.

University School of Cleveland (Cleveland, Ohio)

By the time the Academy first played the University School of Cleveland in 1901, the University School in Ohio was already 11 years old. Although now in a new location, the school continues to offer a quality education for boys in grades K-12. Among its graduates are current Dallas Cowboys Head Coach Jason Garrett, radio talk show host Chris Rose, and Fitbit CEO James Park.

Wayland Academy (Beaver Dam, Wisconsin)

Wayland Academy was originally known as Wayland University when it was founded in 1855. According to the school's web site, it is the country's oldest continuously coeducational boarding school and is thriving in Beaver Dam, Wisconsin. Wayland still fields a football team and lists such visible alumni as George Edwin Taylor, the first African American to run for the United States Presidency; Ric Flair, former professional wrestler; author and Pulitzer Prize winner Zona Gale; and Ray Patterson, former General Manager of the Milwaukee Bucks and Houston Rockets of the National Basketball Association.

RESOURCES

NEWSPAPERS AND MAGAZINES

The Academy News (IL)
The Akron (OH) Beacon Journal
Alton (IL) Telegraph
Altoona (PA) Tribune
The Alumni Quarterly of the University of Illinois
The Arizona Republic
Arlington Heights (IL) Herald
Beverly (IL) Review
Blue Island (IL) Sun-Standard
The Bridgeport (CT) Telegram
The Brooklyn (NY) Daily Eagle
The Cedar Rapids (IA) Republican
Chicago Academy of Sciences
The Chicago Daily Journal
Chicago Daily News
Chicago Daily Tribune
Chicago Evening Post
Chicago Heights (IL) Star
Chicago Herald-American
Chicago Herald and Examiner
Chicago Sun-Times
The Coshocton (OH) Tribune
The Culver (IN) Citizen
The Daily (IL) Chronicle
The Daily (IL) Herald
The Daily (NC) Tar Heel
The Decatur (IL) Herald
Elgin (IL) Courier News
The Evening News (PA)
The Evening Times (PA)

Freeport (IL) Journal-Standard
The Gettysburg (PA) Times
Gibson City (IL) Courier
Greeley (CO) Daily Tribune
The Greene (IA) Recorder
The Hammond (IN) Times
The Indianapolis (IN) News
The Indianapolis (IN) Star
The Inter Ocean (IL)
Iowa City (IA) Press-Citizen
John Hopkins Public Health
Kingsport (TN) Times
The LaGrange (IL) Citizen
The Lemonter (IL)
Life Magazine
The Lima ((OH) News
Los Angeles (CA) Times
Macon (MO) Chronicle-Herald
The Minneapolis (MN) Journal
The Monroe (LA) News-Star
Morgan Park Academy Catalog
Morgan Park (IL) Post
Morning Register (OR)
The New North (WI)
The News-Herald (PA)
The News-Palladium (MI)
The Notre Dame (IN) Scholastic
The Ogden (UT) Standard
Onarga (IL) Leader and Citizen
The Onargosy (IL)
The Osage City (KS) Free Press

The Pantagraph (IL)
The Petaluma Argus-Courier (CA)
The Philolexian (IL)
Pittsburgh (PA) Post
The Pittsburgh (PA) Press
Rock Island (IL) Argus
Salt Lake (UT) Telegram
St. Charles (IL) Chronicle
The San Bernardino (CA) County Sun
The Saturday Evening Post
The Sedalia (MO) Democrat
South End (IL) Reporter
Southtown (IL) Economist
Sports Illustrated
Suburbanite (IL) Economist

Sycamore (IL) True Republican
The Tacoma (WA) Times
The Tennessean (TN)
Time Magazine
The Times (PA)
The University of Chicago Weekly
The Vedette (IN)
The Viatorian (IL)
Washington (D.C.) Post
Waukegan (IL) Post
Wayland (WI) Greetings
The Weekly Review (IL)
The World (NY)

BOOKS

Adler, R. (2004). *Baseball at the University of Michigan*. Mount Pleasant, SC: Arcadia Publishing.
Bowling, L. (2010). *Wallace Wade: Championship Years at Alabama and Duke*. Durham, NC: Carolina Academic Press.
Curtis, B. (2016). *Fields of Battle: Pearl Harbor, the Rose Bowl, and the Boys Who Went to War*. New York, NY: Flatiron Books.
Goodspeed, T. W. (1928). *William Rainey Harper: First President of the University of Chicago*. Chicago, IL: University of Chicago Press.
Grossman, James R. (2004). *Encyclopedia of Chicago*. Chicago: University of Chicago Press.
Holmgren, D. (2009). *"Stewart, David Wallace."* The Biographical Dictionary of Iowa. Retrieved from University of Iowa Press.
Kritzberg, B. (2007). *Morgan Park Academy, A History (Volume I)*. Lincoln, NE: iUniverse, Inc.
Lester, R. (1995). *Stagg's University: The Rise, Decline and Fall of Big-Time Football at Chicago*. Urbana, IL: University of Illinois Press.
Lucia, E. (1970). *Mr. Football: Amos Alonzo Stagg*. New York: A.S. Barnes and Company.
Maggio, F. P. (2007). *Notre Dame and the Game That Changed Football: How Jesse Harper Made the Forward Pass a Weapon and Knute Rockne a Legend*. New York, NY: Carroll & Graff Publishers.
The President's Report: University of Chicago (1903). Chicago, IL: University of Chicago Press.
Pruter, R. (2013). *The Rise of American High School Sports and the Search for Control: 1880-1930*. Syracuse: Syracuse University Press.

Stagg, A. A. (1972). *Touchdown!* New York: Longmans, Green and Co.

Touhy, R. (1959). *The Stolen Years.* Cleveland, OH: Pennington Press, Inc.

Tuohy, J. (2001). *When Capone's Mob Murdered Roger Touhy: The Strange Case of Touhy, Jake the Barber and the Kidnapping That Never Happened.* Fort Lee, NJ: Barricade Books.

University of Chicago Football Yearbook. (2015). Chicago.

University of North Carolina Men's Tennis. (2002). Chapel Hill, NC: University of North Carolina

WEB SITES

Inductees. (n.d.). Retrieved from College Football Hall of Fame. https://www.cfbhall.com

History. (2012). Retrieved from Culver Academies. https://www.culver.org

History. (2017). Retrieved from Morgan Park Academy: www.morganparkacademy.org

Palm Springs Factor Estate! (2016, July 16). Retrieved from TopTen RealEstateDeals.com.

Pruter, R. (n.d.). *A Century of Intersectional and Interstate Football Contests.* Retrieved from Illinois High School Association. https://www.ihsa.org

Illinois High School Glory Days. http://www.illinoishsglorydays.com

COLLECTIONS

Abells, H. D. (1914, August 1). *John E. Anderson Papers.* Retrieved from Chicago History Museum Research Center.

Archives of the University of Notre Dame. UADR 2/122 Folder: Football--Harper, Jesse C. (Notre Dame Football Coach, Manager) 1912.

Burdick, Lloyd, S. Scrapbooks. Box 1. (1911-1949). Record Series 26/20/27, University of Illinois Archives.

Oberg, D. S. (1914, December 1). *John E. Anderson Papers.* Retrieved from Chicago History Museum Research Center.

University of Chicago. Office of the President, Harper, Judson and Burton Administrations. Records, [Box 3, Folder 11]. Special Collections Research Center, University of Chicago Library. (n.d.). Chicago, IL: University of Chicago.

University of Chicago. Office of the President. Harper, Judson and Burton Administrations. Records, [Box 3, Folder 12], Special Collections Research Center, University of Chicago Library. (n.d.). Chicago, IL: University of Chicago.

University of Chicago. Office of the President. Harper, Judson and Burton Administrations. Records, [Box 4, Folder 3]. Special Collections Research Center, University of Chicago Library. (n.d.). Chicago, IL: University of Chicago.

INDEX

256, 265-266, 268-269, 271-272,
280-294, 296-297, 299-300, 314,
346-347, 350, 356, 360, 364, 370,
382, 393, 399

Cutliffe, David, 131

D

Dabbert, Richard, 321, 436-437

Daisley, Dave, 328, 437

Danville High School, 170

De LaSalle High School, 161, 324

Deerfield High School, 110

Dickinson, H.W., 9, 414

Dickinson, Leland, 361, 367, 430

DiCola, Charles, 383-384

Dina, Rich, 359-360, 367, 437

Djikas, Paul J., 395, 402, 405, 438

Djikas, Paul L., 380, 382, 395, 397,
399, 400, 402, 438

Donnelly, Brian, 378

Draper, James, 404-406

Drelles, Leo, 330, 437

Driscoll, Paddy, 311

Droegemueller, Bill, 168-171, 435

Duchossois, Richard, 272, 273, 279

Dudley, Robert, 391

Duncan, Clinton Everett, 105-109

Duzansky, John, 380, 382, 438

E

Earle, Willis, 380, 387, 394-397, 402,
404

East Aurora High School, 40

Eckersall, Walter, 120-121, 136-137,
139

Edmunds, D.B., 69

Eggleston Athletic Association, 22

Eissler, Alfred, 110

Elgin Academy, 64, 104, 167, 203,
216, 239, 243, 246, 250, 261-262,
266-267, 285-288, 299-300, 439

Elgin Junior College, 169, 173

Ellis, Chris, 370-371, 382, 437

Elmhurst Academy, 178

Elmhurst High School, 197

Elmwood Park High School, 370

Encyclopedia of Chicago, 8

Engelman, Richard, 300, 310, 436

Englewood High School, 1-6, 10, 18-
19, 46, 48, 55, 60, 148, 439

Englewood YMCA, 5

Epton, Saul, 283

Etzler, James, 37-38

Evans, Chick, 348

Evanston Academy, 88, 91, 144

Evergreen Park High School, 363

Ewing, Joseph Chalmers, 10, 27, 433

F

Factor, Jerome, 220-224, 226-229,
235-236

Factor, John "Jake the Barber," 222-
236

Factor, Max, 222, 235

Fairbanks, Loriston, 58-59

Falk, Phillip, 306-307

Krysti, Lloyd, 402, 405

L

LaGrange High School, 144, 261

Lake Forest Academy, 9, 10, 19, 22, 24, 36, 41, 77, 83, 91, 95-96, 152-153, 241, 250, 261, 265, 267, 299-300, 305

Lake Forest University, 5, 10

Lake View High School, 39, 60

Lane Tech High School, 142, 145

Lemont High School, 268, 308-309, 315, 362, 382, 399-400, 402

Lenzi, Dan, 382, 395, 400-402, 405, 438

Lester, Robin, 90, 119-120

Leventis, John, 332, 437

Levy, Marshall, 221

Lewis, Mac, 408

Life Magazine, 87, 100, 281

Lincoln-Way High School, 363, 399, 402

Ling, Otho, 149-150, 152, 158, 351, 432

Lister, John, 47-48, 51, 54, 60, 65, 432

Lloyd, Bob, 405

Loomis, Ron, 360-361, 363, 437

Lowenthal, Fred, 5, 12, 40, 43-44, 46-47, 50, 304

Loyola Academy, 110, 148, 165, 213

Lucido, Jack, 340, 431

Luckman, Sid, 351

Luetgert, Mike, 325, 382, 391-392

Luther North High School, 321

Lyman, Link, 182

M

MacLane, Robert, 267, 436

Macomber, Bart, 94-95

Madsen, Ed, 368-370, 375, 378, 385, 437

Maggio, Frank, 29, 122-126

Mahon, George, 205, 213, 216, 218, 239, 268-272, 284-285, 288-289, 291-292, 294, 295, 297-299, 301, 304-305, 311, 314-317, 321-322, 354, 394, 411, 433

Mahon, George, Jr., 360-361, 365, 375, 437

Major, Frank, 305, 436

Mancine, Al, 217

Mann, Ollie, 14,16, 433

Marberry, Jim, 305, 307-308, 433

Marmion Military Academy, 267, 272, 284, 300, 311, 317, 334, 381

Marshall, Gene, 315-317, 321

Martin, Howard, 312

Martin, Irwin, 285, 291, 294-295, 436

Maryville Academy, 360, 362, 369, 380, 396, 439

Maser, Adam, 45

Matray, Ron, 396-397, 400, 402, 405, 438

McAfee, Bill, 168-170, 435

McClure, Jim, 373

McClure, Michael, 403-405

McCormick, Macon, 3

Portsmouth Spartans, 182-183, 185

Pratt, Pete, 326, 437

Price, Owen, 266-267, 273-275, 278, 436

Pruter, Robert, 3-4, 8, 41

Pullman Tech High School, 161, 167, 178, 191-192, 217, 250, 256, 258-259, 264, 266, 284, 299-301, 305, 309, 311, 314-315, 317, 323-325, 328, 334, 339, 440

R

Reavis High School, 350, 354, 358

Reichel, Bernard, 273-274, 436

Reichel, Betty, 274

Reid, Robert, 264, 436

Richards, Bill, 285, 288, 291, 294, 436

Robinson, Arthur, 82-83, 88, 434

Robinson, William, 74, 81-83, 434

Rockefeller, John D., 8, 71-72, 79

Rockne, Knute, 118, 122, 124-126, 129, 138, 141, 171, 192

Rodie, Gene, 315-317, 321, 323, 345, 350

Rodie, Ruth, 323

Roosevelt Military Academy, 309, 311, 323, 327, 333, 339, 440

Roosevelt, President Theodore, 66-67, 120

Rosi, Bob, 382, 399-400, 402, 438

Rothstein, Arnold, 222

Rusgis, Warren, 363, 437

S

Schissler, Walt, 285, 291-292, 436

Schloesser, Richard, 402, 405, 438

Schmitz, Frederick, 168, 435

Schnur, George, 28, 32-34, 36, 39-40, 42, 433

Schoenbrod, Ray, 253-254

Schoening, Ed, 251, 436

Schroeder, Frank, 28, 32, 433

Schryver, Martin, 25-26, 433

Schulte, Harry, 147-149, 432

Scruggs, Charles, 363, 437

Sharp, Bill, 311, 436

Sheppard, Mercedes Z., 403, 410

Sinclair, Guy, 214, 240, 435

Sinclair, John, 190, 435

Skarin, Nathaniel, 301, 436

South Shore High School, 335, 337, 345, 351, 366, 440

South Side Academy, 25, 32-33, 34-35, 42

Springer, Bill, 405

Sprinkle, Ed, 384

St. Alban's Academy, 154, 167-169, 172, 179, 199, 203-204, 211-212, 216, 242, 357, 440

St. Aquinas, 207

St. Bede Academy, 285, 287, 294

St. Charles High School, 14-16, 326, 328, 332

St. Ignatius College, 75, 88

St. John's Military Academy, 63, 83, 267, 272, 284-285, 299, 305, 309, 311, 323-324, 328, 360, 403-404, 440

St. Rita College (High School), 148

262, 264-265, 267, 363-364, 441

Webb, Jonathan, 20, 30-33, 36, 52, 432, 433

Weckel, Buddy, 291, 294, 436

Wedow, John, 76-77, 434

Wendell Phillips High School, 76

West Side YMCA, 8

Westenberger, William, 353, 357, 437

Williamson, Garry, 54, 56, 434

Williford, Red, 322-325, 437

Wirth, Willie, 325, 382, 397-402, 438

Withington, Frederic, 388-389, 391-393, 401-402, 406-407

Wolniak, Len, 328, 330, 332, 334-335

Woodworth, Wade, 248-249, 251-256, 258, 260-263, 432

Y

Yarrow, Donald, 312

YMCA Secretarial Institute, 32

YMCA Training School, 19

Yost, Fielding, 159, 171

Z

Zaccari, Jerry, 360, 437

Zale, Tony, 348

Zedeno, Julian, 356, 437

Zetas, 385-386

Ziemba, Joe, 310-311, 314-317, 320-323, 325-326, 328, 330-332, 334-337, 339, 341-346, 348-352, 354, 356, 360-361, 363-367, 377-378, 394-395, 398, 402, 408, 411, 433

Zinter, Waldemar, 258-260, 436

Zuppke, Robert, 44, 95, 180-181, 185